BUTSER ANCIENT FARM

Extinctions and Invasions:
A Social History of British Fauna

Edited by

Terry O'Connor and Naomi Sykes

CW00553479

WINDgather
PRESS

Windgather Press
is an imprint of
Oxbow Books, Oxford

© Windgather Press and the individual authors 2010

ISBN 978-1-905119-31-8

This book is available direct from

Oxbow Books, Oxford, UK
(Phone: 01865-241249; Fax: 01865-794449)

and

The David Brown Book Company
PO Box 511, Oakville, CT 06779, USA
(Phone: 860-945-9329; Fax: 860-945-9468)

or from our website

www.oxbowbooks.com

Printed in Great Britain by
Short Run Press, Exeter

Contents

Preface

All books are a labour of love, and this one has been particularly protracted. It has taken longer than usual to bring to press, thanks in part to the usual exigencies of competing demands (and childbirth on the part of at least two contributors), and in part to the developments and new finds that are constantly being made in the field. Even at the time of writing, we are aware of new discoveries that (fortunately) strengthen the arguments made in this volume. Studies of wildlife are becoming more aware of, and informed by, the long-term record provided by historical and archaeological sources, and we hope that this volume will be seen as a timely addition.

We thank the many contributors for their expertise and patience, and thank Windgather Press and subsequently Oxbow Books for theirs, and for supporting the project. We are grateful to staff and students, in particular Tom Hartman and Alex Hyde of the University of Nottingham's MSc in Biological Photography and Imaging, who provided some of the beautiful images for this book. We thank all of those who have given permission for their images to be used here, in particular Julie Curl, whose illustrations for Figures 31 and 40 add art to this work of, we hope, science. Figures 22, 23, 34 and 42 are by TPOC. NS would like to thank both the University of Nottingham and the Arts and Humanities Research Council who supported the period of research leave in which this volume was edited.

Contributors

Umberto Albarella Department of Archaeology, University of Sheffield, S1 4ET

Robin Bendrey Muséum national d'Histoire naturelle, F-75231 Paris cedex 05

Bryony Coles Department of Archaeology, University of Exeter, EX4 4QE

Julie Curl NAU Archaeology, Scandic House, 85 Mountergate, Norwich, NR1 1PY

Paul Davies Quaternary Research Centre, Bath Spa University, Bath, BA2 9BN

Andy Hammon English Heritage, 37 Tanner Row, York, YO1 6WP, UK

David Hetherington Cairngorms National Park Authority, 14 The Square, Grantown on Spey, Highland PH26 3HG

Cluny Johnstone Department of Archaeology, University of York, YO1 7EP

Harry Kenward Department of Archaeology, University of York, YO1 7EP

Andrew C. Kitchener Department of Naural Sciences, National Museums Scotland, Chambers Street, Edinburgh, EH1 1JF *and* Institute of Geography, School of GeoSciences, University of Edinburgh, Drummond Street, Edinburgh EH8 9XP

Anthony J. Legge McDonald Institute for Archaeological Research, Cambridge, CB2 3ER.

Alison Locker Editici L'Ingla, Atic 1a, 58 Avenguda del Pessebre, Escaldes-Engordany, AD 700, Andorra

Jacqui Mulville School of History and Archaeology, Cardiff University, CF10 3XU

Terry O'Connor Department of Archaeology, University of York, YO1 7EP

Aleksander G. Pluskowski Department of Archaeology, University of Reading, RG6 6AB

Kristopher Poole Department of Archaeology, University of Nottingham, NG7 2RD

Kevin Rielly Pre-Construct Archaeology, 96 Endwell Road, Brockley, London, SE4 2PD

Dale Serjeantson Archaeology, School of Humanities, University of Southampton, SO17 1BJ

Naomi Sykes Department of Archaeology, University of Nottingham, NG7 2RD

Nicki Whitehouse Palaeoecology Centre, Queen's University Belfast, Belfast BT7 1NN

Derek W. Yalden formerly School of Life Sciences, University of Manchester; now at High View, Tom Lane, Chapel-en-le-Frith, High Peak SK23 9UN

List of Figures

List of Tables

CHAPTER I

Introduction – The British Fauna in a Changing World

Terry O'Connor

The post-glacial archaeology of Britain is largely conserved and understood as great monuments and evocative artefacts, or as 'ancient landscapes' in which both forms of relic are preserved in abundance. This focus on the man-made is reflected in UK legislation, which gives protection to specific places as Scheduled Ancient Monuments, as Listed Buildings or Archaeological Areas, and which legislates on the ownership of portable antiquities and 'treasure trove', itself a fine linguistic and legal relic. There is another, more widespread and familiar, form of archaeological heritage, namely the landscape itself in which we live, in particular the living communities that share that landscape and that interact daily with human lives. Because other branches of legislation deal with the conservation and management of living organisms in terms of present-day concerns over protecting the vulnerable and managing the problematically-abundant, it is easy to forget that the wildlife around us also has a time-depth. It is as much a reflection of past human activity and decision-making as is Stonehenge or Fountains Abbey. The prehistory and history of the British fauna reflects people and other animals adapting to some environmental changes, causing others by accident or design, but above all adapting to each other.

The story of mutual adaptation and response begins before the chronological remit that this book has set itself. The last 'Ice Age', equated in Britain with the Devensian cold stage, reached its maximum in terms of ice cover around 18–20,000 BP. [That is, 'years Before Present'. Where we use calibrated radiocarbon dates or precise calendar dates, the forms 'cal. BC' and 'AD' are used]. Although it is naive to suggest that the Devensian ice-sheet had a clearly-defined boundary, the southern limit of the ice can be imagined as a line extending roughly from the Severn Estuary to the Humber (Jones and Keen 1993). North and west of that line lay ice sheets, with just the frost-shattered tops of the highest mountains protruding. To the south and east lay a barren land of meltwater streams and lakes, seasonally frozen, and swept by cold winds circulating around the ice sheets. Again, it would be simplistic to imagine even that stark landscape as completely devoid of animal life, but the Devensian ice maximum must have represented a point at which Britain supported only a very sparse fauna of tundra specialists, and much of that perhaps only seasonally (Currant and Jacobi 2001; Schreve and Currant in prep.). The limiting factor was not simply temperature. The dynamic and unstable environment south of the ice could not develop soils of any depth or duration. Without those soils, colonisation by even cold-tolerant plants was severely limited. Without the plants, herbivores could not persist, and without herbivore prey, neither could the predators.

The eventual wasting of the British ice sheet was probably a far more complex affair than is generally allowed, with rapid retreat in places matched by sudden surges of ice advance in others. Suffice to say that extensive wasting of ice cover was underway before any substantial temperature rise, and the collapse of the ice sheets may have had as much to do with a loss of precipitation as with temperature (Lowe and Walker 1997). Between about 15 and 14,000 BP, temperatures in northwest Europe did rise, and quite sharply. A short-lived warm spell (the Late Glacial Interstadial) allowed some recolonisation by temperate flora and fauna, and also seems to have attracted people back into Britain (Barton *et al.* 2003; Blockley 2005; Lord *et al.* 2007). Temperatures then fell, first gradually, then, around 12,500 BP, rather sharply. An acutely cold but dry stage (the Late Glacial Stadial, or Younger Dryas) brought permafrost conditions though relatively little ice cover to much of Britain. Some of the larger animals that had successfully colonised during the Interstadial may have adapted to the periglacial tundra conditions whilst others were rendered at least locally extinct. Finally, a little before 11,000 BP, a sudden climate warming ushered in the present post-glacial period, bringing fully temperate conditions in less than a century.

The important point about the various climate swings of the Late Glacial period is that communities and ecosystems were repeatedly disrupted. From 15,000 BP onwards, the fauna of Britain must have been continuously in a state of disequilibrium. Even when temperatures settled for a millennium or so, vegetation communities would have taken longer to respond, and animal communities were constantly adapting to changes of vegetation cover and distribution, as well as to changes of temperature and seasonality. To that dynamic background must be added a landscape which was itself adjusting to the removal of ice, exposing new terrain and drowning large areas under meltwater lakes, with meltwater channels superimposed onto older drainage systems to produce new patterns of ridges and valleys to confront migratory animals. Finally, the combined effects of meltwater pouring into the oceans and land rebounding following the release of ice pressure led to the relative levels of land and sea undergoing diverse adjustments, one of which eventually allowed the sea to transgress through the wide river valley that we now know as the English Channel to meet up with the flooded lowlands that became the North Sea (Preece 1995). By about 8000 BP, Britain was an island, and patterns of seasonal migration and of recolonisation were radically altered.

Just as a lack of vegetation cover in the Late Glacial must have been a major factor in the fauna of that period, so the recolonisation of Britain by temperate flora, and the development of often transient vegetation communities, must have had a marked effect on the post-glacial fauna. Pollen analysis, often backed up by plant macrofossil evidence, gives us an indication of the broad pattern of events by which tundra became temperate woodland, though the detail clearly varied considerably from patch to patch. A common feature of many pollen diagrams early in the post-glacial is the dominance of birch pollen, sometimes with a secondary component of pine. This is generally taken to indicate a stage of rather sparse woodland, predominantly of birch (*Betula* spp.) as these species produce abundant seeds that are readily spread by the wind, and are well adapted to the colonisation of rather thin, young soils. In most pollen sequences, this birch-dominated phase is quickly followed by one in which hazel (*Corylus avellana*) is abundant, itself superceded by a more familiar mix of deciduous woodland, with oak (*Quercus* spp.), elm (*Ulmus* spp.), and alder (*Alnus glutinosa*). The mixture of species and predominant tree species seems to have varied between localities, with lime (*Tilia europaea*), for example, being a significant component in some regions (e.g. see Fyfe *et al.* 2003).

The palaeontological record for the first couple of millennia of the post-glacial shows a fascinating mix of temperate large vertebrates, such as red deer (*Cervus elaphus*) and wild cattle (*Bos primigenius*), alongside species that may be thought of as more typically Late Glacial relict species that went extinct only rather gradually, such as elk (*Alces alces*) and reindeer (*Rangifer tarandus*). Although that may be an over-simplistic analysis, the key point is that the temperate woodland environment that gradually established during the early post-glacial was populated by a greater diversity of large grazers and browsers than was the case later in the post-glacial. Although the details can only be speculation, it is likely that this browser community had a general effect on the patchiness of woodland colonisation and a local effect on the distribution and extent of some tree and scrub communities. There was probably some establishment of clearings and 'trails' by grazing and browsing pressure alone. Into this environment, too, came people, drawn by the herds of large prey and diverse plant resources inland, and by the diversity of littoral resources on coastlines still equilibriating to changing sea level (Bevan and Moore 2003; Mannino and Thomas 2002). People were a clearance pressure on the vegetation, through fire and deliberate felling, and a predation pressure on the animals. How significant a predation pressure is the subject of speculation and theoretical modelling: here we may note that the three big predators of Late Glacial Britain – brown bear (*Ursus arctos*), wolf (*Canis lupus*) and lynx (*Lynx lynx*) – all persisted into the post-Roman period, which suggests that they survived pressure from human changes to the landscape for millennia before their eventual extinction through habitat loss and active persecution.

Once the colonisation and environmental turnover of the early post-glacial stabilises in the pollen record, it is tempting to equate the near-stasis of that record with environmental stability and predictability. That in turn leads to an attitude that not much happened, at least in environmental terms, through much of the Mesolithic. However, we have to acknowledge that our main source of evidence, the pollen record, is generally useful for large-scale, medium-term environmental change, but usually less useful for spatially-limited, short-term impacts. The period between about 8500 and 6000 BP may have seen frequent local clearances of woodland by people, with consequences for deer, boar (*Sus scrofa*), squirrels (*Sciurus vulgaris*), voles (Microtinae), lynx, woodland birds and leaf-litter invertebrates, or changes caused by fluctuations in browsing pressure, with consequences for people (Mitchell 2005). Only rather rarely is the pollen record of sufficient spatial and temporal precision for us to be confident that we would pick up any such local events, still less for us to be confident that we could rule out the possibility (Davies and Tipping 2004). The post-glacial wild-wood must have undergone patchy clearance through many different agencies, and the impression of stasis that we often get from the palaeoenvironmental record is probably misleading. It is important to keep this point in mind, because the next notable environmental impact in the post-glacial is, according to our point of view, either the most significant environmental change in the entire post-glacial period, or just another form of clearance.

Around 6000 BP, people in Britain began farming and the fauna of Britain was supplemented by the addition of domestic cattle, domestic sheep and (probably) goats (*Capra hircus*), and domestic pigs (*Sus scrofa*): two grazers and a broad-spectrum omnivore that is conspecific with a native species. To qualify that bold statement, the date is only approximate, based on just a handful of sites with early, directly-dated specimens of domestic animals. Furthermore, it is not clear whether the people concerned were immigrants from parts of Europe in which farming was already well-established, or whether they were 'locals' who adopted a new way of life (Rowley-Conwy 2003). And it is not clear whether 'farming' at this early date really means anything more than the casual ranching of some new species alongside the continued hunting of deer and boar, and collection of shellfish (Rowley-Conwy 2004). Finally, it increasingly looks as if farming entered Britain not by way of south-east England, as has traditionally been implicitly believed (after all, it is the bit of Britain closest to the rest of Europe), but through the Atlantic and Irish Sea coasts, probably from Iberia and western France (Haynes *et al.* 2003; Innes *et al.* 2003).

With the first domestic mammals came arable crops, principally barley (*Hordeum* spp.) in the north and west of the country, and more cultivation of wheat (*Triticum* spp.) towards the south and east (Fairbairn 2000). To what extent this led to wholesale clearance of woodland is hotly debated, with the consensus moving away from a 'fields of waving corn' model for Neolithic farming towards something more shifting and intermittent (Jones 2000; Thomas 2004). Even allowing for that adjustment in our understanding, some clearance for arable agriculture evidently did take place, and to that must be added clearance *for* monument construction, clearance *as* monument construction, clearance as a consequence of grazing, and clearance by the extraction of building timber and firewood. By the end of the Neolithic, 4500 years ago, at least the landscape of the southern part of Britain was a substantially more open than it had been when the first domestic animals arrived. Here and there, some evidence for secondary regrowth of woodland has been adduced. For example, on the chalklands of central southern and eastern England, sedimentary sequences from the ditches of Neolithic monuments such as causewayed enclosures and barrows commonly show a phase of scrub or tree regrowth around the end of the Neolithic (Evans 1971; 1990; 1999). This has been interpreted as showing 'abandonment' of the monuments and, by implication, some lessening of clearance pressures in the surrounding landscape. The evidence, of course, relates to the monuments themselves, and it could equally be argued that the regrowth of scrub and trees over and around important places was tolerated, even managed, in a quite deliberate attempt to maintain their visibility and distinctiveness within what was otherwise becoming a more open landscape.

Elsewhere in Britain, two very distinctive landscapes were developing by the Bronze Age. Across the higher ground of northern and western Britain, blanket peat was extending across what had been areas of mineral soils, at least some of which had previously been settled and farmed; for example, at Scord of Brouster, Shetland (Whittle 1986). This peat expansion may have been partly driven by climate change, a shift to cooler and wetter conditions inhibiting the decay of plant litter and thus initiating the growth of peat. Prehistoric land use may also have played a part, in particular the removal of the deep-rooted trees and shrubs that recycle nutrients from deep in the sub-soil to the surface in their leaf litter whilst maintaining drainage through their deep root systems (Moore 1993). Whichever factor drove blanket peat growth in any particular area, the consequence was the development of a highly distinctive and biotically unproductive environment, distinctive today for the dominance of ling (*Calluna vulgaris*) and other ericaceous plants, and a sparse vertebrate fauna amongst which red grouse (*Lagopus scoticus*) is particularly iconic. The other distinctive environment developed along the Atlantic seaboard, most especially along the western coast of Scotland and the Hebridean islands. Here, as sea level change gradually stabilised, wave action and prevailing onshore westerlies led to the accumulation of sand in extensive dune systems (Gilbertson *et al.* 1996). The sand was predominantly derived from comminuted shell, thus giving rise to a soil parent material that is both sharply drained and calcareous, in a part of the country in which mineral soils otherwise tend to be either highly leached or peat-based and acidic. Where the dunes were stabilised by soil formation and plant growth, the distinctive *machair* environment developed, giving rise to some of the most fertile agricultural land in northern Britain. Like the peat uplands, this environment developed its own distinctive fauna, characteristically including corncrakes (*Crex crex*) and, during the last millennium, copious rabbits (*Oryctolagus cuniculus*).

Across much of lowland Britain, later prehistory saw more and more land taken into agriculture and closely managed. The archaeological record shows field systems pushing into upland regions, and colluvial infilling of valleys reflects the instability that repeated ploughing brings to even quite gentle slopes (Allen 1992; Bell 1983; 1990). It is debatable just how much of the original post-glacial woodland had been cleared for farming by the dawn of the Roman occupation, but what remained must certainly have been highly fragmented. That fragmentation, with the consequent isolation of woodland faunas in small patches and small populations, must itself have been of some ecological consequence, leading to local extinction of some woodland species simply through the isolation of unsustainable populations, rather than through any deliberate extirpation. Woodland specialists such as pine marten (*Martes martes*) are likely to have been particularly vulnerable to such fragmentation. Conversely, by the end of the Iron Age, Britain was well-connected to the rest of Europe through sea-borne trade and exchange. House mice (*Mus domesticus*) and chickens (*Gallus gallus*) entered Britain during later prehistory, but it was during the Roman period that the potential for the introduction of new species, either deliberately as cargo or inadvertently in cargo, really increased. In part, this was because of the sheer increase in the volume of human and cargo traffic back and forth between Britain and the near Continent. In part, too, the establishment of a road network must have played a part in allowing species newly introduced through ports and distribution centres such as London, Gloucester, Chester and York to be rapidly disseminated. Just as all roads lead away from Rome, so the road system in *Britannia* tended to lead to and from relatively few foci.

In terms of overall environmental impact, the Roman occupation probably made little difference to Britain. Lowland regions were extensively grazed and intensively ploughed before the legions arrived, and continued to be so through the four centuries of Roman rule. Species that were vulnerable to the loss of woodland habitat or disturbance of grassland through grazing pressure were likely already to have been reduced in number or distribution during later prehistory, and the fragile habitats of the northern and western mountains and islands were hardly touched by Roman management. Even along the line of Hadrian's Wall, a major construction and the base for numerous troops, it is questionable whether the Roman activity had a discernible impact on the surrounding landscape (Dumayne and Barber 1994; 1997; McCarthy 1995). The Roman impact on the British fauna was more in terms of introductions. Some were exotic animals, introduced in small numbers and probably never truly established in Britain as viable populations. As later chapters in this book show, pheasant (*Phasianus colchicus*), guinea fowl (*Numida meleagris*), fallow deer (*Dama dama*) and rabbits (*Oryctolagus cuniculus*) may all fall into this category. One Roman introduction that clearly did settle in, at least for a few centuries, was the black rat (*Rattus rattus*), presumably an accidental introduction (O'Connor 1991a; 1992), and the same inadvertent transport may explain the few records of garden dormouse (*Eliomys quercinus*) (O'Connor 1986a). Vermin and exotic pets aside, the Roman impact was largely in the construction of towns, with the consequent creation of new urban habitats and communities. This was the environment into which black rat moved with evident success, and it is likely that a wide range of invertebrates established themselves in towns. Some of these will have been endemic species that adapted successfully to the new opportunity, whilst others will have been imports such as grain pests (Carrott and Kenward 2001).

Britain is often presented as having entered a Dark Age following the collapse of Roman rule, but in terms of the environment in general and fauna in particular, this is probably misleading. Certainly the towns reduced in population and thus in the nature of the highly specialised environment that they represented. Change in the countryside during the fifth to eighth centuries AD is more difficult to assess, mainly for want of evidence. Farming patterns, and thus the specific pressures on different patches of land, may have changed, but the country was still populated, and a mixed farming economy persisted. By the late ninth and tenth centuries, some of the old Roman town centres were being re-occupied, and new towns were established, giving rise to a diversity of urban habitats and niches. Although it seems likely that lowland Britain was still largely open pasture, meadow and arable, towns such as York could be rebuilt largely in timber, some of it from substantial trees of a considerable age (Hall *et al.* 2004). The next major environmental impact, and the one that finally established rural Britain as we know it from the historical sources, came in the aftermath of William the Conqueror's seizure of the throne in AD 1066. With the establishment of baronial estates came two significant changes: the organisation of substantial tracts of land into hunting forests and, later, the introduction of rabbits. The first embodied the concept that the 'wild' should be managed, a concept that subsequently drove the British gamekeeping tradition and its practice of extirpating species that might compete with or predate the prey animals that were raised and managed for the hunt. The second put into the landscape a small grazing mammal capable of legendary feats of reproduction and population growth, and a serious competitor for endemic grazers such as water vole (*Arvicola terrestris*).

From Norman times onwards, archaeological sources of evidence are joined by textual sources. These include descriptions of places and estates, some of them with accounts of the animals to be found, though it would be unwise to base much on what are often rather vague, second-hand, and of questionable objectivity. Much of what we could reasonably regard as the earliest authoritative texts on the natural history of Britain dates from the early nineteenth century, a generation or so after Gilbert White. Sources such as Bell (1837) had little or no archaeological or palaeontological evidence from which to discuss the time-depth of the species of which they were attempting to set down full and systematic descriptions. Bell includes wild and domestic species, discussing both ecotypes in the case of the rabbit, which species he treats as if it were an endemic native of Britain. In contrast, he includes at least some discussion of the introduction of guinea pigs (*Cavia porcellus*), about which species he is splendidly rude: 'Devoid of sense and docility, though incessantly restless, tame from stupidity, and harmless from impotence, it perhaps possesses as few

claims upon our interest and affection as any animal of equally innoxious habits'
(Bell 1837, 354–5). That digression aside, Bell has some comment on changes of
range and the possibility of extinction. Regarding the wild cat (*Felis silvestris*),
he observes that its reduction in numbers and range has more to do with the
introduction of 'the fowling piece' than with destruction of habitat: '… it falls
so surely before the gun of the gamekeeper or the forester, as to threaten its
extermination at no very remote period' (Bell 1837, 179).

Later sources such as Wood (1864) are more expansive in their scope, but
show little more factual information in their discussion. Wood, like Bell, deals
with the rabbit as if it were endemic, but he does note the former presence of
beaver in Britain, which Bell does not. Wood rather vaguely attributes beaver
to a '… former years, when the wolf and bear inhabited England…', then
asserts with suspicious precision that '… it has not been seen in this country
since 1188' (Wood 1864, 92). That date is given no source, yet it is likely to have
influenced subsequent authors.

A key source, and an ancestor to the present volume, is Harting's *British
Animals extinct within British times with some account of British Wild White
Cattle* (1880a). Harting discusses only five species - bear, beaver, reindeer, wild
boar, and wolf – but gives many sources for the historical evidence that he cites,
and uses such archaeological and palaeontological evidence as was available to
him. Harting also quotes the date of 1188 in connection with the extirpation
of beavers, but makes clear the source (Giraldus Cambrensis), and the number
and quality of textual references that seem to show a later presence of beaver
in Britain (see Coles, this volume). Discussing reindeer, Harting details at
considerable length the numerous finds of that species from what we would
now recognise as Late Glacial and Holocene deposits, and reviews the case for
the presence of reindeer in northern Scotland within historic times (Harting
1880a, 61–75). Harting's one conspicuous weakness is his discussion of the
environmental background to these extinctions. Even as late as early Norman
times, he invokes huge areas of largely uncleared forest: 'Even in the less hilly
districts more than half the country was one vast forest… Between the tenth
and twelfth centuries, great forests came up almost to the gates of London…'
(*ibid.*, 5). This description makes no allowance for, nor even passing mention
of, Roman road and fort building or their great *villa* estates, of which Harting
must have had knowledge. It may in part arise from a familiar misunderstanding
of 'forest' to mean a great trackless expanse of trees, rather than a area of land
given over to hunting, and including both woodland and open terrain.

Through the twentieth century, our understanding of environmental changes
in Britain has become more detailed, more subtle and perhaps more confident.
Obviously, much of that can be attributed to the advances in methodology that
have been a feature of the last few decades. Some credit is due, however, to
earlier sources such as Wilcox (1933) who, despite lacking the quantities of data
available today, none the less managed a highly plausible and closely-argued
account of the former distribution of woodland and marsh in England. Such

reconstructions of past vegetation associations and distribution underpin our knowledge of changes in Holocene environments, and hence of the extent and ways in which those environments were changed deliberately or inadvertently by human activities. Those activities and their consequences contributed to the extinction of some species, and allowed the introduction of others. Ultimately, those introductions and extinctions were the outcome of a subtle interplay between human deliberation and the ecological dynamics of the landscape. That interplay continues, of course, and the future will no doubt see further introductions and, regrettably, further extinctions. The difference is that we are now equipped with the knowledge and practical capacity to assess the likely impact of introductions and to ameliorate the worst impacts on other species. To make best use of that knowledge for the future, we need a thorough understanding of the past, and this volume seeks to make a contribution to that understanding.

CHAPTER 2

The Horse

Robin Bendrey

Introduction

The domestication of the wild horse brought into human control an animal that revolutionised transport, warfare and trade. Because of its significance, horse domestication has been the subject of considerable study and speculation with numerous regions – the Ukraine, Kazakhstan, Eastern Europe and Western Europe – being suggested as the centres of domestication (see Levine 2005; Olsen 2006).

The association between humans and horses pre-dates their domestication, however. During the last Ice Age the wild horse was an important provider of meat and other products to hunter-gatherer communities (Clutton-Brock 1992). Some researchers suggest that over-exploitation by Mesolithic hunters, together with the post-glacial spread of forests, adversely affected horse populations leading to their extinction in Britain and other parts of western Europe (Burleigh *et al.* 1991; Clutton-Brock and Burleigh 1991a). Their re-colonisation of these regions is commonly attributed to human agency and their re-introduction to Britain is thought to have occurred only after eustatic sea-level rise isolated the island from mainland Europe (Burleigh *et al.* 1991; Clutton-Brock and Burleigh 1991b). Recently it has been demonstrated that small localised populations of horses did survive in continental western Europe (Boyle 2006) but there is currently little evidence to suggest the same was true in Britain, although the possibility should not be ruled out. This chapter examines the evidence for the early presence of horse in Britain and considers the factors that led to its establishment as a key part of human society and economy.

Early evidence

Radiocarbon dating evidence for the earliest post-Pleistocene horse remains (Table 1) indicates that horses were present in Early Mesolithic Britain but that they became increasingly scarce in the following millennia. After a hiatus in their archaeological representation the next directly-dated horse find is a Late Neolithic/Early Bronze Age skull from Grimes Graves, Norfolk. A few other horse remains have been recovered from seemingly Neolithic contexts but when directly dated these have often returned earlier or later dates and are therefore

Sample code	Site	14C age	Calibration (95.4%)	Reference
OxA-111	Kendrick's Cave, North Wales	10000±200 BP	10500–8800 cal. B.C.	Clutton-Brock and Burleigh 1991a
BM-2350	Seamer Carr, Yorkshire	9790±180 BP	10100–8600 cal. B.C.	Clutton-Brock and Burleigh 1991a
BM-1619	Darent river gravels, Kent	9770±80 BP	9450–8800 cal. B.C.	Clutton-Brock and Burleigh 1991a
BM-1546	Grimes Graves, Norfolk	3740±210 BP	2900–1600 cal. B.C.	Clutton-Brock and Burleigh 1991b
OxA-6320	Durrington Walls, Wiltshire	3045±50 BP	1430–1120 cal. B.C.	Kaagan 2000
OxA-6654	Fussell's Lodge, Wiltshire	2940±50 BP	1320–1000 cal. B.C.	Kaagan 2000
OxA-6613	Durrington Walls, Wiltshire	2500±45 BP	790–480 cal. B.C. (90.9%) 470–410 cal. B.C. (4.5%)	Kaagan 2000
OxA-6614	Durrington Walls, Wiltshire	2090±45 BP	350–310 cal. B.C. (2.8%) 210 cal. B.C.–cal. A.D. 20 (92.6%)	Kaagan 2000

TABLE 1. Key finds of directly radiocarbon dated horse bone [calibration was carried out using OxCal 3.10 (Bronk Ramsay 2001; 1995) and the INTCAL04 curve (Reimer *et al.* 2004)].

considered intrusive: radiocarbon dating of three apparently Late Neolithic horse bones from Durrington Walls returned later Bronze Age to Iron Age dates as did the purported Neolithic horse tooth from Fussell's Lodge (Kaagan 2000; table 1). Confirming the absence of horses from Britain for much of the Neolithic is thus difficult, but the evidence as it stands does not prove localised extinction: currently there is an absence of evidence, rather than evidence of absence.

Horses begin to occur with increasing frequency on archaeological sites across Europe from *c.* 4000 BP onwards (Clutton-Brock 1992, 58). The association of some of these finds with Bell Beaker pottery, for example at Newgrange in Ireland, has been used as evidence to suggest that the horse was reintroduced

FIGURE 1. Konik ponies from a breeding population in an enclosure at Canterbury, Kent

PHOTO COURTESY OF DR A. E. BENDREY

and spread as part of a Beaker 'package' (Van Wijngaarden-Bakker 1974). For Britain, Bendrey (2007a) was able to explore temporal changes in horse representation by employing a novel quantification method to show how 'rare' or 'common' horses were in a group of assemblages by relating the presence or absence of horse to the sizes of the excavated animal bone assemblages. Results from sites in six counties of southern England show the horse progressively becoming more common from the Early Bronze Age, when horse keeping appears to be 'rare', through an increase in the Middle Bronze Age. By the Late Bronze Age, horse remains are represented in all but the smallest assemblages. This indicates that the horse had become an established part of the fauna of Late Bronze Age Britain, and can be suggested as having widespread use. It may be at this time that the horse brought greatest change to society and economy, rather than the period before this when its rarity may have limited the impact of its use, but ensured its position as a symbol of prestige or status.

When relative frequencies of cattle and horse are considered for assemblages with over 400 bone fragments, there is a clear difference between the representation of horses at Bronze Age and Iron Age sites (Figure 2; Bendrey 2007a). In the Bronze Age the horse contributes a relatively small proportion of individual assemblages (typically less than five per cent of the horse and cattle bones). One exception to this pattern is Late Bronze Age Potterne, Wiltshire (Locker 2000), where their remains constitute 15 per cent (Bendrey 2007a). In the Iron Age, horse is not only present in all but the smallest assemblages, as in the Late Bronze Age, but often makes a more significant contribution to assemblages (Figure 2). This could reflect a mix of phenomena, related to changing attitudes to horses, such as horses being eaten more regularly, access to greater numbers of horses or horses being more commonly deposited as ritual acts.

The use of horses

The very rarity of archaeological horse remains in the earlier periods creates problems for quantifying changes in the level of its use. There is evidence that horse was eaten at some Iron Age sites (Maltby 1996), although how frequently is uncertain. The consumption of domestic horses did not begin in the Iron Age; for example, there is evidence of this from Bronze Age Yarnton, Oxfordshire (J. Mulville pers. comm.). When identified, the exploitation of horse carcasses for food is generally described as being less intensive than those of cattle; in that horse bones are less fragmented or exhibit fewer butchery marks (Maltby 1996, 23). That the horse was initially only represented in small numbers at individual sites indicates it was not a regular part of the diet, and that the earliest use of the horse was not primarily as a food animal (Bendrey 2007a).

The earliest indisputable evidence for the use of horses for work in prehistoric Britain derives from artefacts. Antler cheekpieces, parts of the horse's harness, first appear in the archaeological record in the Late Bronze Age (Britnell 1976).

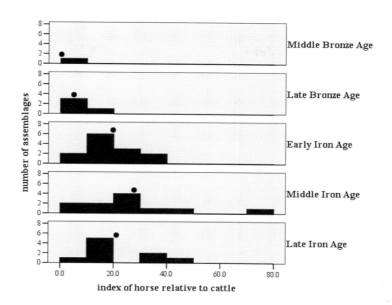

FIGURE 2. Histograms showing the number of identified horse bones calculated as a percentage of the total number of horse and cattle bones (termed 'index of horse relative to cattle') for Bronze and Iron Age assemblages of 400 identified animal bone fragments and over. This is calculated in order to reduce the effects of differential preservation and recovery on intra-site comparisons (see Maltby 1994). Circles represent the mean value for each group of assemblages. [See text for further details, and Bendrey (2007a) for raw data and further analysis].

The presence of chapes in the early first millennium BC suggests a role for horse riding in warfare (Darvill 1987). These winged chapes, from the end of sword scabbards, developed so that a sword could be drawn while on horseback (by hooking the chape under the foot) (*ibid.*, 128). The date at which wheeled vehicles came into use in Britain is also uncertain (*ibid.*, 128). Cunliffe (2005, 538–539) states that although vehicles are known from the Hallstatt period on the continent there is no evidence for their use in Britain at this time (the Late Bronze Age) and suggests that the light two-wheeled vehicle was probably introduced to Britain during the La Tène I period in the late fifth or early fourth century BC. Presumably, therefore, before the arrival of wheeled vehicles, functional use of the horse would have consisted of riding, dragging loads or pack-use. It is probably the case that the importance of riding in the Iron Age has previously been under-represented in the literature (e.g. Cunliffe 2005), largely due to the archaeological visibility of vehicles and vehicle fittings and relative invisibility of riding (Bendrey 2007b).

It is possible to investigate the uses of the horses from the bones recovered from archaeological sites. One avenue of research is to look for 'damage' to the skeletal tissues of the mouth that might show that a horse was ridden or driven with a bit. Brown and Anthony (1998) developed a method for identifying 'bit wear' on the lower second premolar (P_2) through the measurement of bevels on the front part of the chewing surface of these teeth. These bevels were argued as being caused by the tooth being worn down when a horse chews the bit. A problem with this method is that abnormal occlusion with the upper second premolar (P^2) can cause a bevel on the P_2 anterior corner, and the use of a bevel measurement alone as evidence for bitting without comparing the P_2 against the occluding P^2 is insecure (Bendrey 2007c). The method can be used if malocclusion can be discounted, as seen in an Iron Age horse from Kirkburn, Yorkshire (Legge 1991a). In addition, qualitative changes to the occlusal surface may also be used as supportive evidence (Brown and Anthony 1998; Olsen 2006, 254–255).

A macroscopic method that quantifies bitting damage to the 'front' or anterior edge of a P_2 is more successful (Bendrey 2007c). When a horse is bitted the bit is placed in the mouth on the mandibular diastema, the bridge of bone between the front teeth and the cheek teeth. Bands of enamel exposure on the anterior edge of a horse P_2 are argued as deriving from a bit coming into contact with the front edge of the tooth and wearing away a strip of cementum to expose the enamel beneath. More severe bitting damage can also expose areas of dentine below the enamel. However, a note of caution is required - not all enamel exposure on the anterior border of a P_2 is due to bitting. This is a relatively exposed site and other forms of damage can occur, such as dietary wear: interpretations must be based on the size and shape of the area exposed (see Bendrey 2007c). Application of this method to several archaeological assemblages from southern England showed that the majority of Iron Age horses exhibited evidence suggestive of bitting damage (Bendrey 2007c; 2007a). Metal snaffles were in use in Iron Age Britain (Palk 1984), although it is probable that organic tackle was also used. Runnymede Bridge, Surrey presents the earliest evidence for bitting damage from Britain identified to date (Bendrey 2007a). This evidence, dated to the Late Bronze Age/Earliest Iron Age (broadly ninth/eighth centuries BC), predates the use of metal mouthpieces in Britain and may therefore have been caused by an organic mouthpiece such as leather or rope.

Horse breeding and supply

Little evidence for horse breeding has been found at Bronze and Iron Age sites. Harcourt (1979a) interpreted the dominance of mature horses, and absence of immature horses, at Iron Age Gussage All Saints, Dorset, as evidence that horses were not bred there, but rather were rounded up from free-ranging populations, broken in and trained. This interpretation has been frequently used in subsequent publications. Foetal and neonatal mortalities are a significant aspect of the demography of all breeding populations (Mellor and Stafford 2004), although these age groups may be under-represented in archaeological deposits due to conditions of preservation (Levine 1983). The relative absence of horse neonatal remains from many archaeological sites, compared to those of cattle, sheep and pig is a stark contrast (e.g. Grant 1984, 521), and does suggest that horses were not being bred at these sites.

Opposition to this view argues that the horse was too important in the Iron Age not to have been produced by controlled breeding (Palk 1984). Their value may be indicated by the circumstances of some burial deposits (Bendrey 2007a), such as the horse that was buried in its own grave cut in the Iron Age cemetery at Mill Hill, Deal, Kent (Legge 1995). This implies that horses would have been well protected, and were unlikely to have been left to exist as free-ranging herds. Perinatal horse bones have recently been identified from a small number of Iron Age sites, such as Rooksdown, Hampshire (Powell and Clark 1996) and several sites in Cambridgeshire (I. Baxter pers. comm.), and high proportions of immature horses were recovered from Gravelly Guy, Oxfordshire (Mulville and Levitan 2004, 472). There are explanations other than exploitation of free-ranging herds for the lack of young horse bones from a breeding, domestic population. The comparisons made with cattle, sheep and pigs may not be entirely appropriate: horses may have been raised in smaller numbers than these animals and perhaps reared with extreme care (Locker 2000, 105). Differences in representation of perinatal remains between sites may represent differences in horse husbandry skills. If horses were being raised away from settlement sites, then the neonatal death assemblage would not be found at these sites. Horses may have only been raised at some sites, and then traded (Grant 1984, 522). Analyses of strontium isotope (^{87}Sr/^{86}Sr) ratios in horse tooth enamel (which can be related via diet to the underlying geology where the horses grazed) has identified that one horse (aged 9–10 years at death) from Rooksdown was not bred at the site, coming from as far away as Wales, Scotland or the continent (Bendrey *et al.* 2009).

Interpretations of the demography of excavated animal bone assemblages that may have derived from selective or 'structured' deposition (Hill 1995) are also problematic, as it may not represent the true nature of the live population. At Gravelly Guy, for example, horses of different ages are treated differently, with older animals better represented amongst 'special deposit' burials, while younger animals were disposed of with the general refuse (Mulville and Levitan 2004, 472). High ratios of males at some sites have been used as evidence that horses were not breeding there (e.g. Grant 1984, 521), but the preferential selection of stallion skulls or skeletons for deposition in the ground is a common phenomenon that is seen in other geographical areas and archaeological periods (Bendrey 2007a, 65; Olsen 2006, 249).

The importance of horses

The earliest evidence for horse keeping – the Late Neolithic/Early Bronze Age skull from Grimes Graves, Norfolk (Table 1) – provides some indication about the importance of horses in this period. The skull is from an extremely aged mare, probably over the age of 35 years at death, and Clutton-Brock and Burleigh (1991b) suggest that its age at death indicates that it was a highly valued domestic animal, kept with care, as it had lost most of its cheekteeth prior to death and would have been unable to feed.

By the Late Bronze Age, horses appear to have had a critical impact on human society. They then entered widespread use, harness fittings and chapes were first used and largely complete horse skeletons began to appear in what are interpreted as ritual contexts (Bendrey 2007a).

The impact of horses on prehistoric society may be envisaged in several areas. It is in the later Bronze Age that there was a reorganisation of the landscape, with the establishment of permanent settlements, field systems and boundaries (Champion 1999). These changes in the landscape can be related to a number of factors, especially livestock management (Yates 2001). In Wessex, the construction of so-called 'ranch boundaries', systems of linear earthworks, may indicate the importance of cattle management over significant distances (although some may have served as territorial boundaries) (Cunliffe 2004, 74–75; 2005, 50). The locations of some early first millennium enclosures are interpretable as vantage points from which to view livestock, and perhaps other communities (Yates 2001). Horses offered the means of managing territory, cattle and people in this new landscape, and were therefore the means of controlling wealth and exercising power (Bendrey 2007a). In such a scenario the speed, mobility and distances of travel enabled by horse riding could allow the maintenance of land, herds of livestock, and the transport of agricultural and other resources.

Horses would also have enabled raiding over greater distances (Osgood 1998), which would have threatened this wealth and encouraged the construction of defensive sites. It is in the Late Bronze Age that we see the rise of defended settlements. The construction of these early hillforts indicates that a threat existed and that this threat may not have been to the hillforts themselves, but rather to the livestock, a large part of the wealth of these communities (Osgood 1998; Thorpe 2006). Use of horses would have effected major changes to raiding and warfare; horses can be seen as an integral part of warfare in Britain by the end of the Iron Age through the accounts of Julius Caesar.

Conclusion

Current evidence indicates the earliest horse keeping occurred during the Late Neolithic/Early Bronze Age in Britain. Initially a rare animal, it seems to have achieved widespread use by the Late Bronze Age. Horses would have enabled people to travel further and faster than before. The control and management of territory and resources, and wealth accumulation would have been transformed, and the impact on practices of warfare and raiding would also have been widely felt.

The adoption of horse keeping and use may thus be seen as a major influence on the course of economic and social change in Britain during later prehistory. Once established, the use of the horse continued to have a major influence on humans until the mechanisation of transport and warfare (Clutton-Brock 1992; Levine 2005). In fact, it was only during the course of the twentieth century AD that the role of the horse changed from a focus on their economic importance as a source of transport and power, to one centred around leisure and recreation that we are familiar with in Britain today (Hall 2005).

CHAPTER 3

Donkeys and Mules

Cluny Johnstone

....

This chapter investigates the introduction to Britain of a true species, the donkey or ass (*Equus asinus*), and a deliberately bred hybrid, the mule (*Equus asinus* x *E. caballus*). Mule is the term given to the offspring of a male donkey and a female horse, whilst a hinny is the progeny of a male horse and female donkey. Mules (and hinnies) are almost always infertile because the difference between the numbers of chromosomes in horses and donkeys results in an odd number of chromosomes in the hybrid, therefore only first generation crosses exist. As a result of being a hybrid, the introduction of the mule is most likely to be linked to that of the parent species, or more particularly the donkey, which has never been a native British species. For this reason they are considered together in this chapter.

Explanations as to why the donkey has not been native to Britain centre on its environmental adaptations. The wild ass is not naturally adapted to wet and cold climatic conditions and the type of environment which that climate fosters. Horses are specialist grazers which can survive in cold conditions and a degree of wet terrain, whereas donkeys will 'thrive in any dry, stony area where there is scrub vegetation they can graze' (Clutton-Brock 1992, 36). The morphology of the hooves and limbs of asses are adapted to dry, rocky conditions, and the coat will not protect them in cold wet climates. Donkeys are also much more drought tolerant than horses, they require access to water only every few days as opposed to horses, which need water every day (Clutton-Brock 1992). These variations (amongst others) between the two species are evolutionary adaptations to different ecological niches and as a result there are few regions of the world where the two species would have coexisted in their wild state, the possible exception being the Levant area.

Of course the domestication of both species (for horses see Bendrey, this volume; for donkeys Clutton-Brock 1992; 1999; Rossel *et al.* 2008) has to some extent changed the environmental adaptations of the two animals to allow them to coexist in many parts of the world, although not without human care at the margins of the ranges of each species. Britain could well be considered to be at the limit of the environmental tolerance of donkeys. The fact that under human control, the two species can coexist means that the possibilities for breeding hybrids were increased.

Hybrid breeding does not usually happen in nature (Clutton-Brock 1999),

FIGURE 3. Mule
PHOTO BY BARBARA NODDLE

therefore the presence of hybrids suggests some degree of control over breeding by humans. A reason why people went to the bother of enticing donkeys and horses to produce offspring is that mules, in particular, exhibit hybrid vigour or heterosis which means they are likely to be larger, have greater endurance and survive better on poor food than either parent species. This was obviously advantageous to humans, in allowing the transport of heavier loads, over longer distances, for less feed.

Hybrid equids were probably bred from approximately 2500 BC although these were not necessarily the mule but other crosses, including donkey x onager hybrids. Clear evidence for donkey/horse crosses appear in art historical sources at least 1000 years later, with depictions of hinnies in Ancient Egypt and mules in Mesopotamia (Clutton-Brock 1999). By the time of the Roman Empire mules had become 'an essential part of life' (Clutton-Brock 1999, 121) being used for riding, ploughing, drawing carts and carrying baggage. The intensive utilisation of mules by the state (both militarily and publicly) during this period (and possibly also state control of breeding (Johnstone 2008)) is possibly why most of the written evidence and much of the art historical evidence for mules comes from Roman sources. The Romans bred mules in preference to hinnies as they are generally larger, and therefore potentially more useful, as a result of the fact that the size of dam limits the size of the foetus (a horse mare generally being larger than a female donkey) (Clutton-Brock 1992).

Columella and Varro, in particular, provided immensely detailed accounts of mule breeding. As has been alluded to above, breeding mules requires the manipulation of the natural behaviour patterns, as donkeys are territorial and horses are not but instead form family groups (Clutton-Brock 1992). This means that in order to get a jackass to mate with a mare, he has to be trained to respond to a mare in oestrus. Varro (*Rerum Rusticarum* II, 8, trans. Hooper and Ash 1979) suggests that jackass foals destined to breed mules should be reared on surrogate horse mares. Columella (*Res Rustica* VI, 37, 10, trans. Forester and Heffner 1955) also gives details of a 'ramp' system that would allow the smaller donkey to mate with a larger mare. Both of these examples illustrate the lengths to which human ingenuity has been put to obtain these hybrid animals. Another aspect of this is the care with which the parent animals were chosen. The mares that were used to breed mules were second only to those used to produce racehorses (*ibid.* VI, 27) and the jackasses were chosen with equal care. Both Columella and Varro indicate that a first generation cross between a wild ass and a domestic one was ideal because of the size and strength of these individuals. Although the only extant sub-species of wild ass today is the Somali wild ass (*Equus africanus somaliensis*), two other subspecies, the Nubian wild ass (*E. africanus africanus*) and the Algerian wild ass (*E. africanus atlanticus*) were probably still in existence during the Roman period and were likely to have been used for breeding (Clutton-Brock 1999). Indeed, recent genetic research suggests that at least two of these subspecies, the Somali wild ass and the Nubian wild ass, have contributed to the domestic donkey (Rossel *et al.* 2008).

The spread of donkeys from their probable area of domestication in North Africa into Southern (Morales Muñiz *et al.* 1995) and Eastern Europe (Bökönyi 1974) has been documented as happening in the first millennium BC. Mule breeding was well established in the Ancient Greek world and so these animals were already familiar to the Romans. This background information about mules and donkeys in the Roman period is pertinent to the question of their introduction to the British Isles, as it is generally presumed that donkeys were first brought here by the Romans (e.g. Clutton-Brock 1992, 49, 117) and hence, by implication, mules also. Hitherto, records of donkey bones from British archaeological assemblages of any period have been scarce (e.g. Baxter 2002; Bendrey 1999), and those of mules virtually non-existent, with only one published case (Armitage and Chapman 1979). Recent methodological advances in the discrimination of horse, donkey and mule bones have allowed the re-examination of many archaeological equid bones (Johnstone 2004) and this has shown that the paucity of data from Britain is rooted in identification issues.

Details of the methodology developed to differentiate more accurately between horse, donkey and mule bones are given in Johnstone 2004 and 2006. In summary: discriminant function analysis (DFA) was applied to multiple measurements of the long bones of modern reference skeletons of horses, donkeys and mules in order to detect size and shape differences. The most successful element proved to be the tibia (91.9 per cent correct re-classification result), closely followed by the radius,

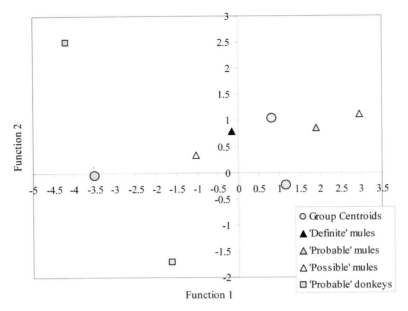

FIGURE 4. Scatter plot showing the results of discriminant function analysis on the mule and donkey metatarsals from Iron Age and Roman Britain.

metatarsal and humerus, with the femur and metacarpal producing slightly less reliable results (76.3 per cent correct re-classification for the metacarpal).

The results of the DFA on the modern specimens of these three animals was then applied to the measurements of archaeological bones to determine their identity. As the differentiation was not perfect for the modern specimens a system of grading the identifications of the archaeological material was employed (Johnstone 2004, 2006). Most of the following discussion is based on those specimens that were graded as 'definitely' or 'probably' belonging to a species, although those with 'possible' identifications are listed for the sake of completeness. Figures 4–6 show the mules and donkeys identified amongst the British bones originally recorded as 'horse' or 'equid', after using the DFA analysis and Table 2 gives the details of these results.

This analysis has identified more donkey and mule bones in the Roman period and also that these animals were present in a small number of possible Late Iron Age contexts. These Iron Age examples include two mules and three donkeys. There are two separate issues to be dealt with before we can say for certain that these represent the introduction of donkeys and mules to Britain in the Iron Age. At two of the sites where these individuals are present, Thorpe Thewles (Rackham 1985) and Skeleton Green (Ashdown and Evans 1981), the occupation sequence is continuous from the Iron Age, through the Conquest period and into the Roman Period. Therefore it is possible that dating of the particular deposits in which these bones were found could be called into question, either as a result of residual datable finds or the intrusion of bones into earlier deposits. A means of confirming or contradicting this would be to go back through the site archives to check the stratigraphy and dating evidence of individual contexts, or by direct radiocarbon dating of the crucial specimens, neither of which has been feasible to this point.

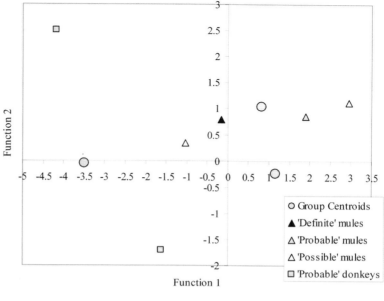

FIGURE 5. Scatter plot showing the results of discriminant function analysis on the mule and donkey metacarpals from Iron Age and Roman Britain.

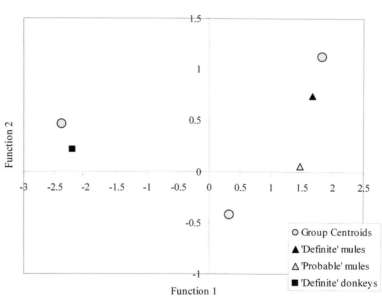

FIGURE 6. Scatter plot showing the results of discriminant function analysis on the mule and donkey femora from Iron Age and Roman Britain.

The second issue relating to these potentially Iron Age specimens is that pre-Conquest contact or trade between the inhabitants of these settlements and the Roman Empire are known (or inferred from artefactual evidence) to have occurred. Therefore, the presence of mules and donkeys can be explained as part of this trade, either as beasts of burden or as trade items in their own right. The site at Thorpe Thewles is known, through artefactual evidence, to have had extensive trade contact with Roman Empire in the pre-Conquest period. Even the site of Danebury (Cunliffe 1984), occupation of which does not extend into the Roman period, had links with the contemporaneous port

Site name	Element/ Bone no.	Date	Probability	Mahalanobis distance	Within 1 sd	Id	Reason for ID level	Reference
Beddington Sewage Farm	MC-416	2nd–3rd C A.D.	0.53	3.96	N	M?	Low probability of group membership and more than 1 sd from group centroid	MOLAS database
Castleford	MT-675	A.D. 85–100	0.63	0.93	Y	M*	Low probability of group membership but within 1 sd of group centroid	Berg 1999
Danebury	MC-433	300–50 B.C.	0.84	6.30	N	D*	High probability of group membership but more than 1 sd from group centroid	Grant 1984
Danebury	MC-437	300–50 B.C.	1.00	6.98	N	D*	High probability of group membership but more than 1 sd from group centroid	Grant 1984
E London RB Cemetery	Fem-101	1st–2nd C A.D.	0.81	0.18	Y	M	High probability of group membership and within 1 sd of group centroid	MOLAS database
Hayton Fort	Fem-347	A.D. 72–85	0.53	1.27	Y	M*	Low probability of group membership but within 1 sd of group centroid	Canby 1977
Longthorpe II	MC-553	A.D. 44–65	0.57	4.50	N	M?	Low probability of group membership and more than 1 sd from group centroid	King 1987
Orton Hall Farm	MT-505	A.D. 225–325	0.72	1.44	Y	M	High probability of group membership and within 1 sd of group centroid	King 1996
Orton Hall Farm	MC-637	A.D. 300–375	0.71	1.01	Y	M	High probability of group membership and within 1 sd of group centroid	King 1996
Orton Hall Farm	MC-638	A.D. 300–375	0.57	1.18	Y	M*	Low probability of group membership but within 1 sd of group centroid	King 1996
Scole-Dickleburgh	MT-445	2nd–Late 3rd C A.D.	0.84	0.11	Y	M	High probability of group membership and within 1 sd of group centroid	Baker 1998
Skeleton Green	MT-431	Early 1st C A.D.	0.69	0.69	Y	M	High probability of group membership and within 1 sd of group centroid	Ashdown and Evans 1981
Stonea	MT-427	E 2nd–3rd C A.D.	0.89	8.26	N	D*	High probability of group membership but more than 1 sd from group centroid	Barker 1976
Thorpe Thewles	Fem-97	LIA	0.97	0.09	Y	D	High probability of group membership and within 1 sd of group centroid	Rackham 1985
Thorpe Thewles	MT-305	LIA	0.55	0.61	Y	M*	Low probability of group membership but within 1 sd of group centroid	Rackham 1985

TABLE 2. Details of British mule and donkey bones identified using discriminant function analysis.

site at Hengistbury Head which has been established as having trading contact with the continent in the pre-Conquest Iron Age (Cunliffe 1978).

The Roman mules fall into two separate groups based on date and site type, with two exceptions. The first group come from first-century AD deposits within military and urban sites. The second group were located in second- to fourth-century AD contexts, mostly from rural locations. It would be expected that some of the first mules to have been brought to Britain would be in conjunction with military activity, so the first group could be explained as

Site name	Element/ Bone no.	Identification	Withers height (mm)	Metacarpal GL/SD index	Metatarsal GL/SD index
Castleford	MT-675	M*	1320.2	-	10.83
Danebury	MC-433	D*	1110.6	13.41	-
Danebury	MC-437	D*	1403.5	10.87	-
Orton Hall Farm	MT-505	M	1351.7	-	10.47
Orton Hall Farm	MC-637	M	1281.4	15.71	-
Orton Hall Farm	MC-638	M*	1452.3	14.71	-
Scole-Dickleburgh	MT-445	M	1403.5	-	11.27
Skeleton Green	MT-431	M	1231.2	-	-
Stonea	MT-427	D*	1178.8	-	-
Thorpe Thewles	MT-305	M*	1267.8	-	10.50

TABLE 3. Withers height estimates and metapodial slenderness indices for donkeys and mules from Britain.

imported military mules. As with many aspects of Romanisation, the spread of new ideas, technologies, goods etc took time to filter down the hierarchy of site types and therefore the presence of mules in later rural settlements can be explained in this way. With these later mules, it seems less likely that they were imported and more likely they were bred here.

Working on the hypothesis that mule breeding was in general linked to centralised wealthy estates whose owners exerted influence over the supply of mules (Johnstone 2008), there are two possible reasons why mule breeding in Britain took time to become established and why it seems to be have happened in the Eastern parts of the country. In the second century the development of the fenlands in East Anglia, Lincolnshire and Cambridgeshire for agriculture was undertaken to supply the northern army garrisons (Middleton 1979). It is possible that mules were bred as transport for this more local supply network, rather than using the ports (Johnstone 2004).

It is also possible that the development of wealthy villa sites in Britain in the third and fourth centuries AD may have created the circumstances for the establishment of mule breeding on a more continental model, i.e. on large wealthy estates (Johnstone 2004; 2008). However, as the number of mule bones currently identified is very small, these are just observations that will be tested as new data become available.

Of the 'definite' and 'probable' identifications, 10 metapodials were present, allowing the calculation of estimated withers heights (using the methods of May (1985)) and slenderness indices. The femora were not included in this analysis as the existing withers height calculation methods have been proven to consistently underestimate the height on this particular element (Johnstone 2004). Details of the results of these calculations are given in Table 3.

For the five mules from conclusively post-conquest deposits, the minimum withers height was 1281.4 mm and the maximum was 1452.3 mm giving a range of 170.9 mm. The mean withers height was 1361.8 mm with a standard deviation of 67.5. Compared to the overall Roman mule average of 1446.2 (Johnstone 2004) it can be seen that the British mules are considerably smaller than their continental counterparts. In addition the mean of the metatarsal

SD/GL slenderness index is 10.9, which is slightly lower than for other areas of the Roman Empire (11.1), indicating that the British mules are not only shorter but also more gracile. There are however, too few cases to statistically test for the significance of these apparent differences.

The Late Iron Age mule from Thorpe Thewles had a withers height of 1267.8 mm and a slenderness index of 10.5, which fits well within the range of the Roman individuals discussed above. It is at the lower end of the range (1220.7 – 1494.5 mm) for all Iron Age mules identified in Johnstone 2004.

The two Iron Age donkeys from Britain had withers heights of 1110.6 and 1403.5 mm, which is quite a range of size. These individuals fit within the range of the Roman continental donkeys (1030.4 to 1507.2 mm), which may indicate that these represent imports from the same stock. The Roman donkey from Stonea (1178.8 mm) also falls within the range of the continental Roman donkeys, but towards the lower end of the range.

The presence of donkeys in Britain, both in the Late Iron Age and Roman Britain is indicative of the importation of these animals from the continent. Indeed the large individual from Danebury, which could represent a 'prize specimen' being gifted or traded as a prestige item is a nice example with which to support this hypothesis. However, it is less clear whether the mules were also imported or were bred here from imported donkeys and local horses. The smaller size of Roman mules from Britain may support the latter theory, if male donkeys were imported and used on smaller local mares, then smaller mules would result. This would also be logistically more sensible than importing mules.

This may also help to explain the small numbers of mules found in Roman deposits from Britain in comparison to the proportions found on the continent. The logistical difficulties of transporting large numbers of animals across the sea may have resulted in small numbers of donkey being imported for breeding but not bringing mules as well. Yet there is still the question of why there were not more mules, particularly given the fact that the north of Britain was a military zone that required supply, which had to be achieved using the road network because the rivers are not well placed for transport (as suggested by Middleton 1979).

In addition to the logistical difficulties of transporting mules to Britain, perhaps environmental factors were also a consideration, with native ponies being better adapted to the colder, wetter climate of northern England than mules (and particularly the donkeys used to breed them). Zoologically, the introduction of small numbers of a species into an area of marginal habitat is unlikely to produce a successful breeding colony (Morales Muniz *et al.* 1995) and once the human interactions that caused their importation have ceased, the species is likely to die out. However, the adage 'absence of evidence is not evidence of absence' may apply here as the equid remains from many northern British sites have not yet been analysed using the new identification methodology (Johnstone 2008).

It is suggested here that the introduction of donkeys and mules to Britain took place as a result of contact or trade with continental Europe and the Roman Empire, with the possibility that this preceded the conquest of Britain in AD 43. Whether mules were imported as live animals or whether just the knowledge of how to breed them was brought in is as yet unclear.

The spread of donkeys and mules could be described as an effect of Romanisation, whilst a few may have come to Britain via trade routes, prior to the conquest, the numbers are greater afterwards. However, there are still proportionately less than on the continent. This has been true of more recent times as well: 'mules were uncommon in only a few countries, including the British Isles, but even in England mule-breeding was practised on a small scale from the time of the introduction of the donkey by the Romans' (Clutton-Brock 1992: 49). As discussed above this may be because of poor environmental adaptation.

There appear to be very few records of donkeys or mules between end of Roman period (exception of one donkey in London (Baxter 2002)) and reintroduction at some point after the Norman Conquest, although the systematic application of the new identification procedures to post-Roman material has not been undertaken. This possible gap in the presence of these animals in the British Isles is something that can be investigated now that the identification problems have been alleviated. Future research can also be directed towards looking more carefully at the distribution of donkeys and mules in Late Iron Age and Roman contexts to determine associations with particular types of site, specific time periods or geographical locations.

Acknowledgements

Thanks to those who provided raw measurement data to supplement that in the published sources quoted in particular, Alan Pipe and Kevin Rielly for allowing me access to the MOLAS database and Jane Richardson for the Castleford data. Thanks to Terry and Naomi for asking me to write this chapter and for their patience whilst I finished it!

CHAPTER 4

The Aurochs and Domestic Cattle

Anthony J. Legge

Taxonomy and distribution

The aurochs, *Bos primigenius*, is a member of the family Bovidae, which includes many species important in the human food economy; cattle, bison, sheep, goats, deer and antelopes. This broad group is divided into superfamilies, cattle being members of the Bovinae. Within this, two genera (*Bos* and *Bison*) hold the recent European species of the aurochs (*Bos primigenius*) and the European bison or wisent (*Bison bonasus*). All modern domestic cattle are descended from the aurochs. The aurochs was widely distributed in the Old World, found throughout Europe and North Africa, extending eastwards though central Asia into China. It was present in India too, but there regarded as a sub-species, *Bos primigenius namadicus,* while in North Africa it was classified into the sub-species *Bos primigenius mauretanicus*. In much of its range in Europe and central Asia the aurochs and wisent shared the same range and similar habitats, though there are significant reproductive barriers between the two species (Gray 1974). Future work on ancient DNA will elucidate the degree of variation throughout this extensive range.

Behaviour

The behaviour of the aurochs can be reconstructed from that of its descendants, modern domestic cattle, and from historical information. Under free-living conditions, cattle form small groups of females and young for much of the year, while the males are more solitary, increasingly so with maturity. The few surviving aurochs in the sixteenth-century Royal Forests of Poland lived in this way, the solitary males joining the female herd only in late summer for mating. In England now, free-living white cattle at Chillingham show the same behaviour, where a dominant male will defend the female herd in the breeding season, resisting challenges from other bulls (Van Vuure 2005, 264–271; Whitehead 1953). However, the dominant bull will accept the younger bulls near the herd as long as their threat is minimal. This behaviour is known as 'linear dominance' in which a herd of both sexes can live together, the younger bulls accepting the rule of the most powerful male. This is behaviour common to those members of the Bovidae that have been domesticated (cattle, sheep and goats) which makes close herding possible (Garrard 1984). The aurochs had a marked breeding season, as with most wild mammals in temperate climates. Contemporary descriptions described mating during the autumn, with births in early summer. Autumn born calves could not survive the severe cold of winter (Vuure 2005, 269).

It is probable that aurochs would have had some degree of seasonal movement in the most open habitats, but probably less where the vegetation was more mixed. The aurochs was found in some numbers at the Mesolithic site of Star Carr in Yorkshire, and was likely to have been largely residential in the valley, in common with the other large mammalian species there. Recent pollen work confirms the nature of the landscape, as '...open birch woodland with dry land' (Mellars and Dark 1998). While the exact nature of the woodland cannot be determined even by pollen analysis, the fauna of red deer, elk, roe deer, pig and cattle would be largely sedentary in such an environment, all finding a suitable habitat within the Vale, showing local movements at most (Legge and Rowley-Conwy 1988, 13–21).

Diet and habitat

Both domestic cattle, and the closely related European wild bison species *Bison bonasus* (Europe and western Asia) are preferential grazers. Cattle are ruminant animals, with a complex digestive system that provides an efficient mechanism for the digestion of a diet that is high in cellulose, especially grasses. Cattle are specially adapted to this diet, followed by sheep and then by goats, which, like deer, are better adapted for a diet that is higher in browse (Hoffman 1986).

On this evidence alone, the aurochs is best regarded as a species that was dependant on grazing, though with the occasional use of open woodland where it would eat forbs and shrubby browse, important as a winter resource. Rangeland cattle in Texas with access to woodland areas seldom browse when grass quality is high (one per cent browse in spring), but rising as grass quality falls, to four per cent browse in summer, 15 per cent in autumn and six per cent in winter. Thus in their selection of feed, cattle and the American bison are at the extreme of grazing adaptation among a variety of wild and domestic mammals (Lyons *et al.* n.d., figure 3, page 5, based on Vallentine 1990). Even the 'woodland' form of the American bison, *Bison bison athabascae*, lived in areas with extensive grazing among open woodlands (Stephenson *et al.* 2001). Indeed, one contemporary observer reported that 'the woodland bison, *Bison americanus*, (sic) is essentially a creature of the grasslands' and as 'beyond doubt almost exclusively an animal of the prairies and woodless plains, ranging only to a limited extent in the forested districts and never seen as a regular inhabitant of the denser woodland' (Shaler 1876, 72).

Historical and recent observations on wild and semi-wild cattle might seem to contradict this view. However, wild cattle and bison survived only in refugia, areas historically preserved as parks or for hunting. These woodlands were of a very open sort, more akin to parkland, with scattered trees, grassy meadows and wetland habitats (e.g. Rackham 1989). These observations led to the aurochs to be considered a woodland animal in some archaeological reports (for example, Cotton *et al.* 2006, figure 11.9, 161: the caption refers to '...the forest dwelling aurochs').

The association of prehistoric aurochs with open land was demonstrated by Higgs (1961), working on the fauna of the Haua Fteah cave in Cyrenaica, Libya. Higgs noted a peak of *Bos* bones at the end of the Pleistocene period, which he equated with woodland recession caused by the cold fluctuation, known as the Younger Dryas, about 12,000 BP. Pollen studies have now confirmed the severity of this cold oscillation, in the Eastern Mediterranean marked by much cooler conditions and low rainfall, with forest recession (Bottema and Van Zeist 1981; Moore *et al.* 2000, in particular pages 73–84 for discussion).

The aurochs can thus be characterised by habitual grazing, but with the ability to use woodland when this was advantageous for winter browse and shelter. An open woodland habitat must be envisaged as only when light can penetrate to the woodland floor will there be worthwhile accessible food. Direct evidence of aurochs diet has now been revealed by studies of the stable isotopes 13C and 15N. Analysis of bone collagen has shown that *Bos primigenius* had '...a diet of grass supplemented by browsing in the light and open pre-boreal environment' (Noe-Nygaard *et al.* 2005, 864). With the rather more closed woodland of the warmer Atlantic period, a higher proportion of shrubs and forbs were consumed, though both the aurochs and the domestic cattle of the early Neolithic in Southern Scandinavia had a diet mainly of grasses.

Osteology and body size

The aurochs were very large cattle indeed, the bulls standing almost 1.8 m in height at the shoulder, and the cows about 1.5 m (Boessnek 1957). The largest assemblage of aurochs bones from a single archaeological site in Britain is that from Star Carr, in Yorkshire, England, described by Frazer and King (1954) and revised by Legge and Rowley-Conwy (1988). The osteology of the aurochs, and the descent of modern cattle from it, was long confused by a belief that two forms of wild cattle, large and small, existed in prehistoric times This idea arose from two misunderstandings. Firstly, bones from Star Carr, as described by Frazer and King (1954), included misidentified elk (*Alces*) bones among those listed as being from the aurochs. This metrical evidence was later discussed by Jewell (1963), who showed the progressive reduction in size from the Mesolithic aurochs, to the domestic cattle of the Neolithic, Bronze and Iron ages. Jewell noted that the Star Carr aurochs bones showed marked variation in size, some being '...much diminished in size when compared to Pleistocene specimens' (Jewell 1963, 83). However, when the misidentified elk bones are discounted, the Star Carr aurochs population has no specimens that are smaller than would be anticipated (Legge and Rowley-Conwy 1988). This natural variation is now

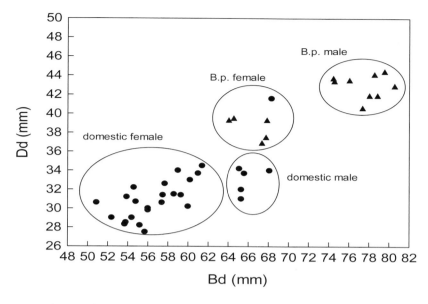

FIGURE 7. Metacarpal measurements – breadth of distal end (Bd) by depth of distal end (Dd) – showing sexual dimorphism in, and separation between, domestic and wild cattle. Triangles denote specimens from Starr Carr, spots denote Hambeldon/Stepleton.

better understood as in cattle, in common with most species where the males are solitary for much of the year, sexual dimorphism is marked, with the male aurochs being very much large than females (Figure 7).

Consequently, the measurements of *Bos* bones can now be used to determine the proportions in which the sexes were killed at archaeological sites. The aurochs bones from Star Carr show both sexes, with rather more males than females. Measurements of the astragali show a ratio of seven males to six females, while the distal metacarpal shows 10 males to five females (Legge and Rowley-Conwy 1988, table 8F and 8H, 131). Figure 7 shows the relationship between two measurements of the distal metacarpal (distal breadth, Bd and distal thickness, Dd) of cattle bones from Star Carr (Mesolithic) and Hambledon/Stepleton (Neolithic). Four groups of bones are evident. Ten very large cattle at the right side of the diagram are the males of *Bos primigenius*. At the left, there are twenty-nine measurements of domestic cows. The group between these have very similar distal width (Bd 63 to 72 mm) but a greater range in the anterior-posterior measurement (Dd 31–42 mm), particularly in relation to each size range. This thickness measurement therefore divides the group into two; the females of aurochs (upper group) and the males of domestic cattle (lower group). This change under domestication was described by Degerbøl and Fredskild (1970), the bone articulations being *less* robust in their anterior-posterior dimension when compared to articular width. The Neolithic site of Selevac in Serbia gave the same pattern with the bones of both wild and domestic cattle (Legge 1990, figure 5.8, 224). It is evident that one female of *Bos primigenius* was also found among the bones from Neolithic Hambledon/Stepleton.

The study of body size in the aurochs must therefore take account of the proportions of males and females in the sample. At Star Carr, an average (or

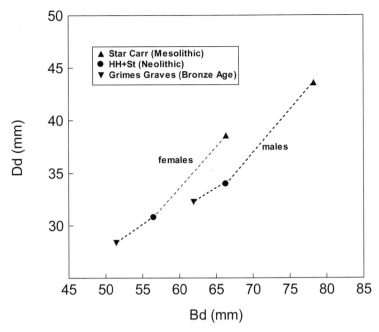

FIGURE 8. Inter-period variation in the size of cattle metacarpals – breadth of distal (Bd) by depth of distal (Dd) – from three archaeological sites.

'mean') dimension for the distal metacarpal will be skewed towards the larger size of the males, as these are more numerous. Conversely, bone measurements from the Neolithic domestic cattle are mainly from females, as these are usually much more numerous in bone samples from post-Mesolithic times (Legge 1981, figure 4, 176–77 and Figure 7 here). In Figure 8, change in body size is shown by the mean dimension of the distal metacarpal, plotted for males and females from three sites in England; Star Carr (Mesolithic, Legge and Rowley-Conwy 1988) Hambledon/Stepleton (Neolithic, Legge 2008) and Grimes Graves (Bronze Age, Legge 1992). The diagram shows a more realistic picture of size reduction, not being biased by disproportions of the sexes in the different samples. It is also evident that the domestication process has only a small influence on the expression of sexual dimorphism in cattle.

Domestication and dispersal

It has long been known that South-west Asia is the region of origin for many of our domestic plants and animals. Recent work has done much to elucidate the process, and place it within a much more secure chronology (Moore *et al.* 2000). The aurochs lived throughout this region, and was domesticated there, though the process is not yet completely understood. The long archaeological sequence at Tell Abu Hureyra in Northern Syria extends from the Mesolithic to the early Aceramic Neolithic, and rather rare cattle bones are present throughout this time, as would be expected in quite arid steppe with little or no permanent water. However, in the later Aceramic Neolithic, cattle bones increase markedly to 10–15 per cent or thereabouts, along with a greater increase in caprines, mainly sheep. There are no environmental or climatic reasons why this would happen naturally. The significance of this is discussed in detail by Legge and Rowley-Conwy (2000, 423–71) and it is sufficient to say here that the sudden increase in *Bos* bones is interpreted as early domestication *c.* 8300 BP. This is supported by the appearance of domestic cattle at the site of Shillourokambos in Cyprus at about this time, an island to which cattle must have been carried by boat (Guilaine *et al.* 2000).

From its first inception in South-West Asia, the agricultural package spread rapidly into Southern Europe, and beyond, reaching northern Europe in no more than 2500 years. Domestic cattle were an integral part of this, being found at all Neolithic habitation sites throughout Europe. Yet while the chronology of this dispersal is well known, its nature is a subject of much contention in archaeology. Sheep, goats, and cereals such as wheat and barley, are not native to Europe and these domesticates had to be part of the dispersal though Europe. But what of native cattle and pigs? Were these part of the dispersed package, or locally domesticated? Figure 8 shows that there is a marked disparity in body size between the local British aurochs and early Neolithic domestic cattle, and this holds true from South-East Europe to Britain. Body size can change rapidly under human control (Widdowson 1980), but the difference here has seemed too great to accommodate 'local' domestication from the osteometric data available. Significant new tools are now available to address this problem though, as yet, findings vary as to the influence of European *Bos primigenius* on the genes of modern European domestic cattle, and conclusions change by the month. Work on ancient DNA supports the dispersal hypothesis, but with some evidence for the local introgression of aurochs genes into Neolithic domestic cattle. Götherström *et al.* (2005) found a distinct difference between the mtDNA of British aurochs and modern European cattle breeds, supporting the external origin for British domestic cattle. They further observed that cattle chromosome haplotypes show a north-south gradient though Europe, with the northern haplotype being common to most aurochs as well as domestic cattle, suggesting some degree of introgression of local aurochs genes. Similar conclusions have been reached by Beja-Periera *et al.* (2006) working with Italian material, though Edwards *et al.* (2007) find these results to '…raise many questions and warrant additional verification.' Anderung (2006) also found evidence for local admixture of aurochs mtDNA. Elsewhere, Kühn *et al.* (2005) examined cattle bones from a Neolithic site in Bavaria, South Germany, finding a remarkable continuity with modern domestic cattle and some genetic distance from the aurochs. Their conclusion was that the population there had little, if any introgression of European aurochs DNA into their lineage. As Anderung and others point out, the introgression of the aurochs DNA would be from males mating with domestic females, making the introgression of aurochs genes an occasional, probably accidental, event, as there is no evidence for local domestication events within Europe involving female aurochs. As Van

Vuure (2005, 267, 269) describes, the few surviving aurochs of the sixteenth and seventeenth centuries would happily mate with domestic cows, though to the disadvantage of the cow's owners. The comparative uniformity of European domestic cattle was emphasised by Bollongino *et al.* (2006), who tested the DNA taken from 33 samples of Neolithic cattle bones from sites throughout Europe, and found that '…the bulk of bovine mtDNA diversity today derives from only a few Neolithic founder chromosomes.' (Bollongino *et al.* 2006, 159). The same group have now expanded this study to a larger scale testing of bones *Bos primigenius* and from early domestic cattle. DNA amplification was achieved in 59 specimens (Edwards *et al.* 2007) and the authors present an emphatic view that European domestic cattle have an origin within South-west Asia. They found that all European aurochs tested have the haplotype designated as 'P' while both prehistoric and modern domestic cattle are of the 'T' haplotype. The authors also identify the 'T' haplotype in cattle from the Aceramic Neolithic (PPNB) site of Dja'de in Syria, which are identified as domestic based on a moderate reduction in size (Helmer *et al.* 2005).

It would appear therefore that the weight of evidence from studies of ancient DNA place the origin of domestic cattle outside Europe, with limited local introgression of aurochs genes. The predominance of the ancient domestic lineage rather implies that later wild admixture was avoided. Interestingly, recent work has also shown the introduction of domestic pigs too from South-west Asia, spreading to the Paris basin by the early fourth millennium BC, though locally domesticated pigs soon displaced the incomers (Larsen *et al.* 2007a; 2007b).

Decline and extinction

The sub-fossil remains of the aurochs are common in sediments from the later middle Pleistocene though to the Holocene in Britain, though few of these are reliably dated. It is well known from Neolithic Causewayed Camps, for example, the Hambledon/Stepleton complex (Legge 1981; 2008), and Windmill Hill (Grigson 2000), though as a small proportion of the bone sample. This need not reflect the abundance of the aurochs as these sites had an apparent social purpose in which hunting was unlikely to be a major concern. The food remains are highly selected, and unlikely to reflect normal domestic usage (Grigson 2000; Jones and Legge 2008; Legge 1981; 2008). It may also be noted that the bones of red deer are rather scarce at the same sites, yet the abundance of red deer antler in Neolithic mining sites could indicate that the species was at least locally common.

When Neolithic farmers occupied the landscape, the wild fauna threatened both their crops and livestock. Neolithic cattle were smaller than the native aurochs, and cattle husbandry was of a specialised form, oriented towards dairy production (Copley *et al.* 2003; Legge 1992; 2006). Interbreeding with aurochs males would be disadvantageous, undoing four thousand years of domestication and threatening the wellbeing of the domestic female by causing the births of

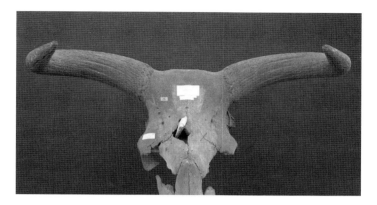

FIGURE 9. Aurochs skull with Neolithic axe, recovered from Burwell Fen (Sedgwick Museum, Cambridge, acc. No. D33, 665a,b).

very large calves. It is probable that the Neolithic farmers killed the aurochs at every opportunity. Large as they were, and aggressive when provoked, they had no defence against a well-aimed arrow. In Britain, powerful Neolithic bows are known, sufficient to deliver a mortal wound to the largest aurochs (Bergman *et al.* 1988). An 80 lb (36 kg.) draw weight was able to deliver 'through and through' wounds to the American plains bison, the arrow tipped with a barbed stone projectile 25 mm wide. When this struck the vital chest organs, the resulting shock and blood loss was quickly fatal (Pope 1925). In Europe, aurochs and deer bones are widely known with severe wounds, some of which were probably fatal, while others had healed (Hallam *et al.* 1973; Legge and Rowley-Conwy 1988; Noe-Nygaard 1975).

An aurochs skeleton excavated at Vig in Denmark had fragments of flint arrowheads embedded in a rib, and three more arrowheads were within the chest cavity (Degerbøl and Fredskild 1970, 9). Piercing wounds have also been found in the scapula (Noe-Nygaard 1975). Burwell Fen, near to Cambridge in England, has yielded the bones of many prehistoric animals, among them numerous specimens of *Bos primigenius*. In 1863, a skull and part skeleton was found there by phosphate miners (Sedgwick Museum, Cambridge, acc. no. D33, 665a, b). The skull was pierced by a blow from a flint axe of late Neolithic form, placed by a Neolithic Captain Marvel, right between the eyes (Figure 9). At the time, the association of the skull and axe was questioned as a possible fraud, being dug up by phosphate miners who were experienced in the sale of antiquities, much to their profit (Fox 1923, 255–58). However, five established geologists examined the skull, and decide that the placement of the axe was genuine (Carter 1874). A preliminary examination of the skull and part skeleton showed no cut marks or other butchery evidence. It would seem that a hunted aurochs was bogged and dispatched by a blow to the skull, commonly suggested as a hunting method for large game. However, Frison and Stanford (1982) reported that American Indian hunting methods did not utilise bogs as traps, as this made handling very difficult and clean butchery impossible; it was more usual for the animals to be chased *out* of boggy areas and killed on dry land.

A site with a single hunting event was been found at Holloway Lane,

Hillingdon, West London (Cotton *et al.* 2006). At Hillingdon, a disarticulated skeleton of an aurochs, rather badly preserved, was found within a deep pit, associated with six barbed and tanged flint arrowheads. The authors interpret this as a 'strike and follow' event, the bones being later placed in the pit as a ritual form of disposal to '...make flesh the tensions inherent in socialising a wildscape' (Cotton *et al.* 2006, 163). Possibly so, though a more prosaic interpretation is at least as likely. Cotton *et al.* (op. cit.) quote Caesar's well-known passage on the status of the aurochs among the German tribes: 'These [the aurochs] the *Germani* capture skilfully in pits, and their young men harden themselves by such labour and exercise themselves by this kind of hunting'. Caesar also noted the value that was placed upon aurochs horns for use as drinking vessels: 'The *Germani* collect them eagerly, encase their edges in silver, and use them as beakers at their most magnificent banquets' (Edwards 1917).

Pitfall traps were also recorded as used to trap aurochs in Eastern Europe in the sixteenth and seventeenth centuries (Van Vuure 2005, 74). The arrowheads at Hillingdon could be both from wounds sustained before the trapping, and the means by which the trapped animal was killed. The difficulty of complete butchery of a massive animal within the confines of a deep pit would also accord with abandonment of articulated bones within the pit. While ritual intent in the bone disposal is possible, the widespread historical use of pitfall taps as a simple, effective and relatively safe means of trapping large mammals makes this interpretation more probable.

The extinction of the aurochs in Britain appears to have happened during the Bronze Age, a time of increasingly dense settlement and land clearance which must have placed the remaining aurochs under pressure. The latest direct radiocarbon dates on aurochs bones are those from a swallow hole at Charterhouse Warren Farm, Somerset (Levitan *et al.* 1988) at about 3245 BP (BM 731). Dates on this and on human bones there place the find securely within the Bronze Age. Only a little older was the find at Lowe's Farm (Shawcross and Higgs 1963) at 3340 and 3850 BP (BM 1443, 1469). Other *Bos primigenius* dates are of the same order; Beckford in Western England at 3578 BP (BM 1445) and Wilburton in Cambridgeshire at 3400 BP (BM 1445). The Burwell skull and skeleton was dated a little earlier at 4200 BP (BM 1525). This cluster of dates in the range 4200–3245 BP suggests that extinction was comparatively rapid. While habitat pressure is evident in the Bronze Age, it is likely that infectious disease was also an agent; as with isolated human populations in historic times, the native British aurochs probably had low immunity to imported diseases. Elsewhere in Europe the aurochs survived into the Roman period (Grant and Sauer 2006) and in Eastern Europe the last were killed only in the seventeenth century AD (Van Vuure 2005). Large drinking vessels made from the horns of aurochs were noted by Caesar as used by the German tribes (see above) and have been found in the Anglo-Saxon ship burial at Sutton Hoo, but here as highly valuable imported objects, suitable for display at a royal court (Bruce-Mitford and East 1983; Oddy and Grigson 1983). A right horn, claimed to be from the last known aurochs to die in 1620, survives mounted as a hunting horn, on display at the museum of Livrustkammaren in Stockholm (Van Vuure 2005, plate 7, 98).

In spite of protection by winter housing and supplementary feed, the last remaining aurochs eventually succumbed to competition for living space, infections from cattle plagues and from hunting (Van Vuure 2005, 53–78). There was little room anywhere for so large an animal. The European bison was rather more fortunate; though reduced in the same way, sufficient animals survived for the population to be gradually restored in special reserves.

In the nineteenth century, the Heck brothers, both zookeepers in Germany, began a programme to breed back the aurochs from modern domestic and semi-wild cattle. Their belief was that modern domestic cattle preserve the genetic make up of the aurochs and that, by selective breeding, they could recover the original species. Their efforts have resulted in an animal that resembles the original in size and colour, though re-creation of the ancestral lineage by this means is scarcely possible (Van Vuure 2005, 323–59). However, with the advent of ever more advanced techniques of genetic manipulation, who knows what could be done in a forthcoming Pleistocene Park?

Acknowledgements

I am grateful to the Sedgwick Museum of Earth Sciences at Cambridge for permission to publish the photograph of the *Bos* skull.

CHAPTER 5

The Elk

Andrew C. Kitchener

Introduction

The elk is the largest living deer and one of the largest ever to have lived. It was formerly regarded as a single species that had an extensive distribution from Europe through the boreal forests of northern Asia, including Mongolia and China, to the northern half of North America. However, differences in karyotype, pelage coloration, and the structure of the premaxillae led Boyeskorov (1999) to distinguish two species, the elk *Alces alces* which occurs west of the River Yenesi in Russia, and the moose, *Alces americana*, which occurs from eastern Siberia to North America.

The elk has a long fossil and archaeological history in Britain, but has been recorded from only 27 localities, mostly in Scotland and in northern England, with none recorded from Ireland (Yalden and Kitchener 2008). The oldest record is from Gray's Thurrock in Essex, which dates from the Ipswichian interglacial about 73,000–135,000 BP (Lister 1984a). A more recent record dates to about 31,000 BP from Kent's Cavern in Devon (Lister 1984a). All other records are from the late Devensian during the Windermere Interstadial, and from the early Holocene until the Bronze Age. These originated from animals that colonised Britain via the land bridge across what is now the North Sea and English Channel at the end of the last Ice Age (Yalden 1999). Until recently, it was widely believed that the elk had become extinct in Britain by the end of the Mesolithic, owing to a lack of subsequent dated finds, an absence from later archaeological sites and no apparent historical record (Yalden 1999). The cause of extinction was widely held to be habitat change owing to a continued warming of the climate (e.g. Clutton-Brock 1991), despite the evident wide range of habitats that elk thrive in today at similar latitudes (Heptner *et al.* 1989; Macdonald and Barrett 1993; Peek 1998). This chapter presents new evidence suggesting that the elk survived until much more recently (Ritchie 1920) and considers the role that humans played in the extinction of the species in Britain.

Archaeological representation

Including those mentioned above, Yalden (1999) lists 27 sites in Britain where elk remains have been recorded, many of which are from northern Britain. However, few are reliably dated, although most are thought to be from the early Holocene. Unless the specimens have been preserved or figured, there may be considerable risk of confusion with the palmated antlers of the giant deer, *Megaloceros giganteus*, reindeer, *Rangifer tarandus*, and even the terminal crowns of large antlers of red deer, *Cervus elaphus*. For example, Ewart (1911) identified an offcut of antler from the Roman site at Newstead, near Melrose, Borders, as being from an elk, which would make this important late evidence for the survival of the elk in Scotland. However, this antler fragment has been recently re-identified as being the crown of a red deer antler (Kitchener *et al.* 2004). Another record from Coldingham in Berwickshire (Reynolds 1934) is probably also from a red deer judging from the published illustration, but the current whereabouts of this specimen are unknown. Even when specimens were available, similar confusion led to the misidentification of red deer antlers as being those from reindeer at many sites in Scotland (Clutton-Brock and Macgregor 1988). The so-called 'Middlestot's bog elk' (Smith 1872) is evidently from a reindeer (specimen in NMS; register no. NMS.Z.1997.85).

The elk does not seem to have successfully colonised Ireland; of four putative fossil finds in peat, two have been radiocarbon dated to the very recent (i.e. about AD 1940), indicating that they are discarded game trophies (Monaghan 1989; Woodman *et al.*1997).

There are two late Devensian (Pleistocene) records of elk from Britain, which both date to the Windermere Interstadial. A complete skeleton of a male with antlers was found in lake or pond muds at Neasham, near Darlington in County Durham in 1939 (Trechmann 1939). The muds were radiocarbon dated from 11,011±230 to 11,561±250 BP. (Blackburn 1952). In 1970 another complete skeleton of a male was found at High Furlong, Blackpool in Lancashire in detritus muds within lake sediments (Hallam *et al.* 1973). Pollen analysis suggested that the muds dated to pollen zones I to III of the late Devensian, but the muds gave radiocarbon dates of 11,665±140 to 12,200±160 BP (12,400 BP in Yalden 1999), which are greater than would be expected. Pollen analysis also revealed that the elk was living in birch woodland with juniper, sedges, grasses and other herbaceous plants of open ground. This would indicate a typical habitat of today's elk. The elk's skeleton had many injuries caused by flint-tipped weapons and bone projectile points from human hunters, and two barbed projectile points were found with the skeleton, but there were no signs of butchery. One of the points had worn a groove in the distal end of the left metatarsal, indicating that it had carried this point for two to three weeks before death: Noe-Nygaard (1975) had disputed this but Stuart (1976) confirmed the original interpretation. Its antlers were just about to be shed, indicating that it had died in the winter between November and February. It is suggested that the animal had fallen through thin ice and had drowned, perhaps after being pursued by human hunters or wolves.

Therefore, although the elk successfully colonised Britain during the Windermere Interstadial, climatic conditions deteriorated once more during the Loch Lomond Readvance (Younger Dryas), thereby presumably forcing the elk out of Britain once more. However, there are two important Mesolithic sites that revealed the remains of elk, indicating early colonisation of Britain after the end of the last Ice Age at about 10,000 BP. Star Carr in Yorkshire has radiocarbon dates of around 9500 BP, whereas Thatcham in Berkshire has a range of dates from about 9600 to 10,050 BP. Pollen analysis shows that the vegetation at Star Carr was primarily birch woodland with some pine and alder. Other pollen, rhizomes and seeds indicated lakeside vegetation, including reeds (*Phragmites australis*), sedge (*Cladium mariscus*), white and yellow water lilies and bog-bean. All in all this represented ideal elk habitat, but elk were relatively poorly represented compared with other deer species. Red and roe deer were initially recognised as the commonest prey of the hunters, but a reanalysis, taking into account the importation of red deer antlers for tool making, led to the conclusion that the remains represented minimum numbers of 26 red deer, 17 roe deer, 16 aurochsen, eight beavers, four wild pigs and 12 elks (Frazer and King 1954; Legge and Rowley-Conwy 1988). Of course larger species such as the aurochs and elk may have been more difficult to hunt and required cooperation between several hunters. There are a number of other factors that make elk difficult to hunt, including their low population density, lack of gregariousness (the commonest association being between calves and their mother, and mating pairs during the rut, but small herds of both sexes may form in the winter led by a female), which may make them harder to find, their ability to escape swiftly over rugged terrain using their long legs, which makes pursuit difficult, their thick hide, which may cause weapons to bounce off, and when cornered they may attack their pursuers (Geist 1998). For example, the High Furlong elk skeleton displayed several injuries caused by human weapons and at Star Carr an elk's scapula has partly-healed fractures caused by a barbed point, suggesting that elk were difficult to kill even if they were successfully struck by weapons (Noe-Nygard 1975). These factors may explain the relative rarity of elk at archaeological sites. Moreover, when hunted successfully, it may have been easier to dismember the carcass where the animal was killed, and remove the meat to make it easy to transport, the so-called schlepp effect (Daly 1969). However, even if elk were rarer and more difficult to hunt, their body weight is considerably greater than that of red deer, so that in terms of edible meat, the elk was a far more important prey item than red deer at Star Carr. Reeves and McCabe (1998) compared the body weights and food yield from various North American ungulates that are traditionally exploited by North American Indians (Table 4). If we equate these with typical European species, we can make a direct comparison of the food yield of the Star Carr assemblage, which

North American Species	European species equivalent	Live weight (kg)	Food yield (kg)	MNI at *Star Carr*	Total food yield at *Star Carr* (kg)	Biomass (kg/km²)
Moose	Elk	500 (550)	344.6 (379)	12	4135.2 (4548)	55–605
Caribou	Reindeer	133.8 (95)	96.2 (68.3)	–	–	38–180
American Bison	Aurochs	627.4 (700*)	425.4 (474.6)	16	6806.4 (7593.6)	2100–8400
Wapiti	Red deer	272.4 (150)	184.8 (101.7)	26	4804.8 (2644.2)	750–1500

TABLE 4. A comparison of the potential food yield (kg) from and biomass (kg/km²) of large ungulates found at the Mesolithic site of Star Carr based on closely related North American species (Reeves and McCabe 1998; Legge and Rowley-Conwy 1988; Kitchener *et al.* 2004). Values in brackets are based on body weights used in Kitchener *et al.* (2004). MNI – minimum number of individuals * – based on European bison body weights.

reveals that the total food yield is about the same or considerably more than that of the prevalent red deer, depending on which body weight is used (Table 4). Given the low population densities, and hence, standing biomass, for elk compared with those of red deer and aurochs, it would appear in fact that elk were selected over other prey by human hunters.

In North America (and probably also in prehistoric Europe) elk and moose were important as sources of good meat and large tough hides, which could be used for clothing or even dwellings (Geist 1998; Reeves and McCabe 1998). However, their antlers were and are rarely used in tool making compared with those of red deer. The long beams and tines and spongy core of red deer antlers allow fine bone points to be worked easily from the antler, whereas the short beams and palms of elk antlers with their dense cores do not (C. Bonsall pers. comm.). Interestingly, although North American Indians traditionally used some parts of the skeleton for tools, antlers were generally not used for tool making (Reeves and McCabe 1998). This may provide another important reason why elk are so rarely recorded at Mesolithic sites and are apparently absent from later sites in comparison with red deer.

The Mesolithic site at Thatcham is situated on a gravel terrace beside a lake on the River Kennet about 3 km from Newbury in Berkshire (Wymer 1962). Here, only one elk was recorded alongside eight red deer, six roe deer, seven wild pigs and two aurochsen, despite the fact that during the period of occupation the vegetation changed from birch through birch-pine to pine-hazel at this site, which would have provided typical elk habitats. Elk was also recorded from the nearby Mesolithic site at Wawcott in Berkshire (Carter 1975). An elk antler from Whittrig Bog, Berwickshire was recently radiocarbon dated to about 7790 BP, providing yet another Mesolithic record (Kitchener and Bonsall 1997).

Survival of elk into the Bronze Age was suggested on the basis of droppings found in peat at Ugg Mere in Cambridgeshire (Godwin 1975). These were radiocarbon dated to about 3260 BP, which would make them the most recent record of the elk in Britain. However, Adrian Lister re-examined these droppings and found them to be too small to be from elk and so this record cannot be sustained (Stuart 1982). Subsequently, Kitchener and Bonsall (1997) published a radiocarbon date of 3935 BP for an elk antler recovered from the River Cree in Wigtownshire in the nineteenth century. Therefore, the elk had survived in this part of Scotland until the Bronze Age. This recent date confirmed that the elk's extinction was most likely to have been caused by a combination of over-hunting by people, deforestation caused by human farming activities and the use of timber for construction and fuel.

Ritchie (1920) suggested that elk could have survived beyond a supposed ninth-century record from Keiss broch in Caithness, on the basis of the survival of two putative Gaelic names, *Lon* and *Miol*. These names apparently refer to a great black or dark deer with a shambling, yet swift, gait, which might well describe an elk. Translations of the Gaelic poems *The aged bard's wish* and *Bas Dhiarmid* also mention the elk as being among the extant wildlife. However, there are some doubts about the association of these names with the elk and no more recent remains have yet been found in Scotland. A now-destroyed rock carving from Michael Cave at Wemyss, Fife was originally interpreted as showing an elk (Childe 1935; Edwards 1933), later as an aurochs (McCormick and Buckland 1997), but has recently been reinterpreted as a seal, which seems more likely given its coastal location (Kitchener *et al.* 2004). It is interesting to note that the most recently dated remains of the aurochs in Britain also come from the Bronze Age, which may suggest that woodland cover and human impact on the populations of elk and aurochs could have caused their extinction at about this time (see Legge, this volume).

It is worth exploring a little further whether the elk could have survived until much more recently in Britain by reviewing its current ecology and behaviour. Elk and moose are mainly inhabitants of boreal forest, comprising mostly spruce, fir and pine (Karns 1998). They rely on frequent disturbances to the tree cover caused by fires, floods, insect damage, diseases and even avalanches to promote regrowth of herbaceous plants and trees, on which to browse (Karns 1998). However, elk can thrive in a wide variety of habitats, including mixed coniferous deciduous forests, delta floodplains with willow, tundra (with small islands or open stands of trees), subalpine shrub and stream valleys (Peek 1998), although Scandinavian elk (which are probably most similar to those that inhabited Britain) are more forest-adapted, feeding principally on pine and spruce (Geist 1998). In Alaska moose populations increased until 17–26 years after fire, whereafter they declined by nine per cent annually as the habitat became less suitable (Karns 1998). It is possible that as forest cover became increasingly fragmented in Britain, elk numbers may initially have risen as more ideal forage became available. Their distribution is limited by the presence of appropriate habitat and forage in the north and by temperature in the south; they become heat stressed at temperatures above 14°C in summer and 5.1°C in winter, so that elk do not occur further south than about 40°N (Karns 1998; Geist 1998), which is still well within the latitudinal limits of Britain. However, our Atlantic climate may be more limiting. Data for mean summer and winter temperatures for Britain for 1971–2000 (Met Office n.d.) show that during summer, mean temperatures greater than 14°C would exclude elk from much of southern and central England, leaving Wales, northern England and Scotland as suitable environments. Mean winter temperatures would exclude the elk only from the southwest and far south of England and the coastal areas of Wales, thus suggesting that there may have been seasonal movements of elk in the Mesolithic when habitats were more contiguous.

Elk are essentially solitary browsers, which feed selectively on highly nutritious young plants, twigs and leaves that contain low fibre, high protein and few anti-herbivory compounds, such as tannins (Bryant and Kuropat 1980; Geist 1998). The diet comprises about 90 per cent browse, eight per cent forbs and only two per cent grass (Renecker and Schwartz 1998). Summer food consists mainly of leaves, herbaceous, riparian and aquatic plants (high in sodium), which allow elk to put on considerable body fat for survival during the winter, when twigs, fallen leaves, conifer needles and bark are the main dietary components. Elk browse on an astonishing number of plant species e.g. 355 in Russia, of which 40 were principal food plants, including preferred browse on willow, aspen and birch (Franzmann 1981; Renecker and Schwartz 1998).

Therefore, elk might easily have survived beyond the Mesolithic perhaps until the Iron Age, when most of Britain was deforested. However, it should be noted that the Highlands of Scotland, with its predominant tree community of Scot's pine and birch, did not become significantly deforested until the eighteenth century (Tipping 1994). The elk's preference for marshy habitats in order to feed on riparian and aquatic plants in summer may have led to a strong association with beaver-modified habitats (Coles 2006; Kitchener 2002). The loss of these dynamic habitats with the supposed extinction of the beaver in Scotland in the mid-sixteenth century (Conroy *et al.* 1997; but see Coles 2006; this volume) could have been an important factor in the demise of any surviving elk populations. The late survival of appropriate habitat in the Scottish Highlands and its possible association with the last beavers leaves us with the tantalising possibility that the elk may well have survived into historic times in Scotland, when it possibly inspired the Gaelic poets (Ritchie 1920).

Even though the actual evidence for the elk in Britain is rather sparse, there is still sufficient to demonstrate a long stratigraphical history, and with our increased knowledge of the habitat and foraging requirements of elk today, it is possible to speculate on its much more recent survival here. New radiocarbon dates have forced us to radically review latest dates of survival and causes of extinction for several large mammals in Britain, including the elk, aurochs and lynx (see Hetherington, this volume), so that human activities rather than climate change are clearly responsible for their more recent disappearance. In an era of ecosystem restoration through reintroductions, which have caught the imagination of the wider public, it is important that a re-evaluation of palaeontological and archaeological evidence for extinct species, such as the elk, now provides a solid basis for assessing the real potential for their reintroduction to Britain. Now that we know that our ancestors were the culprits involved in the elk's demise, we can be certain that there is no over-riding biological barrier, beyond its basic habitat requirements, to prevent the return of the elk.

CHAPTER 6

Red Deer on Scottish Islands

Jacqui Mulville

Introduction

Red deer (*Cervus elaphus*) are the largest surviving indigenous land mammals in the British Isles. They epitomise wilderness; flourishing in areas removed from human activity and are glimpsed in forests, on hills and silhouetted against the skylines of open moorland (Figure 10). During the autumnal rut, males competing for female attention become highly visible, noisy and violent; roaring and clashing they fill the days and the nights with sound and violence. Today British red deer populations are limited to the margins of the modern world, concentrated on Exmoor and in the highlands and islands of Scotland, but in the past they played a central role in human lives. Red deer first arose as a distinct species in the early Pleistocene (Whitehead 1993) and colonised Britain as the glaciers retreated at the end of the last Ice Age. They formed the backbone of human Mesolithic diet and culture, as evidenced by the dominance of red deer bones, teeth and antlers on the majority of sites dating to this period. The establishment of domestic stock in Britain during the Neolithic initiated a decline in the exploitation of red deer and other wild fauna. Over time a combination of environmental and human pressures saw red deer populations dwindle, leading to local extinctions, and it was only with the nineteenth-century rise of deer stalking that many herds were re-established (Staines 1991, 503; Yalden 1999, 177). Today Scotland is home to the largest group of red deer in Europe, estimated to be between 300,000 and 450,000 individuals (Clutton-Brock *et al.* 2004). Most live on the Scottish mainland but small populations exist on some of the larger Scottish islands.

The Scottish islands can be divided into four main groups, each has a different geology and the individual islands vary in size, local topography and soils. Two of the groups are situated off the west coast of Scotland, the Inner and Outer Hebrides (the last also known as the Western Isles), whilst the two groups constituting the Northern Isles lie off to the north-east: the closer Orkney Isles and the more distant Shetland Isles. Although red deer are not found on the Northern Isles today, archaeological evidence demonstrates that they were exploited on the larger Orcadian Isles during prehistory and that in the Hebrides this strategy extended out to the smaller outlying islands (Table 5). The mechanism by which red deer colonised the more distant isles is of particular

FIGURE 10. Red deer stag
© RICHARD FORD, DIGITAL
WILDLIFE

interest. Scotland was denuded of fauna during the last glaciations and recolonisation of the outer islands would have been hampered by rising sea levels
and isostatic changes (Corbet 1961; Fairnell and Barrett 2007; Serjeantson 1990;
Yalden 1982). Red deer can swim up to 7 km, distance enough to gain access to
the Inner Hebrides with ease, but for islands separated by wide or dangerous
straits their movement must have been assisted by humans (Serjeantson 1990).
These windy, exposed islands would have presented a series of environmental
and dietary challenges to colonising mainland red deer, potentially exacerbated
by genetic isolation. For colonising humans too, the islands would have
necessitated the development of new strategies; long term survival on limited
landmasses requires sustainable exploitation of food species. In many respects
the history of Scottish red deer is inter-twined with that of humans and the best
way to examine this mutual relationship is via the zooarchaeological record.

Zooarchaeology: tracking the red deer

The examination of osteological evidence from archaeological sites is possible
only when preservation allows: on mainland Scotland the acidic soil cover
severely limits bone survival; the best evidence is found on the islands. It is

important to recognise that absence of evidence for red deer need not equate to absence of the red deer themselves, only that variables in the preservation and visibility of archaeological sites have biased the data. With these caveats in place it is possible, through the zooarchaeological evidence, to track the spread of red deer from the mainland out to the islands, plotting their expansion, exploitation, management and in many cases their eventual extinction (in the text below the numbers in parentheses relate to the data presented in Table 5). It is possible to distinguish the trade of body-parts (e.g. prepared venison joints or workable antler) from the presence of established herds by a suite of indicators: for instance endemic populations are suggested if red deer assemblages are sizeable, contain a range of body parts and the remains of juvenile animals.

On the Scottish mainland late Mesolithic red deer remains, mostly antler, are recorded from a number of west coast sites (1–5). Out on the islands the archaeological record is sparse with faunal remains reported solely from the small Inner Hebridean Isle of Oronsay (6) with only indirect pollen evidence for large herbivores (probably deer) impacting on vegetation in the Outer Hebrides and Shetland (Edwards 1996; Gregory *et al.* 2005). Where quantifiable, e.g. at Sand (5) and Oronsay, red deer were the most common terrestrial mammal. The presence of juveniles at the former mainland site suggests a breeding population, and metrical data indicates that, at maturity, these animals were similar in size to red deer from contemporary English sites (e.g. Star Carr, Legge and Rowley-Conwy 1988). The island of Oronsay was probably too small to sustain a local population (Mithen and Finlayson 1991); perhaps explaining the absence of juveniles and the restricted range of body parts present: only joints of venison, along with antler and bone for working, were bought to the island (Grigson and Mellars 1987). Interestingly the deer from Oronsay fall into two size groups, the majority are similar to those at Sand and Star Carr with the minority around 30 per cent smaller. Grigson and Mellars (1987) have suggested that the larger animals represent imported mainland deer, whilst the smaller individuals derived from a population living on another (more substantial) island where they have suffered a size reduction due to environmental stresses.

The first substantial island faunal assemblages are associated with the tombs and settlements of Neolithic Orkney (7–15). Although red deer are generally present in small quantities relative to the domestic species, they are dominant in some tombs, e.g. Quanterness (16), Knowe of Ramsay (17) and Yarso, (18). Evidence for calves and older individuals hints that breeding populations were established at this time. Measurements indicate that some of the earliest animals are comparable in size to the large mainland deer. Whilst these specimens may represent imported joints of meat it is equally feasible that they derive from the first live introductions to the islands, before island environmental stresses caused red deer to diminish in size.

By the Late Neolithic/Early Bronze Age a few Orcadian settlements – e.g. the Links of Notland (19), Point of Buckquoy (21) and the Bay of Skaill (22) – had substantial quantities of deer. These animals are noticeably smaller

TABLE 5. Archaeological representation of red deer on the Scottish islands. *Number of Identified Specimens of cattle, sheep, pig and red deer bone (antler has been excluded where possible).

Island Group	No.	Site	Phase	NISP*	% Red Deer	Reference
Mainland and Inner Hebrides						
Mainland	1	Oban Caves	Mesolithic		Present	Kitchener *et al.* 2004
	2	An Corran	Mesolithic		Present	Kitchener *et al.* 2004
	3	Carding Mill Bay	Mesolithic		Present	Kitchener *et al.* 2004
	4	Duntroon	Mesolithic		Present	Kitchener *et al.* 2004
	5	Sand	Mesolithic	143	72	Parkes and Barrett n.d.
	6	Oronsay Middens	Mesolithic	168	66	Grigson and Mellars 1987
	32	Crosskirk	Iron Age	1879	6	McCarthney 1984
Inner Hebrides	24	Killelan	Early Bronze Age	107	12	Serjeantson *et al.* 2005
	25	Ardnave	Bronze age	243	5	Harmen 1983
	33	Dun Mhor Vaul	Iron Age	1232	21	Noddle 1978-80
	34	Dun Ardtrek	Iron Age	1302	28	Noddle 1978
	35	Dun Cul Bhuirg	Iron Age	180	17	Noddle 1978
	24	Killelan	Iron Age	607	18	Serjeantson *et al.* 2005
	36	High Pastures Cave	Iron Age	1352	2	Drew 2004
	37	Iona Vallum	AD 7th Century	100	10	Noddle 1981
	37	Iona Guest House	Iron Age	928	35	McCormick 1981
Northern Isles: Orkney and Shetland						
Orkney	7	Skara Brae	Neolithic	30169	3	Noddle forthcoming
	8	Point of Cott	Neolithic	513	2	Halpin 1997
	9	Isbister	Neolithic	601	4	Barker 1983
	10	Pierowall Quarry	Neolithic	1809	4	McCormick 1984
	11	Midhowe	Neolithic		Present	Platt 1934
	12	Eday	Neolithic		Present	Platt 1937a
	13	Blackhammer	Neolithic		Present	Platt 1937b
	14	Pool	Neolithic	2065	<1	Bond 2007
	15	Knap of Howar	Late Neolithic	6720	1	Noddle 1983
	16	Quanterness cairn	Neolithic	222	8	Clutton-Brock 1979
	17	Yarso	Neolithic		Dominant	Platt 1935
	18	Knowe of Ramsay	Neolithic		Dominant	Platt 1936
	19	Links of Noltland	Late Neolithic	8678	5	Amour-Chelu 1992
	20	Tofts Ness	Neolithic/Early Bronze Age		1	Nicholson and Davies 2007
	21	Point of Buckquoy	Neolithic/Early Bronze Age	188	74	Rackham 1989
	26	Skaill, Deerness	Late Bronze Age	1084	25	Noddle 1997
	27	Tofts Ness	Bronze Age	1323	1	Nicholson and Davies 2007
	28	Moaness, Raasay	Bronze age		1 individual	Mainland unpublished
	38	Howe	Iron Age	1905	28	Smith *et al.* 1994
	39	Warebeth Broch	Iron Age	2098	17	Sellar 1989
	10	Pierowall Quarry	Early Iron Age	219	2	McCormick 1984
	26	Skaill, Deerness	Iron Age	12623	4	Noddle 1997
	40	Mine Howe	Iron Age	10849	6	Mainland *et al.* 2004, Mainland and Ewens 2005

TABLE 5 continued.

Island Group	No.	Site	Phase	NISP*	% Red Deer	Reference
Orkney	14	Pool	Late Iron Age/Pictish	4505	1	Bond 2007
	14	Pool	Pictish/Viking	13535	1	Bond 2007
	57	Buckquoy	Norse (9th to 12th centuries AD)	2738	0	Noddle 1976-7
	57	Brough Road (areas 1 & 2)	Viking	259	0	Rackham 1989
	26	Skaill, Deerness	Viking/Post Viking	5490	1	Noddle 1997
	57	Brough of Deerness	Late Norse/Early medieval	253	0	Rackham 1986
	58	Earls Bu	Late Norse/Early medieval	1263	1	Mainland 1995
Shetland	41	Scalloway	Iron Age	4271	0	O'Sullivan 1998
	42	Scatness	Iron Age	641	0	Bond pers comm.

Outer Hebrides

Island Group	No.	Site	Phase	NISP*	% Red Deer	Reference
Lewis/Harris	22	Northton	Neolithic	608	4	Finlay 1984
	22	Northton	Beaker	726	29	Finlay 1984
	22	Northton	Iron Age	393	57	Finlay 1984
	43	Berie	Iron Age	1878	32	Thoms 2003
	44	Cnip	Iron Age	1489	25	McCormick 2006
	45	Bostadh	Iron Age	351	8	Thoms 2003
	45	Bostadh	Norse	1511	24	Thoms 2003
The Uists	23	Udal	Neolithic	358	3	Finlay 1984
	23	Udal	Early Bronze Age	277	0	Finlay 1984
	29	Rosinish	Beaker	199	21	Finlay 1984
	23	Udal	Iron Age	2399	0	Finlay 1984
	23	Udal North	Iron Age	5504	1	Serjeantson n.d
	46	Sollas	Iron Age	812	1	Finlay1984
	47	Baleshare	Iron Age	2040	1	Halstead 2003
	30	Cladh Hallen	LBA/Iron Age	889	7	Mulville and Powell forthcoming
	31	Hornish Point	LBA/Iron Age	440	1	Halstead 2003
	48	A'Cheardach Bheag	Iron Age	68	13	Finlay 1984
	49	A'Cheardach Mhor	Iron Age	223	2	Finlay 1984
	50	Cille Donnain	Iron Age	4665	2	Mulville and Ingrem forthcoming
	51	Dun Vulan	Iron Age	2882	1	Mulville 1999
	52	Bornais	Iron Age	2890	16	Mulville 2005
	53	Pabbay	Iron Age	2274	3	Mulville 2000
	54	Dunan Ruadh	Iron Age	1423	1	Mulville 2000
	55	Sandray	Iron Age	144	0	Mulville 2000
	56	Mingulay	Iron Age	416	2	Mulville 2000
	23	Udal North	Viking	1942	1	Serjeantson n.d.
	52	Bornais	Norse	13243	6	Mulville 2005; forthcoming
	59	Cille Pheadair	Norse	7115	3	Mulville forthcoming

than mainland deer, suggesting that they derived from an established island population. Elsewhere the few fragments of bone and antler reported from Shetland (Noddle 1986) and the Western Isles sites provide scant evidence for a local Neolithic population. On the latter (23, 24) these animals are reduced in size. Neolithic assemblages have not yet been recovered from the mainland and the Inner Hebrides.

For the Bronze Age it is possible to identify red deer populations on three of the four main island groups (22–31) and all show evidence for size diminution, with deer on the Outer Hebrides being particularly small. On Orkney we are offered an intriguing snapshot into hunting techniques of the period; the remains of an adult stag found on Raasay (28) suggest that the animal was driven into a bog, killed and then (partially) butchered. A different exploitation strategy is evidenced at the site of Cladh Hallan, South Uist (26), where large numbers of skinned and butchered juvenile red deer were recovered. Rather than being hunted, these young animals were probably 'gathered' from the hiding places in which they sheltered whilst their dam grazed elsewhere.

In the Iron Age human activity across the Scottish Isles was widespread and numerous sites have evidence for red deer (10, 14, 22–4, 32–55). For the first time since the Mesolithic there is archaeological evidence available from the west coast mainland with red deer reported from Crosskirk broch (32). Deer remain a persistent part of the animalscape on the Inner Hebrides, with juveniles providing evidence for breeding populations on a number of the islands. On the Western Isles red deer, including juveniles, are reported from a wide range of sites: large quantities have been recorded for the larger islands of Lewis and Harris, with a few fragments noted for the tiny Bishop's Isles lying off the tip of Barra (53–56). Some inter-island differences are apparent. Red deer numbers are generally stable on the Inner Hebrides and Outer Hebrides, with a slight increase in their abundance on South Uist, whilst their presence on Orcadian sites is patchy, some sites (38 and 39) having large quantities of red deer whist others (e.g. 10 and 14) have low frequencies. Records of red deer remain sparse on Shetland (e.g. at Scalloway and Scatness (41–2) where only a few antler fragments, and a single associated skull fragment, have been recovered.

The symbolism of red deer to the Iron Age people of the Inner and Outer Hebrides is demonstrated by their unique appearance as animal motifs on Hebridean decorated pottery and other objects, such as the carved head on a wooden handle from Dun Bharavat, Lewis (Armit 2006, 239 Illus. 7.10; Hingley 1992;). Their significance is also indicated by the use of seventeen overlapping adult deer mandibles to construct a hearth surround at A'Cheardach Bheag (Mulville *et al.* 2003).

From around the ninth century onward there is evidence for the arrival of Scandinavian visitors and settlers across the isles, although assemblages from the Inner Hebrides are rare. On Orkney there is a severe decline in the red deer representation with bones recovered from only two sites (26, 58), and even antler becomes relatively scarce. This decline has been attributed to over-hunting by

Noddle (1982). Red deer are absent from Shetland.

In contrast, the Outer Hebrides remained home to a number of viable red deer herds. On Lewis (45) they increase in importance, on North Uist they re-appear at the Udal (23) and, although their numbers decline, a breeding population persists on South Uist (52, 59). Antler became pivotal as a resource, with the only antler comb production site outside an urban context located at Bornais (Sharples and Smith 2009) on South Uist. On the Inner Hebrides at Iona (37) the medieval monastery continued to exploit the abundant supply of red deer persisting from the earlier Iron Age. In later years it appears that haunches of red deer were imported suggesting decline in the deer population or an increase in demand (McCormick 1981).

There is lack of later assemblages and all we know of the more recent history of the Hebridean deer is that populations persisted on the majority of the larger Inner and Outer isles. The exceptions are Barra, where no population has existed recently and South Uist were the population was eventually hunted to extinction with red deer being re-introduced for sport hunting in the 1970s (Fletcher 2000; Fletcher 2003, 78–52). Legend has it that the destruction of Ormiclate Castle, the home of Clanranald, in 1715 was caused by an accidental kitchen fire whilst roasting the last deer on the island. Red deer were recently re-introduced to Orkney as farmed animals (Orkney Times).

The timing and nature of introductions

As noted above, the diminutive group of individuals present on Oronsay indicates that red deer spread, probably unaided, to the Inner Hebrides during the Mesolithic but in the absence of direct evidence their early introduction further afield remains in doubt. Red deer were present on Orkney in the Neolithic, the large deer associated with the tombs may derive from a founder population, and there is evidence for the introduction of other wild animals at this time (Fairnell and Barrett 2007). In contrast, there is little evidence for an Outer Hebridean red deer population and no other reported faunal introductions at this time. Once established, the Orcadian deer increased in importance but decreased in stature.

Red deer populations were established on the Outer Hebrides by the Bronze Age and these herds remained viable throughout the Iron Age, into the Norse period and beyond. Hebridean deer are, on average, smaller (between two thirds and one half the size of mainland deer) than earlier and contemporary animals found on Orkney (with only a 15 per cent size reduction) or the Inner Hebrides (10–20 per cent size reduction). In common with other island species the reduction in body size may be due to poor nutrition, possibly exacerbated by competition with domestic species for food, and/or genetic changes (Lister 1995). The persistence of the larger size of Orcadian deer may indicate re-introductions throughout prehistory. These populations thrived until the Norse period when, as with other introduced wild animals (Fairnell and Barrett 2007), they died out. The reason for the red deer extinction may be linked to the smaller Orcadian land mass exacerbating increasing human population pressure (at 990 km^2 the Orkneys make up less than one third of either the Inner or Outer Hebrides). The loss of Orcadian red deer during the Norse period is at odds with the evidence from the Western Isles where red deer, and in particular antler, continued as valuable resource.

But why were deer transported out to the islands in the first place? Their early introduction, along with the first appearance of domesticates and settlements, suggests that deer formed an integral part of the animalscape. As a familiar prey species from earlier time, they could be viewed as a self-sustaining source of food and other essential resources, as well as having a wider significance as an essential part of the world. Island inhabitants are unusual in that, in addition to the adoption of farming practises, they continued to hunt, gather and fish to a greater degree than contemporary mainland societies (for example the proportion of red deer on Southern British sites declines to around one percent from the Neolithic onwards). The active management of the deer would have been necessary to minimise their impact on domestic stock and crops (for historical accounts of deer damage see Hull 2007, 260–2) and to sustain these populations for thousands of years (Sharples 2000). On some of the islands (and elsewhere) this delicate balance eventually broke down leading to the extinction of deer herds.

Island lives

This chapter can only begin to examine a small part of the complex interactions between humans and deer that stretch back through time. It is out on the islands of Britain that this relationship remained intimate for the longest period of time and has persisted to the present day. The value of our remaining island deer should not be underestimated; they remain the purest genetic strands of red deer in Britain showing no evidence for hybridisation with Sika deer, unlike the mainland populations. In the long term there is a serious danger that non-hybrid red deer will become extinct, and refugia have therefore been established on a number of islands (Arran, Jura, Islay, Rum and the Outer Isles) to which it is illegal to introduce Sika deer. Although many herds have faced extinction in the past and have been bolstered by re-introductions (e.g. South Uist), island deer remain one of the best hopes for maintaining biodiversity and the active management these animals experience today, as research herds or hunted trophies, serves merely to reflect our long and mutually dependant relationship.

CHAPTER 7

European Fallow Deer

Naomi Sykes

....

Introduction

Visit any stately home and somewhere on the grounds you are likely to find a herd of fallow deer (*Dama dama*). Undoubtedly an elegant sight, they are also one of natural history's puzzles because despite their modern distribution, and despite their name, European fallow deer are not actually of European origin. Fossil records for the last 400,000 years demonstrate that, although different forms of *Dama* inhabited northern Europe during the warm Cromerian, Hoxnian and Ipswichian periods, their intolerance to cold climates saw their distributions pushed south with every glacial. During the last Ice Age (*c.* 40,000–10,000 years ago) *D. dama* became restricted to Anatolia and did not re-colonise north after the event (Lister 1984b; Masseti 1996; Uerpmann 1987).

It is clear from archaeological artefacts, iconography and the remains of the animals themselves that the spread of *D. dama* from Anatolia was almost entirely due to human transportation. Zooarchaeological evidence suggests that fallow deer were introduced to Rhodes as early as the sixth millennium BC, with populations subsequently being established across the Balkans (Masseti

FIGURE 11. Fallow deer buck
© RICHARD FORD, DIGITAL WILDLIFE

1996; Masseti *et al.* 2006; Yannouli and Trantalidou 1999). The Phoenicians are thought to have transported fallow deer around the Mediterranean coast (Millais 1906; Ryder 1975) and by the classical Greek period fallow deer had become incorporated into the Mycenaean and Minoan cultures; they are represented iconographically, mythologically and zooarchaeologically, especially within votive deposits (Boessneck 1973; Poplin 1984; Yannouli and Trantalidou 1999). The first documentary evidence for the management of fallow deer is provided by Roman authors, such as Columella and Varro, and it is to the Romans that the popularisation and spread of the deer management concept should be attributed; there is good evidence that fallow deer populations were established in Roman Italy (MacKinnon 2004), Sicily (Wilson 1990) and Portugal (Davis 2005). Thus far it is possible to piece together the early history of fallow deer and the approximate timings of their movement in southern Europe. More opaque are the issues of when, how and, perhaps most importantly, why this species was taken north and, in particular, introduced to Britain. This chapter seeks to address some of these questions and consider the circumstances and impact of this species' introduction and establishment.

Fallow deer in Britain

Today fallow deer have the widest distribution of any deer species in the British Isles, being found in managed and free-living populations from Southern England to the Hebrides and across to northern Ireland (Chapman and Chapman 1975). Their current distribution is remarkably similar to Rackham's (1997, 124) plot of medieval parks, which is perhaps unsurprising given that it was from these enclosures that most deer escaped when parks became unfashionable and fell into disrepair, particularly during the war years of the early twentieth century. The association between fallow deer and parks is undeniable. Rackham (1997, 123) suggests that in the 1300s there existed over 3000 fallow deer-stocked parks in Britain, and it is clear that both fallow deer and parks were present in Britain by the twelfth century. Writing in *c.* 1180 Alexander Neckham was able to list fallow deer amongst the animals commonly available in Britain (Bartlett 2000, 673). The introduction dates of both parks and fallow deer are, however, the subjects of considerable debate (for up-to-date discussion on park origins see Gautier 2007; Liddiard 2003; 2007). In the case of fallow deer, as with most other non-native species, there has arisen a belief that modern populations descend from animals brought to Britain by invading peoples: originally scholars favoured the Romans (Millais 1906; Lever 1977; Whitehead 1972) but in recent years the Normans have become the more popular proposal (Langbein and Chapman 2003; Rackham 1997; Sykes 2004a). Although these invasion theories are neat and attractive, the actual situation was almost certainly more complex, with no single 'introduction event' but more probably a series of repeated importations. Even in recent history there have been numerous introductions of fallow deer stock – animals were brought from Denmark in the nineteenth century (Whitehead 1950, 153) following prior introductions from Germany in 1661 and from Norway in 1612 (Shirley 1867 cited in Pemberton and Smith 1985, 204) – and there is every reason to suspect the same was true in earlier periods. The circumstances and social meaning of these various introductions are unlikely to have been homogenous, each being a product of its time with a different significance and impact. As such, modern populations of fallow deer, together with their archaeological and historical representation, are a record of human activity with the potential to reveal much about Britain's past societies, their trade networks and even their ideologies.

Chapman and Chapman (1975) were the first to undertake a comprehensive review of the evidence for British fallow deer and to address the human story behind their introduction. The Chapmans' book *Fallow Deer: Their History, Distribution and Biology* remains unsurpassed as a source of information about the species but other scholars have subsequently added to the narrative and clarified some of the facts presented in the volume. Yalden (1999), for instance, reviewed the zooarchaeological evidence for fallow deer, a review which has itself since been updated (Sykes 2004a; 2007). Table 6 provides the most recent data for the earliest reliable examples of fallow deer bones in the archaeological record.

Prior to the twelfth century, the zooarchaeological evidence for fallow deer is scarce, becoming increasingly so as we move back through time. For the Iron Age, just two specimens have been confidently identified and assigned to the period. Both of these are shed antler and, as such, they cannot be taken as positive evidence for the presence of living animals in Britain; the antler could feasibly have been collected in southern Europe and transported north. A similar scenario may account for the shed antler recovered from several Roman-period

TABLE 6. Early representation of fallow deer in the archaeological record (for further data see Sykes 2004 and Sykes *et al.* 2006).

Site	Date	Description of Specimens	Reference
Lydney, Gloucester	Iron Age	shed antler	Wheeler and Wheeler 1932
War Ditches, Cambridgeshire	Iron Age	two pieces of worked antler	White 1964
Scole Dickleburgh, Norfolk	Roman	almost complete shed antler	Baker 1998
St Albans, Hertfordshire	Roman	shed antler	O'Neil 1945
Dorchester-on-Thames	Roman	shed antler	Grant 1978
Catterick Bridge, Yorkshire	Roman	no details	Meddens 2002
Wroxeter, Shropshire	Roman	tibia shaft fragment	Meddens 2000
Walbrook, London	Roman	no details	West 1983
Carlisle, Cumbria	Roman	no details	Stallibrass 1993
Monkton, Isle of Thanet	Roman	antler and several post cranial bones	Bendrey 2003
Whitefriars, Canterbury, Kent	Roman	3 specimens	Bendrey pers. comm
St George's, Canterbury, Kent	Roman	metatarsal	Bendrey pers. comm
Fishbourne Roman Palace, Sussex	Roman	evidence of breeding population	Sykes *et al.* 2006; Allen pers. comm.
Barking Abbey, London	Saxon	no details provided	Rackham 1994
Hereford, Herefordshire	Saxon	3 fragments	Noddle 1985a
Hare Court, London	Saxon	calcaneum	Bendrey 2005

sites, notably St Albans, Dortchester-on-Thames and Scole Dickleburgh (see Table 6). In the past it has been argued that antler may have been collected and transported for functional reasons, possibly as a raw material for bone working (Sykes 2004a). This idea finds support from Scole Dickleburgh specimen, which exhibited clear shaving marks (Figure 12). However, most zooarchaeologists now reject this theory on the basis that the compacta of fallow deer antler is very thin, rendering it problematic for artefact manufacture. Without the option of antler working, the rationale for the curation of fallow deer antler is more difficult to discern. Given that the fallow deer appear to have taken on a religious significance in the classical civilizations of the Mediterranean, it seems possible that the influence of these ideologies was felt further north, with antler being transported and deposited for ceremonial purposes. Alternatively, in his *Natural History*, Pliny the Elder suggested that deer antler had considerable medicinal properties, curing ills from tooth ache to epilepsy when taken in an ashed or powdered form (see Book XXVII, trans. Jones 1963). The shaving of antler to create such a powder could certainly account for the marks seen on the antler from Scole Dickleburgh.

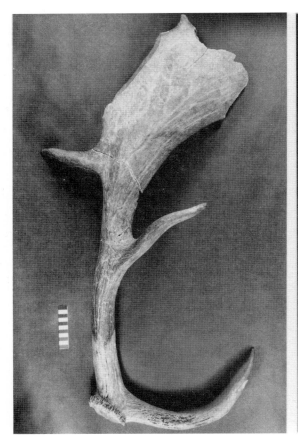

FIGURE 12. Shed antler from Roman Scole Dickleburgh, Norfolk (photo courtesy of Norfolk Museum Service).

Regardless of why fallow deer antler was incorporated into Iron Age and Romano-British deposits, finds of *D. dama* antler add little to the debate about the species' establishment in Britain. To advance the discussion, it is necessary to consider those skeletal parts more likely to represent the presence of the actual animal, although the possibility that bones derive from imported preserved venison cannot always be ruled out. Whilst there is no evidence for post-cranial bones in Iron Age Britain, these elements are better represented on sites dating to the Roman period. Nevertheless, considering the large number of Roman sites that have been excavated, fallow deer remains are rare. But perhaps this is due less to actual absence and more to researchers hesitating to identify Roman specimens as *D. dama* because of the widespread acceptance that the species is an eleventh-century introduction (Langbein and Chapman 2003; Sykes 2004a). It is noteworthy that where zooarchaeologists have actively gone in search of Roman fallow deer, they have not been disappointed. In 2003, for instance, Bendrey published his discovery of nine *D. dama* specimens – two shed antlers, three metacarpals, one metatarsal, two scapulae, and one radius – from a late second to fifth-century rural settlement at Monkton, Kent. Subsequently he noted further examples of foot bones, this time from Roman Canterbury (Table 6). As yet, none of these remains has been radiocarbon dated and it is feasible that they could be intrusive, as was the case with the purported 'Roman' specimen from Redlands Farm (Davis 1997), which was eventually radiocarbon dated to AD 990–1170 (Bronk Ramsey *et al.* 2000). The prognosis for the Kentish specimens is, however, positive, especially given the latest findings from Fishbourne Roman Palace in Sussex, purportedly the residence of the native King Togidubnus (Cunliffe 1998, 109). Recent re-analysis of the animal bone assemblage from the site has identified a substantial collection of fallow deer remains (Sykes *et al.* 2006; M. Allen pers. comm.). Amongst these were two jaw bones, both of which were AMS dated to the around first century AD: one to AD 60 ± 40 years (Beta-201535 2σ Cal BP 1990 to 1820), the other slightly later to about AD 90 ± 40 (Beta-201534 2σ Cal BP 1930 to 1740). These are the earliest specimens recorded for Roman Britain and are the only jaw bones to have been recovered from Roman Europe. As such, their teeth presented a unique opportunity to undertake strontium isotope analysis, a geochemical provenancing technique. The methods and results of this study are presented in Sykes *et al.* (2006) but, in brief, the analyses demonstrated that the *c.* AD 60 individual was imported to Fishbourne as a fawn. From where this animal was brought is currently uncertain but southern Gaul seems a plausible source given the apparent absence of fallow deer in the rest of northern Europe (Sykes 2004a). Results for the *c.* AD 90 individual indicate that the animal was born and raised at Fishbourne, and it is tempting to suggest that it descended from the earlier import. As exotic animals it seems likely that the deer would have been managed within an enclosure near the palace; indeed, on the basis of the evidence it has been possible to tentatively identify a park, or vivarium, within the southern part of the complex.

Game parks were common in Italy from the late Republic onwards (for an overview see Anderson 1985; Starr 1992; Toynbee 1973) but this is the first evidence for an equivalent in Roman Britain. Explanations as to why the Romans went to such efforts to transport and maintain fallow deer can be found in the writings of classical authors. Columella (*De Res Rustica* Book IX, I.1 trans. Forester and Heffner 1955) stated that

> 'wild creatures, such as roe deer, chamois and also scimitar-horned oryx, fallow deer and wild boars sometimes serve to enhance the splendour and pleasure of their owners'

Sometimes the feeding of park animals was choreographed to entertain guests as they dined *al fresco*: according to Varro (*Rerum Rusticarum* Book III.13.1 trans. Hooper and Ash 1979) emparked deer and boar were trained to assemble for food when a horn was blown, much to the delight of the audience. Ownership of wild animals appealed to the Roman mindset, which saw human control over nature as a sign of sanctity (Cartmill 1993, 52). The beliefs of the pre-Roman population, however, were seemingly different and there is some evidence to suggest that wild animals were deliberately avoided in Iron Age Britain (King 1991, 16). If Fishbourne Palace was indeed the residence of Togidubnus, the presence of fallow deer at this site would suggest that the native elite were beginning to adopt Roman ideals, the ownership of game parks perhaps signalling membership of the Roman Empire. As such, the importation of fallow deer in this period cannot be linked to an invading population but was more probably the result of peaceful cultural exchange and political negotiation.

Whilst the specimens from Fishbourne Palace provide conclusive evidence that fallow deer were maintained and bred in Britain during the Roman period, there is a big step from the localised breeding of exotic tame animals to their establishment as a naturalised fauna. Currently the evidence suggests that fallow deer died out with the withdrawal of the Roman Empire; perhaps due to the decline of Roman ideology but perhaps because of climatic deterioration (Dark 2000, 27). Occasionally it has been suggested that fallow deer were present in Saxon period Britain but the evidence for this is currently slim. For instance, *Aelfric's Colloquy* is often cited as referring to fallow deer, or *dammas*, but this is actually a mistranslation – the Saxon word for roe buck '*rann*' having been confused with the Latin *dam* (Yalden 1999,153). Similarly, Hough's (2001) argument that the place-name elements *fealu*, *pohha* or *pocca* refer to 'fallow deer' is unconvincing (P. Cullen and D. Parsons pers. comm.). Nor is there currently any substantive zooarchaeological evidence to suggest that fallow deer were widespread in the Saxon period: a few site reports do mention the possible presence of fallow deer but nearly all the specimens are either antler fragments (Jones and Ruben 1987), dubiously identified or poorly dated (see Sykes 2004a for a review of the evidence). The specimens recorded for Barking Abbey, Hare Court and Hereford (see Table 6) are worthy of further investigation and we should not rule out the possibility that animals were occasionally imported and maintained in the early medieval period. Trade in exotic animals was commonplace amongst the medieval elite, animals often being exchanged between leaders to cement political relationships: the most famous example being the elephant sent to Charlemagne by the Abyssinian Caliph (Hodges 2000, 36). Yet, even if the purported Saxon period *D. dama* specimens prove to be correctly identified and dated, the case for fallow deer living free in the Saxon landscape would remain weak.

Today most scholars agree that it was the Normans who brought and successfully established fallow deer in Britain. Motivation for their introduction has been linked to the Norman's 'love of the chase' and their desire to introduce the type of hunting parks that were, perhaps, common in pre-Conquest Normandy (Gautier 2007; Gilbert 1979; Rackham 1997, 123; Yalden 1999, 153). Certainly the post-Conquest rise in park numbers – from the 32 recorded in the Domesday Book to thousands by AD 1300 – does parallel the zooarchaeological increase in fallow deer representation from the late eleventh century onwards (see Sykes 2004a). The timing of these shifts would appear to implicate the Normans as responsible but is improbable that Normandy was the source of the imported animals: a survey of the zooarchaeological literature indicates that, in the eleventh century, breeding populations of *D. dama* were confined to southwest Asia and southern Europe (Sykes 2004a). When this distribution is considered against the political map of the time, Sicily is the logical source population; the island being the southern kingdom of the Norman Empire. The connections between Norman England and Norman Sicily were particularly strong in the late eleventh century and there is good evidence that concepts of animal parks as well as new hunting traditions were brought from the southern kingdom to Britain (Sykes 2007). Henry I's park at Woodstock is thought to have been based on Sicilian models and, according to William of Malmesbury, it contained a suite of exotic animals – camels, lions, leopards, porcupines and deer – that Henry had been given by foreign kings (Clark 2006, 18–9). This collection, which is the direct ancestor of London Zoo, was not simply a frivolity; it was a metaphor for the Norman Empire, a statement that the Norman kings had power not only over the wild creatures in their possession but also over the countries from which the animals derived.

In all probability it was this symbolic significance of fallow deer, rather than their potential as quarry, that prompted their eleventh-century introduction to Britain. For the first few decades after their arrival, fallow deer would have been a rarity, to be displayed and admired rather than chased and eaten. But it did not take long for the meat-hungry aristocracy to recognise and harness the venison-producing qualities of fallow deer: records for the twelfth century demonstrate that lords were laying out deer parks for precisely this reason (Hoppitt 2007, 157). Desire to participate in the aristocratic culture of hunting and game-eating saw large numbers of fallow deer being imported and farmed with live animals being moved across the country to stock the burgeoning number of parks (Birrell 1992, 120; Rackham 1997, 123). Thomas (2001) has noted that the foot bones of medieval fallow deer often demonstrate pathologies that he has attributed to their rough handling during their capture and transport.

The fashion for fallow deer emparkent reached its zenith in the fourteenth century, when parks covered approximately two per cent of the English landscape (Rackham 1997, 123). From this point, as with most fashions, the popularity of fallow deer-keeping began to decline but the legacy of their medieval introduction can still be seen in the form of parks, which now provide an important ecological resource for wildlife conservation (Rotherham 2007).

Conclusion

Fallow deer have held a special status in human societies ever since the Neolithic period. Their beauty and temperament inspired many peoples, particularly the social elite, to capture, transport and breed them far from their homeland of Turkey. Britain represents the northernmost limit of their distribution, both in antiquity and the present day, but it is also the area where their introduction has been most successful. There is now clear evidence that fallow deer were imported to Britain on a number of occasions, each time for a different reason and with different consequences.

Currently, the earliest evidence for the establishment of a breeding population dates to the first century AD and the zooarchaeological record charts their presence until the end of the fourth century AD. It is notable that most of the Roman period sites from which *D. dama* remains have been recovered are villas suggesting that, as in the rest of the Roman Empire, the owners of these rural estates were keen to demonstrate their social and cosmological status through the possession of exotic animals. If ownership of fallow deer signalled membership of the Roman Empire, it is perhaps unsurprising that the species apparently died out in Britain at the end of the Roman occupation. Evidence for the presence of fallow deer in Saxon period Britain is currently weak; however, it seems possible that this is an artifice of identification: fallow deer were also scarce in Roman deposits until researchers began to *look* for them. What is undeniable is that the records of fallow deer, both zooarchaeological and historical, become increasingly abundant from the end of the eleventh century. It is reasonable to conclude that the Normans were responsible for their reintroduction, initially brought as exotica to emulate the lifestyle of their Sicilian cousins but later bred to sustain an aristocratic hunger for venison. Fallow deer soon became an icon of social position, their consumption and management in privatised parks forming elements of the package through which the elite sought to distinguish themselves from the lower classes. The impact of their introduction continues to this day, having left an indelible mark on the cuisine and landscape of Britain.

CHAPTER 8

The Wild Boar

Umberto Albarella

Introduction

On 7 January 2004 the British Broadcasting Corporation (BBC) reported the news that a wild boar had been spotted in a supermarket in a Gloucestershire town. Apparently the animal had already knocked over an elderly lady and eluded the attention of the supermarket staff. Anybody who spotted it was supposed to alert the police.

Sightings of wild animals in unusual places are not particularly rare – foxes are regularly spotted in human environments, including shops. The interesting aspect of this particular story is, however, that the wild boar had been extinct in Britain – as a free-living species – for centuries. This news, one among many of this sort (Goulding and Roper 2002), was indicative of the fact that the wild boar was back and had once again become a regular feature of British life (Figure 13). Animals escaped from wild boar farms established in the 1980s and 1990s had eventually led to the re-establishment of viable free wild boar populations in the south of the country and were obviously not especially afraid of direct exposure to the human species.

The interest that the return of the wild boar has generated (no less than 107 media articles in six years; Goulding and Roper 2002) justifies our curiosity regarding the past life of this species and how eventually it came to be lost to the British countryside. In this chapter I will briefly report on what is known

FIGURE 13. A small group of wild boar recently re-established in Britain
PHOTO BY MARTIN GOULDING

about the archaeology and history of the British wild boar, its origins, heyday, decline, demise and eventual return.

Origins

According to Yalden (1999, 15) the earliest known occurrence of the wild boar (*Sus scrofa*) in Britain dates back to the Cromerian interglacial (Lower Pleistocene, 600,000–450,000 BP). Remains of the species were found at the site of West Runton (Norfolk), which typifies the period in Britain. Evidence of the presence of wild swine is again found in the Hoxnian and Ipswichian interglacials (Yalden 1999, 17–18), and then in the Late Glacial, when it was never particularly common (Yalden 1999, 60–1). The role played by the wild boar in the life of Palaeolithic hunters in Britain is by and large unknown.

In the Mesolithic the wild boar was – with red deer (*Cervus elaphus*) and aurochs (*Bos primigenius*) – one of the three most common game species. It is relatively uncommon at Star Carr (Legge and Rowly-Conwy 1988) but abundant at the other early Mesolithic site of Thatcham (King 1962). It is the predominant species at Faraday Road (Ellis *et al.* 2003), a possibly slightly later site. There is no chronological pattern to the variation in abundance of the wild boar in the British Mesolithic (Albarella and Pirnie in prep.) and its relative frequency is therefore likely to be related to local environmental conditions and hunting preferences.

In the British Mesolithic the wild boar seems to have been relatively small. In Figures 14 and 15 the size of these animals is compared with that of Mesolithic wild boar from other European areas and to modern wild boar (data from Albarella *et al.* 2009). Both tooth and postcranial bone measurements indicate that British wild boar were smaller than their Danish and, to some extent,

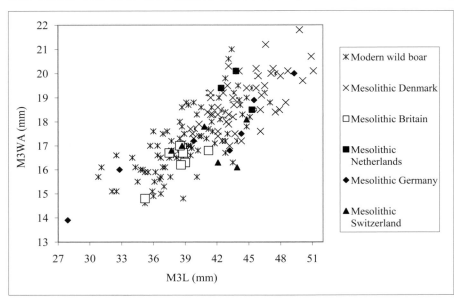

FIGURE 14. Size of lower third molar in British Mesolithic wild boar compared to other Mesolithic specimens and to modern European wild boar. Modified from Albarella *et al.* 2009.

central European counterparts. They also tend to plot towards the lower half of the distribution of modern European wild boar.

Wild boar hunting in farming societies

With the beginning of the Neolithic and the introduction of the domestic pig, the archaeological record for the British wild boar becomes elusive. It is difficult to say to what extent this is due to a genuine rarity of the wild species, the difficulty in distinguishing wild and domesticated forms or the frequent interbreeding between the two populations. A combination of these factors may well represent the best possible explanation.

The domestication of the pig is known to have brought about – at least in the long term – a reduction in the size of the animals. The size of the wild boar cannot, however, be assumed to have remained stable, as a post-Mesolithic size increase has been proved for some other European areas (see Albarella *et al.* 2006a and Albarella *et al.* 2006b, where possible explanations for this phenomenon are discussed). There is some evidence that this occurred in Britain too but the situation for the Neolithic is not particularly clear, due to the scanty biometrical record.

The presence of the wild boar in the early Neolithic is claimed at a few sites. Some large humeri are present at Hambledon Hill (Legge 2008) but the claimed wild boar from Ascott-under-Wychwood (Mulville and Grigson 2007) are of a size that could also be compatible with domesticated forms. The main evidence for the late Neolithic comes from Durrington Walls, where a detailed biometrical analysis of a large pig dataset has revealed that the wild boar was – if at all present – exceedingly rare (Albarella and Payne 2005). Other late Neolithic sites provide evidence that is consistent with Durrington Walls (e.g. the West

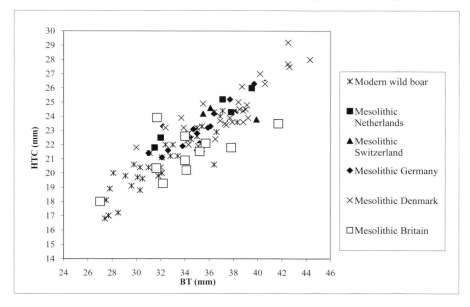

FIGURE 15. Size of distal humerus in British Mesolithic wild boar compared to other Mesolithic specimens and to modern European wild boar. Modified from Albarella *et al.* 2009.

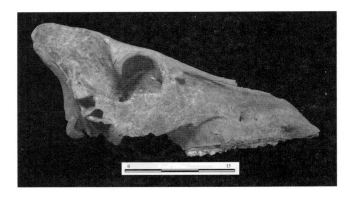

FIGURE 16. A wild boar skull from the late Bronze Age site of Welland Bank Quarry, Lincolnshire
PHOTO BY SHANE EALES

Kennet Enclosure; Edwards and Horne 1997). A lower third molar from the late Neolithic levels at Windmill Hill is larger than any found at Durrington and may well belong to a wild boar, but at this site too the species seems to be far from common. Wild boar is also claimed at late Neolithic Fengate (Harman 1978) and Puddlehill (Grigson 1976) but the evidence is not entirely unambiguous (Albarella and Pirnie in prep.). The most interesting finds are from Mount Pleasant (Harcourt 1979b), where a huge *Sus* astragalus and canine were discovered. This suggests that large wild boar – morphometrically distinct from domestic pigs – did indeed exist in the Neolithic of Britain, but were rare or rarely hunted. Such large specimens also suggest that, as elsewhere in Europe, Neolithic wild boar were larger than their Mesolithic counterparts.

In later prehistoric times the evidence for the occurrence of the wild boar becomes even thinner. The possible presence of the species is mentioned for the Beaker site of Poors Heath (Cornwall 1976) and at late Bronze Age Runnymede, where Serjeantson (1996) mentions the occurrence of some very large, though not measurable, *Sus* specimens. In late Bronze Age levels at Welland Bank Quarry an almost complete skull of large size and typical wild boar profile was found (Albarella *et al.* in prep.) (Figure 16). The presence of the wild boar is also mentioned at the lakeside settlement of Glastonbury (Yalden 1999, 104), among a few other Iron Age sites.

The wild boar in historic times

Studies of large animal bone assemblages from Roman times reveal either no sign of the presence of the wild boar, such as at Colchester (Luff 1993), or the occasional large specimen found among a multitude of smaller pig bones, such as at Exeter (Maltby 1979). Most interesting is the evidence from Wroxeter (Hammon 2005) and Chedworth Villa (A. Hammon, unpublished data), where some specimens are of an exceptionally large size and clearly stand out from the rest of the *Sus* measurements. Considering the propensity of the Romans to export exotica it could be argued that these may represent imported animals from the European continent. The occurrence, however, of large wild boar in prehistoric times in Britain indicates that the post-Mesolithic size increase of this species is more likely to represent an indigenous phenomenon. In Roman times large wild pigs could have therefore still been found naturally in the British countryside.

Analysis of the mitochondrial DNA of the specimens from Wroxeter and Chedworth, indicates that the British wild boar was genetically indistinguishable from that present in central Europe, but different from the animals living in Italy and outside Europe (Larson *et al.* 2007).

From Anglo-Saxon times onwards the archaeological evidence can be integrated with that deriving from written sources. This is the period when pig breeding reached its hallmark, with most animals kept free range (Albarella 2006). Such abundance of free pasturing domestic pigs must have increased the probability of interbreeding with wild boar, a phenomenon historically documented by later sources (Goulding 2003, 26). Nonetheless, the Anglo-Saxons made a clear distinction between the domestic pig and the wild boar, using different terms for the two forms (Rackham 1997, 36; Yalden 1999, 131). That the wild boar still existed in the Anglo-Saxon countryside of Britain is made further clear by the fact that soon after the Norman Conquest William I made a deliberate effort to protect the species, together with other wild game (Goulding 2003, 16). The existence of the wild boar in this period in the British Isles is also documented by Welsh (Rackham 1997, 36) and Irish (Kelly 2000, 281) written sources.

Archaeologically, the occurrence of the wild boar in the second half of the first millennium AD is suggested at a few sites, but not all of them provide conclusive evidence. Perhaps most remarkable is the apparent complete absence of the wild boar in the very large early Saxon animal bone assemblage of West Stow (Crabtree 1989). The occurrence of the wild boar is suggested for York (Coppergate and Fishergate; O'Connor 1989 and 1991b), Lincoln (Flaxengate; O'Connor 1982), Aylesbury (Walton; Noddle 1976) and Southampton (Melbourne Street; Bourdillon and Coy 1980). The stray find of a Middle Saxon (ninth century) isolated pig skeleton, interpreted as a wild boar on the basis of its size, at Stanstead Abbots (Ashdown 1982) is backed up by more detailed biometrical evidence. This is a truly large pig, in the range of the wild boar from the Roman sites mentioned above.

Extinction

By medieval times (i.e. after the Norman Conquest of AD 1066) the documentary evidence becomes more abundant and detailed. The wild boar was protected and its hunting rights restricted to the aristocracy (Grant 1988, 168; Yalden 1999, 150 and 166). The species is therefore not likely to occur in archaeological sites of lower status. Wild boar are, however, more difficult to fence than deer (Rackham 1997, 37), providing thus the occasional opportunity for poaching.

There is general agreement that 'by the Middle Ages wild swine were very rare' (Rackham 1997, 36), which perhaps explains why their hunting did not receive the status or popularity that it had in other European countries such as Germany, Spain (Cummins 1988, 97) or France, where the famous hunting treatise of Gaston de Phoebus provides plenty of descriptions and illustrations of the wild boar hunt.

The final demise of the native British wild boar probably occurred in the second half of the thirteenth century. The best record of this gradual disappearance comes from the Forest of Dean. Here wild boar were still chased for Henry III between 1251 and 1257, but Rackham (1997, 36) believes that 'the dozen which Henry III ordered killed for a friend in the Forest of Dean in 1260 were the last free-living wild swine in England'.

This is probably not far from the truth but it may not be entirely accurate as a few more populations may have managed to linger on until the end of the century. Woolgar (1999, 115–6) reports the hunting of wild boar between the end of the twelfth and the beginning of the thirteenth century in the western part of Essex, where they had by then become rare. He has, however, also two records for the very end of the thirteenth century, though one of them was a gift and it could have conceivably come from the Continent.

Goulding (2003, 19) has a later record than Rackham's for the Forest of Dean (1282), but he also mentions that a request by Edward II (reigned 1307–1327) for wild boar from the Forest of Dean could not be fulfilled, suggesting thus that by that time the species had disappeared.

In Scotland the wild boar may have become extinct at a later date (Goulding 2003, 25), but it was already sufficiently rare in the latter part of the thirteenth century to require management and deliberate feeding (Smith 2000, 706). In Ireland it was, according to Giraldus Cambrensis, still common in the twelfth century but it did not survive for much longer (Kelly 2000, 281–2).

The archaeological evidence reflects the rarity of the species as portrayed by the documentary sources. The best diachronic evidence derives from Dudley Castle (Thomas 2005). Thorough biometrical analysis carried out on *Sus* teeth from this high status site demonstrates the occurrence of a single large outlier (a probable wild boar) in phase 5 (dated 1262–1321), but none are present in the four following phases (dating up to 1750). Postcranial bones show no obvious large outliers, but in phase 5 there is a certain degree of bimodality in the distribution of the measurements, possibly indicating a mixed population with domestic pigs integrated by a wild component. This evidence is remarkably consistent with the historical data as it shows that throughout the medieval sequence wild boar were always rare, and completely absent by the fourteenth century onwards.

The rarity of the wild boar is confirmed by its apparent absence from the animal bone assemblages of Okehampton Castle (twelfth-fourteenth centuries) (Maltby 1982) and Launceston Castle (thirteenth and fifteenth centuries) (Albarella and Davis 1996). This is significant when we consider that these sites produced large samples, which were subject to careful biometrical analysis. In addition both assemblages contain a substantial amount of remains of wild species, particularly deer and wild birds. There are occasional other claims of the presence of the wild boar in the medieval archaeological record, such as at Bewell House, Hereford (Noddle 1985b) and at a few other urban sites (Sykes 2001, 158) but these add little to the story.

Sykes (2001, 158 and 2006, 166) suggests that wild boar specimens identified from British medieval sites may represent imported animals. This cannot be ruled out and it is likely to be the case for the later Middle Ages. In earlier times, however, it does not need to have been so, as large wild boar survived in Britain, though in small numbers, until the thirteenth century. These, as we have seen, can be tracked down throughout the whole prehistoric and historic archaeological sequence.

It is likely that the wild boar disappeared from Britain as a consequence of a combination of habitat depletion (mainly woodland), over-hunting and eventually inter-breeding of the final relict populations with free ranging domestic pigs. Britain suffered woodland loss more than the rest of Europe (Rackham 1997, 37) and, being an island, could not easily be replenished with animals moving in from other areas. Wild boars are strong swimmers (Nowak 1999b) but the Channel was probably too wide and treacherous to be negotiated easily. Loss of habitat alone is unlikely to represent a sufficient explanation for the extinction of the British wild boar, as in Scandinavia, despite the abundance of forest, the species encountered a similar fate, having become extinct by the later Middle Ages (T. Tyrberg pers. comm.). The Scandinavian wild pig populations, however, shared with those of Britain their relative isolation. Although Scandinavia is not an island, a reduction in wild boar numbers in that region could only be compensated with animals coming from the far north. But this area is located outside the natural distribution of the species, which is notoriously vulnerable to deep snow conditions (Nowak 1999b).

Reintroduction and further disappearance

The British countryside did not remain devoid of wild boar for very long, because soon after its disappearance the aristocracy tried to reintroduce the species by using continental stock. It is possible that the park of Cornbury, Oxfordshire had wild boar as early as 1339 (Yalden 1999, 157), though it is difficult to establish whether these were part of a relict population of native animals or they rather represented introduced stock.

Most interesting is a debate occurring in the second half of the fifteenth century between a French and an English herald, which is reported by Cummins (1988, 97). The French herald teases the English for not having in their countryside fierce animals that require bravery to hunt, such as the wolf, the lynx and the wild boar. The English herald replies that although they are lucky not to have wolves they do indeed have the wild boar. Such inconsistency of views suggests that in this period the status of the wild boar in Britain was dubious. The most likely explanation is that the species had indeed become extinct but had eventually been reintroduced for hunting purposes.

In the earlier part of the sixteenth century Henry VIII received from Francis I some live wild boar, but also with instructions on how to maintain and breed them (Williams 1998, 86–7). The introduction of these animals in the sixteenth century is also documented for the Savernake Forest (Wiltshire), Chartley Park (Staffordshire) (Rackham 1997, 37) and the palace of James V in Scotland (Smith 2000, 706).

In the first half of the seventeenth century James I and Charles I introduced wild boar to Windsor and the New Forest from France and Germany (Goulding 2003, 25; Rackham 1997, 37; Yalden 1999, 168). Further reintroductions from Germany are documented until the end of the seventeenth century, but were met with little enthusiasm by local people, who persecuted the animals and eventually contributed to the final disappearance of the species by the end of the century (Goulding 2003, 26).

By the eighteenth century the wild boar – either native or introduced – could no longer be found in the country, and its meat had disappeared from the British tables. Two of the classic British cookery books of the nineteenth and twentieth century (Beeton 1982; Hartley 1954) make no mention of wild boar venison in their recipes.

Archaeologically, the presence of the wild boar is claimed in late fifteenth-mid sixteenth century levels from Worcester (Chaplin 1968–9) and, more tentatively, for the early sixteenth-eighteenth century from Great Linford village, Milton Keynes (Burnett 1992). Since both finds are not backed up by any biometrical evidence they cannot be relied on. The partial skeleton from Great Linford may even belong to a relatively modern improved animal, which would explain its large size. In the absence of any substantiated identification, we must thus assume that the archaeological record confirms the disappearance of the native wild boar in this period. If any bones of this species will in the future be found in late medieval or post-medieval contexts, they will probably turn up at high status, rather than urban or village, sites.

Conclusions

Uncommon in the Palaeolithic, the wild boar was widespread in Britain in early post-glacial times, and one of the favourite preys of Mesolithic hunters. As in other European areas, in this period the wild boar was of a relatively small size. With the introduction of farming the wild boar becomes elusive in the archaeological record, partly due to the difficulties in distinguishing it from the domestic pig, but mainly due to its rarity as a hunted species. From the beginning of the Neolithic until the Middle Ages the wild boar archaeological record in Britain is remarkably consistent. The species remains rare throughout, with the occasional very large animals cropping up at a few sites. If the scarcity of the species in prehistory might partly be attributed to hunting preferences, by post-Roman times documentary evidence clearly indicates that the species was genuinely rare in the countryside. This eventually led to its complete disappearance by the end of the thirteenth century. The following four centuries saw various attempts at reintroduction with the aid of continental stock (mainly from France and Germany), but these eventually run out of steam by the end of the seventeenth century, when the species can be regarded to have become finally extinct. This was, at least, the case until the 1980s, when escaped animals from wild boar farms led to the establishment of viable free living populations in the South of Britain. The return of the wild boar has not always been met with great favour by local farmers (Goulding and Roper 2002) and the animals have genetic characteristics which are mixed and of rather uncertain origins (Goulding 2001). They cannot replace what we have sadly and irremediably lost, but they still remain an interesting and rather majestic addition to our countryside.

Acknowledgements

I am grateful to Naomi Sykes and Terry O'Connor for inviting me to contribute to this interesting project. I would also like to thank Chris Dyer, Barbara Harvey, Chris Woolgar and Tommy Tyrberg for advice; Andy Hammon for allowing me to refer to unpublished information; and Martin Goulding for kindly providing copyright permission to reproduce the photograph in Figure 13.

CHAPTER 9

The Wolf

Aleksander G. Pluskowski

....

Introduction

With the exception of humans, the wolf is the quintessential terrestrial predator of the northern hemisphere and one which outlasted the other large carnivores once native to the British Isles – bears and lynx (see Hammon and Hetherington, this volume). Today, wolves can be seen in zoos and conservation centres across the country, and their re-introduction to Scotland is a subject of current debate. By the beginning of the fifteenth century, the wolf was almost certainly extinct in England, following a sustained and systematic campaign of extermination that would only be matched several centuries later across Continental Europe and North America. This extinction was first systematically documented in James E. Harting's (1880b) seminal work *A Short History of the Wolf in Britain*, subsequently revisited and refined by Anthony Dent (1974) and Derek Yalden (1999). Whilst these authors grappled with reconstructing the complex biogeography of wolves in medieval Britain, others sought to understand the motivation behind the persecution in more depth. The most influential work to date is Barry Lopez's juxtaposition of Native American and European responses to wolves in his *Of Wolves and Men*, first published in 1978. Whilst Harting's interest in the wolf (and other extinct British fauna) was antiquarian, Lopez adopted a conservationist perspective, blaming the medieval Church – and Christian ideology – for the origins of wolf persecution in Europe, and ultimately North America. But although the popularity of Lopez's thesis has not waned, current understanding of human responses to wolves – essential for planning their future management – recognises their diversity resulting from complex interactions between different social, political and ecological contexts (Kruuk 2002). This shift in perspective is exemplified by the publication of the first comprehensive survey of wolf attacks on humans in Europe (Linnell *et al.* 2002), which linked sporadic incidents and specific historical episodes of actual predation with an ecological understanding of wolf behaviour. After decades of research on medieval European society coupled with the holistic ecological perspective central to modern environmental archaeology, it is possible to return to the experiences of wolves in Britain and begin to answer a fundamental question: in a European society sharing a comparable world-view structured by Christianity, why was the wolf exterminated in medieval England and not elsewhere?

Reconstructing the history of human responses to wolves, and the complex web of inter-related predator-prey relationships, requires a detailed synthesis of multiple strands of evidence. No strand can be removed from its particular context, but when placed alongside each other they begin to form a clearer picture of changing responses to wolves on either side of the Norman Conquest – an event which represents a watershed in the ecological history of the British Isles. Our understanding of the wolf in prehistoric and historic Britain is necessarily limited to human responses to this animal. However, modern ecological and ethological models offer potential analogues for expanding this understanding beyond the keyhole of the human ecological niche. It is of course impossible to estimate the numbers of wolves in the past; biologists with years of experience in the field and extensive tracking equipment find it difficult enough to estimate numbers of wolves in regions of the world where they thrive today. As highly mobile and adaptable carnivores, living in packs, the biogeography of wolves was intimately linked to the movements of their prey, in turn linked to climate, topography, vegetation and the dynamic influence of seasonality, the impact of other carnivores on prey populations, the territoriality of other wolf packs and a host of other variables (Fuller *et al.* 2003). Nonetheless, a number of broad observations can be made concerning the changing status of the wolf in the British Isles. In order to highlight the impact of the Norman Conquest, this chapter considers responses to wolves in three chronological sections: the first millennium AD, the late-eleventh to late-fourteenth centuries and, briefly, the post-medieval era.

FIGURE 17. Wolf
PHOTO BY TOM HARTMAN

Experiencing wolves in the first millennium AD

Compared to other animals, the wolf made a limited impression on societies across Britain in the first millennium. Roman colonisation introduced the imperial insignia of the she-wolf and twins, and the occasional archaeological remains of *Canis lupus* represent sporadic hunting (Yalden 1999, 146–147). The remains include occasional teeth, skull and limb bone fragments; however given the similarities between wolf and dog skeletons, particularly the potential for morphological variation in both, they are difficult to positively identity (Pluskowski 2006a). In fact, the exploitation of wild fauna appears to have been limited in the latter half of the first millennium; Anglo-Saxon migrants did not introduce or develop an intensive hunting culture, and occasional examples of canid claws included as grave goods which may potentially be from wolves, coupled with ambiguous remains in settlements are outnumbered by examples of bear, wild boar and beaver remains (Meaney 1981). Appropriations of the wolf were sporadic and localised; although a lupine motif on applied Anglo-Saxon art, originating in Scandinavia, has been identified by Nielsen (2002), the only clear representation appears on artefacts from Sutton Hoo, perhaps reflecting a local family affiliation with the animal (Pluskowski 2006b,144). Certainly later literature records 'wolf' as a recurring personal name, but its popularity (let alone social function) is very difficult to quantify. The she-wolf and twins was also sporadically adopted, represented on a handful of artefacts and reflecting a Christianised resonance of *Romanitas*, one that would fade into obscurity by the end of the millennium. Scandinavian colonisations in the ninth and tenth centuries introduced further localised and short-lived conceptualisations of the wolf as an apocalyptic force (Pluskowski 2004), and if the animal had played an important role in earlier Anglo-Saxon society, its use was rapidly superseded by the new Christian semiotic system which deployed other, already well-established, animals – most notably the lion.

At the same time, aristocratic culture was developing in both England and Scotland focusing on deer as the prey of choice (Sykes 2001; Sykes, this volume). Although this was small-scale, it coincides with the first potential indication of widespread wolf hunting. This indication is not, as traditionally cited, King Edgar's receipt of a tribute of three hundred wolf pelts in AD 957 from the north and south Welsh kingdoms (Harting 1880b, 16). This legendary episode is first documented by William of Malmesbury in the early-twelfth century (*Gesta Regum Anglorum* 2, 155, trans. Mynors *et al.* 1998, 255). However, analysis of the distribution of wolf place names in England led Aybes and Yalden (1995) to conclude the animal had been driven from the south by the time of the Conquest. There is not enough evidence to support the details of the wolf hunts in early medieval Wales, or even Scotland, where there is limited iconographic evidence of Pictish familiarity with wolves and wolf hunting (Henderson 1998, 112–113). In fact, one of the earliest references to wolf hunting in England is found in Ælfric Bata's colloquies, written at the start of the eleventh century

(*Colloquy* 28, trans. Gwara and Porter 1997, 195). This early wolf persecution may have become twinned with the development of aristocratic hunting culture, although direct evidence for sustained wolf hunting in England becomes documented only after the Norman Conquest.

The Norman Conquest and the war against the wolf

The Norman Conquest established a new ruling class which defined itself, in part, through the construction of a new hunting culture revolving around the control and management of deer in areas designated as forest (*foresta/forestis*) (Sykes 2001). Although they were contested and active spaces, forests consisted of initially identified and then actively maintained habitats for deer, and in doing so restricted settlement, woodland clearance and permanent human activity – particularly in the Peak Forest and Dean. The presence of significant herds of deer in these areas undoubtedly attracted wolves – both animals would have affected each other's distribution and behaviour to varying degrees – with the result of providing alternative and undoubtedly irritating competition to the royal chase. Indeed, from the late-eleventh to late-thirteenth century, royal forests became the major theatre of a protracted war waged against the principal competitor for prohibited venison.

How was the wolf perceived by the aristocracy, its principle persecutors? In documentary sources, wolves were overwhelmingly categorised as vermin (Dent 1974; Fisher 1880, 187–188; Harting 1880b; Owen 1841, 358). But whilst the animal is virtually absent in Middle English hunting literature (Rooney 1993, 3), it was employed as a popular symbol of nobility (albeit fallen nobility) in Anglo-Norman fables (Salisbury 1994, 130). The royal huntsman William Twiti's *Art of Hunting* (*c.* 1327) defined the wolf as one of four beasts that is chased, whilst *The Boke of St. Albans* (1486) included it in its list of beasts of venery together with the hart and hare (Danielsson 1977, 31). But even if the wolf was occasionally described as a noble animal, any limits on its pursuit were an extension of royal control over hunting space. By the twelfth century, only royal officials were legitimately allowed to hunt wolves within the bounds of forests, but this was not so much about preserving wolves, as the integrity of Forest law, which Henry II's *Carta de Foresta* clearly states (Dent 1974, 111).

Thus, Walter de Beauchamp had to be given royal permission to hunt wolves in the Forest of Feckenham, Worcestershire (Wilson 2004, 8), whilst a charter of *c.* 1241 in the Cartulary of Rievaulx Abbey gives pasture in Swaledale with the right to take wolves (Atkinson 1889, 304). This principle extended to private forests, but elsewhere the Crown also encouraged the pursuit of wolves; from at least the late-eleventh century in England, it was common royal practice to grant land in exchange for, amongst other things, obligations to keep it free of wolves. Robert de Umfraville was granted lordship of Riddesdale in Northumberland by William I on condition of defending the region from 'enemies and wolves' (Harting 1880b, 20). Robert Ferrers the Earl of Derby was granted lands at

Heage by the Crown in the early-twelfth century in return for driving wolves out of Belper, within Duffield Chase (Derbyshire), which afterwards became a royal forest (VCH Derby I, 405). Although lands continued to be held by serjeanty of killing wolves into the reign of Henry VI, the overwhelming evidence points to a significant depletion of the wolf population in England by the late-fourteenth century, and the obligation to hunt wolves was probably preserved as a sinecure (Fisher 1880, 190; Rackham 1997, 35).

However, whilst there is evidence for opportunistic wolf hunting in Britain, bounties were most frequently collected by the king's attendants at royal hunting grounds in the south, west and Welsh border counties, and successful wolf hunters became specialists; a description of the royal household from the 1130s indicates that the king's wolf hunters or *luparii* required horses, packs of dogs and retinues for their work (Bartlett 2000, 671). References to dogs specifically used to hunt wolves (*canes luporarios*) are frequent (Harting cites a number of instances). The value of such specialist hunters is demonstrated in the pipe roll of Henry II for 1167–8, which lists a payment of 10s. for the travelling expenses of two wolf trappers from the Peak, to cross the sea and take wolves in Normandy – indeed, during the English occupation of Normandy in the mid-fifteenth century, a special office of (largely ineffective) wolf hunters was created (Cox 1905, 33; Halard 1983, 195). In the 1280s, systematic wolf hunting was assigned to members of the knightly classes such as Richard Talbot and Peter Corbet (Chancery Papers, Patent Rolls (C66) 1272–81, 435). In Scotland, where an aristocratic hunting culture comparable to England developed in the south-east, a similar approach to wolf hunting was taken by the Crown. Here, alongside the aristocratic hunt, the trapping of wolves seems to have been particularly popular (Gilbert 1979, 57). Wolf hunting was permitted when other types of hunting were not, as in Eskdale and Pluscarden (1165–69, Innes 1837, 39, specifying traps; 1230; Macphail 1881, 69, 199), and professional wolf hunters were appointed, for example at Stirling in 1288–1290 (Stuart and Burnett 1878, 38). In medieval England, where sustained wolf hunting was predominantly conducted by royal officials and opportunistic trappers, the role of local communities in this process is impossible to gauge. It was probably not considered extraordinary enough to be recorded in official documents, but would have been sporadic and, compared to organised campaigns, largely ineffectual.

Tracking the extinction of the wolf in England is not easy, but the intensity of hunting appears to shadow the management of forests. Although established in the late-eleventh century, the forest institution only became fully operational on a national level by the mid-twelfth century and reached its height in the thirteenth century. The evidence indicates that wolves were caught as far south as Hampshire, where in 1156, the county sheriff arranged for an allowance from the Exchequer to pay for the livery of the royal wolf hunters operating in the New Forest and the Forest of Bere (Madox 1969, 204). Their efforts to reduce wolf numbers in the county were limited – in 1209, one wolf was captured at Gillingham (Dorset) and Clarendon, a roll from 1212–1213 refers to a payment of

5s in May 1212 for a wolf caught within the bounds of the Forest of Freemantle, also in Hampshire (Britnell 2000, 671). In the same year, payments are listed for two wolves captured in the Forest of Irwell in Lancashire (Harting 1880b, 25), and most wolf hunting in forests during the twelfth and thirteenth centuries appears to have taken place in the counties bordering Wales (Britnell 2000, 671). Patent rolls for 1280 indicate that John Gifford was empowered to destroy all wolves within royal forests (Harting 1880b, 28). In 1281, wolf depredations are recorded at Cannock Chase in Staffordshire (VCH Shropshire 1, 490 note 51), and in the same year, Richard Talbot was given license to hunt wolves with nets in the Forest of Dean, so long as no deer were taken and no warrens were coursed (Hart 1971, 37), and lastly – and perhaps most famously – a writ of aid was issued for Peter Corbet to destroy all wolves in the *foresta*, parks and 'other places' in Gloucestershire, Herefordshire, Worcestershire, Shropshire and Staffordshire (Calendar Patent Rolls, May 14, 1281). Wolves remained in Dean; a year later, the Forest Eyre fined two men for taking venison mauled by wolves, whilst the most detailed account of wolf hunting is dated to 1285 (*ibid.*). That wolves were still active in northern England in the late-thirteenth century is suggested by an assemblage of roe deer bones discovered in Rawthey Cave, Cumbria, interpreted as being accumulated by wolves and dated to no later than *c.*1300 (Hedges *et al.* 1998, 440–1). There is a marked decrease in the number of documented wolf hunts in the fourteenth century; the last reliable reference to wolf trapping in England is dated to 1394–6, from Whitby Abbey in East Yorkshire, where the monks paid 10s 9d for tawing fourteen wolf skins – here monastic rather than royal interests were perceived as under threat from wolves (Rackham 1997, 35). In Scotland, comparable persecution of wolves by the Crown is only evident from the high medieval period with a reference to a wolf hunter in Stirling in 1283 – in close proximity to a number of royal parks – whilst more extensive laws for the destruction of wolves were passed in the fifteenth century (Gilbert 1979). The population of wolves, probably isolated in the north-west highlands, survived into the seventeenth century.

Extinction and exoticisation

Today, a European wolf pelt is a rare and expensive commodity. In medieval Britain, as across Continental Europe, the wolf had comparatively little commercial value. There is some evidence for trading wolf pelts; the setting of wolf traps in north Yorkshire on the lands of abbeys such as Rievaulx and Whitby has been associated with supporting local tanners and exporting pelts (Waites 1997, 159), and wolf skins were shipped between eastern Ireland and Bristol (Carus-Wilson 1967, 24), supported by the presence of their lower limb bones at Waterford (McCormick 1997, 837). However, within the context of an international fur trade dominated by the luxury pelts of small mammals – particularly squirrels and mustelids – these are exceptional examples. When coupled with the idea of wolf hunting as opportunistic incidents or short-lived campaigns, it is perhaps unsurprising that very few bones of *Canis lupus* have been identified in medieval archaeological contexts, although this trend must also reflect the problem of confident identification of wolf remains (Pluskowski 2006a). The only identified wolf bone to date from high medieval England was discovered at Lyveden in Northamptonshire and associated with the Forest of Rockingham (Steane 1985, 167). But by the end of the sixteenth century, the English wolf was considered exotic and valuable enough to find a place in the royal collection of animals at the Tower of London. Here, in 1599, a 'lean, ugly' lupine is described as 'the only one in England', sharing cramped quarters with the Tower's traditional collection of big cats (Hahn 2003, 74).

Rather than being misled by the popularity of the predatory relationship between wolves and sheep in medieval Christian literature to explain the inclination to exterminate this large carnivore, the fate of the wolf in Britain is better understood as being inextricably linked to the fate of deer. Its persecution became systematised as a response to its competition, but ironically its extermination did not stop the significant depletion of wild deer herds by the fifteenth century – the result of over-hunting by humans, increasingly poor management of *foresta* and a growing preference for using parks for hunting (Pollard 2004, 60–61). The campaign to re-introduce wolves into Scotland with the aim of controlling deer overpopulation has reversed this medieval impulse.

Despite its extinction, or perhaps because of it, the wolf continues to grasp the imagination of people in the British Isles. Today, its popularity can be partly attributed to the common currency of the 'fairy tale wolf' and werewolf in Western culture, and partly to a growing public interest fostered by UK-based conservationists and biologists. The story of the wolf in medieval England has been used as an exemplar of responses to the animal in contemporary European societies. In fact, the systematic persecution of the wolf resulting in the animal's virtual extinction was a unique episode which can be linked to the unusually elaborate hunting culture that developed after the Norman Conquest. Across Europe, wolves were employed and widely recognised as negative symbols in religious and vernacular literature, but this cannot be used to explain the variation in responses to the physical animal in the landscape, anymore than the overwhelming cultural role of the lion across medieval Europe reflected any form of ecological reality. The Norwegian wolf hunts at the start of the twenty-first century demonstrated how difficult, time-consuming and expensive it was to hunt one of the most successful predators in the northern hemisphere, despite contemporary technological advantages. As such, the extinction of the wolf in England is testimony to the extraordinary success of persistent hunting episodes funded by the Crown. Unlike the recent wolf hunts in Norway, these took place within comparatively accessible environments, and were ultimately driven by an institutionalised desire to preserve deer for exclusive predation by the ruling elite.

CHAPTER 10

The Lynx

David Hetherington

Introduction

This chapter examines the relationship between humans and the smallest of Britain's three top predators. Until very recently, the Eurasian lynx *Lynx lynx* was seen as a victim of the changing British climate, vanishing from the island several millennia ago long before a cultural association with humans could have been forged. Recent radiocarbon dating, however, has forced a dramatic reappraisal of this view. It is now possible to detect the historical footprints of Britain's most elusive large carnivore, not only in the fossil record, but also from linguistic and literary evidence.

The Eurasian lynx is the largest of the four extant lynx species and differs from the other three by feeding primarily on small ungulates, typically roe deer *Capreolus capreolus*. Characteristics of the two intact lynx skulls recovered in Britain, from Reindeer Cave, Sutherland and Beeston Tor Cave, Staffordshire, suggest that the lynx of the British Holocene were of the larger, ungulate-hunting, Eurasian species, rather than the smaller, lagomorph-specialising species such as the Iberian lynx *Lynx pardina* (Kurtén and Granqvist 1987; L. Werdelin pers. comm.). However, like Britain's other native large carnivores, the wolf *Canis lupus* and the brown bear *Ursus arctos*, the lynx is no longer part of the wild fauna of Britain. Theories on the causes of lynx extinction in Britain had, until recent years, focused on natural processes, such as climate change in the early- or mid-Holocene (Clutton-Brock 1991; Curry-Lindahl 1951; Guggisberg 1975). Jenkinson (1983) suggested that early deforestation had brought about the extinction of the lynx by the end of the Mesolithic period. Until recently then, the lynx was considered to have become extinct in Britain before human activity was likely to have been a significant factor in their ecology.

Elsewhere, the species continues to have a very broad geographical range, occurring from western Europe to the Pacific coast of Siberia, and from the Arctic tundra north of 70° to the mountains of the Middle East and the Himalayas (Von Arx *et al.* 2004). Such a broad range suggests that in common with many large carnivores, the Eurasian lynx does not appear to be particularly sensitive to climatic variation. Unlike cursorial predators such as wolves, lynx rely on cover to get close enough to their prey to launch an ambush attack. Although lynx are known to hunt amongst rocks and scrub on Central Asian mountainsides,

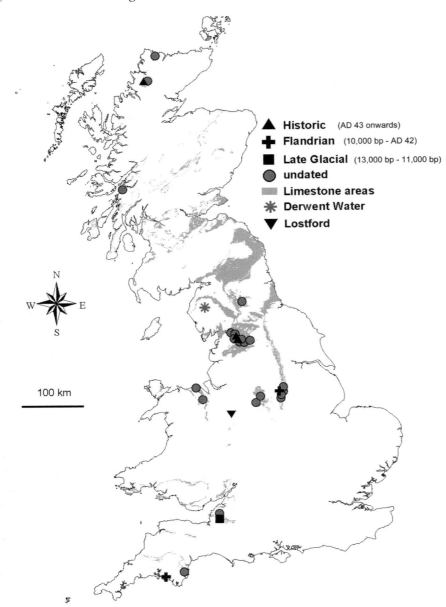

FIGURE 18. Distribution of cave sites in Britain where lynx bones have been recovered. The locations of Derwent Water and Lostford are also marked. Limestone information from 625K Bedrock Data by permission the British Geological Survey.

woodland is the core habitat for Eurasian lynx across Europe and Siberia, where their feeding strategy is reliant on roe deer and the provision of cover from which to hunt (Jedrzejewski *et al.* 1993; Von Arx *et al.* 2004). It is likely then that the fate of lynx in Britain was closely tied to that of its forest habitat and prey.

The palaeontological evidence for British lynx

The past occurrence of lynx in Britain is known from bones found at various cave sites (see Figure 18; Coard and Chamberlain 1999). A limited number of radiocarbon dates on lynx bones from caves from the period 9570–8930 BP demonstrate that lynx were present in Britain well before rising global sea levels eventually separated Britain from continental Europe around 8500 years ago (Shennan *et al.* 2000). Prior to that separation, increased temperatures and low sea levels around 10,000 years ago would have permitted the colonisation of Britain by woodland biotopes, roe deer and lynx, from continental Europe. The bone evidence tells us that lynx continued to be part of the British fauna right through to the early historical era. Skeletal remains of a lynx from Reindeer Cave in Sutherland, northwest Scotland gave a surprisingly young radiocarbon age of 1770 ± 80 years BP (Kitchener and Bonsall 1997). This date indicated a much more recent extinction of the lynx in Britain than previously thought and suggested that climate change was not responsible for the species' demise. The existence of historical-era lynx occurring elsewhere in Britain was recently confirmed through the radiocarbon dating of lynx bone from two sites in the Craven area of North Yorkshire. A tibia from Moughton Fell Cave gave a radiocarbon date of 1842 ± 35 years BP (calibrated to AD 80–320), showing that the lynx had lived in the Yorkshire Dales during the Roman period (Hetherington *et al.* 2006). A femur from Kinsey Cave gave the result 1550 ± 24 years BP (AD 25–600), represents the youngest date yet for lynx in Britain (Hetherington *et al.* 2006). Together, these two dates show that lynx inhabited the Craven area both during and after the Roman period and most likely continued to do so for some time afterwards.

The cultural evidence for British lynx

Just 80 km north west of Kinsey Cave, in the Lake District, lies Derwent Water, considered to be the setting for Pais Dinogad, a lullaby contained within the Book of Aneirin, thought to have been written in the first half of the seventh century AD (Gruffydd 1990). Written in Cumbric, an ancient British language similar to Welsh, this lullaby celebrates Dinogad's father's hunting prowess and refers to him killing several species including roe deer, red deer *Cervus elaphus*, wild boar *Sus scrofa*, grouse, and fish. Interestingly, the second last line of the lullaby lists one of the game that Dinogad's father killed with his spear, as *llewyn*, considered to be the Cumbric word for 'lynx' (Jarman 1988: Loth 1930). According to Jarman (1988, 68) therefore, the last few lines of the lullaby should be translated as:

> 'Of all those that thy father reached with his lance,
> Wild boar and lynx and fox,
> None escaped which was not winged.'

Aelfric's Anglo-Saxon Vocabulary of the tenth century gives the word *lox* for lynx (Wright 1884). However, this in itself is not evidence of the existence of lynx in tenth-century England, especially as the same vocabulary includes words for clearly non-native animals such as camels and elephants. Several attempts have been made to reconstruct the former distributions of locally extinct species in Britain using place-name evidence (Aybes and Yalden 1995; Boisseau and Yalden 1998; Webster 2001). There are several place-names in the former Anglo-Saxon region of Britain which are prefixed by *lox*, for instance Loxley. However, it is believed that the prefix lox-, for the most part, means 'of the person called Locc' (Ekwall 1960; Gelling 1984). Other lox-prefixed place-names are thought to derive from the old Celtic word for a winding stream (Ekwall 1960). But one place in Anglo-Saxon Britain does seem to have been named after lynx. The name of Lostford in Shropshire has evolved since the original Saxon through a process called metathesis. This involves the swapping round of adjacent consonant sounds, so that the *ks* sound represented by the letter 'x', becomes an *sk* sound instead. Prior to becoming 'Lostford' the hamlet was known as Loskesford, and prior to that, Lox's Ford thus 'ford of the lynx' (Ekwall 1960; Gelling 1984). That even one lynx-related place-name exists could be significant. In Lithuania, a country where lynx have existed for many centuries and continue to do so today, only three lynx-derived place-names have been found, while 97 exist for wolves, 43 for bears and 53 for foxes (Balčiauskas and Volodka 2001).

In Old Gaelic, the oldest form of a language spoken across Ireland, Scotland and the Isle of Man during the period approximately AD 600–900, there was a word *lug*, meaning 'lynx' (Dictionary of the Irish Language 1913–1976, L: 235, 33–56). This is entirely cognate with Cumbric *llew* and indeed Welsh *Llew* and Old Gaelic *Lug* were the names given to the Celtic god of light (A. Price pers. comm.). There appears to be a connection running through much of the Indo-European group of languages between 'light' and 'lynx', probably due to a widespread perception of the powerful sight and shining eyes of lynx (Onions 1966; Partridge 1966). After AD 900, *lug* underwent a sound-shift to *lugh* but then it is commonly used in heroic literature to mean 'hero' or 'warrior'. Some of the pre-900 instances, in compound words such as *lug-léimnech*, meaning 'lynxlike-leaping', can only be interpreted with the meaning 'lynx', not 'hero', and the latter is taken to be a transferred meaning from the original 'lynx'. That the Gaels had an adjective meaning 'lynxlike-leaping' suggests that the people were familiar with the way the living animal moved and not simply with imported lynx pelts. But no examples of the word referring to 'lynx' occur after about AD 1200, and no other word appears with that meaning until the modern Gaelic dictionaries, where the English word is borrowed. The linguistic evidence therefore suggests that lynx inhabited Scotland in the period AD 600–900. It also suggests that they may have become progressively scarcer, with the word being used less and less to describe the animal, suggesting that by AD 1200, the lynx was not a common or widespread species.

If lynx existed during the time-scale suggested by the Gaelic language, then they may have been recorded by the Picts, the indigenous people of northern Scotland, who commonly depicted animals on early mediaeval, Christian cross-slabs. One engraving of a hunting scene, on the late ninth-century cross slab found at Kildonnan on the Inner Hebridean island of Eigg, appears to depict a large felid, along with a probable boar, bull and deer being chased by a horseman with hounds and a bird of prey (Figure 19). Although Hebridean in location, some elements of the cross incorporate the style of crosses from eastern mainland Scotland (Fisher 2001). Unfortunately the rear end of the animal has been weathered so that it is not possible to check for the diagnostic short, stubby tail of a lynx. While it is possible that the felid is a biblically-influenced depiction of a lion *Panthera leo*, the creature does appear to have ear tufts and mottled fur. In addition, given this is a hunting scene depicting other species that would have been known to the Picts, the carving suggests that lynx were known and hunted in the Pictish lands of northern Scotland. This is quite possibly, therefore, a representation of a native lynx being pursued by a hunter. It should be borne in mind that lynx were widely regarded in historic European societies as being an elusive predator, more rarely encountered than the bear and wolf (Breitenmoser 1998). Certainly, lynx are one of the least frequently depicted animals in the history of European art (Dent 1976 cited in Bartosiewicz 1993, 14). It is likely that remnant lynx were simply not well known enough during the medieval period to warrant widespread depiction in artwork.

Following the loss of a word for lynx in Gaelic after AD 1200, there appear to be no more direct, documented references to lynx in Scotland. However, the sixteenth-century English chronicler, William Harrison, in his *Description of England*, originally written in 1577, devotes a section to 'Savage beasts and vermines' (Harrison 1805). He describes how wolves were still widespread in Scotland, but also notes the presence of a large felid in northern Scotland:

> 'Lions we have had verie manie in the north parts of Scotland, and those with maines of no lesse force than they of Mauritania were sometimes reported to be; but how and when they were destroied as yet I doo not read.' (Harrison 1805, 379)

He goes on to say that these creatures are no longer heard of. While it is possible that a reference to 'lions' is used as a device to emphasise how wild the north of Scotland was, it may, in fact, be a reference to a recently extinct Scottish

FIGURE 19. Hunting scene from the late 9th century Kildonnan cross-slab, Island of Eigg. The animal at the top right of the hunting scene may be a lynx.
CROWN COPYRIGHT: RCAHMS.

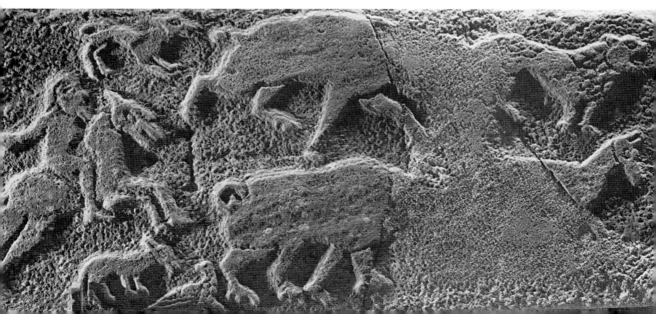

population of the only large cat ever to have occupied northern Europe in the historical period, the Eurasian lynx.

The lynx with people

Eurasian lynx are not often encountered in archaeological contexts (Bartosiewicz 1993; Van Bree and Clason 1971) and none of the lynx bones from British cave sites is known to carry signs of butchery (T. O'Connor pers. comm.). However, as seems to be depicted by Pais Dinogad and the Kildonnan cross slab, humans in Britain did hunt lynx, as they still do in parts of Europe today. The prime motivation for hunting would likely have varied in both time and space, and indeed there may have been several motivations operating at once. Lynx are likely to have been persecuted as a form of pest control when their depredations on woodland-grazed livestock or valued wild game were seen as intolerable, or simply because they were perceived as ferocious beasts of the forest. We know from Germany that in 1818 the last indigenous lynx in the Harz Mountains was tracked for eleven days by 200 hunters before being killed (F. Knolle pers. comm.). They may have also been hunted for sport while carcases would have provided commodities such as thick warm pelts, particularly in winter, as well as meat. Lynx meat is certainly edible, and has been considered a delicacy by those of high status. In eighteenth-century Germany, one game manager felt that lynx would soon disappear from the forests because their meat was so highly prized by the nobility, and several lynx were served at a sumptuous feast attended by European aristocracy at the Congress of Vienna in 1815 (U. Breitenmoser pers. comm.). Clearly, humans were hunting lynx, not just in Britain, but throughout Europe and would have been doing so for millennia.

The available evidence shows that lynx still occurred in the Highlands of Scotland, the Lake District, the Yorkshire Dales, and possibly Shropshire, during the early historical era, and perhaps survived in some of these areas into the late medieval period. This is considerably later than had been previously thought. However, in comparison to other areas of continental Europe, this is an early local extinction. In 1800, Eurasian lynx were still thought to exist right across the Alps, in the Pyrenees, Massif Central and Jura, and in the mountainous areas of Germany and the Czech Republic (Kratochvil 1968). If the persecution and hunting of lynx was commonplace across Europe, why was it that upland areas of Britain, which have acted as refuges for several other carnivorous species, lost their lynx populations, while other, similarly mountainous and thinly populated parts of continental Europe, continued to support lynx up until the nineteenth century? Breitenmoser (1998) noted that the Eurasian lynx had become extinct in southern European areas where the wolf continued to exist, while in Scandinavia the lynx clung on. He concluded that this disparity was due to the lynx's requirements for the cover provided by woodland, in which to stalk its prey of small ungulates. Southern Europe experienced greater anthropogenic deforestation than did Scandinavia with consequent declines in populations of forest dwelling ungulates such as roe deer. High densities of domestic livestock grazing in the remaining forests would have placed more pressure on already diminishing deer populations, and the residual lynx population would have turned to killing the sheep and goats of peasant farmers, increasing persecution of the lynx and ultimately driving its extinction over most of southern Europe. Britain seems to follow the southern European model of losing the lynx early, and before the wolf. This is very likely to be tied to the human impact on woodland, which is not typical for northern Europe. Mather (1990) contended that the pattern of deforestation of the British Isles, where the forest almost disappeared before a twentieth-century reafforestation commenced, resembles that of the Mediterranean Basin, and not that of most central and northern European countries. The last major landscape-scale clearance of woodland in Britain affected the pinewoods of the Cairngorms area around 1700 (Birks 1988). The overall woodland cover of Scotland had declined from a maximum of around 75 per cent in the mid-Holocene, to about 4 per cent by the latter half of the eighteenth century (Stewart 2003; Warren 2002). As in southern Europe, Britain is likely to have seen an early lynx extinction driven by anthropogenic and landscape-scale forest clearance, which commenced in the Neolithic and continued into the early decades of the twentieth century (Birk 1988; Mather 1990; Rackham 1993; see also Kenward and Whitehouse, this volume). Consequent upon this deforestation would have been declines in the populations of forest-dwelling deer. British roe and red deer populations almost became extinct, existing only in remote areas of the Scottish Highlands by the end of the eighteenth century (Ritchie 1920; see also Mulville, this volume). It seems probable then that the Grampian Mountains, and in particular the Cairngorms area, having been last to relinquish its large forested areas and among the last to support wild ungulate populations, would have been the final stronghold of the British lynx. Wolves were not threatened by the severe deforestation to the same extent, as they do not require cover for hunting, and their favoured prey, the red deer, had adapted to the deforestation of the Scottish Highlands by inhabiting the open moors. Instead, a sustained campaign of persecution forced the wolf into extinction in the eighteenth century, at a time when Britain had already been largely disafforested for some centuries (Ritchie 1920; see Pluskowski, this volume).

Back to the future

With climatic processes ruled out as a cause of the extinction of lynx in Britain, and anthropogenic processes such as forest clearance and persecution implicated instead, the Eurasian lynx qualifies ethically as a candidate for reintroduction. Indeed, the Eurasian lynx is listed on Annex IV of Article 22 of the EU Habitats and Species Directive (92/43/EEC), which obliges member states, including the UK, to study the desirability of its reintroduction. Eurasian lynx have been restored to several upland areas of western and central Europe in recent decades, including the Swiss Alps, Jura Mountains, Harz Mountains, Bavarian Forest, Vosges and Dinaric Alps. The IUCN guidelines on reintroductions state that the factors responsible for a species' extinction must be identified and eliminated before a reintroduction can be considered (IUCN 1998). A better understanding of the history of the Eurasian lynx in Britain strengthens arguments for the reintroduction of the species. The return of the lynx may restore natural ecological processes to the forests of Britain, which have been missing since large carnivores were driven to extinction several centuries ago. Areas such as the Scottish Highlands, which, throughout the twentieth century have witnessed continuing large-scale reafforestation, albeit with exotic conifers, as well as the rapid, and at times problematic, growth of deer populations, both native and exotic, have created suitable conditions for a viable lynx population once more (Hetherington and Gorman 2007; Hetherington *et al.* 2008). The continued restructuring of agricultural subsidies to reward farmers for enhancing wildlife and landscapes, could allow lynx to be restored to the human-modified landscapes of Britain, just as they have been elsewhere in Europe. In any case, the vast majority of woodland in Scotland no longer supports grazing livestock and therefore depredation by lynx on sheep would likely be very small-scale and localised. By way of comparison, in Switzerland, where sheep are grazed in open pasture, the lynx population of 120 killed just fifteen sheep in 2006 (KORA Livestock Damage Statistics 2007).

Regardless of suitable ecological conditions, the reintroduction of lynx in Scotland will only succeed if the human population is closely involved and is willing to co-exist with the species. However, there is today much greater human tolerance of, and respect for, wildlife in general, and large carnivores in particular, than in previous societies. People are now willing to pay money to conserve large carnivores and to be able to observe them and experience the wild landscapes they are perceived to inhabit (see Figure 20; Goodwin *et al.* 2000; Hetherington 2006). The return of the lynx to Britain could see the species develop a set of new relationships with its modern human inhabitants, where instead of being persecuted and deprived of its habitat and prey, it is valued as a predator of deer and foxes, a wildlife tourism icon, and perhaps a managed game resource.

FIGURE 20. 'The Lynx back in the Harz.' The lynx is used as a key marketing symbol for the visitor economy of Germany's Harz mountains.

HARZ NATIONAL PARK

CHAPTER II

Wildcats, Domestic and Feral Cats

Andrew C. Kitchener and Terry O'Connor

Introduction

An account of cats in the British fauna is both a tale of introduction and of near-extinction. In common with much of Europe, mainland Britain in the early Post-Glacial had a diverse carnivoran fauna that included the wildcat, *Felis silvestris*. Although there are an estimated nine million domestic cats in Britain today, our last remaining indigenous felid, the Scottish wildcat, may be down to a mere 400 surviving individuals (Kitchener *et al.* 2005). However, in the Mesolithic the domestic cat was unknown, the wildcat was not exclusively Scottish and it shared Britain with the now-extinct lynx, *Lynx lynx* (see Hetherington, this volume). The histories of the wildcat and domestic cat in Britain are thus inextricably linked over the last two or three millennia, from whenever the moggy was first recorded from our shores (Harcourt 1979a; Smith *et al.* 1994). Until then the wildcat reigned supreme and was one of the earliest colonisers following the end of the last Ice Age. For example, at Thatcham in Berkshire its remains have been dated to around 9600 to 10,050 years ago (Wymer 1962), soon after the ice had melted and the first woodlands had become established in the south of England. The taxonomy of wildcats and domestic cats has long been controversial, but the current consensus among zoologists is that they represent two distinct species, following the decision of the International Commission on Zoological Nomenclature (Opinion 2027) to fix the names of wild ancestors of domestic mammals, including the wildcat, *Felis silvestris*, as distinct from those of their presumed domestic descendants, including the domestic cat, *F. catus* (Gentry *et al.* 2004). Indeed the taxonomy of the wildcat remains uncertain with the recognition of between one and three species, although most zoologists regard *Felis silvestris* as a polytypic species, with European (*silvestris* and related subspecies), African (*lybica* and related subspecies) and Asian (*ornata* and related subspecies) wildcats differing in details of pelage (i.e. fur length, colour and pattern) and skull morphology (Clutton-Brock 1999, 133–40; Pierpaoli *et al.* 2003; Yamaguchi *et al.* 2004).

The aim of this chapter is to review the evidence that we have for the reduction in numbers and range of the wildcat and the introduction of the familiar moggy to Britain. As will quickly become apparent, this is a far from simple undertaking. Three major reasons can be identified. First, cats are usually 'top predators' in whatever food web engages them, and are accordingly scarce

FIGURE 21. Scottish wildcat
© ALEX HYDE, ALEX HYDE PHOTOGRAPHY

in the zooarchaeological record. Second, their social and functional relationship with people means that aggregated deaths of cats are exceptional, unlike those of food animals such as sheep, thus further exacerbating their relative scarcity. Third, the confident distinction of domestic cat from wildcat is a subtle challenge, particularly when dealing with isolated and fragmented skeletal elements. To sum up, although archaeological sites often yield a few cat bones, few sites yield a useful sample, and we may have difficulty in distinguishing wildcat from domestic cat. As mainland Britain has both wildcats and domestic cats, it must also be at least a possibility that there has been regular gene flow between the two, although it is likely that this occurred only sporadically when it was favoured by specific social and ecological conditions. Modern Scottish wildcat populations are under threat of extinction in part from degradation and loss of habitat and persecution, and in part because introgressive hybridisation with domestic cats has rendered the wildcat almost extinct (Kirk 1935; Kitchener *et al.* 2005; McOrist and Kitchener 1994; Yamaguchi *et al.* 2004). The presence of hybrids in several parts of Europe, including Switzerland, Hungary and Scotland (Daniels *et al.* 2001; Pierpaoli *et al.* 2003), would seem to raise the possibility that the archaeological record will not necessarily yield the bones of two distinct felids, but could yield a continuous range of morphology, making it difficult to say anything definitive about the prehistory of wildcats and domestic cats. However, biometrical comparisons of modern wildcats and domestic cats, and application of those comparisons to archaeological samples, seem to show that the greater size of wildcats allows their bones to be cautiously distinguished from those of domestic cats in many cases (O'Connor 2007a). Neutered male domestic cats may grow to a very large size, making their limb bones difficult to distinguish from those of wildcats, but their cranial volumes are the same as those of domestic cats and neutering is likely to have been a recent phenomenon in controlling the breeding of domestic cats (Van Bree *et al.* 1970). The location and context of individual finds may also provide important confirmation of the wild or domestic status of the cats to support the size or morphology of the bones, a point to which we return later in this chapter.

Wildcats in Britain

There are few records of wildcats in the fossil and archaeological records in Britain (Stuart 1982; Yalden 1999). The possibility of confusion with the remains of domestic cats is very high from at least Roman times onwards, and is not helped by the sometimes ambiguous nomenclature used by earlier authors. A good example of this comes from the normally quite precise William Boyd Dawkins. Summarising the then-known vertebrate faunas of 'Mid-Pleistocene' and Late Pleistocene Britain, Boyd Dawkins (1910) refers explicitly to 'Wild cat', which he then attributes equally explicitly to *Felis catus* L., which was the preferred name of the wildcat during much of the nineteenth and early twentieth centuries until Pocock (1951) established the nomenclature we use today. The oldest record from Britain appears to be a lower fourth premolar found at the Cromerian site at West Runton, which was identified by Kurtén (1965) as being the ancestral wildcat *Felis (silvestris) lunensis*. Wildcat was also recorded from the Hoxnian interglacial at Swanscombe, Kent (Sutcliffe 1964) and the Ipswichian interglacial sites of Joint Mitnor and Tornewton in Devon (Sutcliffe 1960; Sutcliffe and Zeuner 1962). There is a Late Pleistocene record from Langwith Cave, and several postglacial cave occurrences, including Cales Dale, Robin Hood's and Steetley caves (Yalden 1999), and Victoria Cave (Figure 22). The Neolithic site at Windmill Hill yielded 52 bones attributed to wildcat compared to a meagre two for badger, eight fox and three aurochs bones (Jope and Grigson 1965), and wildcat was also recorded at the Iron Age lake village at Glastonbury (Dawkins and Jackson 1917). Sites in Scotland that have yielded wildcat bones include the Creag nan Uamh caves and Loch Borralie cave in Sutherland, and Dunagoil on Bute (Lawson 1981; Ritchie 1920; A. Kitchener pers. obs.). However, none of these finds has yet been radiocarbon dated. A roof tile with a putative wildcat footprint in it was found at the Roman fort at Mumrills near Falkirk (Macdonald and Curle 1929). Although the European wildcat is a woodland animal, it is widely assumed that it once occupied all of mainland Britain, where suitable habitat existed, only avoiding high mountains, exposed coasts and open habitats (Easterbee *et al.* 1991). The archaeological find

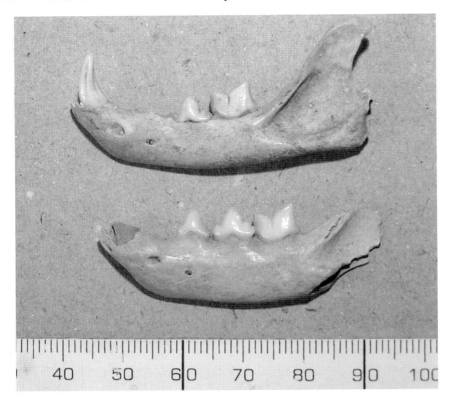

FIGURE 22. Domestic and wildcat mandibles from Victoria cave, Yorkshire.

on Bute suggests that it also occupied at least some, if not all, of the major Inner Hebridean islands, including also most likely Arran, Mull and Skye. There are two putative nineteenth-century records from Skye, but it is possible these may have been feral cats or even hybrids. Cats have also been recorded from the Isle of Man (Garrad 1972), but it is unclear whether they were introduced or indigenous. Finds of cats from prehistoric contexts in the Northern Isles of Scotland tend to be attributed to wildcats without further comment, for example from Late Iron Age Jarlshof, Shetland (Platt 1956). In Orkney cats are recorded from Late Iron Age contexts at Pool, Sanday (Bond *et al.* 2006), and from a similar date at Howe, Mainland (Smith *et al.* 1994). The Howe specimens were published as wildcat, but one of us has recently argued that they include both wildcat and domestic cat (O'Connor 2007a). The same survey notes the probable presence of a few wildcats, though greatly outnumbered by domestic cats, in tenth/eleventh-century AD deposits in York and Lincoln, though appreciably later survival in northern England is shown by the presence of several large wildcats amongst domestic cats, rats, mice and other 'vermin' debris in late medieval deposits at Kilton Castle, North Yorkshire (*ibid.*).

There was until recently some uncertainty over whether the wildcat once occurred in Ireland. Finds from Edenvale and Newhall Caves, Co. Clare were identified by Scharff (1906) as being those of African wildcats (i.e. *Felis silvestris lybica*), although Stelfox (1965) re-identified them as being from domestic cats. Today we would probably regard those identifications as being synonymous. However, Savage (1966) reported wildcat from Edenvale Cave and wildcat remains have been found elsewhere in Ireland. For example, Van Wijngaarden-Bakker (1974) recorded wildcat from the Late Neolithic/Early Bronze Age sites of Newgrange, Co. Meath and Lough Gur, Co. Limerick. The earliest record in Ireland dates to the Mesolithic site at Lough Boora in Co. Offaly (Van Wijngaarden-Bakker 1989), but the wildcat appears to have become extinct by the Late Bronze Age or Early Iron Age. The most recent record was found in a sealed Late Bronze Age context at Chancellorland, Co. Tipperary (McCormick 1999). The cause of the wildcat's extinction in Ireland is unknown, but probably relates to a combination of habitat loss (deforestation) and hunting, as elsewhere in the British Isles.

Wildcat to domestic cat

The wildcat is a solitary hunter, about 25 per cent bigger than a domestic cat; in other words female wildcats are about the same size as male domestic cats. The wildcat is essentially a striped tabby with a thick bushy, blunt-tipped tail, whereas domestic cats may display a wide variety of coat colours and patterns and always have a tapering tail. These differences reflect the quite different origin of the domestic cat and the ecology of its ancestors. Whereas the wildcat has a long fossil history in Europe dating back to almost two million years ago (Kurtén 1965) and is a woodland animal, the domestic cat is widely believed to have arisen in Ancient Egypt about 4000 years ago, its ancestor being the local African wildcat, *Felis silvestris lybica*, which has a lighter build and a tapering tail (Clutton-Brock 1999; Malek 1993). It has also been suggested that domestic cats may have had multiple origins in North Africa and southwest Asia, whereby Asian domestic cat breeds probably arose from Asian wildcats, *Felis silvestris ornata* and related subspecies (Kratochvil and Kratochvil 1976).

However, there is archaeological evidence that cats were associating with people at a much earlier date, suggesting a different and much earlier origin for the domestic cat. A tooth found at Jericho and dating from about 8700 BP is thought by some to represent an early domestic cat or at least early attempts at domestication (Zeuner 1963). A jawbone found at Khirokitia in southern Cyprus and dating from around 8000 BP is particularly interesting as wildcats have never occurred on the island (Davis 1987; le Brun *et al.* 1987). However, if this animal was domesticated, its size was still as great as its ancestor, the African wildcat. Nonetheless, it is difficult to see how the Khirokitia cat could have reached Cyprus without human intervention. A more recent find at Shillourokambos, near Limassol in Cyprus is even older (9500–9200 BP) and suggests that domestic cats were important in this local Neolithic culture. The Shillourokambas cat was found buried alongside a human skeleton and a variety of artefacts. It is currently the earliest evidence suggestive of a domestic cat, although Vigne *et al.* (2004) make the point that the large size of the buried cat is inconsistent with post-Neolithic cats from Cyprus.

In Egypt cats have been reported from Pre-Dynastic burials at Mostagedda and Hierakonpolis (Linseele *et al.* 2007 but note Linseele *et al.* 2008)). The status of these cats is somewhat debatable (tamed wildcat, or tolerated camp-follower, or domesticated house-cat?), but they at least show that a close association between people and cats existed in the eastern Mediterranean early in the Holocene. This archaeological evidence is consistent with recent research into the molecular genetics of modern European domestic cats, which shows that modern domestic cat populations are derived from Middle Eastern wildcats found today in Iraq, which would be consistent with the archaeological evidence for early associations between cats and people in the Middle East and Cyprus (Driscoll *et al.* 2007). This is an important result, as it places cat domestication in the same part of the world and the same millennia as the domestication of sheep, goats, cattle and crop plants. It calls into question local domestication of cats in other regions, though the genetics of present-day cats need not and probably do not represent the full range of the domestic-cat gene pool in ancient times. However, Faure and Kitchener (2009) have recently suggested that full domestication only occurred in Egypt using imported tame Middle Eastern individuals, but that tamed wildcats may have been widespread in the Middle East and Mediterranean before then. The presence of putative wildcats on some Mediterranean islands, including the Balearics, Corsica, Sardinia and Crete, has been questioned by Vigne (1992), who suggests that they represent feral populations of early domesticated cats, whose archaeological record on Corsica stretches back to only 700 years ago, but which may have been introduced as far back as 2500 years BP.

When and how did wildcats make the shift to becoming domestic cats? A number of earlier writers have made the case that cats were probably 'self-domesticating', though few so clearly as Todd (1978). Todd's case is essentially that there was no discernible process by which people could have deliberately initiated and managed the domestication of cats, and little reason for people to have done so. Thus, argues Todd, the impetus for cats to adopt a synanthropic habit must have come from cats exploiting the feeding and shelter opportunities offered by settled human communities. However, the pest-control benefits of cats are often over-stated: Charles Elton's classic field observations showed that although cats may have a limiting effect on the growth of rat and mouse populations at lower densities, they are ineffective at reducing abundant populations (Fitzgerald 1988). Indeed, domestic cats are only able to kill juvenile rats, adults being too formidable as prey (Childs 1986). Subsequent research has also shown that cats may tend to predate voles in preference to mice when both are abundant, although voles would not have been an alternative prey in the Middle East or North Africa (Fitzgerald 1988). Todd proposes that cats were firstly opportunistic predators around human settlements, taking advantage of local concentrations of small-mammal prey also attracted by the feeding opportunities of grain stores and other foods. As settlements grew, it became possible for cat populations to be supported largely by urban scavenging and some predation. A third stage was reached when scavenging was largely replaced by deliberate hand-outs of food from the human population, a point that may only have been attained relatively recently. From the human perspective, the transition from tolerated scavenger to deliberately fed 'domestic' animal may be a significant step. For the cats, food hand-outs are just a more convenient and predictable form of scavenging. Given the limited impact that small felids have on rodent prey populations, it seems much more likely that wildcats were attracted mainly by scavenging opportunities at middens and that human selection for wildcats for domestication was based on a less practical reason such as coat colour mutations that probably arose owing to inbreeding in the commensal wildcats. Hemmer (1990, 108) has suggested that the African wildcat was pre-adapted to domestication, because its cranial volume was lowest among wildcats and most similar to that of domestic cats. Experiments in Russia that selected for tameness in foxes, *Vulpes vulpes*, showed that coat colour mutations became commoner as these animals adapted to human presence over surprisingly few generations (O'Regan and Kitchener 2005). Perhaps, tolerating human presence combined with inbreeding led to the initial proliferation of coat colour mutations that are characteristic of the domestic cat today.

The process outlined above requires one particular behavioural adaptation on the part of the cat: a reduction in intra-specific antagonism. Wildcats, like most felids, have a dispersed social system, whereby there is usually little intrasexual tolerance, although male home ranges overlap two or more female ranges (Kitchener 2000). However, felids show a high degree of flexibility in the pattern of their home-range use; Liberg and Sandell (1988) suggested that where prey and mates are evenly distributed within the environment, there should be little overlap, but where food and mates are concentrated in clumps, a high degree of overlap should be expected. Given that the defence of territory is largely in order to defend an exclusive hunting range, where prey are evenly spread (or in the case of males, to defend females from other males), the availability of concentrated prey and scavenging opportunities around human settlements provided "ecological" conditions for a high degree of home-range overlap, which led to selection for greater tolerance between normally solitary hunters. In short, human settlements reduced the need for cats to defend an exclusive territory and made a reduction in intra-specific antagonism positively beneficial. By tolerating each other, and adapting to us (Nicastro 2004), cats could exploit a resource-rich environment.

The model of cat 'domestication' that emerges is of an uninvited dinner guest that became a tolerated lodger, and then a member of the family. That is uncontroversial: the important point is that this process could have happened at any time from the formation of the first human settlements. Given that domestic cats do seem to derive from Middle-Eastern wildcat populations, that process could have had its origins anywhere from Anatolia to the Horn of

Africa, and any time from the Late Pleistocene onwards. Other opportunistic commensal species, such as house mice (*Mus* spp. see O'Connor, this volume) and sparrows (*Passer domesticus*), were evidently rapid colonisers of Natufian and Neolithic settlements in the Levant, and predators of those small commensals, including cats, may have responded to the consequent concentration of prey. Furthermore, those early settlements probably provided an opportunity to scavenge from refuse middens, a behaviour that is familiar from feral cats today. Therefore, it is possible that domestic cats reached Britain during prehistoric times, and at an earlier date than is generally assumed. Sommer and Benecke (2006) reviewed the Pleistocene and Holocene history of felids in Europe without attempting to distinguish wildcats and domestic cats. They pointed out that there are many more records of *F. silvestris* from about 5000 years ago than in the preceding millennia, and discuss this point in terms of rising sea-levels severing the land-bridge between Britain and the rest of Europe. However, that explanation makes no allowance for deliberate or inadvertent translocation of cats by people. Perhaps the apparent increase in records of cats from British archaeological sites from the Neolithic period onwards actually reflects the beginning of the appearance of domestic cats in human settlements.

Cats and us

Whatever the early prehistory of the domestication by people of cats, the Ancient Egyptians seem to have taken the domestication of the wildcat most seriously, so that domestic cats became common household pets by 3500 years ago. Before then cats are shown in tomb frescos as hunting animals, but afterwards they are depicted as homely pets. The male domestic cat was associated with the sun-god, Ra, because it was believed that Ra adopted the form of a tomcat during his daily battles with Apep, the serpent of darkness (Lumpkin 1991; Malek 1993). This may have been inspired by seeing cats killing and eating snakes. About 3000 years ago in Ancient Egypt the female domestic cat became associated principally with the goddess Bastet, who was the "Lady of Life" associated with fertility and maternity, but also with a darker side linked to the spirit world and death (Lumpkin 1991; Malek 1993). In particular Bastet was associated with the moon and the Earth's fertility, linking together the 28-day lunar and menstrual cycles. Bastet was originally represented by a lion, but this changed to a domestic cat as its popularity spread. Domestic cats had reached the peak of their popularity 2450 years ago, when Herodotus visited Egypt and described the magnificent temple at Bubastis (Tel Basta), including the annual festival to celebrate Bastet that was attended by 100,000 people. By this time cats were regarded as sacred animals. Intentional killing of a cat could result in the death penalty, whereas unintentional death would result in a fine from a priest. If a cat died, the members of a household would shave off their eyebrows as a mark of respect. Domestic cats were even used as weapons of mass distraction, when in 525 BC a horde of domestic cats was used by the Persians during the siege of Pelusium (Budiansky 2002). The Egyptians succumbed to this ploy, because they were afraid of harming the cats during the battle.

Dead cats were mummified and buried in the cat cemeteries at Bubastis and elsewhere. Most of the cats were domestic cats, but a few jungle cats, *Felis chaus*, have also been found there (Clutton-Brock 1999). One such cemetery discovered in 1888 was said to have contained more than 80,000 cat mummies. A recent study of mummified cats has shown that many were young animals of one to four months of age, probably bred in temple catteries, that were deliberately killed for mummification (Armitage and Clutton-Brock 1981). Many hundreds of thousands of mummified cats have been excavated, but most were turned into fertiliser during the nineteenth century. For example, only a single skull survives from a shipment of 19 tons brought to Manchester, England (Clutton-Brock 1988). Recently, cat cemeteries have been discovered at Saqqara and Beni Hassan (Tabor 1991). It must be hoped that these mummified cats will be the subject of fertile research, not fertiliser.

Apart from shedding light on the origin of domestic cats (above), the genetics of modern cats reflects the history of the peoples with whom they associated. Todd (1977) analysed the frequency of occurrence of different alleles for domestic cat coat colour in order to determine their origins and pattern of spread. The non-agouti allele, giving rise to black cats, arose in the Middle East and probably spread through the Rhone and Seine valleys to Britain, where it has become very abundant, especially in urban areas, perhaps as an example of industrial melanism (Clark 1976). The sex-linked orange allele also arose in the Middle East and spread along the Mediterranean, probably with the assistance of Phoenecian traders. The blotched tabby allele appears to have originated in Britain and spread around the world. As the British Empire expanded over time, proportions of blotched tabby cats in former colonies have come to reflect the abundance of this allele in Britain at the time of colonisation (Todd 1977). Therefore, blotched tabbies are less abundant in North America (colonised in the mid-seventeenth century) compared with Australia (mid-nineteenth century), mirroring the proportion of blotched tabbies in the British population at these times.

Returning to the archaeological evidence, domestic cat bones occur frequently at Roman sites in Britain, though seldom in abundance. That said, a quantified comparison of sites with and without cats would be misleading. Cat bones are small enough to be highly vulnerable to poor recovery or rapid excavation, so their absence from some excavated assemblages may not reflect absence from the original death assemblage. Roman Britain also had house mice (see O'Connor, this volume) and black rat (*Rattus rattus*; see Rielly, this volume), so cats could certainly have had a role to play. Ryder (1996) has even tentatively identified an early example of the cat-flap at Housesteads Fort on Hadrian's Wall, though with less than serious intent. Whether cats were actively kept as pest-exterminators, or whether cats opportunistically attached themselves to towns and villas where scavenging opportunities and rodent prey were abundant, is an interesting question. An exceptional example is Portchester Castle, Hampshire. Grant (1975) notes that the nature of the excavation militated against the recovery of small bones, yet the late third to early fourth century AD assemblages yielded appreciable numbers of cat bones – two-three per cent of identified specimens. Grant notes the significance of the abundance of cats, concluding that they were 'pets and strays living in and around the fort' (*ibid.*, 405). Several whole cat skeletons were found in wells and pits at Portchester, which Grant takes as further evidence for their domestic status. There is no published metrical analysis of the Portchester cats, so their identification as domestic cats rests on their context.

A carefully-argued use of context comes from Harcourt's analysis of the bones from the Iron Age settlement of Gussage All Saints, in Dorset (Harcourt 1979a). Harcourt introduces the report by noting '… the presence of what is almost certainly domestic cat of earlier date than previously found and the earliest house mouse (*Mus musculus* [=*M. domesticus*]) of which both the identification and the stratification are beyond dispute' (Harcourt 1979a, 150). Note the subtle distinction that Harcourt draws between his identification of the cats ('almost certainly') and the mice ('beyond dispute'). The mice are identified on unambiguous anatomical grounds; the cats by context. Specifically, all but one of the cat bones from the site were from immature animals, and from one feature came remains of at least five neonatal kittens. Harcourt notes that size is the usual criterion ('rightly or wrongly', *op cit.*, 154) for distinguishing wildcats and domestic cats, and that the immature bones could not be usefully measured. Instead he argues that the immature nature of most of the bones, and especially the group of kittens, indicates domestic status, as what would be the point of in bringing a litter of wildcat kittens back to the settlement? If wildcats were being exploited for fur, more of the bones would have been of adults. It is not a conclusive argument, as Harcourt quite properly acknowledges, but the balance of probabilities supports the conclusion that the Gussage cats were domestic cats, living in and around the settlement, a conclusion that contradicts the assertion that domestic cats were introduced to Britain 'by the Romans'. Cat bones were also recovered from the Iron Age hill-fort at Danebury, though in very small numbers (Grant 1984, 525), including the remains of a kitten. There is no diagnosis of the wild or domestic status of the cats, though the brief discussion of them is grouped with the domestic livestock in Grant's report, not with the 'wild animals'.

Although domestic cats have been in Britain since at least the Iron Age, for much of their early history here they may have been rare and closely associated with people until relatively recently. Wildcats, being dependent on woodland cover, would have declined steadily as tree cover was lost, especially in England and the lowlands of Scotland. Wildcats were also hunted for sport and their fur, which almost certainly led to their local decline in combination with deforestation (Kitchener 1998). However, it was probably the arrival of the rabbit (*Oryctolagus cuniculus*; see Sykes, this volume) and its subsequent escape from warrens that led to a significant change in the dynamic between wildcats and domestic cats. Rabbits adapted well to Britain's countryside and provide a significant source of food for both wildcats and feral cats in Scotland today (A. Lamb pers. comm.). This is in stark contrast to mainland Europe, where wildcats are predominantly predators of mice and voles (Schauenberg 1981). It was perhaps this abundant food source in concentrated patches that allowed domestic cats to spread widely and come into contact with wildcats. This probably led to local hybridisation with wildcats, especially where wildcat numbers had been reduced by hunting, persecution and habitat loss. Hybridisation has become the major problem facing the continued survival of the wildcat in Britain today.

Domestic cats, meanwhile, have found towns to be very much to their liking. Medieval towns throughout Britain have yielded cat bones in some quantities. There is some debate regarding the status of cats in medieval towns (O'Connor 1992). Because of their 'pet' status today, and because the medieval period is recent and deceptively familiar (O'Connor 2007b), it is easy to regard the bones of a cat found in a medieval backyard in the same way as one might inadvertently unearth a former pet whilst digging the garden. However, the age distribution of some urban cat assemblages, with a high proportion of cats approaching one year in age, is more consistent with a feral population of relatively untended cats than with cared-for pets. Some cat bones also show superficial cut-marks consistent with the animals being skinned, and McCormick (1988) has drawn attention to the commercial importance of cat skins in medieval Britain and Ireland. Several explanations were offered for an apparent mass-killing of cats in medieval Cambridge, though they were certainly skinned (Luff and Moreno Garcia 1995). Pets, feral vermin, or 'farmed' for their fur? Even medieval cats manage to retain some ambiguity.

From being deities in ancient times, cats became associated with the devil and witchcraft during Medieval times, owing to their association with the ancient pagan cults of female goddesses (Budiansky 2002; Clutton-Brock 1999; Tabor 1991). It was believed that witches were able to transform themselves into domestic cats and so the cats became surrogate victims. Domestic cats, especially black ones, were treated barbarically and often tortured to death as witches. However, Budiansky (2002) has pointed out that the oft-repeated historical scenario of domestic cats being transformed from gods to devils is too simplistic and that their relationship with people was more complex. For example, in tenth-century Wales cats with known rodent-killing prowess were as valuable as a weaned pig or a ten-month-old calf! Until as recently as the early nineteenth century dead cats were often built into the walls, floors or ceilings of new buildings, sometimes with mice or rats, to protect the house against vermin (Clutton-Brock 1999). However, during the eighteenth century, the Enlightenment brought a change in attitude to the domestic cat and by the late nineteenth century the cat became revered once more, but this time as fancy breeds. More than 400 breeds are recognised today with many colour varieties and hair lengths, and new breeds are even being developed by hybridisation with wild felids. For example, the Bengal breed has arisen from matings between male domestic cats and female leopard cats, *Prionailurus bengalensis*; such hybridisation has also apparently been recorded from the wild. However, Bengals can only be maintained by crossing with domestic cats, as the male hybrids are almost invariably sterile.

While the fortunes of the domestic cat have been in the ascendancy over the last few hundred years, the wildcat's could have hardly fared worse. By the early nineteenth century the wildcat was found only sparingly in Wales, northern England and the lowlands of Scotland, and the Highlands remained its stronghold (Langley and Yalden 1977). By 1850 as sporting estates began to be established, especially in the Highlands, and the breech-loading gun was introduced for shooting game, the wildcat's situation had worsened considerably (Tapper 1992). It was found only in a small area of west central Wales, an even smaller patch of Northumberland and was beginning to decline dramatically in its Highland stronghold. By the 1880s the wildcat was confined to the northwest Highlands and by the beginning of the First World War, it was heading towards extinction (Langley and Yalden 1977). The main causes of this catastrophic decline were continuing deforestation, particularly in the Highlands, and the rise of sporting estates with incessant persecution as vermin brought about by gamekeepers (Lovegrove 2007; Tapper 1992; Yalden 1999). The advent of the First World War brought about a significant reduction in persecution as gamekeepers were never to return in such numbers after the war, owing to changed economic circumstances (Tapper 1992). Much needed woodland habitat began to be restored when the Forestry Commission was established in 1919. Between the World Wars the wildcat appeared to recover strongly from its putative northwestern refuge, although reanalysis of records from the literature (A. Lamb pers. comm.) suggested that small pockets of wildcats may have survived elsewhere. By the 1950s the wildcat had recovered much of its former distribution north of the central belt running between Glasgow and Edinburgh, and this distribution has remained the same at least until the 1980s when the last national survey was carried out by Easterbee *et al.* (1991).

Recently, it was estimated that about 3,500 wildcats were living in Scotland in mid-1990s (Harris *et al.* 1995), but this did not take into account the proportion of cats that were likely to be hybrids. Based on a sample of wild-living cats collected mainly as road casualties from a wide area of Scotland in the 1990s (Balharry and Daniels 1998), Kitchener *et al.* (2005) estimated that perhaps only about 400 wildcats survive in Scotland today. Sadly, it would appear that Britain's last indigenous felid is critically endangered and urgent conservation action is required to save it (Macdonald *et al.* 2004).

CHAPTER 12

The Brown Bear

Andy Hammon

Introduction

In 2006 'Bruno', an adult male bear deliberately introduced into the northern Italian Alps as part of a conservation programme, went on a 'sheep-munching rampage' whilst in search of a mate. He gained iconic status but local farmers, keen to protect their livestock, demanded that he be exterminated. The story received global coverage and caught the public's imagination despite the fact Germany was hosting the World Cup at the time. Bruno was eventually stalked and dispatched but the story did not end with his death; indeed it became increasingly politicised when Germany and Italy argued over who owned Bruno's remains (Harding 2006; Spiegel Online 2007). This is not an isolated example; bears are often seen as important symbols on the one hand but vicious predators on the other (see McIlroy 2006). This contradictory attitude towards bears can be traced back through time to the Neolithic period when the relationship between bears and humans changed fundamentally with the advent of agriculture. In Britain this ultimately led to the bear's extinction due to increased habitat loss and over-hunting.

The story of Britain's indigenous bear is enigmatic and the date of its extinction remains unknown. The situation is confused by problems of identification, dating and interpretation, compounded by the importation of European bears, and their body-parts, from at least the early medieval period. This chapter considers the later history of the indigenous bear, focusing on the Neolithic to early medieval periods. Contemporary ecological and biogeographical data from Europe, northern Eurasia and North America, and historical evidence are used to complement the archaeological and historical evidence. Ethnographic information has also been used to outline the bear's likely social significance and changing relationship with the human inhabitants of Britain.

Ecology and biogeography

Today, the bear has one of the greatest natural distributions of any mammal. There has been longstanding debate regarding whether Old and New World bears constitute one species but it is now generally accepted that European brown bears and North American grizzlies are both *Ursus arctos*. Further research will no doubt enliven the debate, such as Matheus *et al.*'s (2004) study of mitochondrial DNA which has shown that northern and southern North American brown bears have been genetically isolated from one another for at least 35,000 years.

Contemporary ecological studies may hold the key to understanding the history of the British brown bear, although the validity of any analogy must be considered. It may be assumed that British bears were of a similar weight to their northern European counterparts but this is far from certain. Siberian and northern European bears usually weigh 150–250 kg (Nowak 1999a, 685–6), although the average weight of southern European animals may be as little as 70 kg (Grzimek 1975 cited in Nowak 1999a, 686). Bears also demonstrate considerable sexual dimorphism (Iregren and Ahlström 1999, 241) and some measurements are age dependent, for example those of the cranium (Iregren *et al.* 2001; Zavatsky 1976).

MacDonald and Barrett (1993, 105) consider mixed woodland to have been the natural habitat of the European bear, even though the species is now generally restricted to spruce forests because of persecution. This would suggest that the bear could potentially have been distributed across the whole of Britain's land-mass in the past. Estimating the bear population for any period in British history is extremely problematic as numbers would have been influenced by land-use, the extent of mixed deciduous woodland and the size of the human population – variables that are themselves elusive. Contemporary European bear densities vary considerably between seasons, bears moving from their usual solitary status to groups as they search for food and mates (MacDonald and Barrett 1993, 106).

FIGURE 23. Late glacial bear skull from Victoria Cave, Yorkshire.

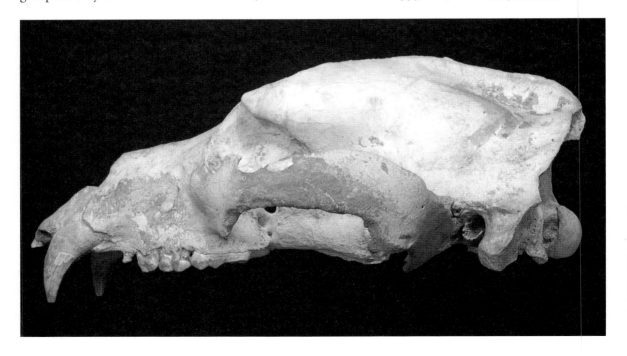

Bears in Britain

The archaeology and history of the British bear is piecemeal and difficult to interpret.

Documentary evidence for bear in Britain is scarce, perhaps reflecting the scarcity of the animal itself, and the geographical focus of the sources allows only generalised statements to be made. Furthermore, early medieval sources are potentially unreliable because most are later than the events they recount. Place-names also add little information about the likely distributions of the brown bear because few examples demonstrate a clear connection; Barham (bear village) in Kent, for instance, probably reflects the founding of a settlement by someone named Bear rather than the presence of the animal (Yalden 1999, 112). Place-names can also be misinterpreted; indeed previous studies have suffered from confused over the Old English for bear, '*beras*', and domestic pig, '*bar*' (Dent 1974, 35–36).

Zooarchaeological evidence provides an additional strand of evidence but this is not without problem. Misdentification can be an issue because bear bones are superficially similar to both human and dog remains. This is especially true where pre-depositional treatment, such as cremation, renders specimens unrecognisable: Schönfelder (1994, 218) has suggested that bear claws in pre-Roman cremations may have been overlooked for this reason. Dating and the determination of stratigraphic associations can be equally problematic, particularly in the case of cave sites which have complicated depositional histories. For instance, Lord *et al.*'s (2007) re-analysis of three cave assemblages from the Craven area of North Yorkshire discounted the previously-accepted association between the bear remains and human activity. The complex stratigraphy of urban sites can also lead to questions over dating, as is exemplified by two recent finds – a scapula recovered from a 'mixed deposit' from Victoria Road in Cirencester, Gloucestershire (S. Warman pers. comm.) and a third phalanx from a medieval deposit from Chester Amphitheatre, Cheshire (I. Smith pers. comm.) – both of which could have derived from earlier deposits. Even where well-dated specimens are identified with certainty, it is not always clear what the remains actually represent; they may derive from 'natural' fatalities, locally-hunted animals or transported body parts such as teeth and skins, although the latter may be inferred from the presence of metapodials and phalanges. With these caveats in place, it is possible to turn to the evidence for the British bear.

Table 7 outlines archaeological specimens recovered since the publication of Yalden's *The History of British Mammals* and should be used in conjunction with his table 4.3 (Yalden 1999, 113–15). The mandibular canine retrieved from a structured fill of a Neolithic barrow ditch at Eynesbury, Cambridgeshire, has been interpreted in symbolic-terms by Sykes (2004b, 90) and is considered to have been analogous to the specimen from a ritual deposit at Down Farm in Cranborne Chase, Dorset (Legge 1991b). A similar interpretation may explain the male canine from a Neolithic pit at Etton in Cambridgeshire, although

Location	NGR*	Period	Element(s)	Reference
Etton, Cambridgeshire	TF 142 076	Neolithic	Canine	Wallace 2005
Eynesbury, Cambridgeshire	TL 180 585	Neolithic	Mandibular canine	Sykes 2004b
Maxey Quarry, Cambridgeshire	TF 127 078	Neolithic / Bronze Age	Two maxillary molars	Philip Armitage pers. comm.
Eton Rowing Lake, Windsor and Maidenhead	SU 968 779	Neolithic / Bronze Age?	Scapula	Gill Jones pers. comm.
Westward House, Chichester, West Sussex	SU 843 048	Late Iron Age / early Romano-British	Phalanx	Ingrem n.d.
Catterick Bridge, Catterick, North Yorkshire	SE 226 995	Third / fourth century A.D.	Tibia	Meddens 2002; Stallibrass 2002
Fullerton, Hampshire	SU 374 400	Late Romano-British	Scapula, humerus and ulna	Hammon 2008
Courage Brewery, Southwark, London	TQ 323 804	Romano-British	Femur	Pipe 2003
Kinsey Cave, North Yorkshire	SD 804 657	AD 420–610	Cervical vertebra	Terry O'Connor pers. comm.
Plantation House, City of London	TQ 332 809	AD 1050–1150	Radius, tibia and calcaneus	Kevin Rielly pers. comm.
The Lanes, Carlisle, Cumbria	NY 402 559	Twelfth / thirteenth century A.D.	Mandible	Stallibrass 1993
Coppergate, York, North Yorkshire	SE 604 517	Thirteenth century A.D.	Third phalanx	Bond and O'Connor 1999
Gaol Street / Bath Street, Hereford, Herefordshire	SO 513 400	Late thirteenth century A.D.	Humerus	Sheila Hamilton-Dyer pers. comm.
Amphitheatre, Chester, Cheshire	SJ 408 662	Medieval	Third phalanx	Ian Smith pers. comm.
Seal House, Southwark, London	TQ 329 794	Medieval?	Scapula	Kevin Rielly pers. comm.

Wallace (2005) did not proffer it. Further cranial elements have been recorded from Maxey Quarry, Cambridgeshire, where two maxillary molars were recovered from a Neolithic/Bronze Age feature (P. Armitage pers. comm.). A fragmented scapula has also been recorded from a Neolithic/Bronze Age feature at Eton Rowing Lake, Windsor and Maidenhead (G. Jones pers. comm.).

TABLE 7. Neolithic to medieval brown bear specimens recovered since the publication of Yalden (1999). * National Grid Reference.

Similar deposits have been found across central and southern Europe where it has been suggested that, by the sixth millennium BC, the bear was adopted as a symbol of motherhood (Gimbutas 1982, 195). This association probably occurred for a number of reasons: bear milk has the highest known fat content of any terrestrial mammal (McLaren *et al.* 2005, 7), cubs stay with their mothers for extended periods of time and the most aggressive bears are females with young (Nowak 1999a, 687). The bear's mythical importance is also intimated for later prehistoric Britain: according to Dent (1974, 35) the 'Helvetian' celts worshipped the goddess Artio (she-bear) whose name has been incorporated into Welsh place-names, thought to denote celtic shrines. This symbolic importance apparently continued into the pre-Roman Late Iron Age, as Schönfelder (1994, 217) attributed ritual meaning to bear claws from the Welwyn Garden City and Baldock cremation burials, in addition to their value as prestige commodities.

Ethnographic evidence provides an insight into how bears may have been incorporated into the belief systems of Europe. In northern Eurasia and North America, for instance, there are many rituals associated with bear hunting and the treatment of the physical remains: there are distinct methods of butchery, 'bear feasts' are surrounded by etiquette, skulls are disposed of in 'special' ways and the skins are often stuffed. The rationale for such veneration is complex and is difficult to elucidate. Hallowell's (1926) definitive work on bear ceremonialism (quoted in McClaren *et al.* 2005, 12 and 14) evaluated a variety of possible psychological (the bear's human-like form when skinned), economic (the high utility of the carcase) and historico-geographic (human migration and population diffusion) reasons for this universal appeal, but did not ascribe pre-eminence to any one factor. Schönfelder (1994, 222) certainly interpreted the cremation examples in terms of prestige objects essential to the maintenance of later prehistoric social and political structures.

By the Roman period the bear's ritual significance may have been on the wane because King's (2005) review of animal bone assemblages from Roman temple sites noted no specimens. It is possible that, as an indigenous tradition, bear veneration was not practiced at Romanised settlements. Alternatively the bear may simply have slipped from the collective consciousness due to its scarcity, although the iconographic evidence from the period suggests that the bear retained some social significance. For instance, the production of Yorkshire jet-carved miniatures appears to have been a sizeable industry; miniatures have been recovered from Malton and York, North Yorkshire, and Colchester, Essex, but also as far afield as Rhineland, Cologne and Trier in Germany (Toynbee 1973, 99–100). Bears are depicted on several Roman mosaics dating to the fourth century AD, such as the example from Newton St Low in Somerset (Cosh and Neal 2005, 275). Most depict the legend of Orpheus, which Cosh and Neal (2005, 20) suggested provided a striking visual scene that would have appealed to the aestheticism of the mosaicists. Hunting for pleasure had become fashionable for the upper echelons of society by the late Roman period (Hammon 2005), possibly making depictions of wild animals even more appealing. In some mosaics the portrayal is ambiguous and the presence of bear is not definitive, as at Winterton in Lincolnshire. Here Cosh and Neal (2002, 8–9) suggested that the mosaicist, although thoroughly cognisant with the story of Orpheus, was less familiar with the animals involved, hence their stylised and similar body-forms. This might indicate that brown bears were already absent in parts of Roman Britain.

The zooarchaeological evidence for the Roman period indicates that, even if bear numbers were low, breeding populations were still in existence in some areas. At Fullerton in Hampshire, for instance, three disarticulated specimens (a scapula, humerus and ulna) were recovered from a Late Roman ditch. All three displayed traces of ephemeral burning but no butchery evidence, and it was not possible to determine whether they were intentionally or accidentally heated. They appear to derive from one individual and probably represent a complete carcass from an animal that was presumably, although not necessarily, caught locally (Hammon 2008). The tibia from third/fourth century AD Catterick Bridge, North Yorkshire, was also considered to have come from a whole animal because of its anatomical position in the skeleton, and Stallibrass (2002, 400) suggested that Yorkshire and the Pennines may have formed one of the last relict bear populations in Britain. Certainly this would concur with the historical evidence, in particular Martial's reference to Scottish bears being imported to kill criminals in the Coliseum after Agricola's conquest in the first century AD (*De Spectaculis* vii, 3 (Tertullianus 1977). The status of other Roman specimens is more ambiguous, such as the single phalanx from a late Iron Age/early Roman deposit at Westward House in Chichester, West Sussex. Given that this site is located adjacent to Fishbourne Roman Palace, where other wild animals have been noted in abundance (Ingrem 2004; Sykes, this volume), this could be evidence for the presence of a locally-available animal, although Ingrem (2004) interpreted as an imported skin because of the cut marks it exhibited.

On the basis of the evidence available to him at the time, Yalden (1999, 112) suggested that the bear probably died out in Britain before the end of the Roman period. Documentary sources provide little opposition to this theory as most of the references to bear are unreliable. Dent's (1974, 36) critique of the historical evidence concluded that the popular belief in a tenth/eleventh century extinction date was overly optimistic because bears were not mentioned in the Laws of Hywel Dda (died in AD 942). Similarly Dent dismissed the contemporary Y Naw Helwriaeth (The Nine Huntings), which describes bear as a 'beast of the chase', because it was based on bardic poetry recanting earlier times. According to Dent (*ibid.*) the only potentially reliable reference to bear is that made in the *Glossary* of Aelfric, dating to the tenth century AD; however, as has been argued by Hetherington (this volume), the document also refers to exotic animals and so must be viewed with suspicion. Zooarchaeological evidence for the survival of indigenous populations in Saxon Britain is also scarce. Most of the bear remains from this period derive from funerary contexts and apparently represent skins, claws and teeth, most likely imported for amuletic purposes (Sykes forthcoming). Recently, however, a bear vertebra was recovered from Kinsey Cave, North Yorkshire, and has been radiocarbon dated to between the early fifth and early sixth centuries AD (T. O'Connor pers. comm.). This specimen is exceptionally important because it is the latest securely-dated specimen of what must have been an indigenous bear, demonstrating that, in this isolated location at least, bears were able to survive a few centuries into the post-Roman period.

All the current evidence suggests that the indigenous bear population had become extinct by the early medieval period and so all later archaeological specimens (Table 7) are likely to derive from European imports, brought into the country for bearing-bating or to satisfy the growing demand for 'exotica'. The volume and extent of this trade is difficult to gauge. Schönfelder (1994, 224) has suggested that body-parts may have been imported to Britain as early as the Iron Age, although he considered it unlikely. Certainly by the Roman period bears are thought, by Toynbee (1973, 93), to have been the most ubiquitous captive animal, perhaps suggesting that their trade was substantial. Dancing-bears of Anglo-Saxon gleeman were almost certainly imports and by the time of Henry I (reign IIOO–II35) *custos ursorum* (bear keepers) were listed amongst the court's officers (Dent 1974, 35). Similar officers served Henry VIII (reign 1509–1547) and looked after bears imported from almost 'anywhere', including the Savoy, Béarn and Abruzzi areas located in the French-Italian border region (*ibid.*). This implies that Europe still maintained viable bear populations. It is not clear when the bear became extinct in Ireland, although a 'curious' ninth century AD document stated that bears were capable of slaughtering young pigs, which suggested a certain familiarity with the habits of bears (McCormick 1999, 359). The latest specimen from Belgium comes from a twelfth-century deposit at the Grimbergen fortification in Flanders (Ervynck *et al.* 1999, 401). Elsewhere in Belgium the bear may have survived for longer, such as the heavily forested region of Wallonia (*ibid.*) and it reputedly survived in adjacent areas of Germany until the nineteenth century (Müller 1971 cited in *ibid.*).

There is considerable evidence for bear importation in the later medieval and post-medieval period, especially in London where numerous sites have produced tantalising evidence for the exploitation of bears, for instance those connected to the Tudor Theatres Project: New Globe Walk and Riverside House, Bankside (Liddle forthcoming; Rielly forthcoming). Other evidence includes a minimum of five individuals displaying skinning evidence from nineteenth-century deposits at Vintry House, Vintners Place, assumed to be a furrier's shop. However, archives of archaeological finds also include misidentifications that have been perpetuated in the literature, such as the specimens purported for Benbow House in Skinmarket Place, Bankside and Eagle Wharfe Road, Hackney (K. Rielly pers. comm.). If any synthesis is considered in future, it will be imperative to re-examine both the specimens themselves and primary records.

Reasons for decline

Ervynck *et al.* (1999, 401) summarised the reasons for the bear becoming extinct in Belgium and the same reasons – habitat destruction, over-hunting and deliberate extermination – are likely to apply to Britain. All three appear to have been connected to the advent of agriculture and the resulting change in attitude towards large predators. Bears seem to have become increasingly uncommon during the Neolithic, probably being targeted because of their perceived threat to livestock (Yalden, 1999, 105 and 111). Dent (1974, 36) reported that the herdsman of Slovakia, the Carpathians and the Bosnian mountains regarded bears as a greater threat to their herds of managed wild horses than wolves. Bears are also reputedly the most dangerous animal in North America (Nowak 1999a, 687). This perception of the bear might have been more imagined than real, since bears are omnivorous and predominantly vegetarian, although they do occasionally dig for rodents and hunt larger mammals (MacDonald and Barrett 1993, 105–6; Nowak 1999a, 686; *ibid.* 686).

A more economic explanation might account for their decline and persecution; for it is primarily in areas of intensive ranching in North America where the bear has been eliminated (Nowak 1999a, 687). The same might have been true of Britain where the last indigenous bears, such as the individual from Kinsey Cave, seem to have been pushed as a consequence of woodland clearance to the less densely-populated western and northern peripheries. The bear's life-cycle may also have contributed to its decline because, as stated by Iregren and Ahlström (1999, 240), it reaches maturity late, has long breeding intervals and high levels of infant mortality which result in a slow rate of reproduction. The bear is therefore especially vulnerable to the depradations placed upon it by human activity.

It has been argued that the bear's decline in medieval Belgium can be charted because their remains are visible in the 'consumption' refuse of the bear-hunting social elite (Ervynck *et al.* 1999, 401). If bear-hunting carried a similar cachet in Britain, a review of the evidence from high-status Roman and medieval sites might provide our best opportunity to pinpoint the indigenous bear's final decline. As Ervynck *et al.* (1999, 401) have pointed out, however, the lower classes also exterminated smaller carnivores that were perceived as threats to livestock, but these animals may be under-represented archaeologically for a number of reasons: first if the carcasses of slaughtered bears were not utilised as a resource their remains may not have been transported to dwellings at all; second, low-status sites have not been routinely excavated so the evidence is simply unavailable. We therefore encounter a problem of differential visibility in the archaeological record depending on whether the brown bear was treated as a high-status hunting trophy or as a threat to livestock to be controlled and discarded as necessary.

Whilst many historians and archaeologists have suggested that bears were deliberately extirpated, the techniques employed remain a mystery prior to the medieval period. An essential prerequisite in successfully hunting bears would have been a good understanding of their behaviour, particularly in relation to hibernation and trail use (McLaren *et al.* 2005, 6). Three general methods appear to have been used (Hallowell 1926, 42 cited in *ibid.*): locating the bear in its den before forcing it out and killing it, attacking and killing the bear in the open, and trapping using a variety of devices. Toynbee (1973, 95) quoted Oppian's account of capturing, rather than killing, bears in Armenia using the den technique. Not only did season dictate hunting method, but may have also partially determined how carcases were utilised. Bear meat is less tough during the spring and summer months, whereas hides are of better quality in early winter because of fat deposits laid down prior to hibernation (McLaren *et al.*, 2005, 21). Bear meat may be responsible for trichinosis (*Trichinella spiralis*) infections when eaten and this may have led to its prohibition (see Simoons 1994, 351–2).

Discussion

For much of European pre- and proto-history the bear appears to have had a mystical significance whilst still being utilised as a valuable source of meat, lipids, fur and other products. Even in the historic period, when the bear had become a traded commodity and was exploited for entertainment, a ceremonial aspect persisted. Artisans taking part in a carnival in the City of Romans (AD 1580) expressed their 'collective consciousness' by parading as various animals, including the bear which represented spring (Le Roy Ladurie 1979, 240–241 cited in Cohen 1994, 68).

The later history of the indigenous bear is enigmatic and the date of its final extinction remains unclear due to problems of the identification and dating of bear bones but also because historical and iconographic evidence is often ambiguous. It would appear that the bear became extinct in the early medieval period, having been in decline since the Neolithic. The importation of European bears and their body-parts, which reached its height in the medieval and post-medieval periods, may have occurred as early as the Late Iron Age. By Roman times it was a two-way process, with Scottish bears making their way to the Coliseum.

As the archaeological and historical records are incomplete, difficult to analyse and are open to interpretation, other avenues have to be explored. Fortunately there is a multitude of analogous data and information due to the bear's ubiquity; however, as with any analogy, the validity of the application of these data is open to question. Ethnography provides a rich source of material to contextualise archaeological data; the cluster of Neolithic finds from East Anglia considered in conjunction with North American accounts provides a greater appreciation of prehistoric bear ceremonialism, for instance. If we are to gain a fuller understanding of the indigenous bear and its later history a scientific dating and provenancing programme (stable isotope and mitochondrial DNA analyses) should be instigated. Just such a programme of analysis is under way at Trinity College Dublin at the time of writing, focussed on Late Pleistocene bears.

Acknowledgements

The author would like to thank the following people for providing published references and unpublished material: Umberto Albarella, Martyn Allen, Philip Armitage, Polydora Baker, Julie Bond, Pam Crabtree, Vicky Crosby, Simon Davis, Charly French, Louisa Gidney, Sheila Hamilton-Dyer, Claire Ingrem, Gill Jones, James Kenny, Jacqui Mulville, Terry O'Connor, Hannah O'Regan, Kevin Rielly, Diane Siebrandt, Ian Smith, Sue Stallibrass, Chris Swaysland, Naomi Sykes, Sylvia Warman and Fay Worley.

CHAPTER 13

The European Beaver

Bryony Coles

In Britain, in the mid to later twentieth century, most people knew about *Castor canadensis*, the North American beaver, but few were aware that beavers had once also lived in Europe. In recent years, however, more and more people have come to know something of *Castor fiber*, the European beaver, as it has spread from a few small refuge areas to re-colonise many of its former habitats, from Spain and Portugal to the Netherlands, Denmark and Sweden including most countries in between. In Britain, as this book goes to press, a trial release of beavers into the wild is underway in Knapdale, in south west Scotland. There is ample evidence that beavers are native to this island, having first colonised before any of our human ancestors and, to take an archaeologist's time perspective, they became extinct only quite recently. In this chapter, I will outline the nature of that evidence and briefly examine a few of its many implications. Readers who wish to know more about European beavers should turn to Kitchener's *Beavers* (2001) and Blanchet's *Le Castor et son Royaume* (1994), while their archaeology and history is explored in more detail in *Beavers in Britain's Past* (Coles 2006).

The nature of the evidence

The archaeological record for the presence of beavers in Britain (Figure 24) consists mainly of bones, but there are several other relevant sources of information, perhaps more varied than for any other mammalian species apart from *Homo sapiens*. The earliest beaver bones that we know of pre-date the arrival of humans by many millennia: both *Trogontherium*, the Giant Beaver, and *Castor fiber*, the European Beaver, are known from the late Pliocene onwards. Our first human forebears are thought to have arrived some 700,000 years ago, and the Giant Beaver disappears from the record around 400,000 BP, so for some 300,000 years humans co-existed with the two species of beaver, but this chapter is concerned only with the smaller *Castor fiber*. The earliest record of wood that may have been gnawed by beavers comes from Stoke Newington on the northern side of London, and dates to the earlier Pleistocene; recorded in a drawing made by Worthington Smith in the late nineteenth century, the two pieces of birchwood are shown with pointed ends similar to those made by beavers.

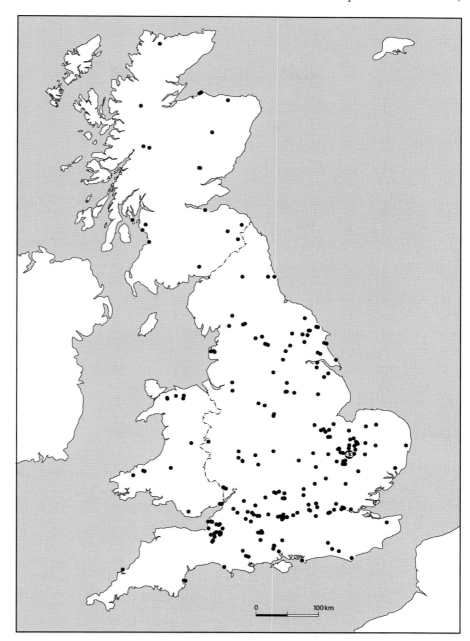

FIGURE 24. The distribution of beaver evidence in Britain from late in the last Ice Age to recent times. Many of the dots represent finds of beaver bones and others beaver-gnawed wood, beaver structures and beaver place-names, with a few other rare categories of evidence.
DRAWN BY MIKE ROUILLARD FOR *BEAVERS IN BRITAIN'S PAST*

At the height of the last Ice Age, for several thousand years from about 20,000 BP, both humans and beavers along with most other animals retreated south from what is now Britain, and both began to spread northwards again as temperatures rose and the ice sheets wasted. From about 13,500 BP, conditions in Britain were warm enough and vegetated enough for beavers to return from their various southern refuges (Figure 25), as did humans. The first evidence for beaver structures comes from a little later, early in the Holocene, with indications

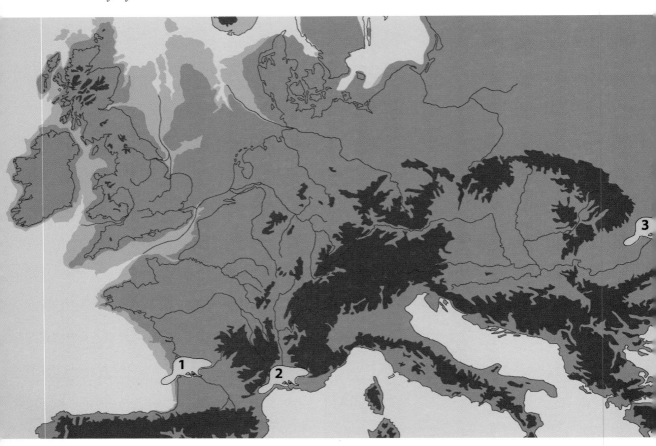

of relic channels and burrows, probable lodges and foodstores and undoubtedly beaver-chewed wood. Later in the prehistoric period, the first probable dams are known, and from the first millennium AD there is an unexpected survival of beaver fur. Throughout the millennia beaver bones occur, often in conjunction with human activity and sometimes clearly the result of human predation. With the introduction of writing, humans enlarged the record with occasional references to beavers, most notably the late twelfth-century account of beavers on the River Teifi given by Gerald of Wales, and also with later mentions in legislation, recipes, and travelogues. The most recent of the records for beavers in Britain comes, prosaically, from a parish account book.

Beavers and their habitat

Beavers live in small family groups, an adult pair together with their young of the current and previous years, maybe five to seven individuals all told. They establish a territory around a lake or along a river or stream, taking about 500m to 2000m of water's edge per territory. An adult beaver (Figure 26) is relatively large for a European rodent, weighing 20–25kg and measuring 1–1.25m from

FIGURE 25. Map of Europe showing how beavers could have spread overland from their southern glacial refuges (marked by the yellow beavers) to the land which is now Britain. In due course, rising sea levels created the insurmountable saltwater barriers of the Channel and North Sea, since when beavers have not been able to reach Britain from the continent unless aided by humans. Ireland was separated from Britain by saltwater at an early stage, and has no known records of beaver presence.

DRAWN BY MIKE ROUILLARD FOR *BEAVERS IN BRITAIN'S PAST*

nose to tail. Their reddish-brown pelt is exceptionally thick, insulating and waterproof, and they have a generous amount of body fat as befits a semi-aquatic mammal. Beavers are at their most fast and agile in water, but emerge frequently onto land, especially to feed. Their diet is entirely vegetarian, consisting of herbaceous plants and the leaves, twigs and bark of trees and shrubs. They are well-known for their practice of felling trees by gnawing at the trunk with their sharp incisors, to obtain the topwood twigs and the bark, but much of their diet in fact comes from vegetation they can reach at ground level or in the water, such as the fleshy stems and rhizomes of rushes, flag iris and waterlilies. In the autumn, they build up an underwater store of branches by their den entrance, to feed on should ice and snow prevent access to their normal food sources.

Beavers make an underground den in the river bank, reached via a burrow dug from below water level to provide protection from predators. If water levels fall, the family is at risk, and on streams and small rivers beavers may therefore build a dam of wood, mud, stones and uprooted plants, to pond back enough water to ensure their safety. On rivers that are too wide or fast-flowing to dam, they do not settle unless there is water deep enough year-round to shelter the den entrance. Beavers also need enough height of ground above the water table for a dry den, and where this is not available they may build a lodge on the ground surface, using the same materials as for a dam to make a very solid shelter.

Beavers have regular paths on dry land, which may become worn down and flooded, and sometimes they dig out their routeways, effectively creating canals leading to their feeding areas or cutting across a stream meander. They normally feed within 30 m or less of the water's edge, and over the years their regular browsing creates patches of dense shrubby cover. This is because many of the tree and shrub species that they feed on, such as willow, hazel, ash and dogwood, react by producing a crop of new shoots and a natural coppice system develops, providing further food for the beaver family.

FIGURE 26. An adult European Beaver (*Castor fiber*) in the southeast of France.
PHOTO BY RENÉ NOZERAND

On the small rivers and streams where beavers build dams and create ponds, they can have a significant impact on their immediate surroundings. The ponds act as silt and nutrient traps, thereby boosting local biomass and biodiversity. Along a stream, the beaver territories are often visibly richer in plant and animal life than the stretches in between, and the effect spreads into the surrounds with many animals drawn to drink at the ponds, or to graze and browse on the lush vegetation. Predatory species, including humans, are likewise attracted to the concentrations of food whether or not they prey on the beavers themselves.

In other conditions, along lake shores or the banks of deep rivers for example, the beaver effect is less marked, although there is some underwater enhancement of conditions for aquatic insects, fish and mammals which enjoy the shelter and food associated with sunken wood stores and water-filled burrows.

Beaver influence on humans

One way of tracing the interactions of beavers and humans is to examine the archaeological record for evidence of beaver influence on humans, as well as for the perhaps more expected human influence on beavers. One of the earliest sites of human activity in Britain is Boxgrove in Sussex, where some 500,000 year ago people exploited the animals that came to a water source to drink. There were beavers amongst them, and quite possibly the water was in fact a beaver pond which attracted hunters and hunted alike. No doubt there were numerous similar situations throughout the Palaeolithic.

When the record expands after the last Ice Age, the indications increase that humans were attracted to beaver territories. At the well-known Maglemosian site of Star Carr, situated on the shores of the former Lake Flixton in what is now the Vale of Pickering, human activity was concentrated around a wood-strewn area which was interpreted by the original excavator, Grahame Clark, as a platform that people had built to consolidate the marshy ground. Among the animal bones that people had discarded were several from beavers, youngsters as well as adults, and it seems likely that the people had hunted or trapped beavers for their meat, fat and fur (Clark 1954). But what was only realised later (Coles and Orme 1982) was that the spread of wood included beaver-gnawn pieces, suggesting that people's choice of the specific location was influenced by the presence of a beaver lodge or food store that provided convenient firm ground on the edge of the lake.

Along the Thames in the same period, people were similarly attracted to beaver territories. At sites along the River Kennet around Newbury, such as Thatcham (Wymer 1962) and Faraday Road/Greenham Dairy Farm (Ellis *et al.* 2003), beaver bones have been found amongst the debris of human presence, and features interpreted as 'gullies' are likely to have been beaver burrows or canals. In addition, the investigations at Thatcham produced evidence of ponded water, later interpreted as probably due to beaver dams (Evans 1975, 88). Again, it looks as though the people who settled for a while by the river chose to do so within a beaver territory. These were not the only places that Mesolithic peoples lived, but perhaps the only environment heavily modified by a species other than themselves that they deliberately sought out.

With the advent of farming in Britain, at around 4000 BP, the picture might be expected to change. Humans, after all, were attracted as foragers and predators to the plant and animal life of a beaver territory, and one might expect the needs and interests of farmers to be somewhat different. Yet people still headed deliberately for beaver territories. Sometimes the evidence suggests that it was for the wild resources, as at the Baker Platform on the edge of an island in the marshy Somerset Levels. Here (Figure 27) a dense spread of wood proved to be a mixture of humanly-cut and beaver-gnawed pieces (Coles *et al.* 1980; Coles and Orme 1982) and the beaver wood was concentrated in the lower centre of the spread, suggesting a former lodge or food store. Radiocarbon dates indicate occupation of the site intermittently over many centuries in the fourth millennium BC, and quite possibly humans and beavers alternated or co-existed in their use of the location, each refurbishing the structure as and when they saw fit.

A similar co-existence of beavers and humans is suggested by the evidence from Eton Rowing Lake at Dorney (Allen *et al.* 2004). Here, beavers had settled along the former back-channels and tributaries of the Thames, and early in the Neolithic farmers also settled along the banks and on the islands. What is interesting is that in the early years the human activity was very much concentrated within 50m of the water's edge, essentially within the beaver territory, suggesting that it was specifically the beaver-modified land that these farmers sought. The attraction may have been the tree-free organic-rich soils that had accumulated in beaver ponds; in North America both indigenous farmers and the early European colonists used former beaver ponds to grow their crops (Cronon 1983). Equally, the farmers may have known that shrubby beaver pasture provided good browse for their cattle. Both would have been particularly valuable for pioneer farmers, at a time when much of Britain was otherwise tree-covered.

Elsewhere, there are indications that people were using beaver territories for other types of activity. At Mossgarth in the Lake District recent palaeoenvironmental work has revealed that people who secreted a cache of stone axe blades did so in still shallow open water with woodland and marsh and plentiful dead wood nearby (Davis *et al.* 2007). The axes may be an early example of consigning a votive deposit to water, a practice well-known from later prehistory, and the local conditions including the dead wood are suggestive of beaver activity. In Lancashire, at Briarfields, a human skull dating to the Bronze Age was found in the peats of a wetland area most probably created by beaver dams (Wells *et al.* 2000), and this too has been interpreted as a votive or ritual deposit. The archaeological record must contain other examples, as yet unrecognised, of humans using beaver ponds in this way, and a more thorough study might reveal whether people had a preference for ponds created

FIGURE 27. The Neolithic Baker Platform in the Somerset Levels, a mass of cut wood including pieces gnawed by beavers (top left) and pieces cut by humans using a stone blade (top right).
BAKER PLATFORM PHOTOS SOMERSET LEVELS PROJECT

by beavers, or whether it was simply the accessible open water that attracted them (Figure 28).

Humans continued to be drawn to beaver territories for many centuries, probably well into the first millennium AD. In England, evidence from a number of Anglo-Saxon settlements indicates that people made use of diverse wetland animals, including waterfowl and amphibians as well as beavers: at West Stow in Suffolk watervole, frog, pike, crane, swan, greenshank and many other species of waterfowl were identified in addition to beavers (Crabtree 1985). Other resources enhanced by beaver activity are discussed in Coles (2000).

Beavers were important in the Welsh and English mental landscapes of the

FIGURE 28. Two Breton beaver ponds, similar to the contexts suggested by the evidence from Mossgarth (5a) and Briarfields (5b).
PHOTOS BEAVER WORKS PROJECT

period too. In North Wales, where the beaver were known as *afanc*, *Llyn yr Afanc* on the Conwy and *Sarn yr Afanc* on the Ogwen can be translated as the Beaver Pool and Beaver Dam (or Causeway) respectively. In England, streams such as Bardale Beck in Yorkshire and Beverley Brook in Surrey were named after beavers, while from the Yorkshire town of Beverley to the Thames island of *befer ige*, a variety of other places in the landscape acquired beaver names. Beaver activity may have stimulated human thought processes in other ways too, providing ideas and models for aspects of human water engineering from dams as causeways to canals as transport routes. The practice of coppicing and the use of decaying plant matter to enrich soils may also have been inspired by observation of beavers.

Human influence on beavers

It will be obvious already that humans influenced beavers by preying on them. They were hunted with bows and arrows and spears, and later perhaps guns, or caught in nets and traps. In Britain, humans were probably the chief predators of beavers, with wolves, bears, otters, eagles and pike also keen to eat them, especially the young. For people, the carcass of a young adult beaver provided about as much meat as a roe deer of the same age, and beaver fat would have been particularly valuable in late winter when other supplies were short. The cut-marks on beaver bones indicate that people butchered them from Mesolithic Star Carr to Iron Age Glastonbury, while written recipes from the later Middle Ages show that they were still being consumed though probably only rarely and by the very rich. A late example, describing how to serve beaver tail as a Lenten food, comes from the mid-fifteenth century *Boke of Nurture* written by John Russell, whose master was Humphrey Duke of Gloucester, a very wealthy royal prince. There are several other references to beaver tails as a fast-day food: living in and under the water, and with their apparently scaly black tails, in dietary terms beavers were regarded as honorary fish.

People preyed on beavers for their castoreum sacs. Castoreum is an oily secretion produced both by females and by males from a pair of internal sacs that lie near their anal glands. It is used, as far as a human can tell, for territorial marking and for individuals to communicate their presence and status to other beavers. For humans, until quite recent times, castoreum has been an important medicine to assuage fevers and treat a variety of ills. Its composition, and thus its quality as a medicine for humans, varies according to the beaver's diet. It is apparent that a far-flung trade in castoreum was well-developed when William Harrison (1805) wrote of its import from Persia. The antecedents of the trade go back at least to classical times, and it may well have had a long but so far untraceable prehistory. Thus, in Britain, by later prehistory castoreum may have been imported as were wine and other luxuries. However, it would be surprising if local sources had been neglected by those without access to expensive imports. The castoreum glands can be removed from a dead beaver without leaving any cut-marks on its bones, meaning that there is very little chance of identifying its use from the archaeological record.

The dense fur of beavers was another reason for people to kill them. The desire for beaver pelts was so strong that, when European beavers became scarce in early modern times, the trade in Canadian beaver skins became one of the driving forces of European expansion in North America. Before this there is good evidence, in the form of Acts of Parliament to impose tolls, for the export of various furs from Britain to mainland Europe. In the earlier twelfth century AD an English Act set tolls for exports from Newcastle upon Tyne, including beaver skins. A century later, a Scottish Act set a toll of four pence per pack (tymmr) of beaver skins exported. Earlier legislation from Wales, the tenth-century Laws of Hywel Dda, indicates that beaver fur was highly valued and used to trim the King's clothes.

Archaeologically, evidence for human use of beaver fur comes mainly from the skinning marks on bones, in particular the characteristic knife cuts that show where the pelt was freed from the skull. Such marks occur on a skull from Anglo-Saxon Ramsbury on the River Kennet (Coy 1980), and on bones dating to the later Neolithic from Burwell Fen near to Cambridge. In addition there is the exceptional find from Sutton Hoo dating to the earlier seventh century AD: scraps of beaver fur were found preserved on fragments of wood in one of the burial mounds (Stoves 1983). The wood has been interpreted as the remains of a lyre, the fur as the remains of the beaver-skin bag that protected it, and the burial chamber as that of Raedwald, a king of the East Angles (Carver 1998). Recently a replica of the bag was made for display, revealing that at least two and probably three skins would have been needed to make the original (A.Wainwright pers. comm.).

Having taken a beaver's skin, tail, fat, flesh and castoreum sacs, and reduced the carcass to a heap of bones, there was still something left of value to humans (Figure 29). Beaver bones are squat and strong, and in North America are known to have been used for tools in recent times. In the archaeological record from Britain, the lower jaw is the skeletal element most frequently used to make artefacts. Complete with molars and incisor, a mandible makes a good woodworking tool to use as rasp or chisel. Examples are known from the later Neolithic to the Iron Age, including a couple from Meare Lake Village in the Somerset Levels. Incisors can also be used on their own as a chisel or scraper, as might be the case for the one found in Sculptor's Cave, Covesea, on the Moray Firth (Benton 1931). However, from the early-to mid first millennium AD there are examples of incisors with a gold or bronze collar and suspension loop that seem less likely to have been woodworking tools. They come mainly from amongst the grave goods of pagan Anglo-Saxons, as at Wigber Low in Derbyshire where an Anglo-Saxon burial was inserted into a Neolithic mound along with a rich array of artefacts including two gold-mounted beaver incisors. Where the associated human skeletons can be aged and sexed, they are often found to be those of women or children, leading archaeologists to suggest that

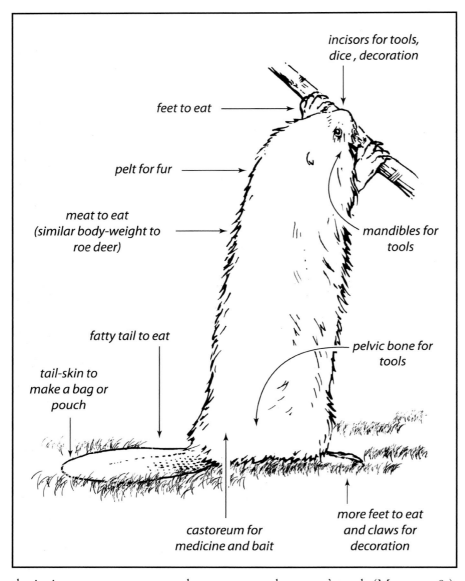

incisors for tools,
dice , decoration

feet to eat

pelt for fur

meat to eat
(similar body-weight to
roe deer)

mandibles for
tools

fatty tail to eat

pelvic bone for
tools

tail-skin to
make a bag or
pouch

castoreum for
medicine and bait

more feet to eat
and claws for
decoration

FIGURE 29. An indication of the resources that a human predator might take from a beaver.
DRAWN BY MIKE ROUILLARD FOR *BEAVERS IN BRITAIN'S PAST*

the incisors were worn as amulets to protect the owner's teeth (Meaney 1981), although this is just one of various possibilities.

The path to extinction

Humans influenced beavers indirectly, as well as by the direct impact of predation, although the evidence can be more difficult to identify and interpret. Today in western Europe, beavers are found living close to humans, as in the River Drôme where it flows through the towns of Die and Crest. On the outskirts of Grenoble where factories, trading estates and a spaghetti-junction of roads dominate the landscape, there are beavers below in the River Drac. In Bavaria, in a region of relatively intensive farming, beavers inhabit the watercourses and ditches amidst the cultivated fields. Thus, we should not assume that in Britain in the past beavers shunned areas of dense human settlement. What is perhaps more likely is that as humans developed their own skills as water engineers, from the later Middle Ages onwards, they came increasingly to see beavers as a nuisance rather than as a living package of valuable commodities. The people who invested time and money in the development of water meadows or canals would not have wanted beavers to move in.

Perhaps it was a change of attitude such as this which prompted beavers to be included as vermin in the Acts for the Preservation of Grayne, first passed in the mid sixteenth century. The Acts listed a surprising variety of birds and mammals considered to be vermin, and provided for bounty to be paid on them (Lovegrove 2007). The system continued into the nineteenth century, with payments made and recorded by churchwardens, and it is from these records that we have the last indication of a live beaver in Britain, or rather a recently dead one for a bounty of two pence was paid on its head. The record comes from the parish of Bolton Percy, on the River Wharfe to the south-west of York, and it dates to 1789.

For long, people have assumed that beavers became extinct in Britain several centuries earlier than this, but there is evidence to support the validity of the Bolton Percy record. To the west of Harrogate, and within 50 km of Bolton Percy, there is an oral tradition of the late survival of beavers in the vicinity of Oak Beck, together with place-names Beaverdyke and Beaverhole. Similar traditions from western Scotland and from northern Wales raise the possibility that there were in fact several pockets of beavers in Britain that survived well beyond the late Middle Ages, in the waters of Loch Ness and the Lochaber region and in rivers such as the Wharfe and the Ogwen.

As with several of the other animals examined in this book, the last beaver we know about was not necessarily the last of its species in Britain, and they may have survived into the earlier nineteeth century. The places where they would have done so, hidden from human persecution, were not so much the small upland streams as the high-banked, deep-pooled lowland rivers such as the Wharfe. My reason for suggesting this is that, where beavers need to build dams to raise water, and lodges to ensure a dry den, their presence is easily detected by humans, but where they can live in underground dens protected by a deep natural pool they do not need to build; in these circumstances they can go about their lives virtually unnoticed by the human eye. If they had inhabited a particular stretch of such water for many beaver generations, and developed patches of shrubby beaver pasture sufficient for a sustainable food supply, few of their chief predators may have be aware of the night-swimming beavers, in the days before electric torches and street lights.

CHAPTER 14

The Rabbit

Naomi Sykes and Julie Curl

Introduction

The European rabbit, *Oryctolagus cuniculus* is one of the worlds' most successful mammals and today the species is established throughout Britain, regardless of environment, from Cornwall to Caithness and on the larger offshore islands (Thompson 1994). Rabbits have not only become incorporated into human culture – as foodstuffs, pets and popular icons – but they are also, along with cattle and sheep, a prime architect of the British landscape, responsible for maintaining the country's close-cropped fenland, grass heath and chalk downland (Thompson 1994, 85). Rabbits have established themselves so successfully within our lives and landscape, it is easy to forget that the species is not native to Britain. There is much 'received wisdom' concerning their introduction; ask any school child, or even their parents, who was responsible and the reply will invariably be 'the Romans'. However, the actual circumstances of the rabbit's introduction and establishment are far from clear, as is exemplified by the academic literature on the subject: scholars have argued variously that rabbits are native (Warry 1988), were imported by the Romans (Sheail 1984), the Normans (Bond 1988; Rackham 1997; Rowley 1997; Yalden 1999) and the Angevins (Lever 1979).

The uncertainty surrounding their introduction is due largely to the ambiguous nature of the iconographic, historical and archaeological evidence. It is notoriously difficult to differentiate rabbits from hares in early iconography and, often, depictions can be classified only as 'lagomorph' (Callou 2003, 196–204). Etymologists also find it difficult to confirm the identity of animals mentioned in early texts and place-names because terms of reference have changed over time and space. For instance, in Britain, rabbits have only been referred to as such for the last two hundred years, prior to this they were known as 'conys' (from the Latin *cuniculus*, also meaning underground passage) and only juvenile animals were called 'rabbettes' (Thompson 1994, 64). In the Roman world rabbits and hares appear to have been referred to collectively as 'lepus' (Warry 1988), and even today in German-speaking countries, hutched rabbits are referred to as hares (*Stalhasen*) whilst only wild individuals are called rabbits, '*Kaninchen*' (Van Dam 2001, 159). Thompson (1951) and Brown (2002) have highlighted similar etymological problems for tracing the history of the rabbits' nemesis, the ferret (*Mustela putorius furo*) whose story is inextricably linked to that of the rabbit and will also be considered briefly in this chapter. Even where historical references are indisputably to rabbits and ferrets, the earliest documentary records can be viewed only as a *terminus ante quem*, the animals most probably arriving prior to the first accounts. Whereas for other species zooarchaeology offers an important source of corroborative evidence, both rabbits and ferrets are difficult to deal with archaeologically. Ferrets are skeletally almost indistinguishable from their wild progenitor, the polecat (*Mustela putorius*) and it is seldom possible to identify archaeological remains with confidence. For rabbits, their propensity to burrow down into archaeological deposits has confused our understanding of their ancient biogeography. When *O. cuniculus* remains are recovered from contexts dating to periods in which rabbits are, conventionally, not thought to be present, they are often misidentified because researchers are not expecting them or dismissed as 'intrusive' (Crabtree 1990; Miles 1984; Sykes 2007). On other occasions, contexts containing rabbit remains may actually be re-phased to agree with historically-based introduction dates (e.g. Jones 1993; Sutermeister 1976). This is clearly an unsatisfactory, circular situation and there is a need for a critical re-assessment of the evidence. On the continent, such work – incorporating historical, metrical and DNA analysis – has already begun to reveal important insights into the ancient biogeography of rabbits (see for instance Callou 2003). Whilst a similar study for Britain is some way off, this chapter seeks to provide a starting point, considering first the evidence for continental Europe and then reviewing the evidence for Britain against this backdrop.

Rabbits on the continent

Fossil records suggest that the modern species of *O. cuniculus* evolved in southern Spain, where its remains have been documented in deposits dating to the Middle Pleistocene (Lopez-Martinez 2007; Rogers *et al.* 1994). The species spread to northern Europe and their bones and teeth have been recovered from deposits dating to the Hoxnian Interglacial in Suffolk (Yalden 1999, 17). When the Wolstonian Ice-Age advanced around 330,000 years ago, the rabbit seemingly became extinct, along with many of the other warm-loving species, across northern Europe and relict populations appear to have survived only in Iberia and southern France (Branco *et al.* 2002; Lopez-Martinez 2007, 42).

Butchered rabbit remains have been recovered from many prehistoric and historic sites across Portugal and Spain (Davis 2005). The presence of rabbits on the Iberian peninsula was first documented by the Phoenicians who colonised the coastal regions around 1100 BC (Zeuner 1963, 410). It has been suggested that the Phoenicians transported rabbits around the Mediterranean, although it is possible that rabbits were introduced to the Balearic Islands as early as the Neolithic period (Reumer and Sanders 1984). Outside Iberia, the earliest reference to rabbits dates to the second century BC, the Greek historian

FIGURE 30. Rabbit
© RICHARD FORD, DIGITAL
WILDLIFE

Polybius mentioning their presence on the island of Corsica, although Callou (2003, 230) argues convincingly that the text is actually referring to another lagomorph *Prolagus sardus*. By the first century BC rabbits were being managed in Italy: Varro (116–27 BC) recommended that they be kept in *leporaria*, stone-walled pens or parks, where they could be hunted (*On Agriculture* Book III, xii, trans. Hooper and Ash 1979, 491). Writing slightly later both Strabo (63 BC–AD 24) and Pliny the Elder (AD 23–79) recounted that a plague of rabbits on the Balearic Islands was dispatched using ferrets, or at least a ferret-like animal (Thompson 1951, 472). The idea of using ferrets to catch rabbits was reiterated in the seventh century by Isodore of Seville (Owen 1969, 490). By this point rabbits must have been already established in France because in AD 590 Bishop Gregory of Tours is said to have scorned the Lenten consumption of foetal rabbits, or *laurices*. These had become a popular fast-day food because, as they came from the 'watery' environment of the womb, they were considered to be 'fish' rather than meat (Zeuner 1963, 413). The desire of monks to acquire foetal rabbits is seen as one of the main driving forces of rabbit domestication (Nachstein 1949). It has been suggested that between the sixth and tenth centuries, rabbits were bred within the walls of French religious houses and that the practice gradually spread from monastery to monastery (Van Damme and Ervynck 1988; Zeuner 1963). Certainly in 1149 the abbot of the Benedictine monastery of Corvey, on the Wesser (Germany) asked the abbot of Solignac, in south-west France, for two pairs of rabbits (Nachstein 1949). Surely it can be no coincidence that the earliest archaeological records of rabbits in central and northern Europe have been recovered from monastic sites: those from the eleventh- to twelfth-century site of Charité-sur-Loire in France (Audoin 1984), and the late twelfth/thirteenth century specimens from the Belgian sites of Ename Abbey (Ervynck *et al.* 1999) and Dune Abbey (Gautier 1984).

From monastic beginnings, rabbits gradually became associated with the secular elite. According to Gautier (2007, 56), *garennae* (warrens) became an important part of seigneurial culture in northern France from the eleventh century. However, the work of both Clavel (2001) and Callou (2003) demonstrates that rabbit remains are rare in northern French archaeological assemblages dating before the twelfth century, suggesting that the term *garennae* cannot be linked specifically to rabbits but was more probably a landscape for hunting a variety of small game animals. Two rabbit femora were recovered from an eleventh/twelfth-century context at Valkenburg Castle in the Netherlands but, on radiocarbon dating, both were found to be thirteenth/ fourteenth century intrusions (Lauwerier and Zeiler 2001). It is from the thirteenth/fourteenth century that rabbits begin to appear more frequently in the archaeological record of northern Europe and we also find the first clear archaeological evidence for ferrets: two partial skeletons, including an individual whose teeth had been filed down to prevent damage to their quarry, were recovered during excavations of Laarne Castle in Belgium (Van Damme and Ervynck 1988). The presence of both rabbits and ferrets in thirteenth century Germany is clearly demonstrated by several documents, including the work of Albertus Magnus and the texts relating to Emperor Frederick II's hunting animals (Thompson 1951, 476).

Rabbits in Britain

If rabbits were rare across northern Europe before the twelfth century, it may seem unlikely that the species was present in Britain at an earlier date. However, there is some evidence to suggest that this may have been the case.

The main sites on which early-dated rabbits have been recorded are listed in Sykes (2007) and will be summarised here. The specimen from the Mesolithic site of Thatcham, Berkshire, is a classic example of the effects of bioturbation, radiocarbon dating confirming the specimen as an eighteenth-century intrusion (Gowlett *et al.* 1987, 127). Similarly, the Bronze Age deposits from Brean Down, Somerset, were noted as being disturbed by rabbit burrows (Levitan 1990) and the rabbit remains from Barton Court, Oxfordshire (Miles 1984) and West Stow, Suffolk (Crabtree 1990) are also thought to be intrusive. In most cases these conclusions have been based on the abundance of partial, often juvenile, skeletons, suggestive of a situation where infant rabbits have died in their burrows. The assemblage from the Roman site of Carne's Seat in Sussex also contained large number of juvenile lagomorph bones, again recorded as intrusive (Beech 1986).

For many years the only early specimen that was not obviously intrusive or misidentified was that from the Roman villa at Latimer in Buckinghamshire

(Hamilton 1971); however, as with fallow deer (Sykes, this volume), new evidence supporting a Roman introduction has recently come to light. At Lynford in Norfolk, six rabbit bones, probably from a single adult animal, have been recovered from an undisturbed pit containing a large amount of pottery dating from the Middle and Late Iron Age, as well as wheelmade forms dating to the 1st century AD (Figure 31). All the rabbit bones are butchered to some degree; the proximal tibia and distal femur have been chopped off, and further fine cuts were noted when the bones were viewed using a microscope (S. Parfitt pers. comm.). The Lynford rabbit may have been brought into the country either as a live animal or as a carcass for meat (and possibly for the skin). It would have been highly unusual at the time and may have been eaten as part of a special feast or used as a ritual offering. Two further rabbit bones, one darkened by charcoal in the earth, have been recovered from a late third-century fill of a disused bathhouse at Beddingham Roman villa, East Sussex (D. Rudling pers. comm.). Whilst neither sets of remains have, as yet, been radiocarbon dated, the secure contexts from which they derive and the fact that they demonstrate post-mortem modifications (butchery and burning) suggests that they are unlikely to be intrusive. Furthermore, it is interesting to note that measurements of the specimens suggest that the individuals were noticeably smaller than modern British animals, closer to the size exhibited by Mediterranean populations. It has been demonstrated repeatedly that the geographic variation in rabbit size obeys Bergman's (1847) Law, with animal size increasing with latitude (Callou 2003, 78). This suggests that the Roman specimens from Lynford and Beddingham were imported directly from southern Europe, again indicating that no populations existed in the northern part of the Roman Empire. It is possible that the Romans or the indigenous population of Britain attempted to breed rabbits; the climate of Roman Britain, which was warmer than today, would

FIGURE 31.
Reconstruction of the Lynford rabbit and its associated pottery.
DRAWING BY JULIE CURL

have been less of a shock to these Mediterranean creatures. Indeed, the presence of a *leporarium* has been proposed for Whitehall Villa in Northamptonshire, but this was based on the large number of hare remains recovered from the site, no rabbits were identified (Sykes in prep). There are, however, no documentary references to *leporaria* or warrens in Roman Britain.

The earliest reference to a warren comes from the Domesday Book which records a '*warenna leporum*' at Gelston in Lincolnshire. Bond (1988) has suggested that this should be regarded as an enclosure specifically for hares but Warry (1988) has argued that the term '*lepus*' may have been used to refer to both hares and rabbits. In support of this he cites the Roman author Varro who mentioned that there were three kinds of *Lepus*, of which *cuniculus* was one (*Rerum Rusticarum* III, xii, trans. Hooper and Ash 1979). With this argument Warry raises an important point, that we should not unthinkingly project modern terms and systems of classification back onto past societies. Nevertheless, in this case there is very little evidence to suggest that rabbits were present in Anglo-Saxon period Britain and Bond's (1988) argument seems more convincing. Anglo-Saxon vocabularies had no term for rabbit (Yalden 1999, 158) and there is just one potentially early historical reference that may relate to the species: the Marksbury charter, dated nominally to AD 936, mentions 'conigrave', meaning 'rabbit grove'. This document is, however, an unreliable source, possibly a thirteenth-century forgery (Grundy 1932). The zooarchaeological record for rabbits in Anglo-Saxon period Britain is equally sketchy. *O. cuniculus* remains have been claimed at a number of Anglo-Saxon sites but recent re-analysis has suggested that many of these remains are intrusive or misidentified (Sykes 2007). More convincing is the single butchered rabbit bone that was recovered from a Saxon pit at Southampton (Bourdillon and Coy 1980, 44; Jones 1985, 171). On the basis of current evidence this specimen most probably represents a one-off import, perhaps simply a joint of preserved meat; certainly it is insufficient to suggest that rabbits were being bred in the country at this point.

Iconographic evidence is frequently cited in support of a Norman introduction date for rabbits: lagomorphs are famously depicted in the Bayeux Tapestry and also on one of the corbels of the twelfth-century Romanesque Church in Kilpeck, Herefordshire (Figure 32). It is debateable whether these representations are actually rabbit or hare; the latter seems more likely, given the association with hounds – the traditional 'hound and the hare'. Zooarchaeologically there is, apparently, more evidence for the presence of rabbits in Norman period assemblages but this may simply be the creation of researchers who, understandably, accept misidentifications or intrusive specimens because the pattern fits with traditional notions of a Norman introduction. Many of these Norman examples, such as those from Brighton Hill South in Hampshire (Coy 1995), are clearly intrusive and are documented as such. Others, notably those from Castle Acre in Norfolk (Lawrance 1982), look suspicious and warrant re-analysis. A large number of rabbit remains

FIGURE 32. The so-called 'rabbit' depicted on a corbel from Kilpeck Church, Herefordshire.
PHOTO BY RICHARD JONES

were recovered from 'Norman' contexts at Faccombe Netherton, Hampshire (Sadler 1990). Most are thought, with good reason, to be intrusive but a few specimens were retrieved from undisturbed contexts within sealed features dating to between AD 980 and 1180. Sykes (2007) examined these specimens and found that their preservation and appearance was consistent with the wider assemblage and, although none exhibited butchery, gnawing or burning marks, one specimen (a femur) was measureable. As with the Roman specimens from Lynford and Beddingham, it is rather small compared to the later medieval rabbits and whilst the data are extremely limited, it is tempting to suggest that it represents an early generation import from southern Europe. The same may be true for a specimen recovered from a late twelfth-century context at Clay Hill Castle, Sussex (Sykes n.d.). In this case the specimen was a humerus which came from an undisturbed level and was confirmed as contemporary with the deposit on the basis that it had been burnt. Again, measurement showed it to be small compared to later medieval and modern rabbits. The dating of the Clay Hill example puts it beyond the Norman period and whilst the date range for the Faccombe Netherton assemblage spans both the Late Saxon and Norman periods it seems most probable that the bone dates to the later part of the range, the late twelfth century.

If the Faccombe Netherton and Clay Hill specimens are of twelfth-century date, this does not mean that rabbits were being bred extensively, or even at all, in England at this point. Indeed, Alexander Nequam's list of English wildlife, written in the 1180s, makes no reference to rabbits, although notably fallow deer are mentioned (cited in Bartlett 2000, 673). Instead, rabbits appear to have been maintained on, and imported from, small off-shore islands: for instance rabbits were recorded on Drake's Island in 1135 (Hurrell 1979), a warren was mentioned on the Isles of Scilly in 1176 (Sheil 1971) and between 1183–1219 a tenant was given entitlement to take 50 rabbits a year from Lundy island (Veale 1957). Potentially the earliest reference to rabbits on the mainland comes from a deed, dated to between 1135 and 1272, relating to the Dartmoor warren (Henderson 1997, 105). The next reference, dated to 1187–94, comes from a grant of land by Simon le Bret to the canons of Waltham in Essex that mentions the area once contained a *cunicularium* (Bartlett 2000, 672). More tightly dated is the reference in the *Close Rolls* for 1235, which records that Henry III gave a gift of 10 live rabbits from his park at Guildford (Veale 1957, 88). This low figure indicates that rabbits were in short supply; however, seven years later in 1242, the Guildford cunnery was able to provide 30–40 rabbits, suggesting that populations were beginning to flourish (Veale 1957, 88). Interestingly the animal bone assemblage retrieved during excavations of the Royal Palace at Guildford shows that rabbits are represented in increasing numbers, especially relative to hare, from the *c.* 1230–1268 levels onwards (Sykes *et al.* 2005). By 1251 Henry III was able to provide his Christmas dinner guests with 450 rabbits, along with hundreds of other exotic game animals including 290 pheasants and 120 peafowl (Rackham 1997, 119 and see Poole, this volume). Veale (1957, 88) highlighted 1230 to 1250 as the period when the practice of rabbit-keeping spread quickly across mainland Britain; certainly by 1264 warrens were being constructed as far north as Scotland (Gilbert 1979).

Despite the rise in warren numbers, it should not be assumed that the establishment of rabbit colonies was an easy task, far from it. There are ample records demonstrating the lengths that warreners had to go to – including creating artificial burrows and planting food crops – in order to settle these Mediterranean animals into their colder British surroundings (Sheil 1971, 39–57). Bailey (1988, 12) has shown that early warrens often operated at a financial loss, so the motivation for their construction must have been beyond mere economics. It would seem that the initial increase in rabbit farming was driven primarily by the elite, keen to secure access to luxury meats. Early warrens were usually located close to monasteries, castle and manors, particularly within the grounds of parks (Bailey 1988, 4). As such, rabbits and warrens became an important symbol of lordship, along with fishponds and dovecotes (Williamson 2006, 7). However, Stocker and Stocker (1996) have argued that rabbits were maintained not simply as icons of status but also for metaphorical reasons – their fecundity, subterranean habitat and surface emergence being viewed as an allegory for human life, death and Christian salvation respectively. Rabbits are frequently incorporated into religious iconography and it may be for this religious symbolism that rabbits were favoured by ecclesiastics. Another possibility is that, in a period when monks were keen to hunt but forbidden from doing so, the chasing and capture of rabbits was deemed an acceptable activity for men of the cloth. Certainly rabbiting was not considered to be true hunting, indeed the *Master of the Game* suggests that it was a distinctly low pursuit, more suitable for ladies than respectable lords (Cummins 1988, 236–7). This is reflected in the iconographic evidence, which frequently shows women engaged in catching rabbits, as in the Queen Mary's Psalter (Royal 2B VII, dated to 1315) where two ladies are depicted rabbiting with ferrets. The association between women, rabbits and ferreting became so strong that, by the later medieval period, ferrets were a symbol of aristocratic ladies, as is evidenced by the portraiture of the period.

According to Owen (1969) ferrets were first recorded in Britain in 1223, a date consistent with the zooarchaeological representation of the species: Fairnell's (2003) survey of fur-bearing animals demonstrates that ferret and polecat remains are increasing common on archaeological sites dating from the twelfth/ thirteenth century onwards. Partial polecat/ferret skeletons have been recovered from a number of medieval sites; significantly, examples from the 'Norman' (980–1204) and medieval (1260–1356) contexts at Faccombe Netherton manor (Sadler 1990), the thirteenth/fourteenth-century urban site of Southampton (Noddle and Bramwell 1975) and the late fourteenth-century contexts from the parker's residence at Lodge Farm (Locker 1994) were found associated with rabbit remains. By coincidence, manorial accounts for Lodge Farm state that a ferret was purchased in the year 1391–2 (Locker 1994, 108). There is a dearth of published polecat/ferret remains in contexts pre-dating the thirteenth century, especially when compared to the considerable representation of pine marten, stoat and weasel remains. Brown (2002) has argued on etymological grounds that polecats, as well as ferrets, may not be native species, instead being introduced to Britain as part of the newly developed 'coney culture' (Van Dam 2001, 162). Until we have either a body of well-dated pre-Norman polecat specimens, or sufficient evidence to be confident of their absence, this question cannot be resolved.

Whilst rabbits were originally managed to supply great households with luxury meats, Bailey (1988) has shown that the socio-economic changes accompanying the Black Death heralded a great shift in rabbit husbandry. As human population and labour force declined so too did arable farming; however, the comparatively low labour cost involved in running a warren made rabbits an attractive prospect for lords, representing a form of agricultural diversification (Williamson 2006, 7). Warren management was made easier by the bout of warm weather between the 1370s and 1390s that allowed rabbit populations to flourish. At the same time the improving living standards and purchasing power of the masses increased demand for rabbit meat and fur, the latter being particularly valued as other fur-bearing animals became scarce or extinct. The net result was that large numbers of commercial warrens were established during the fourteenth and fifteenth centuries, many of which held rabbit populations capable of sustaining an annual cull in excess of 2000 individuals (Bailey 1988, 6). As rabbits became more numerous their luxury status declined; Rackham (1997, 48) shows how the price of rabbits, relative to daily wage, dropped from the thirteenth to nineteenth century. Nevertheless, rabbits were still sought after for feast day menus. For instance, in 1395 rabbits were purchased for a feast at Merton College in Oxford; zooarchaeological evidence unearthed during excavation of this early college property confirms that rabbits were consumed in increasing numbers at the site (Worley and Evans 2006).

Inevitably, as rabbits became more abundant and acclimatised to their British habitat, they were able to thrive without human assistance and, by the mid-fourteenth century, warren escapees were beginning to impact on the landscape and livelihood of local residents. The *Nonae* of 1340 for Sussex records the complaints of West Wittering's parishioners whose wheat crops had apparently been devoured year after year by the Bishop of Chichester's rabbits, whereas in Ovingdean 100 acres of arable land are said to have been annihilated by Earl Warenne's rabbits (Blauuw 1847, 62). Similar accounts can be found across the country, particularly in East Anglia (Bailey 1988, 6–7). By 1555 feral populations of rabbits were so numerous that Conrad Gesner, the Swiss naturalist, wrote that 'there are few countries wherein coneys do not breed, but the most plenty of all is in England' (Veale 1957, 90), a statement that is as true today as it was then.

Conclusion

In many respects, the story of the rabbit in medieval Britain is similar to that of any luxury good. Originally rabbits were socially exclusive and sought after for their meat, fur and symbolic value. However, in establishing warrens to secure supplies of this species, the elite increased the availability to such an extent that the rabbit's luxury status gradually diminished. This slide down the social scale continued as rabbits began to escape from warrens and gradually became the naturalised animal so familiar within the landscape today. This later history of the British rabbit is well known and well rehearsed. Less clear is when the species was originally introduced to Britain. When the historical, iconographic, zooarchaeological and landscape evidence are considered together, the obvious conclusion to draw is that modern populations descend not from animals introduced by either the Romans or Normans but from individuals brought to Britain as part of a fully-fledged and pan European 'coney culture' that included warrens and ferrets, all of which appear in Britain at approximately the same time: the late twelfth century. There is very little evidence to suggest that rabbits were present in Britain prior to this point, the records for the Norman and Saxon period being dubious to say the least. It has often been suggested that the Romans were responsible for introducing rabbits and, whilst this theory has lost favour over the last decade, this chapter has presented some convincing evidence to suggest that introductions may have been attempted whilst the country was under Roman rule, perhaps by individuals keen to emphasise their Roman identity by following the fashions of the southern Empire. Debate concerning the ancient biogeography and introduction of rabbits will, no doubt, continue until a comprehensive programme of radiocarbon dating and DNA research has been undertaken. We should perhaps look to the work being done in France and the Mediterranean to see the benefits of this kind of approach.

CHAPTER 15

The House Mouse

Terry O'Connor

Introduction – why mice matter

House mice are one of the most familiar of wild animals, yet their close association with people tests the meaning of 'wild' to its limits. They live with us, in our houses and outbuildings, seldom far from human settlement, and have travelled with people throughout the world. They are significant socially, both as cartoon characters and as an indicator of poor house-keeping, and significant economically, as they consume and foul stored food and are a vector of various diseases. Their indirect significance could also be measured by the large numbers of cats that share our homes, whether it was us or the cats who instigated that relationship (see Kitchener and O'Connor, this volume).

In archaeological terms, house mice have another significance. As a species that is not native to northern Europe, they have needed our inadvertent help as sources of food and transport in order to spread across the Continent. For the British archipelago, the first arrival and subsequent persistence of house mouse populations provides a proxy record of the degree of contact between these islands and continental Europe, contact measured in terms of the frequency and volume of ship-borne cargo. Once established here, house mice became a well-adapted and quite specialised part of the commensal fauna, the community of species that relies upon people for food and shelter. As such, they are a significant component of the ecosystem that develops around and within a settlement, taking their share of food from our crops and wastes, and providing food to support the predators such as cats and owls that hunt within and around our homes (O'Connor 2000). Whatever our personal feelings about house mice, they are always with us.

A bit of mouse biology

House mice are placed in the genus *Mus*, differentiated from other small murine rodents such as the field mice *Apodemus* species, and the larger murines mostly placed in the genus *Rattus*. A number of anatomical and behavioural attributes separate the murines from other rodents, notably their tendency to be omnivorous. This trait is reflected in their teeth. The anterior dentition consists of the chisel-edged and constantly-growing incisors typical of all true rodents,

FIGURE 33. House mouse
© RICHARD FORD, DIGITAL
WILDLIFE

whereas the premolars and molars have rounded cusps quite unlike the more specialised herbivorous dentition of voles (Cricetinae). Amongst the mouse species known from postglacial Britain, *Mus* upper incisors are readily identified by a distinct notch in the occlusal surface, and the upper and lower molars by a cusp pattern quite distinct from that of *Apodemus* or the appreciably smaller harvest mouse *Micromys minutus* or hazel dormouse *Muscardinus avellanarius*. As with all rodents, the post-cranial skeleton is more problematic. There are diagnostic features on the pelvis (Clevedon Brown and Twigg 1969), which I have found to be quite consistent and useful on archaeological specimens, and some consistent features around the proximal part of the femur. In general, though, confident identification is largely based on the skull and dentition.

Palaeontological and phylogenetic studies indicate that house mouse originates in the Middle East, probably as a nocturnal species of open habitats, feeding on the large-seeded wild cereals and pulses typical of that region and environment, and on small invertebrates. House mice are famously prolific breeders. Females typically have four to eight young per litter, and can produce five to ten litters per year. Fecundity is closely linked to population density; in very dense populations, breeding may cease altogether (Corbet and Southern 1977, 227–34) Lifespan is obviously highly dependent on predation pressure; house mice attain several years of age in artificial conditions, but this is a poor indication of the life expectancy of a typical mouse. House mice are behaviourally flexible, allowing them to adapt their social behaviour according to the availability of space and food. This adaptability can be shown in modern house mouse populations (Ganem and Searle 1996), and was probably an important factor in the adoption of a commensal niche by some mouse populations, as non-commensal populations typically show a higher incidence of agonistic behaviour (Frynta *et al.* 2005).

The taxonomy of house mice has been troublesome (Macholán 2006; Marshall and Sage 1981; Suzuki *et al.* 2004;). Linnaeus named them *Mus musculus* (the mouse like a mouse). Subsequently, zoologists have recognised a number of other *Mus* species. In an influential paper, Schwarz and Schwarz (1943) reviewed what they termed 'the wild and commensal stocks of the house mouse', giving subspecies status to a number of forms differentiated on pelage colour and pattern, on size, and on attributes such as the relative lengths of tail and body. To cut a long story short, Schwarz and Schwarz differentiated a Western European form that they termed *M. musculus domesticus* (from *Mus domesticus* Rutty 1772, described from type specimens from Dublin), from an Eastern form *M. musculus musculus* (as described by Linnaeus, from type specimens from Uppsala). Subsequent research has proposed that these two forms should be regarded as distinct species (Marshall and Sage 1981). As the type specimen named by Linnaeus derived from the Eastern form (Degerbøl 1940), the Western species takes the name *Mus domesticus* Rutty. The point about this taxonomic digression is that *M. musculus* and *M. domesticus* are very difficult to distinguish on skeletal features, making the identification of archaeological specimens problematic. In the published literature, therefore, we find house mouse remains from Britain attributed to *M. domesticus* by some writers (e.g. Yalden 1995), but to *M. musculus* by others (e.g. Coy 1984). In the latter case, it is seldom clear whether the author intends a specific separation from *M. domesticus*, and is proposing that (eastern) *M. musculus* formerly occurred in Britain, or (more likely) that the author is following Schwarz and Schwarz, and many recent authors, in separating the two forms only at subspecific level. Confusing, isn't it? For the remainder of this chapter, the vernacular term is used throughout, and should be taken to indicate 'a commensal *Mus* species' unless clearly indicated otherwise.

People and mice: a long story in brief

It would be no exaggeration to say that human settlements have had house mice for as long as people have lived in houses. Some of the earliest 'villages' of which we have archaeological evidence are settlements of the Natufian period in the Middle East. Scattered throughout the Levant, Natufian sites date to the very end of the Pleistocene, around 12,000 years BP, and consist of clusters of house structures with hearths, grindstones and, often, human burials (Belfer-Cohen and Hovers 1992; Boyd 2006) Despite the apparently sedentary nature of the settlements, the economic base was essentially hunting and gathering, exploiting mosaic environments for animal prey, principally gazelle, and a wide range of plant foods that included wild cereals. In a gradual process, best seen in the sequence at Tell Abu Hureyra (Moore *et al.* 2000; Willcox *et al.* 2009), cereal cultivation supplemented, then replaced, plant gathering, to be followed by the domestic husbandry of caprines and cattle in the Pre-Pottery Neolithic. From their earliest phases, then, Natufian and PPN settlements would have stored cereals and pulses and disposed of organic garbage, providing feeding opportunities for adaptable commensal species (Hardy-Smith and Edwards 2004). The work of Tchernov, in particular, has shown how rapidly house mice and house sparrows (*Passer domesticus*) seized this opportunity (Auffray *et al.* 1988; 1990; Tchernov 1984; 1991; 1993; 1994). The extensive Neolithic site of Çatal Hüyük, in Anatolia, was clearly infested with house mice (Brothwell 1981). It would be easy to imagine that house mice then followed cereal agriculture across Europe as an inevitable part of the Neolithic 'package'. However, as Cucchi *et al.* (2005) make clear, the spread of house mice through the Mediterranean region and into Western Europe was gradual and rather intermittent, only truly successful in the last few centuries BC. Although the spread of arable farming, and of the large-seeded crop plants on which it was based, extended the niche which house mice came to adopt, it took the advent of large-scale maritime trade to provide a dispersal mechanism that could move mice sufficiently far and often, and in sufficient numbers, to allow the establishment of successful populations (Cucchi and Vigne 2006). Morales Muñiz *et al.* (1995) link the spread of house mice and house sparrows through the Iberian peninsula to the increase in Phoenician trade during the last few centuries BC. Furthermore, house mice did not have the commensal niche to themselves. Evidence from the Mediterranean region, together with ecological and ethological observations, show that wood mouse *Apodemus* spp., endemic to the British Isles from at least the early Holocene, may have been opportunistically commensal (Berry *et al.* 1982; Cucchi *et al.* 2006, 438–9). To some degree, then, the arrival of house mice in the British Isles is proxy evidence of the degree of integration of the archipelago with continental Europe.

Earliest archaeological records from Britain

A review of house mouse records from Britain is fraught with challenges. First, there is the problem of archaeological recovery. House mouse bones are very small, and their consistent recovery can only be expected if samples of archaeological deposits have been sieved on meshes of no greater than

2mm aperture (a point further discussed by O'Connor 2001; O'Connor and Barrett 2006). Second, even if rodent bones are successfully recovered, their identification is problematic, for the reasons discussed above. In short, the presence or absence of house mouse can only be assessed from a minority of the bones in a typical assemblage. Third, the dating of rodent material is notoriously difficult. Rodents burrow, and so may introduce themselves into deposits with which they are asynchronous, and the small size of their bones makes it possible for them to move passively down through a coarse, clast-supported sediment (O'Connor 2003). That small size also makes it unlikely that a single bone would yield sufficient collagen to allow direct radiocarbon dating. We depend, therefore, on indirect dating, and on careful taphonomic analysis of small vertebrate assemblages to give us satisfactory evidence of the introduction of house mice to Britain.

That said, the earliest credible records from Britain date from the Iron Age. Coy (1984) reported house mouse from all phases at Danebury, albeit in samples that also yielded rabbit bones. Coy briefly discusses the intrusive rabbit, but reports the house mouse bones as if there were good grounds to consider them to have been of authentic Iron Age date. Accepting that, the occurrence of the species in the earliest phase at Danebury is of some interest, as it implies that the species was already present in central southern England, and not acquired from further afield as the hillfort grew and extended its trading links. A further record from an Iron Age site in southern England comes from Gussage All Saints, in this case from a well-sealed context (Harcourt 1979a). On the other hand, the hillfort at Winklebury was systematically sampled for small vertebrates and yielded no specimens of house mouse (Rackham 1982), though the predominance of common shrew in the Winklebury records suggests some form of selective deposition. These Iron Age records should not surprise us, for two reasons. First, despite contemporary Roman propaganda to the contrary, prehistoric Britain was not some isolated backwater. Some parts of England, notably the central southern counties and East Yorkshire, show clear evidence of regular trade with, and appreciable cultural influence from, the near Continent. House mouse may have been present just across the North Sea well before the late centuries BC, if the Bronze Age records from Bovenkarspel, Netherlands, are reliably dated (Ijzereef 1981). Second, one of the defining features of Iron Age archaeology, especially in southern England, is the presence of structures inferred to have been used for storing grain, including storage pits and above-ground granaries. These stores would have constituted an ideal niche for house mice, and the relatively dry consistency of stored grain may have given house mice just enough of an advantage over native wood mice, which have greater water demands.

Beyond the hillforts, house mouse was present right through the sequence of deposits at Ossum's Eyrie Cave, Staffordshire, including what are at least arguably pre-Roman contexts, underlying the stratigraphically-lowest contexts to include Roman pottery (Yalden 1977; Bramwell *et al.* 1990). If the dating of this sequence is secure, then it not only gives us an early record for house mouse, but also for rats, bones of which were present throughout the sequence. However, caves are notoriously difficult places in which to model the deposition and subsequent movement of small bones with any confidence. In the absence of direct dating of the house mouse bones from Ossum's Eyrie, this record must be treated with due caution.

Spreading around the country

Having established themselves in at least southern England during the Iron Age, house mice seem to have taken the Roman conquest in their stride, and have been found at many Roman sites across England. It is a fair generalisation to say that house mice are found at most Roman sites where bone preservation and recovery makes it possible for small rodent remains to have been recovered. Presumably the degree and frequency of cargo movements between Britain and the Continent increased, at least periodically, facilitating the 'topping up' of native mouse populations by new immigrants. This is the period in which the differentiation of *Mus musculus* and *M. domesticus* becomes critical. It would be easy to assume that the geographical separation of these two species dates back to the original colonisation of Europe by house mouse. However, in the near-absence of reliably and consistently identified material of Roman date, we cannot exclude the possibility that *M. musculus* was formerly more widespread across Europe, and replaced in Western Europe in more recent times by *M. domesticus*. The long programme of excavation in York, supported by systematic sieving programmes, has yielded a good record of house mice through the Roman period. The species is essentially ubiquitous, with some indication that it arrived in York a little before the ship rat *Rattus rattus*. This is not surprising given the evidence that house mice were already established in Britain, whereas rats were a new arrival in the second century AD. In the one instance in which there was sufficient well-preserved cranial material to attempt a species separation, house mice from Roman York were shown to conform with *M. domesticus* in the form of the zygomatic bone, but that record is based on a small minority of specimens from one location, and should not be taken as representative of Roman Britain as a whole.

The record from York also shows that house mice persisted in the city through the post-Roman period, whilst the archaeological record indicates that rats may have undergone extirpation, to be reintroduced in the late ninth century as Scandinavian settlement re-established urban occupation and regular sea-borne trade (Rielly, this volume). To date, there has been little investigation of fifth-century material from York, or from any other major Roman town in Britain, so we have little direct evidence of how the abandonment of *Britannia* by the Empire affected the ecology of those towns. An interesting hint comes from a substantial accumulation of small bones on the floor of the abandoned *frigidarium* of the legionary fortress baths at Caerleon, southeast Wales. The bones are arguably of post-Roman date, and probably accumulated as a result of barn owls occupying the building (O'Connor 1986b). A wide range of small vertebrates is represented, including house mouse alongside wood mice, field voles *Microtus agrestis* and shrews *Sorex araneus*, *S. minitus* and *Neomys fodiens*. The assemblage gives the impression of an essentially 'rural' ecology, in which house mice continued to find a niche, presumably as a stable population not subject to repeated immigration from a source population. Perhaps it is the capacity to sustain an isolated population that explains the post-Roman persistence of house mouse but not of ship rat. Given the close association of rats with urban sites in Roman Britain, it is quite possible that rat populations were repeatedly supplemented by new introductions, and were extirpated when this repeated immigration ceased.

Beyond mainland Britain, house mice successfully accompanied people around the British archipelago. One of the earliest off-shore records is from Iron Age Shetland, in the form of a solitary os coxa from the broch site at Scatness. This important specimen was identified by the present author as *Mus* (*in litt.* to P. Barber 18/9/2000) based on comparative specimens and the characters given by Clevedon Brown and Twigg (1969). Perhaps this rapid movement to offshore islands should not surprise us, given the evidence that it was transportation, as much as habitat, which facilitated the spread of house mice across prehistoric Europe. At some time during the last two millennia, house mice reached the remote Hebridean outpost of St Kilda, and have successfully accompanied ship-borne people to such far-flung outposts as South Georgia (Long 2003, 202–4).

To sum up, house mouse reached these islands as part of a rapid, trade-borne spread across western Europe during the last few centuries BC. The successful establishment of the species in Britain must have been facilitated by the close integration of Iron Age Britain with Atlantic Europe, and by the bulk storage of cereals at many Iron Age sites. House mice have been highly successful. They persisted through the temporary collapse of urban living in the post-Roman period, and have adapted with great success to the distinctly challenging environment of the modern city. And we have adapted to them. Quite apart from their place in story and folklore, house mice have been involved in many of the medical advances of recent decades, and their capacity to breed rapidly in captivity has made them essential to genetics research. It has been a long journey from the Natufian, and a long story of mutual adaptation.

CHAPTER 16

The Black Rat

Kevin Rielly

Introduction

Present knowledge about the early history of Britain's black rat (*Rattus rattus*) is based almost entirely on information gleaned from archaeological excavations of the last 30 years. Before 1970 it was generally agreed the species was introduced in the late eleventh century by returning Crusaders (Barrett-Hamilton and Hinton 1910–1922, 582). Then came two breakthrough archaeological discoveries, the first from St Magnus in the City of London where a juvenile rat femur was identified from a late tenth-century deposit (Armitage 1979) and the second from Skeldergate, York, where fourth-century well fills yielded several rat bones including a complete skull (Rackham 1979). Subsequent finds occasioned a series of articles on the species (Armitage *et al.*1984; Armitage 1994; Dobney and Harwood 1998; McCormick 2003; O'Connor 1991a) and their accumulated evidence has pushed back the introduction date suggesting that rats arrived shortly after AD 43. It is now thought that, although black rats

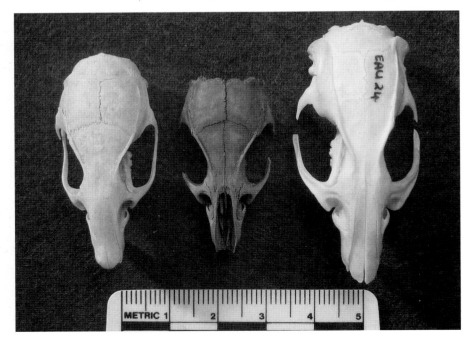

FIGURE 34. Medieval black rat skull (*centre*) compared with modern black rat (*left*) and brown rat (*right*).

Century A.D.	England	Wales	Scotland	Ireland	Isle of Man
1st	6				
2nd	10				
2nd/3rd	2	1			
3rd	1				
3rd/4th	9				
4th	7				
4th/5th	1				
6th/7th					
8th/9th	2				
9th/10th	3				
10th/11th	8				
10th–12th					1
11th/12th	13				
12th	2			1	
12th/13th	13		1		
13th	10				
13th/14th	6			2	

TABLE 8. Inter-period variation in the number of sites on which rat are represented (source Rielly in prep. a).

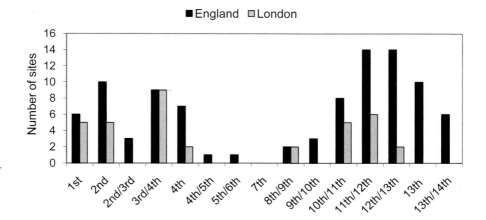

FIGURE 35. Inter-period variation in the number of sites which rat are represented (source Rielly in prep. a), separating London from the rest of England.

were distributed throughout Late Roman Britain, their population collapsed in the Early and Middle Saxon period, only becoming re-established in the late Saxon and/or early medieval period.

This chapter reviews the Roman and early medieval evidence for the black rat's introduction and spread. Discussion is based on an extensive dataset, synthesised from both published and grey literature (Rielly in prep a) and summarised in Table 8 and Figure 35. The dataset's reliability is dependent on issues of identification, dating and recovery. Here it has been assumed that the researchers whose records have been collated for this study made every attempt to differentiate black *Rattus rattus* from brown rat *Rattus norvegicus*, as well as from their similarly-sized relative, the water vole *Arvicola terrestris*. In general, it is easier to separate rat from vole than black from brown rat, the greater level of identification dependant on skeletal part and completeness (Lawrence and Brown 1973, 196, Wolff *et al.* 1980 and Armitage *et al.* 1984). For this study problems of misidentification are alleviated somewhat by the fact that the brown rat was not introduced to Britain until the eighteenth century (Yalden 1999, 183); for this reason specimens identified only to *Rattus* spp have been included in this study. It is possible that either re-deposition or the burrowing habit of the brown rat could affect dating of the specimens. In order to limit these factors, the study has only included specimens from well-sealed deposits containing associated dateable materials covering no more than 200 years. It is more difficult to account for burrowing because such diggings rarely show in the archaeological record; however the deep post-medieval overburden seen on urban sites should have guarded the Roman and medieval against the more recent activities of the brown rat.

Sieving is invaluable for the recovery of small mammal bones (see Brothwell and Jones 1978, 48), and it is no surprise that the major discoveries, summarised above, coincided with the onset of systematic sampling. The efficacy of this retrieval method varies according to sampling procedure and the size of the sieves' mesh but most of the specimens detailed in this report were retrieved using mesh of 2mm or less. Sieving is important not only for indicating the presence of rats but also for highlighting their absence. Negative evidence is particularly pertinent when comparing the species' distribution with areas outside England and also when illustrating the apparent lack of rats from Early and Middle Saxon deposits. The sample evidence has also been used as an approximate indicator of relative abundance, essentially limited to York and London, noting the proportion of samples with rat bones (after O'Connor 1988, 105).

Distribution of rats from Roman times to the medieval period

Rat bones from Roman levels are no longer limited to the third- and fourth-century examples described by Armitage *et al.* (1984, 375) and there is now clear evidence that black rats were established in Britain at an earlier date (Figure 36). The earliest securely-dated rat bone (a pelvis identified by Philip Armitage), was recovered during excavations at 168 Fenchurch Street from an occupation deposit within a multi-roomed mud-brick building, which was burnt to the ground during the Boudican revolt of AD 60/1 (Dunwoodie 2004, 15–20; Rielly 2004, 59). The means whereby this particular animal, or a close relative, was imported to London may be indicated by the concentrations of carbonised grain found in an adjacent room within the same building. While these grain samples were dominated by wheat, with some barley and oats, there were also

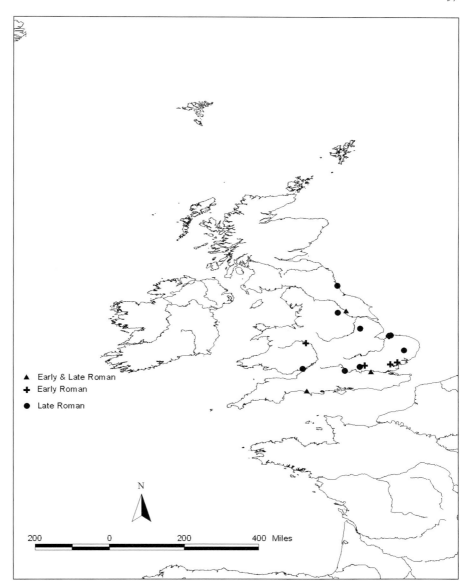

FIGURE 36. The distribution of Roman sites with rat bones (source Rielly in prep.).

▲ Early & Late Roman

+ Early Roman

● Late Roman

N

200   0   200   400   Miles

small quantities of lentils, einkorn and bitter vetch seeds. The last two were essentially Southern European crops and their presence strongly suggest that the grain was imported, most probably from the Mediterranean or Near East. It is logical to assume that the rats were carried along as 'unwelcome companions' (Davis 2004, 56–7) and, after disembarking from the ships, quickly exploited the sources of food and habitation offered by the restaurants and warehouses of Roman London. This is exemplified by other first-century examples from London which include a tentatively-identified axis from a dump deposit at 1 Poultry (Pipe in prep) but also a more substantial collection (19 bones from at least three individuals) recovered from Fish Street Hill. These remains came from a well, located in a small enclosed yard, that contained large quantities of rubbish (fine wares, glass and other objects, as well as large concentrations of food waste, especially bird and fish bones, cereals, spices and fruit seeds), interpreted as the refuse from a nearby inn (Rielly and Davis in prep). In this deposit the rats were accompanied by the remains of at least 15 house mice, suggesting the efficacy of this feature as a pit-fall trap and perhaps the presence of a notable rodent population in this area at this time. Certainly the species appears to have colonised the main suburb of Southwark by the end of the first century, as evidenced by the single black rat femur recovered from the Southwark Cathedral site (Armitage in prep).

The first-century date of introduction in London is reflected in other parts of England. For instance rat bones were recovered from a Romano-British enclosure settlement unearthed at Ivy Chimneys, near Witham, south-west of Colchester in Essex (Luff 1999). Shortly after the Conquest this settlement was bisected by the London to Colchester Roman road, which would have offered a perfect route for the inadvertent export of rats from London. At Wroxeter in Shropshire a rat skull and mandible were recovered with several other small mammal bones and it is assumed these represent the remains of one or more owl pellets (O'Connor 2002, 62). They were located amongst the ruins of the legionary fortress, abandoned in the late first century. A similar date may apply to these remains; however, it is always possible that these ruins were used as a convenient owl roost or perch for some years following their abandonment. Another possible early find is the rat from the enclosure settlement at Thornham near the north Norfolk coast (Lawrence 1986). The site has been generally dated to the first century, but the rat bone(s) as Romano-British.

Rat remains have been recovered from a greater number of second-century sites. For London almost all the specimens come from the suburb of Southwark, with the exception of a single bone from a pit possibly associated with a building at 2–12 Gresham Street (Ainsley 2002; Rielly in prep b). These rat bones were all recovered from sites within the southern part of the Jubilee Line Extension (JLE) project, with excavations adjacent to London Bridge Station. A notable feature of these sites and, in particular, from the Main Ticket Hall, Borough High Street, was the recovery of dumps with copious quantities of carbonised seeds (Gray 2002, 249). There is no evidence for foreign imports (einkorn or bitter vetch) amongst these grain dumps, so it cannot be deduced whether the Southwark rats were independently introduced or if they spread to this locality from the city across the river. However, it can be supposed that this 'concentration' of rats may bear some relation to the storage of grain in this area. Most of the JLE rat bones were recovered from deep features (wells and pits), apart from one bone taken from an occupation deposit associated with a building at the Area 8 site.

Beyond London, the second-century distribution of the black rat extends from York in the north to Dorchester in the south-west. The evidence for black rats from the more westerly and northern areas of Britain is rather sparse, with just one find from the Roman town at Caerwent (*Venta Silurium*) in Wales, where deposits within the forum-basilica provided two late third-century rat mandibles and a third possibly dated to the second century (M. Maltby pers. comm.). The absence of rats from other Roman settlements in Wales may relate to the acidic soils found in certain areas, particularly in North Wales. Recovery methods are also likely to have biased the archaeological representation of rats because, although large collections of animal bones have been retrieved from Welsh sites, they tend to pre-date the active use of sieving, as for example during the 1975–9 excavations of the Roman fort of *Segontium*, near Caernarfon (Noddle 1993).

Where rats are present, the range of sites they occupied is of interest, including not only the urban centres of York and Colchester but also the villa at Gorhambury and a rural settlement on the outskirts of Dorchester (Locker 1990; Rielly 1997). At the latter site a series of structures and agricultural features dating to the third century suggest the presence of a villa-like settlement (Smith *et al.* 1997, 304). It would certainly appear that rats had both the ability and the inclination to settle in areas other than in close proximity to highly populated ports of entry. The earliest rats at York, from late second-century deposits, probably date to within a decade or two of the establishment of the main civilian *Colonia* (O'Connor 1988, 68). In contrast, the *Colonia* at Colchester was founded in AD 49, but the earliest rat is from a second-century level (Grimm in prep). This absence could relate to a lack of sieving at several sites, but sampling programmes have been in operation at a number of sites within the city, including Culver Street that featured well stratified first- to fourth-century occupation levels (Crummy 1993, 34; Luff 1993, 11–12).

The third and fourth centuries appear to have witnessed the greatest distribution of rats in the Roman era, with further evidence from York and Dorchester, at other urban centres such as Lincoln as well as sites towards the northern periphery of Roman rule – the fort at South Shields and the villa at Dalton Parlours in West Yorkshire (Dobney and Harwood 1998). Again, these bones were found in a variety of settlement types, including a number of rural sites. Sieving is cited as an issue regarding the lack of rats from earlier levels at Lincoln, where amongst a variety of sites only those from the late Roman waterfront area where routinely sampled (*ibid.*). The quantity of rat bones from these sites tends to be rather small, with the exception of the General Accident site at York (O'Connor 1988) and also from the earlier phase at Dalton Parlours. While it is difficult to ascertain the reason(s) for the good recovery of rats at this York site, the late third/early fourth-century collection at Dalton Parlours are clearly associated with a granary, these levels providing a minimum number (MNI) of 20 rats as well as 60 mice (Huntley and Stallibrass 1995, 145). It is of interest that rats were also found in a later context within this granary, dating to the late fourth century, but following the abandonment of this structure. This change of usage undoubtedly had an effect on the rodent population, as suggested by the recovery of a MNI of 2 rats and 6 mice. It can be seen that the density of rats found at the General Accident Site appears to increase by

Location	Date (centuries AD)	N	N1	% (N/N1x100)
London	1st–2nd	10	78	12.8
	3rd–4th	12	59	20.0
	10th–11th	5	105	4.8
	11th–12th	15	135	11.1
	12th–13th	6	72	8.3
York (GA)	Mid-late 2nd	1	51	1.9
	Late 2nd–early 3rd	5	25	20.0
	11th–12th	1	4	25.0
	12th–13th	10	58	17.2
York (CG)	Late 9th	11	59	18.6

TABLE 9. Relative abundance of samples with rat bones from the General Accident Site (GA) and Coppergate (CG), York and a combination of sites from London, where N is the number of samples with rat bones and N1 is the number of samples with animal bones (London information taken from Rielly in prep and York data from O'Connor 1988, 107 and 1991b, 257).

the third century (see Table 9), perhaps indicating a general increase in the rat population within the *colonia*. An expansion in rat populations is also indicated by the evidence for third/fourth-century London, which appears to suggest an expansion in their distribution, with rats bones found at several occupied as well as abandoned sites in both the centre and periphery of the City. For instance, rats were found alongside or just outside the eastern perimeter in the area of the east London cemeteries, areas that were clearly used as city dumps and that would have attracted scavenging rats.

No sooner had rats become established than their population seems to have crashed, reflected by the clear paucity of finds dating between the fifth and ninth century (Figure 37). In London, there appear to be just two finds from this long period, both dating to the late eighth/mid-ninth centuries, each taken from sites within the Middle Saxon settlement of Lundenwic (Rackham *et al.* 1989). This small number of bones is highlighted by the large number of excavations undertaken in this area, based on modern day Covent Garden, many of which were extensively sampled. The rest of England is similarly bereft, as particularly shown by the well-sampled excavations in York, with rats not appearing until the later ninth century, at Coppergate (O'Connor 1991a). Neither York nor London can offer much evidence for fifth- to seventh-century occupation. However, the absence of rats at the early sites of West Heslerton (Berg 1998; pers. comm.; Dobney and Harwood 1998, 378) and West Stow (Crabtree 1989; 1996), of which only the former was sieved, is probably significant. Further negative evidence is provided by the large bone collections derived from the extensive excavations at the Middle Saxon era sites of Flixborough in Lincolnshire, plus Wicken Bonhunt, Brandon and Ipswich, all in East Anglia (Crabtree 1996), and then in Southampton (Hamwic), the sites of Melbourne Street (Bourdillon and Coy 1980), Six Dials (Bourdillon with Andrews 1997) and the Friends Provident St Mary's Stadium (Hamilton-Dyer 2005). With the exception of Melbourne Street and Wicken Bonhunt all of these sites were sieved and, although there is insufficient evidence to warrant firm conclusions concerning the initial decline of the rat population, there is little doubt that the nationwide density of this species had declined dramatically by the seventh/eighth centuries.

It is of interest that their probable re-emergence coincides with the period of Viking contact, evidence from York strongly suggesting that this species was

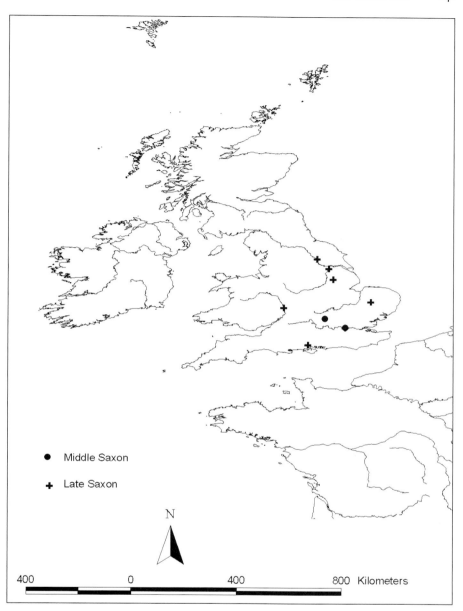

Middle Saxon

Late Saxon

N

400   0   400   800   Kilometers

FIGURE 37. The distribution of Saxon period sites with rat bones (source Rielly in prep.).

reintroduced via Viking trading ships (O'Connor 1991b, 257). The density of rats at the Scandinavian settlement at Coppergate in York (see Table 9) is similar to that observed at the later levels at the General Accident site and also within Late Roman London. It can perhaps be proposed that favourable conditions and/or a sizeable introduction outweighed the initial limitations on population expansion that might be expected for a newly arrived species. While the evidence regarding this introduction is rather slight in other parts of England, the number of sites dated to the ninth and early tenth centuries with rat bones,

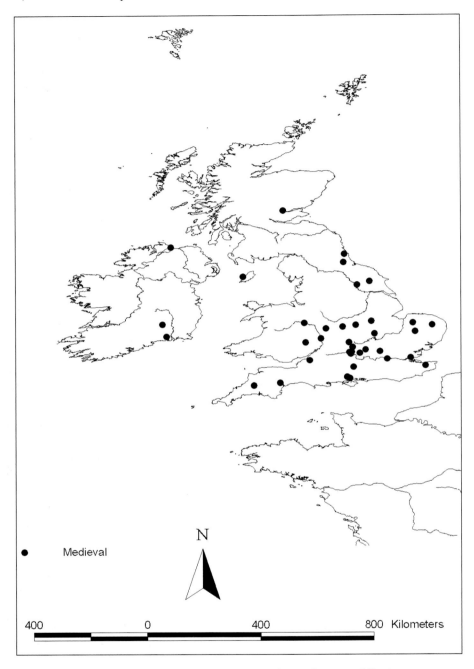

FIG 38. The distribution of medieval period sites with rat bones (source Rielly in prep.).

in comparison with the extensive negative evidence from Middle Saxon sites in the same localities, does appear to indicate a general trend.

The following two centuries are marked by a steady increase in rat representation (Figure 38). London is clearly well populated with rats by the eleventh/twelfth centuries as shown by their wide distribution, extending from the City into Southwark and also at one of the outlying monastic houses, at Merton Priory (Pipe

2007). This resurgence of rats in London was probably supported by the extensive rubbish deposition and the stalling/feeding of domestic animals (Bowsher *et al.* 2007, 83; Hill and Rowsome 2008). Rats were similarly well distributed around England by this period, although perhaps not re-attaining Roman densities until the thirteenth/fourteenth centuries. In comparison to the Roman period, these rats had obviously occupied a wide selection of settlements, from farmsteads and monastic houses to castles and major urban centres. While widespread, the quantities of rat bones recovered were invariably quite small, with the notable exception of the 36 bones from the eleventh/twelfth-century castle at Middleton Stoney, described as deriving from a stone-lined shaft (Levitan 1984).

For Wales, during this later period, it is necessary to turn to historical and linguistic evidence. Giraldus Cambrensis, in his *Journey Through Wales* written in 1188, describes 'a large species of rodents, called rats' referring to a story he had 'read somewhere', which shows he knew of the existence of this creature but not necessarily that it occupied Wales during this time (Thorpe 1978, 170). Perhaps of greater significance is the Welsh word for rat '*llygoden mawr*' or '*llygoden ffrengig*' which translate as large mouse or French mouse. The latter name could derive from the fact that it entered, or possibly re-entered, Wales with the French-speaking Normans, which may have been as early as the late eleventh century coinciding with the Norman invasion of South Wales.

The same twelfth-century author and traveller has a little more to offer concerning the presence of rats in Ireland, when he refers, in approximately 1180, to 'larger mice that are commonly called rats' eating the books of the Bishop of Ferns (O'Meara 1982, 81). This would appear to be the earliest written reference to rats in Ireland (McCormick 1999, 366), coinciding with the arrival of the Normans in the twelfth century. It is of interest, in this respect, that the Irish name for the rat, following the Welsh name, is French mouse *luch francach*. The earliest archaeological evidence is represented by a skull from a mid twelfth-century deposit within a site interpreted as the remains of medieval tenements at 2–4 Peter Street, Waterford (McCormick 1997, 837). There is undoubtedly a great potential for an earlier introduction, most notably via the Viking settlements. The lack of such evidence could again relate to the absence of sieving, although ironically, the Waterford example was hand-collected. However, the numerous samples taken from Viking Age deposits from Dublin (*c.* 917 to 1030 AD), admittedly for botanical rather than zoological purposes, were described as containing 'no bones of rats or mice' (Geraghty 1996, 55). Later finds of rat bones include examples from Kilferagh, a small rural settlement in County Kilkenny (McCormick 1987, 99–100) and a single pelvis from a dump possibly associated with the medieval castle at Greencastle, County Down (Beglane 2007), again all hand-collected.

The Isle of Man evidence is limited to a few bones taken from deposits associated with a Norse settlement on St Patricks Isle, Peel, dating between the eighth and twelfth centuries and just predating the late twelfth/early thirteenth-century construction of the Cathedral of St German on the same site. Unlike Ireland and Wales, there is no obvious indication either from the local name for rat or from historical texts to suggest whether this animal was present during the medieval period. While outside the remit of this report, it is worth mentioning that the Black Death, which ravaged most of Britain in 1348–50 (Horrox 1994, 10, 81–2 and 85), was not mentioned in the *Chronicle of Man* (yearly accounts between 1249 and 1374) for 1348 (Coakley 2008). The Peel example suggests that rats were present on the island in the early medieval period. However, they may have either become extinct or perhaps never attained the population density necessary to trigger an epidemic (see McCormick 2003, 2–4). Alternatively, they may not have carried the vector flea, *Xenopsylla cheopis* to the island. Of interest also is the linguistic evidence, where the Manx *rodden* for rat is apparently derived from northern English, probably entering the local vocabulary in the fifteenth century with the arrival of the Stanley lords or possibly a little later via merchants (Ball and Fife 1993, 283).

The single example from Scotland was provided by a deposit associated with a row of houses facing the High Street in early medieval Perth. There would appear to be no corroborative evidence, either historically or otherwise, to confirm whether rats were introduced at or prior to the thirteenth century in Scotland. However, as mentioned above, concerning the spread of plague, it can be assumed that rats were relatively plentiful in certain areas of Scotland by the later fourteenth century (Horrox 1994, 85).

Discussion

Rats entered this country as early as the mid first century, most probably as unwelcome guests accompanying grain imports from the eastern Mediterranean, becoming well-established throughout England and extending into Wales by the Later Roman period. A point worth considering is the means whereby the rat population was maintained. By the later second century, there was less trade between the Mediterranean and Britain, suggesting that the rat population must have been self-sustaining or at least reliant on transfers from rat colonies in other parts of north-west Europe, where trade continued into the later Roman period (see Fulford 1991, 44).

In sharp contrast to the Roman period, there follows an uninterrupted dearth of rats, right up to the mid-ninth century. The timing of their demise is as yet poorly understood, but the negative evidence from sites such as West Heslerton would suggest it took place either coinciding with or soon after the end of the Roman era. A major reason for the population collapse may be the dismantling of the Roman infrastructure, which had provided optimal conditions for this 'warmth-loving' species that had adapted to a purely commensal existence in the north European limits of the Roman empire (after Armitage 1994, 233–4 and McCormick 2003, 11). Climate change may have also played a part, given that records suggest cooler temperatures and prolonged wetness in the years between the early fifth and eighth centuries (Armitage 1994, 234).

There is a question concerning whether the rat population suffered a major decline rather than extinction. However, it can perhaps be assumed that if any rats had survived, they would have been restored to something like their former glory within the concentrated and waste littered urban centres set up by the seventh/eighth centuries in various parts of England, from York in the north to Southampton in the south (Hill 2001, 3). The evidence regarding the subsequent discovery of black rats at ninth-century York and at a few other sites, dated to the ninth or tenth centuries, has been used to suggest a reintroduction, most probably by Viking traders. An interesting aspect of this event, as found at Coppergate, is the notably large density of rats. This is clearly different to the first-century Roman evidence from London or indeed to the initial occurrences of this species at York. The greater quantity of rats could relate to the method of introduction, with a direct transfer by ship from rat-infested Scandinavian ports (note the early ninth-century occurrence of this species at Birka in Sweden as described by Bengt Wigh 2001, 54 and 125–6 taken from McCormick 2003, 7) compared to the more arduous overland route via the east coast of Spain and then along the Rhone/Rhine or Rhone/Loire rivers as used by first- and second-century Roman traders (Peacock 1978 cited in Milne 1985, 112).

There are relatively few tenth- to eleventh-century sites with rat bones, perhaps suggesting initially a rather slow rate of colonisation. However, they were certainly better represented by the twelfth century, when they reached the Irish ports, and had extended beyond the major urban centres in England to smaller settlements as the villages of Thrislington and Wharram Percy by the thirteenth/fourteenth centuries. This widespread distribution clearly provided the means whereby, in 1348, the plague was able to cause such devastation across Britain.

Acknowledgments

The gathering of data for this report was facilitated by the generous donation of information by a host of archaeozoological colleagues. These include Umberto Albarella, Ian Baxter, David Berg, Keith Dobney, Lorraine Higbee, Louisa Gidney, Jessica Grimes (Wessex Archaeology), Sheila Hamilton-Dyer, Philip Armitage (including identification of the pelvis from 168 Fenchurch Street), Alison Locker, Jacqui Mulville, Sue Stallibrass, Ian Smith (Chester Archaeological Service), Naomi Sykes, Dale Serjeantson and Sylvia Warman (Cotswold Archaeology); Fay Worley, Andrew Hammond, Tessa Pirnie and Umberto Albarella (English Heritage); Mark Maltby (for the only rat from Wales); Finbar McCormick, Fiona Beglane, Jonny Geber and Auli Tourunen (Irish rats). Thanks are also due to Dave Bowsher at Museum of London Archaeology (MoLA) and Cath Maloney at the London Archaeological Archive Resource Centre (LAARC) who facilitated access to various unpublished reports, Daphne Hills (Mammal Section, BMNH) for help with the identification of British rat-sized rodents, to James Gerrard and Josephine Brown at Pre-Construct Archaeology (PCA), for production of the distribution maps and to James again as well as Kevin Hayward (also at PCA) and Alan Pipe (Museum of London Archaeology) for helpful comments in the writing and editing of this report.

CHAPTER 17

Extinct Birds

Dale Serjeantson

Introduction

There were major changes in the avifauna of the British Isles at the end of the Pleistocene which accompanied the vegetation changes summarised in Chapter 1. In the early Holocene the British Isles was colonised by a suite of birds substantially similar to that of the present today (Harrison 1988), but including some large species which later disappeared. As more finds are excavated from archaeological sites, we can see that some of these species were quite common in the past, while others seem always to have been sparse.

The species discussed here are the great auk (*Pinguinis impennis*), the common or Eurasian crane (*Grus grus*), the Dalmatian pelican (*Pelecanus crispus*), the white stork (*Ciconia ciconia*), the spoonbill (*Platalea leucorodia*), the great bustard (*Otis tarda*), and the white-tailed eagle (*Haliaeetus albicilla*). Of these, the great auk is totally extinct, and others became extinct as breeding birds in Britain. Three doubtful species will also be mentioned: a gadfly petrel (*Pterodroma* sp.), the gyrfalcon (*Falco rusticolus*), and the pygmy cormorant (*Phalacrocorax pygmaeus*). Remains of these last three have been found in excavations, but whether they ever bred in the British Isles is in doubt. A recent detailed survey of the history and archaeology of the British avifauna (Yalden and Albarella 2009) shows that there may have been further species present at one time in the Holocene which then became extinct. There is a possible Iron Age find of an eagle owl (*Bubo bubo*) and a small number of medieval records of the night heron (*Nycticorax nycticorax*) and the little egret (*Egretta garzetta*) from sites in London which may be of breeding birds or vagrants.

Several authors have surveyed the historical evidence for birds in the British Isles (e.g. D'Arcy 1999; Cocker and Mabey 2005; Gurney 1921); others have looked at place-names (Yalden 2002) and at illustrations in medieval manuscripts (Yapp 1981). Before the tenth century AD however the only source of information on the status of birds in Britain is their remains. These are found mainly in three places: caves, fens and archaeological sites. The evidence is unevenly distributed. Remains in caves are often raptor prey, those from fens are mostly natural deaths, and those from archaeological sites are mainly – but not exclusively – birds which were eaten. As people rarely ate birds on inland sites before the Roman times, archaeological deposits earlier than the later first millennium BC contain few birds, except on coastal sites in Scotland, where farmers living near the coast caught and ate seabirds (Baldwin 1974; Fenton 1978; Randall 2005). From the Roman period onwards sites do have remains of wild birds as well as domestic chickens and geese. Wild birds are invariably present in the rubbish pits of wealthy Medieval households, though not in those of the poor (Serjeantson 2006a).

This chapter is based on records from *c.* 225 sites with one or more of the species discussed. It has been compiled from reports on archaeological assemblages, information from individuals who have kindly allowed me to cite unpublished records, and earlier surveys (Albarella and Thomas 2002; Albarella and Yalden 2009; D'Arcy 1999; Kitchener 2007; McCormick and Buckland 1997; Parker 1988; Serjeantson 1988; Yalden and McCarthy 2004,). All but one of the birds discussed here have quite large bones, readily recovered during excavation, and most are sufficiently distinct to be identified reliably. Nevertheless, the record is certainly incomplete, especially for Ireland and Wales, and will rapidly become out of date as more remains are excavated.

Great auk

The only bird that has become extinct in Europe in the past 500 years is the great auk. This goose-sized seabird, was the penguin of the northern hemisphere. Flightless and using its wings only for swimming, it spent most of its life at sea, and came on land only to breed. In historical times – by which time it was already quite scarce – the great auk bred only on a few islands off the east coast of North America and Iceland. As it never evolved fear of humans, it was easily captured. The last authenticated live birds were a pair killed off Iceland in 1844 (Fuller 1999; Grieve 1885).

A book written on the great auk soon after it became extinct mentions only a handful of poorly-dated records from British archaeological sites (Grieve 1885), but a hundred and twenty years later, the great auk has been found on more than 60 sites. The earliest record from the British Isles is from the 500,000 year old site at Boxgrove, Sussex, where a great auk humerus was found in the vicinity of butchered animals; so even at this early date the great auk could have been human food (Anon 1994). All other finds from the British Isles are from Holocene coastal sites, most around the north and west of Scotland, but a few come from England, Ireland, and the Isle of Man. The great auk was one of the most frequent species at the Mesolithic shell middens on Oronsay (Grigson 1981) and the Neolithic settlements at Knap of Howar and Tofts Ness in Orkney. As late as the first millennium AD in Orkney island sites, the great auk was the third most frequent species after the gannet (*Sula bassana*) and cormorant/shag (*Phalacrocorax carbo* and *aristotelis*), according to an unpublished survey by Paul Mead.

Excavated bones from many sites exhibit butchery marks, so there is no doubt that great auks were deliberately caught for food. As the great auk only came ashore to breed, people must usually have killed it during the six weeks or so it spent on shore laying and incubating its single egg and rearing the chick. That birds were killed at this time is confirmed by bones of chicks as well as adult birds at Halangy Down in the Scilly Isles and Cnip in the Hebrides, which were probably caught at sea.

Wherever great auks were regularly predated, numbers declined. At Tofts Ness and Pool, both sites on the island of Sanday in Orkney, the percentage of great auks among the birds declined in successive phases from 19 per cent at the time the island was first occupied in the Early Neolithic to eight per cent in the Late Bronze Age, two per cent in the Iron Age and just one per cent in the Medieval period. From the first millennium AD onwards, no site anywhere has more than one or two bones, so by then the great auk had clearly become very rare around the British Isles. The severe decline at this time probably coincides with the increased use of boats and offshore fishing. The latest find is from a seventeenth-century rubbish pit at Castle Rushen on the Isle of Man, contemporary with the earliest illustrations of the bird (see Figure 39).

Two sightings, one off Orkney and one off St Kilda in the Outer Hebrides, suggest that one or two birds may have bred around the British Isles into the eighteenth century. The last authenticated sighting was in 1844, but a description of a pair of birds seen in Belfast Lough in 1845 is convincing, which would make these the last great auks ever seen alive (D'Arcy 1999).

Crane

Before the seventeenth century the common crane was a summer migrant which came to Britain to breed but spent the winter in southern Europe or North Africa. Some of the bones from Ice Age sites in France are much larger than those of today's birds, which prompted Milne-Edwards, a nineteenth-century palaeontologist, to propose that there was formerly an extinct giant crane in Europe, *Grus primigenia* (Harrison and Cowles 1977). Remains of very large birds have since been found from as late as the Iron Age in Glastonbury, Wales and the Outer Hebrides. A recent metrical analysis has shown that the common crane was formerly much larger and has diminished steadily in size. The very large specimens therefore may not be from a separate species, but from large common cranes (von den Driesch 1999). As even modern cranes stand almost as tall as a human, the species has always been conspicuous. About three hundred place-names in the British Isles include an element meaning crane, suggesting that it was familiar all over the country (Boisseau and Yalden 1998). According to Geraldus Cambrensis, cranes were particularly common in medieval Ireland. The crane was often illustrated in medieval bestiaries (Yapp 1981). Hawking manuals and menus for feasts at the tables of households of high rank frequently refer to the crane. For instance, in 1465, 204 birds were commanded for a great feast in Durham, and in 1520 Thetford Priory presented the king with a gift of cranes (Stone 2006).

The place-name and historical evidence is supported by many archaeological records. Cranes are the most frequent of the species discussed here: a survey in 1998 tracked down 78 sites on which bones had been found (Boisseau and Yalden 1998) and that has now risen to nearly 90. Cranes have been recorded in Scotland, Ireland and Wales as well as England. It is likely that they were caught on migration as well as at their breeding sites, but – as with the great auk – breeding is confirmed by occasional finds of immature birds in England and also in Ireland. One skeleton of an immature crane was found in what had been a waterlogged ditch around the Late Iron Age settlement at Haddenham in Cambridgeshire. It was complete down to the unfused epiphyses of the tarsometatarsus and tibiotarsus and feather impressions. The lack of damage makes it likely that this was a natural death (Serjeantson 2006b). Cranes are equally common on prehistoric, Romano-British, and early medieval sites, but – despite the demand for cranes for banquets – the remains become less common on late medieval sites (Albarella and Thomas 2002; Sykes 2005). There is little doubt that over-hunting in the Middle Ages seriously diminished crane populations, a blow that was compounded by fenland drainage which reduced their habitat to the point that they could no longer breed in this country (Harrison 1988).

White stork

The white stork is a large wading bird which nests on trees and on artificial elevated platforms such as chimneys. In continental Europe today it breeds on houses as well as in the wild. It is an occasional vagrant in Britain but there has been only one historical description of breeding, a pair which nested on St Giles Cathedral in Edinburgh in 1416 (Harrison 1988). The white stork is convincingly illustrated in two medieval manuscripts, which suggested to Yapp (1981) that the artist has actually seen the bird, either in England or elsewhere, but – perhaps significantly – it does not appear on the menus of medieval banquets.

There are fewer than 20 archaeological finds, of which three are from the Pleistocene. The most northerly is from Bronze Age Jarlshof in Shetland. Four of the finds are from Medieval towns in the south of England. A specimen from Winchester may have been a falcon's prey, as it was found in the area of the Royal Mews, close to remains of gyrfalcons and cranes. The numbers are many fewer than for the crane, but they seem too frequent to suggest that all were vagrants and they are as numerous as some species which are known to have bred in the British Isles, such as the bittern (Albarella and Thomas 2002). The stork probably did breed, but perhaps intermittently.

Spoonbill

The spoonbill is a fairly common vagrant today which breeds in southern Europe. It has been recorded in the past in Wales, west London and Norfolk, the last historical reference to breeding birds dating from the seventeenth century. The medieval illustrations, interestingly, are all from manuscripts created in either Somerset or the Fens, both places where the illuminator no doubt saw the bird (Yapp 1981). It was also known in the Middle Ages as the 'shoveler', under which name it was served at Henry VIII's banquet for the King of France in Calais in 1532 (Bourne 1981), but these birds might have been procured locally in France or the Low Countries. A statute of 1533 made it illegal to take the eggs of spoonbills between 1st March and 30th June (Stone 2006), which certainly suggests that spoonbills nested in England at the time.

Despite the historical records, archaeological finds are rare. I know of remains at just three medieval sites: Eynsham Abbey in Oxfordshire, Castle Rising in Norfolk, and Southampton, Hampshire. Like some of the other waterfowl discussed here, it seems that the spoonbill did not survive the drainage which took place from the seventeenth century onwards (Harrison 1988); it was probably never common.

Dalmatian pelican

The largest bird to have bred in Britain since the last glaciation is the pelican. Pelican bones have been found in natural contexts in the Fens, but remains were first found in a cultural context in the Iron Age 'Lake Village' at Glastonbury in Somerset. They were identified as coming from the Dalmatian pelican, rather than the white pelican (*P. onocrotalus)* (Andrews 1917) and subsequent finds have been of the same species (Serjeantson 2006).

The Dalmatian pelican breeds in large colonies on islands in the shallow waters of fens, lakes and deltas, near the coast and also inland. Today it does not breed nearer than the Danube delta and northern Greece, but until recently was widespread in southeast Europe (Snow and Perrins 1998, 96). In the first millennium BC it was formerly found in wetlands much further west; the Roman naturalist Pliny wrote that it bred in the estuaries of the Rhine, Scheldt and Elbe (Harrison 1988). This is confirmed by archaeological finds from the Low Countries.

All but one of the find spots in Britain have been in the Somerset Levels, with three sites, or the Fenlands, with at least seven sites; some were natural deposits and some archaeological. Beyond those two areas, a bone was recovered in Hull docks (Forbes *et al.* 1958). The securely-dated records are from the first millennium BC; the latest, from the site of Camp Ground, Earith, Cambridgeshire, is from the third or fourth century AD. A pelican bone was found during excavations of Medieval Glastonbury (Coy 1977), but without confirmation from a radiocarbon date, it is best regarded as reworked from the Iron Age.

Andrews (1917) concluded that the pelican 'was used for food by the people of the lake-dwellings' at Glastonbury and this was certainly the case at Haddenham, Cambridgeshire, as there were cut marks on a humerus from that site which indicated that the birds had been butchered for meat and also to remove feathers. The archaeological evidence for breeding is unequivocal: some of the bones from the Fens and also from Glastonbury are of immature birds.

The reason why the Dalmatian pelican became extinct in Britain is not hard to find as it requires a large undisturbed area in which to breed. 'If disturbed, it abandons the nest even when there are partly grown young in the nest' (Harrison 1988, 20). The Fens were canalised and partly drained in the Roman period, and the cause of its extinction in Britain was probably loss of habitat and disturbance rather than direct predation.

Great bustard

The great bustard has quite different ecological requirements to the waterfowl just discussed: it favours undisturbed steppe, grassland or open agricultural land, thus its range today is restricted largely to Hungary and Iberia. During the Windermere Interstadial, however, tundra conditions were widespread and at that time bustards were present all over Europe, including southern England (Cuisin and Vigne 1998). Remains from that period have been found in caves in Cheddar Gorge and south Wales (Harrison 1988). These were not necessarily human prey, though many from elsewhere in Europe most certainly were. Later, when the British Isles became heavily wooded, it is likely that the bustard died out and did not recolonise until farming restored the open landscape. There are no more archaeological or palaeontological records until the Middle Ages. Some bones were originally identified as bustard at Fishbourne Roman Palace in Sussex (Parker 1988) but recent re-analysis has shown that the specimens are actually cranes (Allen and Allen 2009).

In later historical times the bustard was mostly found on the Downs and Wolds of southern and eastern England. It is mentioned in a few medieval sources: for instance, Thetford Priory presented bustards to the Duchess of Norfolk in the 1520s (Stone 2006) and Henry VIII commanded 48 for his Calais feast, many fewer than the waders on the list, no doubt reflecting the fact that bustards were scarcer. Despite the historical references, very few later remains have been excavated: just one from medieval London and one from seventeenth-century Norwich, the latter with other remains of a feast. The paucity of records suggests that the bustard has never been very common since the end of the last glaciation.

White-tailed eagle

In the British Isles the golden eagle (*Aquila chrysaetos*), which is a bird of mountains and moorlands, has survived, while the white-tailed eagle, sometimes called the sea eagle, was killed off. It is thought that people did not make a distinction between the golden and the white-tailed eagle before the seventeenth century. Place names which include 'erne' or 'earn' are abundant in lowlands as well as uplands, confirming that the eagles were common everywhere. In Ireland the names 'Iolar' and its corrupt form 'Iller' are also found all over the country. Eagles were frequently illustrated in medieval manuscripts; those depicted with a fish in the beak must have been drawn by a painter who had seen white-tailed eagles (D'Arcy 1999, 62). It became extinct as a breeding bird in Scotland in 1916 and in Ireland in 1898.

The archaeological evidence indicates that the white-tailed eagle was ubiquitous in the past. Its remains have been found on at least 80 sites in England, Wales, Scotland and Ireland, of which six are Pleistocene caves. They are distributed widely in time and space. In the prehistoric period they are found on both domestic and ritual sites. The most spectacular collection was more than 600 bones from about 20 birds found in the Neolithic burial mound of Isbister (Bramwell 1983).The excavators originally interpreted the skeletons as a ritual deposit contemporary with the human burials in the tomb, but recent radiocarbon dating has shown that the birds died nearly 1000 years later than the humans buried in the tomb (Pitts 2006). It is hard to see the eagles as other than anthropogenic, but their origin remains highly enigmatic.

Some prehistoric settlements in Orkney, including Links of Noltland and Point of Cott, have large numbers of bones but it is more usual for just a few to be present. In the Romano-British period white-tailed eagles are one of the wild birds most often encountered. They have been found on more than 20 sites. Skeletons were found at Winchester and Colchester, apparently buried deliberately, and large numbers were recovered from the Roman forts at Caerleon in Wales. Intriguingly, 57 bones were excavated at Dragonby in Lincolnshire, a Late Iron Age settlement on the Humber estuary. At this time the settlement may already have been within the influence of the Roman world across the channel. Remains are also quite common on Early Medieval sites, but – outside Norse Scotland – only four date from later than the eleventh century AD, and none is later than the fifteenth century.

The previous species discussed here were all caught for food, but, like all raptors, eagles were rarely eaten, so why have remains been found associated with human settlements? Unlike the golden eagle, the white-tailed eagle feeds on carrion as well as live prey, so once farming began in the fourth millennium BC, their scavenging habits probably led them to become commensal around human settlements (Mulkeen and O'Connor 1997) (Figure 40). More sinister, white-tailed eagles descended on battlefield corpses, a habit they shared with ravens (Harrison 1988). This is described in a Viking funerary inscription in Sweden which praises a warrior because he 'gave the eagle food' (Baxter 1993). Burial practice in prehistoric Britain seems to have included exposure of the dead as a prelude to final burial, so corpses would have been exposed to avian scavengers, just as in the Parsee religion today. This in turn would have given the

FIGURE 40. White-tailed sea eagle over an Anglo-Saxon village. The white-tailed sea eagle seems to have been a commensal bird until the end of the first millennium AD
DRAWING BY JULIE CURL

birds ritual associations, as well as enhancing numbers. Eagles also had special significance for the Roman army, so their presence may have been encouraged around army camps.

This however does not fully explain the bias towards finds in the Roman-British period. Another possible reason for the capture of eagles was to supply feathers, as feathers of both golden and white-tailed eagles were used as adornment on military helmets. Eagle feathers have always been sought after for the power they conferred by the association with the top predator of the avian world, rather than for their physical qualities. Indeed, for this reason, the desire for feathers may go back into prehistory (Clark 1948). Bones, too, gained significance from the association, no doubt the reason why the ulna of a white-tailed eagle was selected to make a bone point buried in one of the barrows at Radley, Oxfordshire (Barclay *et al.* 1999). A single claw found at the Late Bronze Age site at Potterne in Wiltshire must have been used for ornament, as it had been perforated for use (Lawson 2000).

The white-tailed eagle survived human predation, increases in the human population, early agricultural intensification, and the beginnings of urbanization. Numbers may well have been helped along by all these things. It seems to have declined only in the Middle Ages, eventually failing to survive an onslaught by sheep-farmers, poultry keepers and gamekeepers in the nineteenth century.

The success of recent reintroduction confirms persecution rather than habitat change as reason for extinction.

Doubtful species

A few isolated bones have been found on archaeological sites of birds where there is real doubt as to whether they were from a breeding population. Remains of a gadfly petrel, either Fea's petrel (*Pterodroma feae)* or a closely similar species which is now extinct, have been found in three Scottish middens. Ten bones have been recovered from a minimum of six birds from contexts of various dates between the second century BC and the twelfth century AD. These could be accidentals, but, given the numbers and spread in dates, it is more likely that a gadfly petrel, like the great auk, formerly bred on some of Scotland's offshore islands (Serjeantson 2005). A pair of carpometacarpi from a pygmy cormorant was excavated from a fifteenth/sixteenth-century pit in Abingdon, Oxfordshire (Cowles 1981). Though the possibility was raised that there was a small local breeding population, there is no confirming evidence that its range ever extended as far as the British Isles, so, until further finds turn up, this is probably best regarded as an accidental. In Winchester, bones from two gyrfalcons were found close to the Royal Mews (Coy in press). There are many descriptions of how gyrfalcons were imported for hawking from Norway and Iceland in the Middle Ages (Gurney 1921, 42), so the origin of these birds is clear.

Conclusions

Though relative numbers of finds from archaeological sites do not reflect numbers in the landscape they do suggest that some species must have been more common than others. If we consider excavated remains only, rather than historical references, we have to revise some conclusions about the past status of some of the birds discussed here. The great auk, the common crane, and the white-tailed eagle must all have been common breeding species in the past. The great auk almost disappeared at the end of the first millennium AD, but the crane survived well into the early Middle Ages and the white-tailed eagle into the eighteenth century. The pelican, spoonbill, white stork and bustard appear to have been much rarer and were probably only intermittent breeders, the great bustard, for instance, bred only in those periods when there was open country, and the pelican only at times when the Fens and the Somerset levels were inundated. The gadfly petrel too may have been a rare and intermittent breeder.

The wetland species discussed here became extinct in Britain thanks to the combination of predation and drainage of wetlands, but some are returning, with and without human assistance. In the past 50 years reserves have been created which are suitable for many of the species discussed here. Cranes and spoonbills have recently bred in eastern England, though Britain, like the rest of

Western Europe, no longer has space for the Dalmatian pelican. The landscape of southern England may now be suitable for the bustard, but the density of human population and road traffic does not bode well for its future here. The more versatile white-tailed eagle, successfully reintroduced to western Scotland, may yet be seen again over Ireland, Wales and England.

Acknowledgements

I am grateful to the very many people who have provided information. I would especially like to thank Derek Yalden who made unpublished records available, as did Umberto Albarella, Ian Baxter, Julie Curl, Sheila Hamilton-Dyer, Lorraine Higbee, Jen Kitch, Terry O'Connor and Lena Strid. The hard work put into unpublished dissertations by Rebekah Davies and Paul Mead is also gratefully acknowledged.

CHAPTER 18

Bird Introductions

Kristopher Poole

Introduction

The variety of birdlife in Britain today results largely from a process of extinction and arrival stretching over 2500 years. Humans have been complicit in many of these changes, several species disappearing through predation (Serjeantson, this volume), whilst over three hundred have been intentionally imported (Dudley *et al.* 2006). Although many of these species have had little impact on peoples' lives, others have developed closer relationships with humans, a statement perhaps more true of the Galliformes than any other order. This chapter focuses on the most notable Galliformes: domestic fowl (*Gallus domesticus*), common pheasant (*Phasianus colchicus*), blue peafowl (*Pavo cristatus*), turkey (*Meleagris gallopavo*) and helmeted guinea fowl (*Numida meleagris*). Understanding the timing and motivations behind each arrival is complicated by problems of identification in the archaeological (they are osteologically similar and the remains of domestic fowl and pheasant, and peafowl and turkey are notoriously difficult to separate), documentary and iconographic records. It is only by combining these sources that we can begin to tell the story of how these particular birds became so important in human history.

Domestic fowl

Although widely used for food today, domestic fowl may initially have been more important as sacrificial and fighting birds (Simoons 1994, 145). Yalden and Albarella (2009, 99–102) have recently summarised archaeological and genetic evidence for the species, which suggests that these birds were first domesticated in south-east Asia in the sixth millennium BC, from where they spread gradually, perhaps through southern Russia, to south-east Europe (Figure 41). According to Benecke (1993, 21) domestic fowl arrived in the Mediterranean around the eighth century BC, and central Europe by the seventh century BC. In Britain, the earliest records date to the Early Iron Age, as at Blackhorse Road, Hertfordshire (Legge *et al.*1989) and Houghton Down, Hampshire (Hamilton 2000). At the latter site, one pit was found to contain the skeletons of a cockerel, a hen and a few possible immature fowl bones, indicating that breeding may have been taking place in Britain, although there is little evidence to suggest

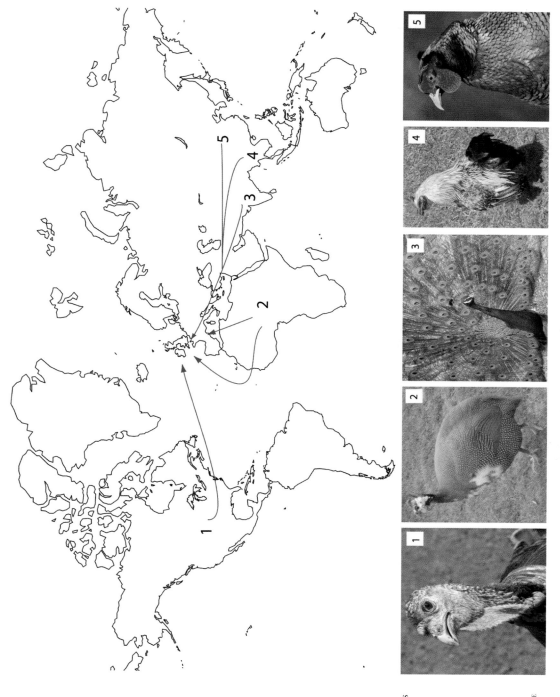

FIGURE 41. Origins and route of bird introductions:
1) Turkey,
2) Guineafowl,
3) Peafowl,
4) Domestic fowl
5) Pheasant

1 BY TOM HARTMAN
3 BY KIM VICKERS
5 © ALEX HYDE, ALEX HYDE PHOTOGRAPHY

that populations were established at this point. Indeed, the scarcity of domestic fowl in Early Iron Age Britain may be the very reason that the Houghton Down animals were selected for burial; animal burials are a feature of European Iron Age sites and are often interpreted in ritual terms (Hill 1995).

As Yalden and Albarella (2009, 101 and especially table 5.1) show, it is not until the Late Iron Age that domestic fowl begin to appear more frequently on British sites, their increased representation reflecting the Roman influence which saw fowl-keeping become common across continental Europe (Benecke 1993, 24). Domestic fowl had been present in Italy since at least the sixth century BC (West and Zhou 1988, 525). By the second century BC they were being used for sport (Toynbee 1973) and intensive poultry rearing was well established by the first century BC (White 1970, 322–327). They also acquired great religious significance, the cockerel being associated with the cult of Mithras and the god Mercury.

Escalating trade between Britain and continental Europe from around 100 BC or before (Potter and Johns 1992, 26) was probably linked to the native elite's increasing desire for exotic food and drink, which they utilised as a marker of social distinction (Hill 2002). Although domestic fowl remains are still scarce on Late Iron Age sites, it seems that fowl keeping was beginning to become established in Britain, domestic fowl finds from across the country suggesting multiple introductions. Whether domestic fowl were initially exploited in quite the same way as elsewhere is unclear. Many researchers quote Julius Caesar's words from *Gallic Wars*, that Britons did not regard it right to eat chickens, geese and hares, but the reason he gives, '*animi voluptatisque causa*', is ambiguous. Butchery marks on domestic fowl bones from archaeological sites around the time of Caesar's visit indicate that if he was implying that their consumption was taboo, this was not strictly applied (Albarella 2007, 396). Coupled with the fact that the word 'voluptas' refers to sports, shows or festivals, it is highly likely that Caesar was referring to cockfighting (Serjeantson 2000a, 499).

This sport was certainly popular in parts of the Roman Empire, and the high numbers of cockerels at late Roman Silchester, Hampshire, for example, may indicate birds used in this way (Serjeantson 2000a, 499). The religious significance of cockerels in Roman Britain is attested by large numbers of their remains recovered at the Uley shrines in Gloucestershire, which were dedicated to Mercury (Levitan 1993). Birds, especially chickens, were also by far the most common offering in Romano-British graves (Philpott 1991, 201). On settlements, chickens are more frequent in major towns, military sites and villas, than rural and nucleated sites (Maltby 1997, 412), perhaps due to their use to feed the non-productive population (Grant 1989, 144). From this period through to the Middle Ages and beyond, chickens featured regularly in diets, although some areas were slow to adopt fowl husbandry, such as north and west Scotland where chickens were rare until the later Middle Ages (Serjeantson 1988). The overall picture, however, is of these birds becoming firmly entrenched in everyday British life, a legacy that endures into the present day.

Common pheasant

The common pheasant is seen by many as the quintessential English game bird, a fact belying its natural range, which probably stretched in a wide, discontinuous belt from the Pacific Ocean to the Black Sea (Blank 1984, 312). Present in Greece at least since the fifth century BC, the pheasant was first mentioned in Roman Italy by Pliny, Statius and Martial in the first century AD (Zeuner 1963, 458), likely spreading from there to other parts of the Empire. For Roman Britain, pheasant remains have been reported at a small number of sites: Yalden and Albarella (2009, 107) list eight, to which can be added finds at Clausentum (Macdonald 1958) and Silchester (Maltby 1984), both in Hampshire, and Chilgrove in Sussex (Outen 1979). Notably, most identified pheasant remains have been recovered from high-status settlements, perhaps suggesting that pheasants were imported as 'luxury' goods – certainly they were employed as a motif on mosaics of elite residences, although Witts (2005, 106) has argued that some of the pheasant-like birds may represent peacocks. There is currently little evidence to indicate that breeding populations were established in Roman Britain but it is possible that their distribution was wider and has simply been obscured by the problems of identifying their remains.

Pheasant remains are rarer still for the Saxon period, which led Yapp (1981, 31) to argue that the term *fasianus*, found in eighth- and tenth-century AD vocabularies, referred to capercaillies rather than pheasants. Since the publication of Yapp's (1981) book, however, pheasant remains have been reported at Fishergate in York (O'Connor 1991a) and at Flixborough (Dobney *et al.* 2007) and Lincoln (Dobney *et al.* 1996), both in Lincolnshire. Yalden and Albarella (2009, 107) also mention the purported specimen from Lewes, Sussex (Bedwin 1975), but this should be viewed with caution as the assemblage is largely post-Conquest in date, and re-analysis of the material revealed a high level of misidentification in the original analysis (N. Sykes pers. comm.). Of the Anglo-Saxon specimens that are confidently dated and identified, it may be significant that they come from sites with evidence for long-distance trade, perhaps suggesting that pheasants were occasionally imported as exotica. It is still unclear, therefore, whether pheasants became established in Britain shortly before AD 1066 (as suggested by Yalden and Albarella 2009, 107) or shortly after the Norman Conquest (Rackham 1997, 50). Until a comprehensive and detailed review of the zooarchaeological evidence is undertaken, it seems unlikely that this question will be answered (Sykes 2007, 63). As with chickens, pheasants were probably introduced later to Scotland than England, the earliest reference dating to AD 1578 (Lever 1977, 337–8), although probable pheasant feathers were recovered from fifteenth century AD Pluscarden Priory (Cerón-Carrasco 1994, 414).

Whilst the introduction date of the pheasant is unknown and may remain so, both the historical and archaeological evidence point to an increasing representation of pheasants through the course of the medieval period (Yalden and Albarella 2009, 101, table 5.1). For England, a charter from AD 1098 assigned 16 pheasants to monks in Rochester; a licence dated 1100 granted the Abbot of Malmesbury permission to kill hares and pheasants; and in 1249 the Sherriff of Kent was commanded to produce 24 pheasants for a feast for Henry III (Lever 1977, 336), although for Henry's 1251 Christmas feast, the number had risen to 290 (Rackham 1997, 119). The large numbers of pheasants mentioned in the historical sources are not mirrored in the archaeological record but this must surely be related to problems of identification. It seems likely that sizeable pheasant populations were maintained in the parks that became so common in the landscape from the twelfth century onwards (Rackham 1997, 123). The remains of three pheasants (two male, one female) recovered from thirteenth-century levels at King John's Hunting Lodge, Writtle, Essex (Bramwell 1969), which had a park, may be an example of this. Within these spaces, access to pheasants could be controlled, and the aristocracy could hunt them with hawks. Yet by the late fifteenth century the Crown had given legal protection to pheasants (Lever 1977, 377), suggesting that they had already established feral breeding populations. Through a mixture of these feral birds, and those bred for sport, the pheasant has become so widespread that it is now almost synonymous with the British countryside.

Blue Peafowl

Unlike pheasants, blue peafowl have never become established in Britain, retaining elite associations throughout their tenure. A native species of India, they were imported into Mediterranean countries from at least the time of the Persian Empire, gradually spreading west to Roman Italy, where they were bred in huge flocks during the late republican and early imperial periods (Toynbee 1973, 250). Peacock feathers were likely desirable items in themselves, and in many areas people could have been familiar with these before the live animal (Jackson 2006, 21), but feathers are seldom preserved archaeologically, a rare example being recovered from a mid-fourteenth century context in London (Egan 1998).

From Italy, live birds were distributed throughout Europe, although their bones are rare: there are only three examples for Roman France (Lepetz and Yvinec 2002, 35), three for Roman Britain, and two for Saxon Britain (Table 10). In contrast, peafowl remains on five sites dating to within a hundred years of the Norman Conquest support the idea of a Norman re-introduction (Sykes 2007, 63). The number of subsequent examples (Table 10) indicates that breeding populations must have been established soon after 1066. At Henry III's 1251 Christmas feast, 120 peafowl were served, and 104 peacocks were consumed at a feast for the Archbishop of York in the fifteenth century (Mead 1967, 33). That peacocks were high-status birds is clear from manuscripts, the iconographic evidence (e.g. the Bayeux Tapestry shows two peacocks in association with William I's palace), and the fact that peafowl bones are overwhelmingly recovered from high-status sites, in Britain and France (Sykes 2007, 63). However, it was not enough for a person simply to own a peacock; they also had to be *seen* to do so (Appadurai 1986, 31), the bright, distinctive plumage making them particularly attractive for display. A Roman recipe, adopted in the medieval period, recommends carefully removing the feathers before roasting the bird whole, then replacing the skin, and presenting the bird, often with considerable ceremony (Mead 1967, 88). Peacocks, however, had more than a purely aesthetic appeal; since early Christian times, they were considered symbolic of eternal life and Christ, and often depicted in funerary contexts. This may explain the use of peacock feather fans in Christian liturgical contexts, both in Italy and in England where one was in the possession of St Paul's Cathedral, London in AD 1295 and another at the abbey of Bury St Edmonds in AD 1429 (Green 2006, 45). However, attitudes to peacocks were also ambivalent, for their habit of strutting around displaying their tail feathers meant they were considered to symbolise the sin of Pride (Jackson 2006, 105). 'Proud as a peacock' is a well-known saying, and this bird continues to stand out from others. Whilst society has changed since it first arrived, its status as an exotic bird arguably has not.

Turkey

Turkeys also initially enjoyed an elevated status, although today they are seen as much more mundane. Imported from North America, these birds were originally thought to be either guinea-fowl, being termed *meleagris*, or a cross between a rooster and a peafowl, hence the term *gallopavo* (Crawford 1984, 326). Similarly, the name 'turkey' was also used to refer to the guinea fowl (Donkin 1991, 79) and so it is difficult to be certain to which bird the records relate. The earliest *certain* documentary evidence we have for turkeys dates to AD 1511 in Spain (Crawford 1984, 325), and 1541 in England, with the earliest bone finds dating to the mid-sixteenth century (Table 11). As suggested by Zeuner (1963, 457), the arrival of the turkey seems to have signalled a decline in the popularity of peacock, a shift in tastes that is reflected in the zooarchaeological record with the greater representation of turkey bones on post-medieval sites. However, peafowl were still served on special occasions in the eighteenth century AD, according to Oliver Goldsmith (Grahame 1984, 317). Turkey breeding populations seem to have been established quickly in many parts of Europe, with large flocks kept on the lower Rhine in 1571 (Zeuner 1963, 459). It is reasonable to assume that breeding was also taking place in Britain, with fragments of both turkey bones and eggshell recovered from 1560–1635 contexts at the Royal Navy Victualling Yard, London (West 1995).

As with pheasants and peacocks, the turkey's initial popularity amongst the upper classes likely derived from its relative rarity. From there, it gradually became more widely available, first appearing on the English Christmas menu in 1585 (Zeuner 1963, 459), and becoming a traditional Christmas food at some point in the early eighteenth century (Simon 1944).

Site	Site type	Date of specimen(s)	Reference
Portchester Castle, Hampshire	Fort	Late third-fourth century A.D.	Eastham 1975
Great Staughton, Cambridgeshire	Villa	Fourth century A.D.	Bramwell 1994
Winterton, Humberside	Villa	Roman	Hamilton-Dyer & Serjeantson pers comm.
Wicken Bonhunt, Essex	Rural/high status	A.D. 650–850	Crabtree 1996
Thetford, Norfolk	Urban	Late Saxon	Jones 1984
Nantwich, Cheshire	Urban/Castle	Tenth-early twelfth century A.D.	Fisher 1986
Westminster Abbey/Palace	Urban/Royal	*c.* A.D. 1040–1150	Reilly 2006
Faccombe Netherton, Hampshire	Manorial	A.D. 1070–1204	Sadler 1990
Carisbrooke Castle, Isle of Wight	Castle	Eleventh century A.D.	Serjeantson 2000b
Ludgershall Castle, Wiltshire	Castle	Early-middle twelfth century A.D.	Poole n.d.
Hereford, Herefordshire	Urban	Late eleventh-thirteenth century A.D.	Bramwell 1985
Guildhall, London	Urban	*c.* A.D. 1140–1230	Reilly 2007
16–22 Coppergate, York	Urban	A.D. 1150–1250	Bond & O'Connor 1999
Eastgate, Beverley, Humberside	Urban	Twelfth-fourteenth century A.D.	Scott 1992
Windsor Castle	Castle – Royal	Twelfth-fourteenth century A.D.	Baker pers comm.
Canterbury Cathedral Precincts, Kent	Urban/Ecclesiastical	Late twelfth–early fourteenth century A.D.	Driver 1990
Rattray Castle, Aberdeenshire	Castle	Early thirteenth–fifteenth century A.D.	Hamilton-Dyer *et al.* 1993
Manor of Beaurepaire, County Durham	Manorial	A.D. 1250–1400	Gidney 1995
York Minster, York	Urban/Ecclesiastical	Thirteenth century A.D.	Rowland pers comm.
Pevensey Castle, Sussex	Castle	Thirteenth-fifteenth century A.D.	Powell & Serjeantson n.d.
Cuckoo Lane Site A, Southampton	Urban/Wealthy	A.D. 1300–1350	Bramwell 1975a
Dudley Castle	Castle	A.D. 1321–1647	Thomas 2005
BC72 Site, London	Urban/Wealthy	Mid fourteenth century A.D.	Egan 1998
Wells Museum Garden, Somerset	Urban/Ecclesiastical	A.D. 1360–1370	White n.d.
Kingston Lacey Estate, Dorset	Manorial	Fourteenth-fifteenth century A.D.	Locker 1994
Brighton Hill South, Hampshire	Village	Late fourteenth-mid/late fifteenth century A.D.	Coy 1995

TABLE 10: Results of literature survey for sites where peafowl have been identified.

Helmeted Guineafowl

More than any other of the birds discussed here, the history of guinea fowl in Britain is beset by documentary and skeletal identification problems. Originating from Africa, where they are/have been known in sub-Saharan areas and the Atlas Mountains, and possibly present in the Nile Valley during

Site	Site type	Date of specimen(s)	Reference
1–5 Aldwark, York	Urban	Late fifteenth century A.D.	Bond & O'Connor 1999
Odiham Castle, Hampshire	Castle	Late fifteenth century A.D.	Hamilton-Dyer n.d.
Wickham Glebe, Hampshire	Manorial	Early/Mid Medieval	Coy 1985
Wickham Glebe, Hampshire	Manorial	Late Medieval	Coy 1985
Middleton Stoney Castle, Oxfordshire	Castle	Late Medieval	Levitan 1984
Barnard Castle, County Durham	Castle	Medieval	Jones *et al.* 1985
Castle Rising Castle, Norfolk	Castle	Medieval	Jones *et al.* 1997
Town Ditch, Newcastle-Upon-Tyne	Urban	Medieval	Gidney 1989
Baynard's Castle, London	Urban/Castle	*c.* A.D. 1520	Bramwell 1975b
Castle Ditch, Newcastle-Upon Tyne	Castle	*c.* A.D. 1525–1550	Alison 1981
Finsbury Pavement, London	Urban	Sixteenth century A.D.	Locker & Reilly 1997
Castle Rising Castle, Norfolk	Castle	Sixteenth century A.D.	Jones *et al.* 1997
Royal Navy Victualling Yard, London	Urban	A.D. 1560–1635	West 1995
Camber Castle, East Sussex	Castle	Mid sixteenth century A.D. –A.D. 1637	Connell *et al.* 1997
Eynsham Abbey, Oxfordshire	Wealthy	Mid sixteenth-mid seventeenth century A.D.	Ingrem 2003
Gold Hill, Shaftesbury, Dorset	Urban	Sixteenth-seventeenth century A.D.	Serjeantson 1985
Norton Priory	Wealthy	Late sixteenth-seventeenth century A.D.	Greene 1989
Castle Bastion, Newcastle-Upon-Tyne	Castle	Seventeenth century A.D.	Rackham 1983
Chantry House	Urban/wealthy	Seventeenth century A.D.	Curl pers comm.
York Minster, York	Urban/Ecclesiastical	Seventeenth century A.D.	Rowland pers comm.
London Aldgate	Urban	A.D. 1670–1700	Armitage 1984
Castle Rising Castle, Norfolk	Castle	Post-Medieval	Jones *et al.* 1997
Aldwark, York	Urban	Post-Medieval	O'Connor 1984a
Town Wall, Coventry	Urban	Eighteenth century A.D.	Bramwell 1986
Bewsey Old Hall, Warrington	Wealthy	Eighteenth century A.D.	Roberts 1986
Sackler Library, Oxford	Urban	Early nineteenth century A.D.	Charles and Ingrem 2001

TABLE 10 continued.

Roman times (D. Yalden pers. comm.), these birds had reached Greece by the fifth century BC, and Roman Italy by the first century AD (Zeuner 1963, 457). The only possible evidence from elsewhere in Europe is a mosaic in Cologne, Germany, and 'leg bone' at the Roman frontier camp at Saalburg in Germany (Donkin 1991, 22). Whether this reflects true scarcity or misidentification is impossible to say, although guinea fowl were something of a rarity even in

Site name	Site type	Date	Reference
Hull Magistrates Court	Urban/Ecclesiastical	*c.* A.D. 1310–1600	Dobney n.d.
Castle Mall, Norwich	Urban	Mid/late fourteenth–mid sixteenth century A.D.	Albarella *et al.* 1997
Whitefriars, Coventry	Urban	A.D. 1545–1558	Rackham 2005
Barnstaple, Devon	Urban	Sixteenth century A.D.	Bourdillon n.d.
Beeston Castle, Cheshire	Castle	*c.* A.D. 1500–1600	Dobney n.d.
Manor of Beaurepaire, County Durham	Wealthy	*c.* A.D. 1500–1600	Gidney 1995
Durham Cathedral	Urban/Ecclesiastical	*c.* A.D. 1500–1600	Dobney n.d.
Royal Navy Victualling Yard, London	Urban	A.D. 1560–1635	West 1995
Heigham Street, Norwich	Urban	*c.* A.D. 1575–1625	Weinstock 2002
Hull Magistrates Court	Urban	*c.* A.D. 1500–1750	Dobney n.d.
Preceptory of the Knights Hospitallers, Beverley	Urban	*c.* A.D. 1500–1750	Dobney n.d.
South Castle Street, Liverpool	Urban	*c.* A.D. 1500–1750	Dobney n.d.
Exeter, Devon	Urban	Mid sixteenth century A.D.	Maltby 1979
Camber Castle	Castle	Mid sixteenth century A.D. –A.D. 1637	Connell *et al.* 1997
Hereford, Herefordshire	Urban	Sixteenth century A.D. and later	Noddle and Hamilton-Dyer 2002
Reading Abbey	Wealthy/urban	Sixteenth–seventeenth century A.D.	Coy 1986-90
Castle Ditch, Newcastle	Urban	Late sixteenth–seventeenth century A.D.	Allison 1981
Norton Priory	Wealthy	Late sixteenth–seventeenth century A.D.	Greene 1989
Alms Lane, Norwich	Urban	A.D. 1600–1675	Harman 1985
Royal Navy Victualling Yard, London	Urban	A.D. 1635–1726	West 1995

Italy, according to Roman writers (Zeuner 1963, 457). After the Roman period, there is no evidence of guinea fowl in Europe until the Middle Ages, when late fourteenth- and fifteenth-century French references are thought to be reliable (Donkin 1991, 43). By the sixteenth century they had reached Britain, although confusion over naming means we cannot be certain of the exact date. As today, whilst the turkey was widely adopted throughout Europe for food, the guinea fowl was probably more prized for display (Donkin 1991, 84).

TABLE 11: Results of literature survey for sites where turkey has been identified.

Site name	Site type	Date	Reference
Camber Castle	Castle	A.D. 1637+	Connell *et al.* 1997
Exeter, Devon	Urban	A.D. 1660–1700	Maltby 1979
Worcester Cathedral, Worcester	Urban/Ecclesiastical	Seventeenth century A.D.	Thomas 1999
Castle Bastion, Newcastle-Upon-Tyne	Urban	Mid seventeenth century A.D.	Rackham 1983
Aldgate, London	Urban	Late seventeenth century A.D.	Armitage 1984
Cook's Green, Winchelsea, Sussex	Rural	Seventeenth century A.D.	Clements 1990
St Ebbe's, Oxford	Urban	Seventeenth century A.D.	Wilson 1984
Castle Mall, Norwich	Urban	Late sixteenth–eighteenth century A.D.	Albarella *et al.* 1997
Skeldergate and Walmgate, York	Urban	Late seventeenth century A.D.	O'Connor 1984b
Christchurch, Dorset	Urban	Seventeenth–eighteenth century A.D.	Coy 1983
Alms Lane, Norwich	Urban	A.D. 1720–1750	Harman 1985
Exeter, Devon	Urban	A.D. 1660–1800	Maltby 1979
Castle Mall, Norwich	Urban	Late sixteenth–eighteenth century A.D.	Albarella *et al.* 1997
St Mary's Guildhall, Lincoln	Urban	Late seventeenth–late nineteenth century A.D.	O'Connor 1991c
St Peters Lane, Leicester	Urban	Eighteenth century A.D.	Gidney 1992
Bewsey Old Hall, Warrington	Wealthy	Eighteenth century A.D.	Roberts 1986
Westgate Road, Newcastle	Urban	Mid/late eighteenth century A.D.	Gidney 1994
Launceston Castle, Cornwall	Urban	Eighteenth–nineteenth century A.D.	Albarella & Davis 1996
The Bull Ring, Birmingham	Urban	Eighteenth–nineteenth century A.D.	Baxter 2009

TABLE II continued.

Conclusion

Despite the many problems of identification, the legacy of domestic fowl, pheasant, peacock, turkey and guinea fowl introductions is clear. All have affected British society in some way, whilst their relative importance varied over time. At first, all would have been rare, and sought after by elites as a way of constructing their social position. As some, namely chickens and turkeys, became more accessible to other sections of society, their roles as status markers would have diminished, although they remained significant, both in the diet, and symbolically.

CHAPTER 19

Freshwater Fish

Alison Locker

Introduction

The British marine and freshwater indigenous fish fauna was established at the end of the last Ice Age. Euryhaline species (i.e. fish tolerant of both fresh and salt water) penetrated freshwater via newly established coastal waters as glaciers melted, whilst stenohaline species (salt intolerant) colonised via tributaries of rivers on the land bridge joining Britain to the continent. This chapter concentrates on fish in freshwater systems, which were increasingly altered by anthropogenic factors affecting species reliant on freshwater for all or part of their lifecycle.

Maitland and Campbell (1992, 47) list the indigenous freshwater species of Britain as follows; these are based on Wheeler 1977:

Via the sea (Euryhaline)	**Via the land bridge (Stenohaline)**
Sea Lamprey (*Petromyzon marinus*)	Grayling (*Thymallus thymallus*)
River Lamprey (*Lampetra fluviatilis*)	Pike (*Esox lucius*)
Brook Lamprey (*Lampetra planeri*)	Barbel (*Barbus barbus*)
Sturgeon (*Acipenser sturio*)	Gudgeon (*Gobio gobio*)
Allis shad (*Alosa alosa*)	Tench (*Tinca tinca*)
Twaite shad (*Alosa fallax*)	Silver bream (*Blicca bjoerkna*)
Atlantic salmon (*Salmo salar*)	Bream (*Abramis brama*)
Brown trout (*Salmo trutta*)	Bleak (*Alburnus alburnus*)
Arctic charr (*Salvinus alpinus*)	Minnow (*Phoxinus phoxinus*)
Houting (*Coregonus oxyrinchus*)	Rudd (*Scardinius erythrophthalmus*)
Powan (*Coregonus lavaretus*)	Roach (*Rutilus rutilus*)
Pollan (*Coregonus autumnalis*)	Chub (*Leuciscus cephalus*)
Vendace (*Coregonus albula*)	Dace (*Leuciscus leuciscus*)
Smelt (*Osmerus eperlanus*)	Spined loach (*Cobitis taenia*)
Eel (*Anguilla anguilla*)	Stone loach (*Noemacheilus barbatulus*)
3 spined stickleback (*Gasterosteus aculeatus*)	Burbot (*Lota lota*)
9 spined stickleback (*Pungitius pungitius*)	Perch (*Perca fluviatilis*)

Sea bass (*Dicentrarchus labrax*)

Common goby (*Pomatoschistus microps*)

Thick-lipped grey mullet (*Chelon labrosus*)

Thin-lipped grey mullet (*Liza ramada*)

Golden mullet (*Liza aurata*)

Flounder (*Platichthys flesus*)

Ruffe (*Gymnocephalus cernuus*)

Bullhead (*Cottus gobio*)

The number of indigenous species in Britain is low because of the relatively short existence of the land bridge and the low number of euryhaline species. This 'island effect', particularly in the west and north, compares poorly with continental Europe. Neither Ireland (Fitzsimons and Igoe 2004) or Scotland (Maitland and Campbell 1992, 50) have indigenous stenohaline species, and the number of euryhaline fish is low, fourteen for Ireland and fifteen for Scotland, though not all species are shared. Stenohaline species were initially concentrated in the south and east of England, closest to their continental origins and a few, including burbot, ruffe and spined loach, retained that distribution. Some natural redistribution is likely to have resulted from postglacial changes in land levels, melting ice and flooding. However Jacobi's comment (1978, 328) that 'there is at present very little convincing evidence from England for the exploitation of freshwater fishes in the Mesolithic' remains substantially true 30 years on. Most prehistoric peoples, other than coastal dwellers, appear to have eaten little fish, especially freshwater fish, according to the archaeological record. The Neolithic and Bronze Age bone evidence is poor, with marginally more data from the Iron Age. The Roman evidence is more abundant, favouring eel and salmonids among species from freshwaters, but exploitation would have had little impact on fish stocks (Locker 2007).

At this juncture it is useful to point out that the identification of archaeological fish bones can be difficult, especially when fragmentary, and there are often large numbers of generally nonspecific bones such as ribs and fin rays. The most easily identified bones are usually vertebrae and those from the skull, though it is sometimes difficult to progress beyond family level. A typical example, and particularly relevant here, is the Cyprinidae. This family includes barbel, gudgeon, tench, silver bream, bleak, minnow, rudd, roach, chub, dace and carp. Most cyprinid vertebrae and skull bones are very similar between species, except for the pharyngeal bones. These are paired, with a characteristic shape, number and arrangement of teeth. Cyprinid fish grind the food against horny pads; teeth are absent in the upper and lower jaws. Pharyngeal bones are robust, survive well, and are relatively easy to identify, as are single teeth broken off the main bone, especially carp in which the teeth are very distinctive. The toothed dorsal fin rays of carp and barbel are also characteristic, though in other cyprinids (and many other fish) fin rays are nonspecific. There are many other species with distinctive bones, teeth, denticles, scales or bone texture which aid identification and are too numerous to describe here.

Returning to species dispersal, more recent expansions have been effected by people, some accidentally, for example through canals (Maitland and Campbell 1992, 51) and some deliberately, particularly in Ireland and Scotland, often by anglers both as quarry and live bait (*ibid.*, 50). In the latter case the dates are unknown but later than the fourteenth century. The Scottish and Irish archaeological record is, at best, poor for stenohaline fish. In England the range of these species was initially extended through fish pond culture, which became a sophisticated system of breeding and raising freshwater fish for the table and live fish were transported great distances to stock elaborate pond systems. This was first practised among high-status secular society after 1066, then on monastic estates where it reached its apogee (Currie 1989, 147).

Anthropogenic dispersal is unlikely before the medieval period when evidence from both bones and documents suggests greater fish consumption (Serjeantson and Woolgar 2006, 102). Conversely, the construction of mill weirs, altering watercourses, accelerated from early medieval times. This restricted the access of migrating species, such as salmon, to their freshwater spawning grounds exerting some pressure by the fourteenth century, when documentary sources show the use of weirs was restricted by law. Eels, which as immature 'glass' eels enter freshwater systems to mature and later return to the sea as adults to spawn, were also caught in large numbers. The Domesday Survey in AD 1086 records around 6,000 water mills in England (Wheeler 1979, 11) and these were particularly common in the middle Thames valley. Wheeler (*ibid.*) describing the effects of medieval 'industrialisation' and commercial navigation of the Thames cites thirteen corn mills on the Wandle at Domesday rising to 24 by AD 1610. The addition of fulling mills in the fourteenth century and dyeing mills in the sixteenth and seventeenth centuries increasingly polluted and obstructed parts of the river. Sewage and other domestic waste is potentially fatal to fish that require higher levels of dissolved oxygen, such as grayling, and trout. Others, including some cyprinids, are tolerant of low oxygen, stagnant conditions and will feed on organic waste. These factors, plus silting as increased tillage, both more intensive and extensive, led to exposed soils being washed into watercourses, would have locally influenced the suitability of the most utilised waterways for some species. Growing pressure on freshwater fish stocks has been shown to mirror the expansion of sea fisheries, firstly for herring and then cod, from the tenth century (Barrett *et al.* 2004, 628).

However, the need to conserve stocks by limiting the fishing season and ensuring free passage for migrating fish was recognised. Salmon fisheries in Scotland were regulated by a closed season from AD 1030 by royal edict. The Magna Carta (AD 1215) stipulated the dismantling of the king's fish weir to protect salmon, and in AD 1285 the Statute of Westminster specified penalties for salmon poaching (Montgomery 2003, 62). While numbers of some indigenous species have become very precarious today, only the houting and the burbot are officially extinct in the Britain, both within the twentieth century. They were always minority species, restricted to eastern England. Houting (described below) has not been identified in archaeological deposits. Burbot has been identified, but rarely, for example in medieval deposits at Whittlesea Mere, Cambridgeshire (Irving 1998, 37) and Roman and medieval deposits from Tanner Row, York (O'Connor 1988, 114). Burbot was last recorded in England in 1972 (Maitland and Campbell 1992, 263). A victim of pollution and restricted watercourses, houting numbers have been heavily reduced in the western Baltic (Wheeler 1979, 74). Burbot remains established in rivers and lakes in northern, west and central Europe, northern Asia and North America (Maitland and Campbell 1992, 263).

Euryhaline species

Space limits discussion to a few euryhaline species. Glacial relicts such as the arctic charr, powan, pollan (only in Ireland) and vendace always had restricted distributions and were a very localised source of food. Houting, a non breeding vagrant 'whitefish' and closely related to powan, pollan and vendace, entered brackish waters from the east coast of England. The archaeological record for 'whitefishes' is silent, specific identifications can be difficult, and some may have been generically listed as 'salmonids'. Salmonid bones are particularly friable, especially the skull (Butler and Chatters 1994). The other species have all been exploited for food on a seasonal basis tied to migration. Stickleback occurs in many archaeological samples, though may be incidental being caught with other small fish, or the stomach contents of carnivorous fish such as pike. The adaptation of flounder to brackish water and the lower reaches of rivers is reflected in a prolific archaeological record.

Only one species of sturgeon has been found in British waters, the Atlantic sturgeon, classed as a non-breeding vagrant. This status has been recently challenged, but only on the basis of recorded sightings in rivers usually being in the breeding season (Knight 2007). Once seen occasionally in the lower reaches of rivers including the Severn and the Thames, the archaeological finds are usually the large distinctive dermal scutes and pectoral fin spines, and are more common from post-Roman levels. Much of the skeleton is made of cartilage, like sharks and rays, and does not survive. Sturgeon remains were found at Flixborough (close to the river Trent), in late seventh to tenth-century deposits for which Barrett (2002), in the context of other finds, suggests high status. A royal fish since at least the twelfth century (Hagen 1995, 160), and the property of the crown, it was also elevated by rarity, impressive size and appearance, featuring in medieval menus and household accounts. To meet demand sturgeon was imported in barrels and also mimicked using veal (Hoffmann 1996, 649). Mrs Beeton (1982, 162) included it among her fish recipes in the mid-nineteenth century, but describes it as 'rare in the London market' as by then numbers had seriously declined from pollution. There is evidence of a reduction in the size of sturgeon caught in the Baltic and the Low Countries in the medieval period as a result of blocked waterways and pollution (Hoffmann 1996, 649). Sturgeon finds are too few in Britain to detect a similar trend, but waterways were similarly affected. Although a rare sight today in British waters, sturgeon were once occasional but regular visitors, and a status food.

Prior to AD 1300 the most seasonally abundant euryhaline fish were salmon and eel. Although their need to access freshwater systems was recognised and safeguarded by legislation as early as the twelfth century, salmon suffered from obstructed waterways, overfishing and pollution. Wheeler (1979, 54) considered Thames salmon were virtually extinct by AD 1861, and questioned whether they were ever as prolific there as some of the literature implies. Recent river improvement schemes have helped restore numbers and wild salmon are still found in many rivers, in the west of England and Wales (Ayton 1998), Scotland (Williamson 1991, 39) and Ireland (Vickers 1988, 3), albeit often in low numbers and facing health problems transmitted by farmed fish. A greater risk to salmon numbers today is the large number of smolts that die at sea leaving just 10 per cent surviving to return to their natal rivers in Scotland, a rapid decline since 1960 when almost 50 per cent survived (Graham-Stewart 2007, 25). A complex range of sea changes, in particular a currently high North Atlantic Oscillation Index (Sutterby and Greenhalgh 2005, 14), seem likely to have contributed to this decline and are being researched by the 'Salmon at Sea' (SALSEA) research programme. Today a valuable anglers' fish and a prime food fish, classified as over-fished and at risk (Marine Conservation Society), wild Atlantic salmon have been an important catch in Britain from prehistory. Many traditional methods of capture remain basically unchanged, as shown by the variety of nets and wicker traps used on the Severn (Waters 1987). Salmon (and trout) were totemic animals of Celtic myth, particularly in Ireland and associated with wisdom (Ross 1967, 350), often in association with hazelnuts, both of which were found at Mesolithic sites such as Mount Sandel, on the river Bann in Ireland (Van Wijngaarden-Bakker 1986, 73; Woodman 1978, 343). The only other fish honoured in this way is the eel (Matthews 2002, 152) representing both wisdom and inspiration like salmon, and some Irish myths suggest certain eels could turn into weapons. Both species were mysterious in their migration and for Ireland the most abundant fish in freshwater. This ancient connection may have inspired their totemic value and their Celtic status may have a very ancient origin. However, prior to the medieval period, salmon were unlikely to have been under any significant pressure.

Eel is among the most common of all fish identified in archaeological assemblages. As arriving elvers or departing adults they were trapped in thousands. Young eels were 'grown on' in ponds and so abundant they were used as currency for medieval rents. Eels are robust fish, able to live out of water for some time, slithering across damp areas to find water. Although they were so commonly eaten, there is no evidence of any threat to their numbers before AD 1300.

Stenohaline Species

The prehistoric archaeological record for stenohaline fish is limited; there are fewer inland sites with fish assemblages. The data are greater for the Roman period (Locker 2007) reflected in a larger number of sites. The potential of some species was realised in pond culture which developed from the eleventh century, firstly in England in store ponds. Sophisticated pond systems evolved to provide a year round source of fresh fish for rich landowners, clergy and royalty and were a status symbol. Species tolerant of low levels of dissolved oxygen were particularly suitable. Pike, perch, tench, bream, roach, chub and dace were the most favoured and spread across Britain. Maitland and Campbell (1992, 49) comment on the distribution of pike and perch mirroring ecclesiastical establishments in Scotland and present by the end of the sixteenth century. Both species can be transported live wrapped in damp moss or sacking.

Angling was both a sport, first practised by early medieval landed gentry (Hagen 1995, 161), and a source of food, freshwater fish were exempt from game laws and open to all on public waterways. Promoted as a noble, though more contemplative, pastime along with hunting and hawking, there were many books on angling, the earliest being 'Treatyse of fyssynge wyth an angle' in the *Boke of St Albans*, written between AD 1406 and AD 1450 (Currie 1991, 102). Isaac Walton's *Complete Angler* of AD 1653 (1985), which also satirised the effects of order imposed on Puritan England (Franklin 1996, 441), commended angling over other hunting sports, a perfect compromise between peace and civility and excitement and fraternity (*ibid.*), a gentleman's pastime with specific codes of practice. The popularity of angling as a sport across the social divide was realised with the development of the railways in the nineteenth century, as anglers from increasingly urbanised England could access distant rivers and lakes. Cheaper coarse fishing was associated with the working classes, thus retaining social distinction, and fishing clubs and angling holidays became popular (*ibid.*, 443). It is during this period that some fish were introduced beyond their natural range, such as brown trout to many parts of Scotland. Live bait species, such as gudgeon, minnow, roach and dace, were brought by anglers for pike and other carnivorous fish, following a northerly route as new rail lines expanded the angling landscape (Maitland and Campbell 1992, 49).

Ireland had no indigenous stenohaline species and the first evidence for pike is of interest. The earliest archaeological evidence to date is from Trim Castle in late thirteenth to early fourteenth-century deposits, though Hamilton-Dyer (2007, 113) also considers the possibility these bones may be from stored imported fish. Barbé and Garrett (2007) refer to the use of the Irish name for pike (*lius*) as early as AD 1400 and postulate that pike may have been native. However, the genetic variability of pike from England and Ireland is narrow, the 'founder effect', typical of populations initially from a small number of colonisers, and consistent with dispersal from their native south east England progressively north and west (Maitland and Campbell 1992, 169), thus supporting introduction to Ireland. Recorded Irish exports to England in the late fifteenth and early sixteenth centuries (Longfield 1929, 49), suggest that by that time pike was already well established. No other stenohaline species have yet been identified from archaeological deposits in Ireland within the time frame examined here and Hamilton-Dyer (2007) considers their introduction is twelfth century at the earliest.

Introductions

The only fish introduced to Britain close to the end of the time period is carp (*Cyprinus carpio*). Current evidence places it not earlier than the fourteenth century. Other European imports, such as the goldfish (*Carassius auratus*), possibly Crucian carp (*Carassius carassius,* both included and excluded as native to the SE England, Maitland and Campbell 1992, 47, 186, but now generally viewed as native by biologists), bitterling (*Rhodeus sericus*), orfe (*Leuciscus idus*), Danubian catfish (*Siluris glanis*), and pikeperch (*Stizostedion lucioperca*) are comparatively recent, within the last few centuries.

Before AD 1300 the anthropogenic spread of stenohaline species would have been for food. Species with a tolerance for low oxygen were the prime fish for pond culture, particularly carp, tench and bream, which are cyprinids, as are roach, chub, barbel and dace which were also important. Though not cyprinids, pike and perch were commonly kept and the former highly valued. To date, the documentary evidence for carp is more abundant than the bone evidence. The robust and distinctive pharyngeal bones of this species survive well and their rarity in the archaeological record compared to other cyprinids would seem to reflect a true scarcity. The documentary evidence also provides the earliest record. There is no reference to carp in ponds in Britain before AD 1350, when bream and pike were the most popular fish on royal tables (Currie 1991, 98). The Duke of Norfolk kept carp on his estate in AD 1462 (*ibid.,* 101). Sir John Howard stocked his ponds with carp, as well as bream, tench, roach and perch in AD 1467/8 (Wilson 1973, 37, 36). Prior More of Worcester first stocked his ponds with a few carp as a trial in AD 1531 (Hickling 1971, 120). By AD 1530 there are records of carp in Norfolk, Suffolk, Hampshire, London, Surrey, Worcestershire and Gloucestershire (Currie 1991, 103)

The carp is indigenous to eastern Europe. Hoffmann (1995, 70) maps the pre AD 600 bone and verbal records which cluster round its natural distribution in the Danube basin and cites Cassiodorus (the minister for the kings of sixth-century Italy) who listed Danube carp among fish served to visitors. These Gothic kings would have already encountered carp in its native range. European records from AD 600 chart the movement of carp from the lower Danube westwards (Hoffmann 1995, 73). Prior to the twelfth century there are no references to carp in ponds, which Hoffmann (1994, 142) proposes as evidence that these fish were wild. Carp remains have been identified across Europe and there is a strong documentary record, for example AD 1245 in Northern France and AD 1258 for Paris. The faunal record is not so precisely dated but includes specimens dated to the thirteenth to fourteenth century for Northern Holland and the fourteenth century for Paris (*ibid.* 140). Carp are likely to have been brought over to England either as a gift or by an enterprising pond culturalist. Currie (1991, 102) suggests the Low Countries with a developed aquaculture may have been the source and, with strong connections to East Anglia, the first carp would have been in the south east of England. The earliest written record is from AD 1346 October 13th at Canterbury for eight pike and carp costing 22 shillings from the kitchen accounts of the household of Edward III. They were purchased, so not from the royal fishponds, but there is no indication of the source (NA PRO). The coronation feast of Henry VI in AD 1429 at Westminster featured carp in the third course, with pike in the first and bream in the second courses. Later records of carp in ponds also include letters between the king's commissioners and the new owners of Tichfield Abbey in Hampshire in AD 1537, discussing the stocking of ponds with 500 carp yielding sales of twenty to thirty pounds a year after three to four years (Currie 1984, 21), and Henry VIII ordered carp to be stocked in ponds at Cornbury Park, Oxfordshire (Bond and Chambers 1988, 366). A survey of twelfth to fourteenth-century royal fishponds includes bream, pike, tench and other fish but not carp, supporting a fifteenth-century date of introduction as a pond fish (Steane 1988, 39). Royal fishponds might be expected to be the first to stock these prestigious fish.

The bone evidence from Britain is currently sparse compared to Europe (Hoffman 1994, 140). To date the earliest finds are serrated dorsal spines and circumorbital bones from fifteenth-century deposits excavated at King's School, Ely, Cambridgeshire (Humphrey and Jones 2002). A serrated dorsal spine was identified from a Tudor pit at Little Pickle, Surrey (Bullock 1994, 269). A number of carp bones were identified from Nonsuch Palace, Surrey, of sixteenth and seventeenth century date, including the characteristic pharyngeal bones and serrated dorsal spines (Locker 2005). A serrated dorsal fin spine was also attributed to pre-AD 1538 deposits. These dorsal spines are distinctive, but can be confused with barbel as seems to have been the case at Lincoln in a Roman deposit (Irving 1996, 53) since amended to barbel by Van Neer (pers. comm.). One other carp bone was cited in late medieval deposits at Lincoln, but the date and anatomy remain unconfirmed. In the case of the King's School carp, the authors emphasise the particular care taken with the identifications. Here and at both Little Pickle and Nonsuch Palace the association is likely to be high status, if not royal. There is a carp spine from Higham Ferrers, a Roman deposit, but the provenance is poor and it is likely to be intrusive (R. Nicholson pers. comm.)

Despite the monastic contribution to fishpond culture (McDonnell 1981) the evidence does not place them at the forefront of carp husbandry in Britain, though the King's School site had an association with the Bishop of Ely and Prior More of Worcester recorded carp in his ponds (Hickling 1971, 120). Carp seemingly only became commonplace from the sixteenth century but rapidly became the prize pond fish according to Taverner in AD 1600 (Hickling 1962, 25). Carp mature more quickly than bream, previously the most favoured pond species, and are very tolerant of low oxygen (0.7 mg/l). A limit on their distribution is temperature; the minimum for spawning is 18°C. Some Scottish and Irish populations only breed in warmer summers, and carp activity levels are closely related to temperature. Carp also need a certain level of fat to overwinter successfully (Maitland and Campbell 1992, 182).

Conclusions

There is no evidence that British fish fauna suffered any extinctions before AD 1300, but contemporary legislation suggests that medieval obstruction and pollution of waterways had begun began to impact on fish numbers, contributing to future localised extinctions. The development of pond culture from the Norman Conquest reflects demand for fish when religious 'fish days' comprised half the year. Initially an elite occupation, pond culture gradually became more widespread and commercial. Some species indigenous to south east England were gradually spread through anthropogenic means. The only introduced species is carp, currently dated to the fourteenth century, and integral to pond culture. The archaeological record for carp is poor to date; they are first documented in kitchen accounts of AD 1346. Were these fish bought from local unrecorded pond stocks, or from abroad, salted, fresh or live, transported in wet straw or moss? New data will doubtless emerge and archaeological finds have an important role to play. Carp will continue to thrive in an extending range in rising temperatures, a victor in any global warming.

Acknowledgements.

I would like to thank James Barrett, Sheila Hamilton-Dyer, Jennifer Harland and Rebecca Nicholson for access to unpublished data, Wim van Neer regarding the Lincoln carp, Steven Brindle for the 1346 carp reference, Hannah Russ for drawing my attention to a particular paper and Gordon Copp regarding the status of Crucian carp.

CHAPTER 20

Land and Freshwater Molluscs

Paul Davies

Introduction

Any study of past extinctions and introductions is based upon a sound knowledge of the current distribution of species. From its inception in 1876, The Conchological Society of Great Britain and Ireland had a strong interest in species' geographical distribution and was able to build upon earlier work at a county level (e.g. Lowe 1853, and others quoted in Kerney 1999). In 1961 the Society formally launched its latest major national mapping initiative based upon 10 km national grid squares, with the preliminary results published in Kerney (1976) and a more detailed update published in Kerney (1999). As pointed out in the 1999 update, the level of detail which we know about molluscan distributions in the British Isles and Ireland is probably unparalleled with comparison to any other invertebrate group.

The national mapping scheme has given us a superb database of what species presently live where within Britain and Ireland. Above and beyond that, the scheme has also incorporated fossil occurrences from molluscan studies concerned with late-Quaternary landscape change (e.g. Kerney *et al.* 1980; Preece 1980) and with the setting of prehistoric archaeological sites (e.g. Evans 1999; Evans *et al.* 1988). The combination of modern and past occurrences within the scheme has allowed us to determine whether species are likely to be native (that is, arrived in the British Isles under their own powers of dispersal), probably native (likely to have arrived under their own accord but not definitively proven to have done so by the fossil record), or are introductions (brought here by accident or deliberate introduction, Tables 12 and 13). It also clearly highlights some species that the fossil record shows were here in the past but for which there are no modern records (i.e. they are now extinct in Britain and Ireland, Table 14). However, it is necessary to point out that this has only been possible for those molluscan species with a recognisable shell, since it is the shell that is preserved in ancient deposits. While the present distribution of non-shelled Mollusca (i.e. slugs) is therefore known, the fossil record is unable to shed light on their native or non-native status.

Period in which introduced	Species	Notes
Prehistory	*Cochlicella acuta*	Most probably a late prehistoric introduction. Present in a pre-later Iron Age soil at Stackpole Warren, Dyfed (Benson *et al.* 1990).
	Monacha cartusiana	A 'weed' species present from the Neolithic period onward.
Roman/Romano-British	*Oxychilus draparnaudi*	A Mediterranean species.
	Balea biplicata	Known from a few Roman sites only and presently restricted to the Thames area near London.
	Candidula gigaxii	A 'weed' species.
	Cernuella virgata	A 'weed' species.
	Monacha cantiana	A 'weed' species probably introduced in the late Roman period.
	Helix aspersa	A mainly Mediterranean species probably introduced accidentally via trade routes.
	Helix pomatia	Probably introduced during the Roman period for food.
Medieval	*Oxychilus helveticus*	Known only from Post-Roman sites.
	Cecilioides acicula	A Mediterranean species. Although found in prehistoric deposits the species can burrow to about 2m and it is therefore probably intrusive in pre-Medieval deposits.
	Candidula intersecta	No pre-Medieval records in the UK.
Recent	*Paralaoma caputspinulae*	First recorded in 1985. Originally Australasian.
	Helicodiscus singleyanus	First recorded in 1975. Origin in North America.
	Semilimax pyrenaicus	Found in Ireland only. Probably an 18th or 19th Century introduction.
	Bradybaena fruticum	A 20th Century introduction with a few occurrences recorded in south east England. Now probably extinct.
	Trochoidea elegans	Recorded in 1890 from Kent.
	Cochlicella barbara	Probably introduced in the 1970s. Restricted to a few south-western coastal parts of the UK
	Hygromia cinctella	First recorded at Paignton, Devon in 1950. The species is now expanding northwards.
	Hygromia limbata	First recorded in 1917 in Devon. Now spreading northwards.
	Theba pisana	A Mediterranean 'weed' species probably introduced in the 19th Century.

Late-Glacial and Postglacial faunal changes

TABLE 12. Introduced terrestrial species. Data from Kerney (1999).

Studies of well-dated fossil sequences have allowed a very detailed picture of molluscan colonisation of the British Isles and Ireland since the last glacial period. Kerney (1977) first proposed molluscan biozones (in effect the molluscan equivalent of the well established Late-glacial and postglacial pollen zones) for south-eastern England, and these have since been amended in the light of further intensive study and dating at Holywell Coombe near Folkestone (Preece and Bridgland 1998; 1999). The molluscan biozones are set out in Table 15.

As one would expect, these biozones clearly mirror the climatically-driven vegetation changes in the Late-glacial to mid-postglacial periods, with open-country, cold-climate faunas (Zones *y* and *z*) giving way to shade-tolerant or shade-demanding faunas indicative of mid-postglacial temperate woodland (Zones *a–d*). The most recent zones (*e–f*) show the re-emergence and expansion

Species	Notes
Potamopyrgus antipodarium	Introduced sometime prior to 1852. Probable New Zealand origin.
Physa spp.	One species (*Physa fontinalis*) is native, but other poorly-defined species are probably 19th Century introductions from North America.
Menetus dilatatus	First recorded in 1869, origin probably eastern USA.
Ferrissia wautieri	A very recent (1976) introduction from North Africa.
Musculium transversum	First recorded in 1856, of North American origin
Dreissena polymorpha	An introduction from the Caspian/Black Sea around 1820, probably via timber imported from the Baltic.

TABLE 13. Introduced freshwater species. Data from Kerney (1999).

of open-country faunas, though now temperate rather than cold-climate ones, as prehistoric and historic farming activity transformed the British Isles into a mosaic of grassland, arable and woodland.

Several points are worthy of note. First, some species that colonised the British Isles as the last glacial maximum came to an end, and (relatively) warmer Late-glacial and early postglacial conditions persisted, themselves subsequently became extinct as conditions became warmer still and temperate woodland developed. *Columella columella*, for example, is an arctic-alpine species which was a characteristic element of the Late-glacial and early postglacial periods (Table 15), but which became extinct from the British Isles as conditions warmed further (Table 14). Second, it is also evident that it is not just species that can become extinct: communities or species-associations can too. Notwithstanding the actual geographical extinction of *Columella columella* it is evident that the association of the other species in Zone z has no modern parallel within the British Isles, having only existed for the limited period of periglacial conditions in the Late-glacial and very early postglacial. Third, as vegetation changes followed temperature changes and the landscape became one of temperate mixed-woodland, thermophilous (i.e. warmth-loving) shade-requiring species such as *Spermodea lamellata* were able to move into the British Isles for the first time. The first few thousand years of the postglacial period was therefore a time in which the molluscan fauna of these islands was altering as a result of temperature, and later vegetation, changes. Some of our native species did not finally reach Britain until well into the postglacial period, just before the land bridge attaching the British Isles to the European mainland was cut off by rising sea level. This severing of the land bridge fixed our 'native' molluscan fauna and hindered the migration of other species from the European mainland which otherwise may also have become established here. Finally, it can be said that as a result of later human impacts these islands have a richer molluscan fauna than they would have had had woodland clearance not occurred (Kerney 1968). Without such clearance some of the open-country species which are now widespread and characteristic of grazed or otherwise managed land might well have been marginalised to the point of extinction. In addition, some of the more recent 'accidental' introductions (see Table 12) would not have become so readily established within wooded conditions.

Introductions and extinctions

The species considered as introduced are given as Tables 12 and 13. It is noticeable that 21 terrestrial species are considered as introductions (Table 12), some 20 per cent of the entire current terrestrial molluscan fauna. Only two species seem to have been prehistoric introductions, the other 19 being Roman/Romano-British, medieval or more recent introductions. Only one (*Helix pomatia* – Figure 42) is considered a deliberate introduction, as a food source; the rest appear to have been 'accidental'.

The status of many of the freshwater and brackish species is less certain. Kerney (1999) only lists five species and elements of one taxon (*Physa* spp.) as definite introductions. They are all recent and the dates of first occurrences well documented (Table 13). However, a further 14 freshwater or brackish gastropods and seven freshwater bivalves are only listed as probably native or query (?) native. This uncertainty reflects the relative paucity of well-dated fossil occurrences as compared to terrestrial Mollusca.

Table 14 lists the terrestrial and freshwater species currently considered as once native but now extinct. As mentioned earlier, the majority of these are species that were able to colonise the British Isles during the Late-glacial or early postglacial period but were disadvantaged as temperate woodland conditions became fully established. Although these extinctions seem to be securely recorded, a word of caution is necessary. As the mapping scheme data accumulated, at least one species (*Vertigo genesii* an arctic-alpine species thought to have only inhabited the British Isles during the Late-glacial and early postglacial) was 're-discovered' as an extant species, albeit in a single locality in Teesdale (Coles and Colville 1980). It remains possible that some of

Species	Notes
Cochlicopa nitens	A central and eastern European species which is known only from UK Late-Glacial and early postglacial deposits (see Preece 1992 and Davies 2006).
Columella columella	An arctic alpine species found only in Late-glacial and early postglacial deposits in the UK.
Discus ruderatus	A Holarctic species found in early postglacial deposits but replaced by *Discus rotundatus* between 8630 ±120 and 7650 ±80 BP (Preece and Bridgland 1998; 1999).
Trochoidea geyeri	Seemingly extinct from much of the UK by the early-mid postglacial as open country was replaced by closed woodland. However, it was present at Gwithian, Cornwall, in the Bronze Age but seems to have become extinct shortly after, possibly as a result of competition from other helicellines.
Helicopsis striata	Extinction in early-mid postglacial due to loss of open habitat as woodland cover increased.
Nesovitrea petronella	Presently a boreal-alpine species. Extinction from UK due to postglacial warming.
Margaritifera auricularia	Climatic change (postglacial warming) probably responsible for extinction.
Pisidium vincentianum	A cold water bivalve now found in western Siberia and The Himalayas. Only found in early postglacial lake deposits in the UK.

TABLE 14. Terrestrial and freshwater species becoming extinct from the UK during the Holocene. Data from Kerney (1999) unless otherwise stated.

the other colder-climate species listed in Table 14 may survive as isolated extant populations in remoter areas of the British Isles.

Biozone	Characteristic species and dates
Zone _y_	*Pupilla muscorum*, *Vallonia* spp. and *Vitrina pellucida* dominated faunas. Dated from 13,160 ±400 yr BP to just before 11,530 ±160 yr BP and therefore covering the pre-interstadial phase of the Late-glacial.
Zone _z_	An open ground periglacial fauna with *Pupilla muscorum*, *Trichia hispida*, *Abida secale*, *Vallonia* spp., *Columella columella* and *Neosovitrea hammonis*. Dated from just before 11,530 ±160 yr BP until 9820 ±90 yr BP. Covering the Late-glacial (Windemere or Allerød) Interstadial and (Loch Lomond or Younger Dryas) Stadial phases of the Late-glacial period, as well as the very early postglacial period.
Zone _a_	As _z_ but with *Pupilla* and other bare ground species declining and with ecologically catholic species increasing. Appearance of *Carychium tridentatum*, *Vitrea* spp. and *Aegopinella* spp.. Dated from 9760 ±100 yr BP until before 9530 ±75 yr BP and reflecting increasingly wooded conditions.
Zone _b_	Expansion of *Carychium* and *Aegopinella* and otherwise generally a woodland assemblage. First appearance and expansion of *Discus ruderatus*. Dated from just before 9460 ±140 yr BP until 8630 ±120 yr BP.
Zone _c_	*D. ruderatus* replaced by *D. rotundatus* Otherwise a closed woodland assemblage. Dated from 8630 ±120 yr BP until just before 7650 ±80 yr BP.
Zone _d_	A woodland fauna with the notable expansion of *Oxychilus cellarius*, *Spermodea lamellata*, *Leiostyla anglica* and *Acicula fusca*. Dated from 7650 ±80 yr BP until sometime before 5620 ±90 yr BP.
Zone _e_	Shade species decline. Re-emergence and expansion of open-ground species, particularly *Vallonia costata*. Lower boundary dating to between 5620 ±90 to 3980 ±70 yrs BP, reflecting the diachronous nature of substantial prehistoric woodland clearance.
Zone _f_	As Zone _e_ but with *H. aspersa*. From sometime before 2850 ±70 yr BP.

TABLE 15. Molluscan biozones from south-east England as detailed by Preece and Bridgland 1999.

FIGURE 42. *Helix pomatia.*

Relict, declining and 'migrating' species

Another feature of the national mapping scheme is that it is possible to consider which extant species are relict and which are declining. Relict species are those which were once more widespread under different climatic conditions (e.g. the cooler, drier conditions of the early postglacial) and are now generally disadvantaged but just about maintaining viable populations in a few localities where conditions allow. *Vertigo genesii*, mentioned above, comes into this group. Other examples include *Vertigo modesta, Vitrea subrimata, Sphaerium solidum, Catinella arenaria, Pisidium conventus,* and *Pisidium lilljeborgi.* Declining species are those which were once far more widespread but are threatened by human-induced habitat loss (e.g. *Aplexa hypnorum* and *Lymnaea glabra* suffering from loss of ditches and ponds), the effects of pollution (e.g. *Myxas glutinosa* and *Segmentina nitida*) or climatic cooling since the mid-postglacial climatic optimum (e.g. *Pomatias elegans, Ena montana*).

Some species show very strong evidence of northward migration due to longer-term climate change. Both *Vertigo genesii* and *Vertigo geyeri* are boreal-alpine species intolerant of warmth and have migrated northwards since the earlier postglacial period. Unlike *Columella columella* they have not yet become extinct, but future warming could severely threaten their existence in the British Isles. Conversely, some of the more recent introductions, particularly the 'Mediterranean' species (e.g. *Theba pisana* and *Hygromia cinctella*) which currently have a limited distribution due to frost intolerance may well expand their distributions in the same way that *Monacha cantiana* seems to have done over the last century (Kerney 1999).

CHAPTER 21

Insects

Harry Kenward and Nicki Whitehouse

Introduction

The beetle fauna of the British Isles has changed greatly during the current, Holocene, interglacial. There was an almost complete turnover of insect fauna during the violent climatic convulsions of the Late Glacial period and early Holocene warming. In the Mesolithic and Neolithic, natural succession combined with the effects of climate change and increasing human impact caused substantial changes. Massive human impacts on ecosystems starting in the Bronze and Iron Ages continued until the mid twentieth century, when the most rapid ecological changes since the early Holocene were brought about by the demands of the Second World War and industrial forestry and farming. In contrast, a new phase of invasion brought about by human activity saw the arrival of numerous aliens from the Roman period onwards.

Hammond's (1974) account of the changing British beetle fauna and Buckland's (1981) review of the early dispersal of stored products pests remain essential reading; our review is informed by several decades of new information. Coleoptera nomenclature follows Böhme (2005), and plants Stace (1997). Holocene radiocarbon dates are calibrated (Oxcal v. 3.10, 2005; range calculated to 95 per cent confidence, using the INTCAL 04 curve, Reimer *et al.* 2004), whilst dendrochronological dates are BC. Pre-Holocene dates are given uncalibrated (BP, 1950).

Setting the scene: the end of the last Ice Age

The last glaciation (Devensian in Britain, Midlandian in Ireland) ended about 13,000 years ago. Ice sheets had extended across much of Britain and Ireland, eradicating most of the species present during the previous interglacial and subsequent interstadials (short periods of climate amelioration). During the Late Glacial ice retreat (*c.* 13,000–10,000 years ago), organisms re-colonised. Perhaps half of the present-day fauna arrived during this period (Hammond 1974), especially before early Holocene afforestation (*c.* 10,000 years ago).

Coope (1994) reviewed the arrival of cold-adapted beetles early during deglaciation, before Late glacial warming: starting with Faunal Unit 1, pioneer species living today in barren, tundra-like landscapes. This was followed early in the Windermere Interstadial (*c.* 13,200–12,200 years ago) by Faunal Unit 2, lacking cold-adapted taxa, but with warmth-lovers including plant-feeders and various ground beetles, xerophiles and aquatics. A cooler fauna was present later in the interstadial (*c.* 12,200–11,000 BP, Faunal Unit 3). Cold-adapted beetles re-invaded during the Younger Dryas (*c.* 11,000–10,000 BP, Faunal Unit 4). Finally, at *c.* 10,000 BP, thermophiles again dominated, cold-adapted taxa being lost (Faunal Unit 5) during an abrupt Holocene warming.

This pattern is repeated at numerous sites across the British Isles. In some southerly locations, an insect fauna associated with light forest had started to colonise shortly after 13,000 BP; the birch bark beetle *Scolytus ratzeburgi* arrived on the south-east coast of England, in the earliest part of the Interstadial (Coope 1998). Together with other species often associated with birch and hazel, it suggests light woodland and scrub. Other species indicate a largely dry, sandy landscape, with patchy heather and herbs. Many species apparently did not survive the cold Younger Dryas, warmth-lovers retreating southwards once again.

Mesolithic and Neolithic: building a fauna (9500–2000 BC)

The many Late Glacial fossil insect investigations carried out over the last half century have diverted our attention from our ignorance concerning early Holocene insects (Whitehouse 2006), and the crucial initial interglacial period needs further investigation. In Britain, the most important early Holocene sites include Holywell Coombe (Kent), West Bromwich (Staffordshire), Lea Marsdon B (Warwickshire), Bole Ings (Nottinghamshire), Church Stretton (Shropshire) and Church Moss (Cheshire). Most were raised mire peats or alluvium in fluvial systems. The few Irish studies from this time period are reviewed by Whitehouse (2007); they include an unpublished fauna from intertidal peats in Strangford Lough in Co. Down (Whitehouse and Rodgers 2008) and a small assemblage from Sluggan Bog in Co. Antrim.

Faunas from the earliest stages of warming indicate the almost instantaneous arrival of thermophiles, exemplified by assemblages from Holywell Coombe (Coope 1998). During the first few hundred years of the Holocene swamp fauna dominated, though the presence of bare-ground ground beetles, such as *Carabus arvensis* and *Cicindela campestris*, also indicates open, dry areas. As new tree species colonised and habitats diversified, enriched forest fauna moved northwards over the next few thousand years.

By *c.* 6000–4000 BC, forests reached their maximum, with extensive tracts of lime-dominated forest in lowland England and Wales, oak in the north and west, and birch and pine in northern Scotland (Bennett 1988). In Ireland, oak, elm and pine were well established by about 9000 years ago, with pine the most common, particularly on infertile soils in the west, and oak and elm in the fertile regions, especially the south east and north east. Woodland beetles were at their peak (20–30 per cent of terrestrial fauna), although there are important local variations, suggesting that the landscape remained patchy, with open areas locally, especially in floodplains. Generally, however, open ground and pasture indicators were found at relatively low levels, although there are some exceptions to this (e.g. Runnymede, West Heath Spa, see Whitehouse and Smith 2010). Tree-associated beetles diversified; oak associates were generally more abundant than previously, whilst pine associates remained important. Beetles associated with shade-tolerant trees such as elm and lime increased, indicating a thicker woodland canopy (*ibid.*).

Insect assemblages dated between 4000–2000 BC start to show the effects of deforestation, albeit highly localised, with taxa indicating herbaceous vegetation and open ground diversifying whereas tree-associates decline, though this can vary significantly from site to site (*ibid.*). At many sites specialised wood-associates diminished and open-loving taxa, such as dung beetles, and indicators of herbaceous plants, meadows and disturbed ground increased. This is especially evident towards the end of the Neolithic. Robinson (2000) suggested that the early Neolithic rise of dung beetles probably reflects grazing of woodland by domesticated animals but that clearances were probably limited. It was generally not until the Bronze Age that forest specialists became confined to increasingly isolated pockets of woodland. It is clear that the Neolithic landscape was increasingly heterogeneous, with some areas substantially cleared (e.g. areas of the southern chalklands, such as Silbury Hill), whilst others retained significant woodland cover (e.g. mire woodlands such as those found at Thorne and Hatfield Moors, see Whitehouse and Smith 2010). One of the effects of Neolithic clearance was the initiation of alluviation in some river floodplains, only evident at some sites, such as the Thames Valley, during this earlier period (Robinson and Lambrick 1984), but increasingly important later.

Bronze Age and Iron Age: early extinctions (2000 BC–AD 43)

By the late Holocene, pollen and beetles suggest a significant reduction in primary forest, many assemblages showing the effects of clearance (Osborne 1965). The range of studies is substantially greater than for the earlier Holocene, though with a bias towards 'archaeological' sites and the Bronze Age. There is appreciable variation between locations, but a fairly clear overall picture of increasing human impact. The pattern initiated in the Neolithic intensified, the forest insect fauna being progressively replaced by 'culture-steppe' elements associated with cleared landscapes and pasture. Sites characterising this period include long alluvial 'natural' floodplain successions in the Thames and Trent River systems (e.g. Runnymede, Robinson 2000; Bole Ings, Dinnin 1997), as well as shorter ones (e.g. Pilgrims Lock, Warwickshire, associated with the River Avon, Osborne 1988), estuarine and foreshore successions (Buckland *et al.* 1990; Tetlow 2003) and raised mire and trackway sites (e.g. Buckland 1979; Whitehouse 2004). Also important are assemblages from Bronze and Iron Age settlement sites, such as Meare Heath, Somerset (Girling 1976; 1982), Meare Lake Village, Somerset (Girling 1979; 1982), Tattershall Thorpe, Lincolnshire

FIGURE 43. Fragments of fossil beetles from Bronze Age lake settlement site at Ballyarnet, Co. Derry, Northern Ireland.
PHOTO BY NICKI WHITEHOUSE

(Chowne *et al.* 1986), Mingies Ditch, Oxfordshire (Allen and Robinson 1993), Late Iron age occupation at Fisherwick, on the Trent, Staffordshire (Osborne 1979), and the Iron Age and Roman farmstead at Farmoor, Oxfordshire (Robinson 1979). Well fills of this period are an important source of evidence, such as those at Wilsford, Wiltshire (Osborne 1969; 1989) and Dragonby, Lincolnshire (Buckland 1996).

Dramatic changes in the insect faunas are evident at several sites. At Wilsford, Bronze Age insects from a well dated to *c.* 1880–1430 BC (NPL-74) suggest grazing animals in an almost treeless landscape (Osborne 1969) (though even nearby trees may be under-represented by fossil insects, Kenward 2006). The abundance and diversity of the dung beetles, including *Onthophagus* species, was striking. There were also disturbed ground indicators, e.g. *Stenocarus umbrinus* and *Mecinus pyraster*. In Ireland, assemblages associated with a Bronze Age trackway dated to *c.* 1600 BC at Derryville Bog, Co. Tipperary, indicated surviving ancient woodland locally (Caseldine *et al.* 2001).

By the Iron Age, beetles usually indicate grazing land, the chafer *Phyllopertha horticola*, typical of unimproved grasslands, often being abundant. The similarity of faunas between sites at this time is striking, indicating that the human-made 'historic' landscape was developing, a process which continued into the Roman period. Iron Age assemblages – unless formed in extensive wetlands – mostly consist entirely of species which typify agricultural land today, or perhaps more accurately, until the mid twentieth century, before industrialised farming.

Some sites, e.g. Meare Lake Village, had abundant synanthropes, though these were fairly unspecialised forms (facultative or typical, *sensu* Kenward 1997). The earliest investigated deposits in Ireland with synanthropes were at the Middle Bronze Age Ballyarnet Lake settlement site (Whitehouse 2007), but few sites have been studied and a synanthropic fauna almost certainly started developing earlier. Initial investigations of the waterlogged Mesolithic platform site at Derragh, Lough Kinale, Co. Longford, suggests there are hints of a culturally-favoured fauna here (Whitehouse unpublished). In Britain, synanthropes became evident in the early Neolithic – e.g. at the Scottish crannog, Eilean Domhnuill a Spionnaidh, on North Uist, Outer Hebrides (Worsop 2000). There were synanthropes, including the human flea, *Pulex irritans*, among later Neolithic fauna at Skara Brae (Sadler 1991). Kenward (1997) and Smith *et al.* (2000) suggest that rich synanthropic faunas can develop rapidly on small rural sites through importation of infested materials, overcoming isolation, and indicating that such faunas are not solely restricted to large, urban settlements.

A significant effect of these landscape changes was apparently the extirpation of many beetles from Britain and Ireland. To date, 40 pre-Linnean (pre-nineteenth century) extirpations have been recorded for Britain, and 15, four with their nearest living relatives in Central European forests, for Ireland. Whitehouse (1997; 2000; 2006) discusses the complex issues surrounding these extinctions. Of lost taxa, over 60 per cent (25) are associated with old and dead wood (saproxylics), the rest being from a variety of threatened habitats, including rapidly disappearing wetlands and meadowland. A complex combination of anthropogenic, edaphic and climatic changes caused the extirpation, or at least range reduction, of numerous saproxylics, with a simultaneous and dramatic increase in elements associated with disturbed ground and cleared landscapes. Deforestation and cultivation destabilised soils, changing the sedimentation regimes in major rivers, drastically altering their fauna, especially of riparian beetles (Osborne 1988; Smith 2001; Smith and Howard 2004).

The Roman period onwards: growing ecological impact but surprisingly few extinctions

From the Roman period onwards, faunal change has two contrasting aspects: damage to natural habitats resulting from the agricultural demands of increasing population, and importation of aliens through trade. Information is mostly from towns or forts, with some from rural settlements; natural deposits are almost unrepresented, through a combination of rarity (superficial deposits have often been lost) and a regrettable lack of interest in many quarters. Consequently, synanthropes are prominent. Agricultural development (e.g. Dark 2000) seems not have promoted invasions or extinctions in natural habitats, but the fossil record is poor. However, dung beetle diversity had fallen drastically by the Roman period, *Onthophagus* species suffering especially.

Impact of Roman colonisation

The Roman invasion saw massive changes in the insects exploiting occupation sites. Military supplies, then trade, brought synanthropic insects, especially grain beetles, presumably with substantial economic impact. Only for a few – particularly grain pests – can a clearer history be built up. Timing arrivals from an incomplete fossil record is difficult; species may have been present well before the earliest find. Invaders often have a long period of obscurity before becoming abundant (Williamson 1996). Another problem is post-depositional contamination: aliens believed to have arrived recently sometimes occur in archaeological samples but are demonstrably modern (Kenward 2009).

The absence of pre-Roman grain pests in the British Isles contrasts with records from early sites in the Middle East and mainland Europe (e.g. Panagiotakopulu 2000), though Iron Age population centres with waterlogging are barely studied. Had any alien insects arrived through prehistoric trade? If, as suggested, there was Iron Age grain export from Britain, then surely other goods were being imported, or ships returned in ballast, inevitably bringing stowaway insects. We remain unsure whether some species are native or introduced; prehistoric records of synanthropes are of species often found in natural habitats, and so are probably native.

The most obvious Roman beetle importations are heat-demanding stored products pests, probably mostly infesting grain. The commonest are *Oryzaephilus surinamensis*, *Cryptolestes ferrugineus*, *Palorus ratzeburgi* and *Sitophilus granarius*. They apparently invaded stored grain early in the history of agriculture; their early spread across Europe from the Middle East is reviewed by Buckland (1981) and Panagiotakopulu (2000). Grain pests are known from numerous Roman sites, sometimes in huge numbers (e.g. Kenward and Williams 1979). It seems that they came with the first units of the Roman army, being present very early at some military sites (e.g. in York, Carlisle, and Ribchester, Lancashire). They are usually present even in tiny assemblages from urban or military sites (e.g. the fort at South Shields, Osborne 1994), and got to some rural sites, e.g. Sandtoft, Hatfield Chase (Samuels and Buckland 1978). While they surely infested cereals intended for humans, it seems that the greatest outbreaks of grain beetles were in poor grain used as horse feed, and they are characteristic of stable manure deposits (Kenward 2009; Kenward and Hall 1997).

Natural-habitat insects during the Roman period (or in the later Iron Age) have barely been investigated, but intensification surely had an impact. Only one beetle from the Roman period seems to have become extinct: *Airaphilus elongatus* (Osborne 1974; 1996); with early Holocene records, it was certainly native. *Micropeplus caelatus*, now lost from Britain but still in Ireland, was found in Roman York, but probably came from older peat (Hall *et al.* 1980).

The Dark Ages

The Dark Ages (AD 400–850) are obscure for British beetles too. Preservation is rare, perhaps primarily because most settlements lacked massive accumulations of self-preserving organic waste. Did alien synanthropes survive? There are Anglian or Saxon assemblages with unspecialised synanthropes from York (Allison *et al.* 1996; Kenward *et al.* 1986) Southampton, Buckland *et al.* (1976), Oxford (Robinson 2003) and rural Oxfordshire (Robinson 1981); grain beetles were absent. A restricted synanthrope fauna was predictable in rural settlements (e.g. Kenward *et al.* 2000), but not in proto-urban trade centres, and the rich synanthropic fauna at a seventh/eighth-century farmstead site in Co. Antrim makes the urban data even more surprising (Allison *et al.* 1999; Kenward and Allison 1994; Kenward *et al.* in press).

Renewal of overseas contact: later Saxon and Viking beetles

The Later Saxon and Viking Age (for our purposes, 850–1066) was one of intensified overseas contact. Towns arose in Britain and rich populations of insects developed in them. Myriad samples have been examined from York (Hall and Kenward 2004; Kenward and Hall 1995), so it is surprising that very few 'exotics' have been found. The rare grain beetles noted may be contaminants: more would be expected if they were established (Kenward and Hall 1995). It seems possible that they died out after the Roman period, probably because grain was generally stored and processed on a small scale. In the rest of the British Isles, occupation sites of this period have produced rather few assemblages, preservation sometimes being only by mineral replacement (e.g. at Southampton, Kenward and Girling 1986), or toxic salts (e.g. puparia on a brooch at Sewerby, East Yorkshire, Girling 1985).

After the Norman conquest

Post-Norman Conquest archaeological assemblages are moderately common, typically with grain pests and indicators of stable manure (Kenward and Hall 1997), both surely related to increasing numbers of horses being kept in towns. The changing economic system in Britain probably favoured large centralised grain stores, so pests could thrive and disperse. While grain insects may have survived undetected, it seems as likely that they, and some other species associated with humans, were re-introduced. Some insects became commoner in the fossil record at this time, e.g. the spider beetle *Tipnus unicolor*, which had been common in Roman Britain, but rare or absent from pre-Conquest English settlements. It was perhaps favoured by a trend towards longer-lasting dwellings, though changes in the deposits available for investigation may be a factor.

The Tudor period and later

Tudor and later occupation site beetle communities were much like medieval ones, though typically with fewer species through time as the range of habitats in settlements became restricted. Britain was an active trading nation, so the importation of numerous aliens is predictable; many were established by the twentieth century, but few sites have been investigated and we cannot yet time most arrivals.

There are some 'post-Linnean' archaeological assemblages. These have yielded a range of immigrant species (Carrott *et al.* 1995; Hall *et al.* 2007). Some species may have become rarer, or died out, during the inclement Little Ice Age, though habitat loss may have been at least equally significant (Buckland and Wagner 2001). The large ground beetle *Pterostichus madidus* seems to have inexplicably become commoner during this period. Possibly a Roman introduction (Buckland 1981), perhaps it underwent the period of entrenchment seen in many establishing aliens (Williamson 1996), or was a native that adapted to synanthropic habitats.

Recent extinctions and arrivals

It is difficult to know from the fossil record when species disappeared from the British Isles (Whitehouse 2006). Many last records date *c.* 3000–1000 BC, but are from isolated places such as Thorne and Hatfield Moors. In Ireland, several species seem to have disappeared during the historic period, almost certainly related to aggressive medieval and post-medieval clearances (Whitehouse 2006). Did the beetles exist in the wider landscape? Few woodland deposits of later date have been studied, so perhaps some species persisted locally: *Prostomis mandibularis* from twelfth-century Beverley (Kenward and Carrott 2003), unless redeposited, certainly begs questions about extinction dates, since it was previously thought to have been lost in the Bronze Age!

The longhorn *Cerambyx cerdo* exemplifies the problem of tracing extinctions even of spectacular insects. Fossils from about 4000 years ago, several live records from the earlier nineteenth century, and decreasing nineteenth-century records suggest a contracting population (Duffy 1968; Harding and Plant 1978). Other extirpated species currently dismissed as collector's imports may turn up in old collections or as fossils. The bottom line is that we know very little about the beetle fauna of the last few centuries. This is particularly frustrating, as information could contribute to conservation debates.

The past 150 years, and especially recent decades, have seen a torrent of additions to the lists of Coleoptera for Britain and Ireland, their number greatly exceeding the Holocene extinctions. Some represent taxonomic 'splitting', but many more are immigrants, and arrivals continue unabated, probably faster than at any time since the Holocene began. Some apparently invade naturally as temperatures rise, others are brought by long-distance trade. Our beetle fauna is enriching numerically, but many arrivals are cosmopolitan, often potential pests, illustrating the homogenisation of global biota, a cause for concern among ecologists. Current change in Britain seems more profound than since the end of the Ice Age. The fossil record amply demonstrates the migratory ability of insects, but could they track climate change across fragmented natural habitats, especially woodland? Perhaps Holocene extinctions of forest insects were caused by woodland fragmentation as much as by decreasing area. Current efforts to restore and connect forests, and to a lesser extent heaths and wetland, seem essential to avoid even more drastic losses.

CHAPTER 22

Conclusion

Derek W. Yalden

Introduction

About a decade ago, I was reviewing much of the material then available on many of the questions explored in this volume, as I worked towards writing *The History of British Mammals* (Yalden 1999). Most of the mammalian topics covered here were part of my brief, though none of them could be considered in so much detail as here. It therefore gives a particular pleasure to read comprehensive reviews of such topics as when and by whom fallow deer *Dama dama* and rabbit *Oryctolagus cuniculus* were introduced, and when lynx *Lynx lynx*, elk *Alces alces* and wolf *Canis lupus* became extinct (see also Harris and Yalden 2008). While my views were by no means original, I felt then I was still arguing for the relatively recent notions that the Normans were responsible for both fallow deer (Chapman and Chapman 1975) and rabbit (Sheail 1971; Tittensor and Tittensor 1985). Better archaeological data, e.g. from Launceston Castle (Albarella and Davis 1996) confirmed the importance of Norman exploitation, and moreover demonstrated convincingly that fallow deer were introduced some 150 years earlier than rabbits (see Sykes, this volume). In this conclusion to the volume, I should like to review some of the major changes that have been published since 1999, and suggest where future research into the history of British mammals might be best directed.

Better dates and fossils

One of the more surprising discoveries of the 1990s was how recently the Lynx had become extinct. This was dependant on the specimen from Inchnadamph, Sutherland (Kitchener and Bonsall 1997), radiocarbon dated to 1770 BP (i.e. *c.* 180 AD). More of the (rather few) lynx specimens have since been dated, and two others are also of Roman or later date: Moughton Fell (1842 BP or *c.* AD 108) and Kinsey Cave (1550 BP/*c.* AD 400), see Hetherington *et al.* (2006) and this volume. The earliest known fossils of red squirrel *Sciurus vulgaris* and hazel dormouse *Muscardinus avellanarius*, two species assumed to be native but with no early fossils to confirm this, have now been recorded by Price (2003) in early Post Glacial cave deposits from south-west England: dormouse from Simmonds Yat East and Merlin's Cave, squirrel from Madawg Cave and King

Arthur's Cave (all Wye Valley), and both of them from the Neolithic layers of Broken Cavern and Three Holes Cave (Torbryan, Devon). The harvest mouse *Micromys minutus*, which was considered likely to be a Neolithic human introduction (Corbet and Harris 1991; Yalden 1999), has also now been found as an early Post Glacial fossil at Merlin's Cave (Price 2003). Even more exciting is the addition of at least two, perhaps three, species to the Late Glacial/Early Post Glacial small mammal fauna: grey-sided vole *Myodes rufocanus* and probably bog lemming *Myopus schisticolor* in King Arthur's Cave (Price 2003), birch mouse *Sicista betulina* together with another early *Muscardinus* from a probable Mesolithic site, Chapel Cave in N. Yorkshire (Warren 2004). The scant subfossil record of *Sicista* in western Europe, its occurrence in Jersey during the Riss glaciation, and as near as Belgium during the Late Glacial, had been noted (Yalden 1999) but its discovery in Britain so quickly by an alert student was certainly unexpected.

Genetic phylogeography

Some of the most striking changes to our understanding of the history of British mammals have come not from archaeological work but from genetic studies. Mostly these have compared genetic samples of modern mammals from across their ranges, but occasionally have used archaeological material. An important example of the latter is the study of cattle/aurochs relationships by Troy *et al.* (2001). They examined the mtDNA of 392 extant cattle, from across their range, and also managed to extract mtDNA from four (two Mesolithic, two Bronze Age) specimens of British Aurochs. Modern European cattle were closest to those from the Middle East, with African cattle also closely related. The Aurochs specimens formed a small side branch of their own, equally discrete from European, African and Middle Eastern cattle. The humped cattle (zebu) of Indian origin were well separated from all of these. This genetic evidence confirms the widely accepted view, on archaeological and other grounds (e.g. Grigson 1989), that zebu were domesticated independently, in India, from the local race (*Bos primigenius namadicus*) of aurochs, but that western cattle were domesticated in the Middle East from western aurochs (*B. p. primigenius*), then taken to both Europe and Africa already domesticated. A less dramatic but similarly valuable phylogenetic analysis shows that domestic horses have a very different pattern of domestication, involving not two but many ancestral maternal lineages; horses were apparently domesticated from several closely related populations (Vila *et al.* 2001). This has relevance for British mammals in that the Exmoor Pony nestles comfortably within the complex of domestic breeds; it is not a remnant Late Glacial wild horse. Genetic evidence confirms, to no-one's surprise, that European sheep and goats were domesticated in the Middle East (Wood and Phua 1996; Manceau *et al.* 1999). The importance of new genetic evidence on the source of domestic cats is emphasised by Kitchener and O'Connor (this volume).

It had been widely assumed that temperate mammals survived glacial conditions in refugia in southern Europe, in the Mediterranean peninsulae (Iberia, Italy, Balkans). The earliest relevant genetic evidence became available in the 1990s; it confirmed that, for instance, brown bears *Ursus arctos* and hedgehogs (Western *Erinaceus europaeus* and Eastern *E. concolor*) showed a pattern of variation consistent with this notion. Western forms, probably associated with Iberian glacial refuges, were related genetically through western Europe north to Scandinavia, and eastern forms, probably from a Balkan refuge, occurred northwards through eastern Europe to Finland (Hewitt 1999). However, a very different pattern is shown by small mammals, which vary little across a wide east-west sweep of Eurasia, from Britain and France in the west, across Germany and Poland to Russia, even to Siberia. Genetically, the populations of, at least, *Myodes glareolus* (more familiar as *Clethrionomys glareolus*), *Sorex araneus* and *Sorex minutus* in the southern peninsulae are very distinct. It seems that the widespread genotypes swept across northern Europe from refugia in the east, around the Baltic Sea or even the Caucasus, confining the locally differentiated southern forms in isolation south of the Carpathians, Alps and Pyrenees, and preventing them from spreading back northwards from their refugia (Bilton *et al.* 1998). Subsequent work on the genetics of some of the interesting species has expanded on these findings. The occurrence of pigmy shrew *Sorex minutus* in Ireland has prompted much discussion, since few small mammals occur there, and this one in particular is, given its ecology, a poor candidate for accidental human introduction. Given its northern distribution in Europe, and its wide range (e.g. on the Isle of Man and the Outer Hebrides), an early, Late Glacial or Post Glacial, natural spread seemed possible (e.g. Yalden 1981). However, genetic evidence indicates that Irish pigmy shrews are related, not to their nearest conspecifics in Scotland or Wales (as they would be if they had spread naturally), but to Iberian shrews. By contrast, those on Man are genetically close to English, Welsh and Scottish shrews: either they did spread naturally, or, if they are also accidental introductions, then they came from Great Britain (Mascheretti *et al.* 2003). A similarly revealing analysis of common voles *Microtus arvalis*, including examples of Orkney voles from three of the islands (Mainland, Sanday, Westray), shows that they too are most closely related, not to the geographically nearest Dutch or Danish voles, but to specimens from France and Spain (Haynes *et al.* 2003). An early (Neolithic?) accidental introduction is presumed, since there are archaeological specimens from the Neolithic sites of Skara Brae, Links of Noltland, Quanterness, Maes Howe and Holm of Papa Westray, with radiocarbon dates of 4800 BP and 3590 BP on specimens from Links of Noltland (Thaw *et al.* 2004). However, the possibility that the introduction was not entirely accidental is raised by the suggestion that these large voles might have been carried either as cult animals, or as food for the journey (Thaw *et al.* 2004).

Yet another case where genetic evidence reveals the role of human introduction is the pine marten *Martes martes* in Ireland. Martens have been widely introduced to Mediterranean islands, presumably for their fur - pine martens to Mallorca, Sardinia and Corsica, beech martens *M. foina* to Crete. It had always been assumed to be native to Ireland but, given the erratic nature of the Irish mammal fauna, there was possibility that it was introduced there too. The only two radiocarbon dated specimens, from Foley Cave 2555 BP and Kilgreany Cave at 2780 BP, are not old enough to argue for native status (Woodman *et al.* 1997). As for the pigmy shrew, the genetic evidence indicates that Irish martens are not closely related to Scottish ones, but have an Iberian pedigree (Davison *et al.* 2001). A slightly different story comes from the study of brown hares *Lepus europaeus*. These show that British hares are, like the small mammals discussed above, part of an eastern genetic lineage, which probably survived the Last Glaciation in a refuge near the Black Sea. In southern Europe, the Spanish hare *L. granatensis* and the Italian *L. corsicanus* differentiated in and remain restricted to southern refugia. As a twist to this story, however, British hares have very little variation, implying that a small number, with limited variation, was introduced by humans (while natural spread of a very small colonising group could have produced the same result, this seems unlikely given that brown hares show normal levels of variability on the east side of the North Sea) (Alves *et al.* 2003; Kasapidis *et al.* 2005; Suchentruck *et al.* 2001).

Future Progress

Given the recent advances just indicated, some of the possibilities for future advances are very obvious. New archaeological material, and new dating applied to existing specimens, will resolve some problems. New genetic research will solve other problems. What follows is a very idiosyncratic research programme reflecting my interests.

The dates of extinction of British mammals remain even more enigmatic than the dates of introductions, especially given the good progress in solving many of the latter. It appears that aurochs *Bos primigenius* became extinct in the Bronze Age, with the latest dated specimen being that from Charterhouse Warren Farm at 3425 BP. It is always unlikely that we know the latest specimen of any such species, and its possible survival to e.g. Roman times (Segontium (Caernarvon) and Vindolanda?) was mentioned by Yalden (1999). For brown bear, the latest specimens do seem to be of Roman age (e.g. Colchester), though a few later bones are known; they are presumed to indicate importations of bears for baiting, as dancing bears, or as trade items (e.g. skins). Even the earlier Roman specimens could have been imported, and genetical or molecular studies of some of these specimens (examining oxygen or carbon isotope signatures to determine source areas, for instance) could help to resolve the uncertainties. More puzzling is the apparent failure of the archaeological record to demonstrate survival of extinct species later in Scotland or Wales than England. The latest elk *Alces alces* is Scottish, but the latest brown bear, lynx, beaver and aurochs are probably English (see tables in Yalden 1999, and other contributions here). Given the higher human density in England throughout history, it would be an obvious expectation that the extinct species survived longer in the more sparsely populated north and west. The historical documentation of the wolf does fit that pattern; so might the apparent survival of beavers around Loch Ness to the fourteenth century, but note Coles' (this volume) suggestion of a late Yorkshire record. However, the archaeological record is also predominantly an English one, except, perhaps, for the excellent record from the northern isles where, however, large mammals are unlikely to have been preserved; some redress of this imbalance might well also restore the balance of the archaeological record towards a truer picture of the survival and eventual extinction of these species. Better dating of the beaver quoted from Rattray might do this, for one species, very rapidly. One detail of the Post Glacial extinction of mammals deserves specific study. Small mammal faunas transitional between the "arctic" lemming faunas and the "temperate" wood mouse faunas are barely documented, but the root vole *Microtus oeconomus* (formerly recorded as *M. ratticeps*) seems to occupy such an intermediate position, and would repay further study. It occurs with *Lemmus lemmus*, in particular, in Late Glacial faunas, but it seems also to occur in some early Post Glacial (Mesolithic) sites with wood mouse and other temperate species in a few cave sites (Yalden 1999). Price (2003) suggests that root vole (northern vole) survived to Neolithic times in Broken Cavern, Torbryan, and the species apparently survived to Bronze Age times on Nornour, Isles of Scilly. This is then a species worthy of more study, and particularly of dating evidence.

A more complex story that requires reinvestigation, and perhaps some more archaeological material as well, concerns the history of the hares in Britain. When it was assumed that the brown hare was a native species (e.g. by Yalden 1982), its occurrence in archaeological sites received little or no critical attention. As it became increasingly evident that it was not native, so the inadequacy of this oversight became more striking. There are two related problems. The mountain hare *Lepus timidus* is considered native, in historical times, only to the Scottish Highlands (and, as a well-marked subspecies, Ireland). However, the archaeological record makes it clear that it was widely distributed early in the Late and Post Glacial. Well-dated specimens, many with cut-marks, from Robin Hood Cave, Pin Hole and Church Hole, falling in the Late Glacial 12,600–12,240 BP, attest its early presence in England (Charles and Jacobi 1994); similarly, it was present in southern Ireland at Plunkett Cave at 12,190 BP (Woodman *et al.* 1997). Surely, it was widespread in Late and early Post Glacial Britain, but then its range shrank as tree-cover spread in the Post Glacial, restricting it to the higher ground in Scotland which trees did not cover. However, it is not confined to open conditions in Scandinavia; it can at least tolerate birch scrub, and perhaps even denser woodland. So another thesis is that it was actually displaced from southern Britain by the introduced brown hare. In Sweden, the recently (1890s) introduced brown hare is hybridising with and displacing the mountain hare (Thulin 2003). It would require archaeological data to distinguish these two explanations. Interestingly, Turk (1964) reported both brown and mountain hare bones in a Bronze Age fissure at Hartle Dale, in the Peak District. If both dating and identifications are correct (and the latter certainly seem to be), these may represent both the latest English mountain hares and the earliest English brown hares of which we have record. This and any similar records deserve checking, and certainly merit radiocarbon dating.

The occurrences of island races, and of species on islands, including Ireland, where introduction is suspected, obviously offer a fertile area for further study, both genetical and archaeological. Given the extensive studies by Berry on the epigenetic variation in *Apodemus sylvaticus* skulls, confirming the important parts of his interpretation (for instance, that wood mice on St Kilda, Shetland and the Inner Isles parish are related to Scandinavian, not Scottish, mice; Berry 1969) merits genetical effort. It was argued that Irish wood mice, too, came from Norway, but the discovery of a Mesolithic specimen in a tufa deposit undermines that argument (Preece *et al.* 1986). Fortunately, a genetic study of *Apodemus* is already underway at York and elsewhere (J. Searle pers. comm.). The white-toothed shrews of the Isles of Scilly and the Channel Isles also merit attention. Presumably, the *Crocidura suaveolens* on the Scillies, believed from archaeological specimens to have been there since Bronze Age times, represent, like the Orkney voles, an early accidental introduction from somewhere further south – Spain? France? The fauna of the Channel Isles is hard to interpret. Each island has an idiosyncratic assemblage of small mammals. Jersey is near enough, and with a shallow enough sea between it and France, that it ought to have received a full complement of small mammals. It has a white-toothed shrew, *C. suaveolens*, as well as a red-toothed one, *Sorex coronatus*, has wood mouse and bank vole, but no *Microtus,* nor *Sorex minutus*. Guernsey does have a *Microtus, M. arvalis*, and wood mouse, but has no bank vole or *Sorex*, and has a different white-toothed shrew *C. russula*. Archaeological samples might give us some useful information on when these species arrived (all together? in stages?); genetical information should confirm whether came from the nearest French mainland, as seems likely for the wood mouse (Berry 1973) but unlikely for *C. suaveolens*, which does not occur (now, at least) in northern France. A similar research agenda could be set for the Manx fauna., and the Irish fauna continues to perplex us. The red deer was widely regarded as native until Woodman *et al.* (1997) found it unexpectedly absent from the Mesolithic site of Mount Sandel, and then found no Post Glacial radiocarbon dated specimens earlier than 4190 BP either. Pine marten and pigmy shrew were generally accepted as native until the genetical studies outlined above. If they are not native, which species are? Irish hares and stoats, present in the Late Glacial as well as the Post Glacial, are safely assumed to be native (emerging genetic evidence confirms that both are very variable as well as very distinct (Hughes *et al.* 2007; Martinkova *et al.* 2007)). By contrast, red fox and badger have no early archaeological record, and could instead be introductions, perhaps for fur. An early archaeological record or two might confirm their native status, limited genetic variability might confirm them as introductions. A slightly more challenging genetical study might examine the origins of domestic ducks and geese, combining surveys of the modern forms with, if possible, ancient DNA from archaeological specimens. Were mallard domesticated twice (east and west), like aurochs, or many times, like horses?

One further topic involving broader archaeological interpretation merits discussion. If the Mesolithic period saw deciduous woodland covering the majority of the British landscape, as the map by Bennett (1988) implies, then grazers like aurochs would have had little scope for living here; they would have been restricted, perhaps, to riverine and coastal grasslands and other small clearings (an analysis of the sites where aurochs have been recovered confirms that they are ecologically distinctive (more lowland, less wooded) (Hall 2008)). A modified interpretation of the pollen rain suggests that there might have been more grassland than conventionally allowed (Maroo and Yalden 2000). There is considerable debate about the reality of the notion of extensive woodland cover, the alternative notion being that the landscape might instead have been in a dynamic mosaic, in which the large ungulates themselves played an important part in creating and maintaining open grasslands during part of the cycle, until they scrubbed up and changed into woodlands (Vera 2000). Ungulates would then have inhibited any seedlings from growing in any clearings (as caused by trees falling, or aging), so that grasslands reappeared over perhaps a 500 year cycle. It is not easy to see how archaeological data could contribute to this debate: the relative density of different ungulates and their impact on woody vegetation cannot be assessed. However, better integration of information from large mammals, pollen and insect faunas might allow a better understanding of the possible mosaics of habitat then, and ecosystem modelling, integrating these various lines of evidence, might yield informative results. An alternative examination of the problem by Mitchell (2005) has compared the rate of change in the pollen record in Post Glacial Ireland, where wild boar were the only large ungulates, to that in Great Britain, where there were certainly also aurochs, elk, red and roe deer. The absence of any discernable difference suggests to him that ungulates were not influencing the development of the vegetation.

Clearly, a combination of archaeological, genetical and historical approaches will continue to illuminate the topics discussed here. If progress is as fast as during the last decade, we can expect both profound discoveries and zoological surprises.

Bibliography

Ainsley, C. (2002) 'The animal bones', 259–74 in J. Drummond-Murray and P. Thompson (eds), *Settlement in Roman Southwark: Archaeological Excavations (1991–8) for the London Underground Limited Jubilee Line Extension Project*, MoLAS Monograph Series 12, London

Albarella, U. (2006) 'Pig husbandry and pork consumption in medieval England', 72–87 in C. Woolgar, D. Serjeantson and T. Waldron (eds), *Food in Medieval England: diet and nutrition*, Oxford University Press, Oxford.

Albarella, U. (2007) 'The end of the Sheep Age: people and animals in the Late Iron Age', 389–402 in C. Haselgrove and T. Moore (eds.), *The Later Iron Age in Britain and Beyond*, Oxbow, Oxford.

Albarella, U., Beech, M. and Mulville, J. (1997) *The Saxon, Medieval and Post-Medieval mammal and bird bones excavated 1989–91 from Castle Mall, Norwich Norfolk*, (Ancient Monuments Laboratory Report 72/97), English Heritage, London.

Albarella, U. and Davis, S. (1996) 'Mammals and birds from Launceston Castle, Cornwall: decline in status and the rise of agriculture', *Circaea* 12 (1), 1–156.

Albarella, U, Davis, S., Detry, C. and Rowley-Conwy, P. (2006a) 'Pigs of the "Far West": the biometry of *Sus* from archaeological sites in Portugal', *Anthropozoologica* 40 (2), 27–54.

Albarella, U., Dobney, K. and Rowley-Conwy, P. (2009) 'Size and shape of the Eurasian wild boar (*Sus Scrofa*), with a view to the reconstruction of its Holocene history', *Environmental Archaeology* 14(2), 103–136.

Albarella, U., Marrazzo, D., Spinetti, A. and Viner, S. (in prep.) *A beaver hunting station in East Anglia? Animal remains and worked bone from Welland Bank Quarry (Lincolnshire, England)*.

Albarella, U. and Payne, S. (2005) 'Neolithic pigs from Durrington Walls, Wiltshire, England: a biometrical database', *Journal of Archaeological Science* 32 (4), 589–99.

Albarella, U. and Pirnie, T. (in prep.) *Animals of our past: zooarchaeological evidence from Central England*.

Albarella, U., Tagliacozzo, A., Dobney, K. and Rowley-Conwy, P. (2006b) 'Pig hunting and husbandry in prehistoric Italy: a contribution to the domestication debate', *Proceedings of the Prehistoric Society* 72, 193–227.

Albarella, U. and R. Thomas (2002) 'They dined on crane: bird consumption, wild fowling and status in medieval England', *Acta Zoologica Cracoviensia* 45, 23–38.

Allen, M. J. (1992) 'Products of erosion and the prehistoric land-use of the Wessex chalk', 37–52 in M. G. Bell and J. Boardman (eds), *Past and Present Soil Erosion: Archaeological and Geographical Perspectives*, Oxbow, Oxford.

Allen, M. G. (2009) 'The re-identification of great bustard (*Otis tarda*) from Fishbourne Roman Palace, Chichester, West Sussex, as common crane (*Grus grus*)', *Environmental Archaeology* 14(2), 184–190.

Allen, T., Barclay, A. and Lamdin-Whymark, H. (2004) 'Opening the wood, making the land: the study of a Neolithic landscape in the Dorney area of the Middle Thames Valley', 82–98 in J. Cotton and D. Field (eds), *Towards a New Stone Age: Aspects of the Neolithic in South-east England*, Council for British Archaeology Research Report 137, York.

Allen, T. G. and Robinson, M. A. (1993) *The Prehistoric Landscape and Iron Age Enclosed Settlement at Mingies Ditch, Hardwick-with-Yelford, Oxon*, (Thames Valley Landscapes: The Windrush Valley 2), Oxford University Committee for Archaeology, Oxford.

Allison, E. (1981) 'The bird bones', 231–2 in B. Harbottle and M. Ellison (eds), 'An excavation in the Castle Ditch, Newcastle-Upon-Tyne, 1974–6', *Archaeologia Aeliana* 9, 75–250.

Allison, E. P., Hall, A. R., Jones, A. K. G., Kenward, H. K. and Robertson, A. (1996) 'Report on plant and invertebrate remains', 85–105 in R. L. Kemp (ed.), *Anglian Settlement at 46–54 Fishergate*, (The Archaeology of York 7.1), Council for British Archaeology, York.

Allison, E., Hall, A. and Kenward, H. (1999) 'Technical report. Living conditions and resource exploitation at the Early Christian rath at Deer Park Farms, Co. Antrim, N. Ireland: evidence from plants and invertebrates. Part 1: Text', *Reports from the Environmental Archaeology Unit*, York 99/8, 64 pp. and 'Part 2: Tables', *Reports from the Environmental Archaeology Unit*, York 99/10, 144

Alves, P., Ferrand, N., Suchentruck, F., and Harris, D.J. (2003) 'Ancient introgression of *Lepus timidus* mtDNA into *L granatensis* and *L. europaeus* in the Iberian peninsula', *Molecular Phylogenetics and Evolution* 27, 70–80.

Anderson, J. K. (1985) *Hunting in the Ancient World*, University of California Press, London.

Anderung, C. (2006) *Genetic Analysis of Bovid Remains and the Origin of Early European Cattle*, dissertation of the University of Uppsala, Faculty of Science and Technology 234 (available on-line www.diva-portal.org/diva/getDocument?urn_nbn_se_uu_diva-7201-1__fulltext.pdf).

Andrews, C. W. (1917) 'Report on the remains of birds found at the Glastonbury Lake-Village', 631–37 in A. Bulleid and H. S. G. Gray (eds), *The Glastonbury Lake Village, Vol. II*, Antiquarian Society, Glastonbury.

Anon (1994) 'Earliest great auk', *British Archaeological News* 12 (4), 8.

Appadurai, A. (1986) 'Introduction: commodities and the politics of value', 3–63 in A. Appadurai (ed.), *The Social Lives of Things: Commodities in Cultural Perspective*, Cambridge University Press, Cambridge.

Armit, I. (2006) *Anatomy of an Iron Age Roundhouse: The Cnip Wheelhouse Excavations, Lewis,* Society of Antiquaries of Scotland, Edinburgh.

Armitage, P. L. (1979) *The Mammalian Remains from the Roman, Medieval and Early Modern Levels, St Magnus, City of London*, (Ancient Monuments Laboratory Report 2806), English Heritage, London.

Armitage, P. L. (1984) 'The faunal remains', 131–48 in A. Thompson, F. Grew and J. Schofield (eds), 'Excavations at Aldgate 1974', *Post-Medieval Archaeology* 18, 1–148.

Armitage, P. L. (1994) 'Unwelcome companions: ancient rats reviewed', *Antiquity* 68, 231–40.

Armitage, P. L. (in prep) 'The animal bones', in D. Divers (ed.), *Excavations at Southwark Cathedral; Montagu Close Phases 1 and 2.* PCA Monograph

Amitage, P. and Chapman, H. (1979) 'Roman mules', *The London Archaeologist* B, 339–46, 359

Armitage, P. L. and Clutton-Brock, J. (1981) 'A radiological and histological investigation into the mummification of cats from Ancient Egypt', *Journal of Archaeological Science* 8, 185–96.

Armitage, P. L., West, B. and Steedman, K. (1984) 'New evidence of Black Rat in Roman London', *The London Archaeologist* 4, 375–83.

Armour-Chelu, J. M. (1992) *Vertebrate Resource Exploitation, Biology, and Taphonomy in Neolithic Britain,* unpublished PhD thesis Institute of Archaeology (UCL) and British Museum (Natural History).

Ashdown, R. R. (1982). 'Osteological report on the porcine skeleton from Stanstead Abbots', in A. G Davies, A. V. B Gibson and R. R. Ashdown 'A Mesolithic site at Stanstead Abbots, Hertfordshire', *Hertfordshire Archaeology* 8, 1–10.

Ashdown, R. and Evans, C. (1981) 'Animal bones', 205–37 in C. Partridge (ed.), *Skeleton Green: A Late Iron Age and Romano-British Site*, Britannia Monograph Series 2, London.

Atkinson, J. C. (1889) *Cartularium Abbathiae de Rievalle Ordinis Cisterciensis fundatae anno 1132*, Surtees Society, Durham.

Audoin, F. (1984) *Ossements animaux du Moyen Age au monastère de La Charité-sur-Loire*, Publications de la Sorbonne, Paris.

Auffray J.-C., Tchernov E, Nevo E. (1988) 'Origine du commensalisme de la souris domestique *Mus musculus domesticus* vis-à-vis de l'homme', *Comptes Rendus de l'Académie des Sciences de Paris* 307, 517–22.

Auffray J-C, Vanlerberghe F, Britton-Davidian J. (1990) 'The house mouse progression in Eurasia: a palaeontological and archaeozoological approach', *Biological Journal of the Linnean Society* 41, 13–25.

Aybes, C. and Yalden, D. W. (1995) 'Place-name evidence for the former distribution and status of wolves and beavers in Britain', *Mammal Review* 25, 201–227.

Ayton, W. (1998) *Salmon Fisheries in England and Wales,* Atlantic Salmon Trust, Pitlochry.

Bailey, M. (1988) 'The rabbit and the medieval East Anglian economy', *Agricultural History Review* 36, 1–20.

Baker, P. (1998) *The Vertebrate Remains from Scole-Dickleburgh, Excavated in 1993 (Norfolk and Suffolk) A140 and A143 Road Improvement Project*, (Ancient Monuments Laboratory Report 29/98), English Heritage, London.

Balčiauskas, L. and Volodka, H. (2001) 'Some aspects of human dimensions of large carnivores in north-west Lithuania', 92–102 in L. Balčiauskas, (ed), *Proceedings of the BLCI Symposium 'Human dimensions of large carnivores in Baltic countries'*, Siauliai, Lithuania.

Baldwin, J. R. (1974) 'Sea bird fowling in Scotland and Faroe', *Folk Life* 12, 60–130.

Balharry, D. and Daniels, M. (1998) *Wild living cats in Scotland*, Scottish Natural Heritage Research, Survey and Monitoring Report No. 23.

Ball, M. J. with Fife J. (1993) *The Celtic Languages*, Routledge, London.

Barbé, F. and Garrett, S. (2007) Appendix. 8.0, *Review of Pike Policy in Ireland*, Irish Federation of Pike Angling Clubs and Irish Pike Society. www.angling-in-ireland.com/pages/Appendix.htm

Barclay, A., Serjeantson, D. and Wallis, J. (1999) 'Worked bone and antler', 74–5 in A. Barclay and C. Halpin (eds),

Excavations at Barrow Hills, Radley, Oxfordshire. Volume 1: The Neolithic and Bronze Age Monument Complex, Thames Valley Landscapes Volume 11, Oxford.

Barker, G. (1976) 'The animal bones', 46–8 + tables I–IV in T. W. J. Potter (ed.), Excavations at Stonea, Cambs: Sites of the Neolithic, Bronze Age and Roman Periods. *Proceedings of the Cambridge Antiquarian Society* 66.

Barker, G. (1983) 'The animal bones', 133–50 in J.W. Hedges (ed.), *Isbister. A chambered tomb in Orkney*, British Archaeological Reports, British series 115, Oxford.

Barrett, J. (2002) *The Fish Bone from Excavations at Saxon Flixborough, Lincolnshire*, Unpublished Report.

Barrett, J. H. Locker, A. M. and Roberts, C. M. (2004), '"Dark Age Economics" revisited: the English fish bone evidence AD 600–1600', *Antiquity*, 78 (301), 618–36.

Barrett-Hamilton, G. E. H. and Hinton, M. A. C. (1910–1922) *A History of British Mammals*, Gurney and Jackson, London.

Bartlett, R. (2000) *England Under the Norman and Angevin Kings 1075–1225*, Clarendon Press, Oxford

Barton, R. N. E., Jacobi, R. M., Stapert, D. and Street, M. J. (2003) 'The Late-glacial reoccupation of the British Isles and the Creswellian', *Journal of Quaternary Science* 18(7), 631–43.

Bartosiewicz, L. (1993) 'Late medieval lynx skeleton from Hungary', 5–16 in A. Clason, S. Payne and H. P. Uerpmann (eds), *Skeletons in Her Cupboard: Festchrift for Juliet Clutton-Brock*, Oxbow Monograph 34, Oxford.

Baxter, I. L. (1993) 'Eagles in Anglo-Saxon and Norse poems', *Circaea* 10(2), 78–81.

Baxter, I. (2002) 'A donkey (Equus asinus L.) partial skeleton from a Mid-Late Anglo-Saxon alluvial layer at Deans Yard, Westminster, London SW1', *Environmental Archaeology* 7, 89–94.

Baxter, I. (2009) 'The mammal, amphibian and bird bones', 295–304 in S. Rátkai (ed.), *The Bull Ring Uncovered. Excavations at Edgbaston Street, Moor Street, Park Street and The Row, Birmingham, 1997–2001*, Oxbow Books, Oxford.

Bedwin, O. (1975) 'Animal bones', 189–90 in D. J. Freke (ed.) 'Further excavations in Lewes', *Sussex Archaeological Collections* 114, 176–93.

Beech, M. (1986) 'The animal bones', 45–7 in R. Holgate (ed.), 'Excavations at the Late Prehistoric and Romano-British enclosure complex at Carne's Seat, Goodwood, West Sussex' *Sussex Archaeological Collections* 124, 35–51.

Beeton, I. (1982) *Mrs Beeton's Book of Household Management*, First published in 1861, Chancellor Press, London.

Beglane, F. (2007) *Report on Faunal Material from Greencastle, Co. Down, 057:003, Licence No. AE/01/13*, unpublished report for Centre for Archaeological Fieldworks, Queens University, Belfast.

Beja-Pereiera, A. and 26 others (2006) 'The origin of European cattle: evidence from modern and ancient DNA', *Proceedings of the National Academy of Sciences* 103 (21), 8113–18.

Belfer-Cohen, A. and Hovers, E. (1992) 'In the eye of the beholder: Mousterian and Natufian burials in the Levant', *Current Anthropology* 33(4), 463–71.

Bell, M. G. (1983) 'Valley sediments as evidence of prehistoric land-use on the South Downs', *Proceedings of the Prehistoric Society* 49, 119–50.

Bell, M. G. (1990) 'Sedimentation rates in the primary fills of chalk-cut features', 237–48 in D. E. Robinson (ed.), *Experimentation and Reconstruction in Environmental Archaeology*, Oxbow Books, Oxford.

Bell, T. (1837) *A History of Quadrupeds*, John van Voorst, London.

Bendrey R. (1999) 'A note on the identification of donkey (*Equus asinus* L.) bones from Roman Southwark', *Organ* 22, 7–12.

Bendrey, R. (2003) 'The identification of fallow deer (*Dama dama*) remains from Roman Monkton, the Isle of Thanet, Kent', 15–18 in I. D. Riddler (ed.), *Materials of Manufacture: The Choice of Materials in the Working of Bone and Antler in Northern and Central Europe During the First Millennium AD*, British Archaeological Report, international series S1193, Oxford.

Bendrey, R. (2005) 'The Animal Bone' 64–66 and 103–105 in J. Butler (ed.), *Saxons, Templars and Lawyers in the Inner Temple*, Pre-Construct Archaeology Monograph No 4, Durham.

Bendrey, R. (2007a) *The Development of New Methodologies for Studying the Horse: Case Studies from Prehistoric Southern England*, unpublished PhD thesis, University of Southampton.

Bendrey, R. (2007b) 'Work- and age-related changes in an Iron Age horse skeleton from Danebury hillfort, Hampshire', *Archaeofauna* 16, 73–84.

Bendrey, R. (2007c) 'New methods for the identification of evidence for bitting on horse remains from archaeological sites', *Journal of Archaeological Science* 34, 1036–50.

Bendrey, R., Hayes, T. E. and Palmer, M. R. (2009) 'Patterns of Iron Age horse supply: an analysis of strontium isotope ratios in teeth', *Archaeometry* 51, 140–150.

Benecke, N. (1993) 'On the utilization of the domestic fowl in Central Europe from the Iron Age up to the Middle Ages', *Archaeofauna* 2, 21–31.

Bennett, K. D. (1988) 'A provisional map of forest types for the British Isles 5,000 years ago', *Journal of Quaternary Science* 4, 141–4.

Benson, D. G., Evans, J. G., Williams, G. H., Darvill, T. and David, A. (1990), 'Excavations at Stackpole Warren, Dyfed', *Proceedings of the Prehistoric Society* 56, 179–245.

Benton, S. (1931) 'The excavation of the Sculptor's Cave, Covesea, Morayshire', *Proceedings of the Society of Antiquaries of Scotland* 65, 177–216.

Berg, D. (1998) 'Faunal remains assessment', in D. Powlesland (ed.), The West Heslerton Assessment', *Internet Archaeology* 5, http://intarch.ac.uk/journal/issue 5.

Berg, D. (1999) 'Animal bones', 223–80 in P. Abramson, D. Berg and M. R. Fossick (eds), *Roman Castleford Excavations 1974–85. Vol 2: The Structural and Environmental Evidence*, (Yorkshire Archaeology 5), West Yorkshire Archaeology Service, Wakefield.

Bergman, C. (1847) 'Uber die Verhaltnisse der Warmekonomie der Thiere zu ihrer Grosse', *Göttingen Studien* 3, 595–705.

Bergman, C. A., McEwen, E. and Miller, R. (1988) 'Experimental Archaeology: projectile velocities and comparison of bow performances', *Antiquity* 62, 658–70.

Berry, R. J. (1969) 'History in the evolution of *Apodemus sylvaticus* at one edge of its range', *Journal of Zoology* 159, 311–66.

Berry, R. J. (1973) 'Chance and change in British long-tailed field mice (*Apodemus sylvaticus*)', *Journal of Zoology* 170, 351–366.

Berry R. J., Cuthbert A. and Peters J. (1982) 'Colonization by house mice: an experiment', *Journal of Zoology* 198, 329–36.

Bevan, L. and Moore, J. (2003) *Peopling the Mesolithic in a Northern Environment*, British Archaeological Report, international series 1157, Oxford.

Bilton, D. T., Mirol, P. M., Mascheretti, S., Fredga, K., and Searle, J. B. (1998) 'The Mediterranean region of Europe as an area of endemism for small mammals rather than the major source for the postglacial colonisation of northern Europe', *Proceedings of the Royal Society of London B* 265, 1219–26.

Birks, H. J. B. (1988) 'Long-term ecological change in the British uplands', 37–56 in M. B. Usher and D. B. A. Thompson (eds), *Ecological Change in the Uplands*, Blackwell Scientific Publications, Oxford.

Birrell, J. (1992) 'Deer and deer farming in medieval England', *Agricultural History Review* 40 (2), 112–26.

Birrell, J. (2006) 'Procuring, preparing and serving venison in late medieval England', 176–88 in C. Woolgar, D.

Serjeantson and T. Waldron (eds), *Food in Medieval England: Diet and Nutrition*, Oxford University Press, Oxford.

Blaauw, W. H. (1847) 'On the Nonae of 1340, as relating to Sussex', *Sussex Archaeological Collections* 1, 58–64.

Blackburn, K. B. (1952) 'The dating of a deposit containing an elk skeleton at Neasham near Darlington', *New Phytologist* 51, 364–77.

Blanchet, M. (1994) *Le Castor et son Royaume*, (2nd edition, 1st edition published 1977), Delachaux et Niestlé, Lausanne.

Blank, T. H. (1984) 'Pheasants and partridges', 311–15 in I. L. Mason (ed.), *Evolution of Domesticated Animals*, Longman, London.

Blockley, S. M. (2005) 'Two hiatuses in human bone radiocarbon dates in Britain (17000 to 5000 cal BP)', *Antiquity* 79, 505–13.

Boessnek, J. (1957) 'Funde des Ures, *Bos primigenius* Boj., aus alluvialen Schichten Bayerns', *Säugetierkundliche Mitteilungen* 5, 55–69.

Boessneck, J. (1973) *Die Tierknochenfunde aus dem Kabirenheiligtum bei Theben*. Institut für Palaeoanatomie, Domestikationsforschung und Geschichte der Tiermedizin, Munich.

Boisseau, S. and Yalden, D. W. (1998) 'The former status of the crane *Grus grus* in Britain', *Ibis* 140, 482–500.

Bökönyi, S. (1974) *History of Domestic Mammals in Central and Eastern Europe*, Akadémiai Kiadó, Budapest.

Bollongino, R., Edwards, C. J. Alt, K. W., Burger, J. and Bradley, D. G. (2006) 'Early history of European domestic cattle as revealed by ancient DNA', *Proceedings of the Royal Society Series B* 2, 155–9.

Bond, C. J. and Chambers, R. A. (1988) 'Oxfordshire fishponds', 353–70 in M. Aston (ed.), *Medieval Fisheries and Fishponds in England*, British Archaeological Report, British series 182(ii)), Oxford.

Bond, J. (1988) 'Rabbits: the case for their medieval introduction into Britain', *The Local Historian* 18, 53–7.

Bond, J. (2007) 'The mammal bone', 247–62 in J. Hunter (ed.), *Investigations in Sanday, Orkney, Volume 1, Excavations at Pool, Sanday – A Multi-Period Settlement from Neolithic to Late Norse Times*, Oxbow, Oxford.

Bond J. M. and O'Connor T. P. (1999) *Bones from Medieval Deposits at 16–22 Coppergate and Other Sites in York*, (The Archaeology of York: The Animal Bones 15/5), Council for British Archaeology, London.

Bond, J. M., Nicholson, R. A., O'Connor, T. P. and Cussans, J. 2006. 'The animal bones', 242–62, in J. Hunter (ed.) *Excavations at Pool, Sanday*, Society of Antiquaries of Scotland, Edinburgh.

Bottema, S., and Van Zeist, W. (1981) 'Palynological

evidence for the climatic history of the Near East, 50,000–6,000 BP', 111–132 in J. Cauvin and P. Sanlaville (eds), *Préhistoire du Levant*, (Actes du Colloque Intenational 598), Centre National de la Recherche Scientifique, Paris.

Bourdillon, J. (n.d.) *Introduction to the archive of animal bones for 4 sites in Barnstaple, North Devon (BAF86, ND020, ND127, ND150)*, unpublished report.

Bourdillon, J. and Coy, J. P. (1980) 'The animal bones', 79–120 in P. Holdsworth (ed.), *Excavations at Melbourne Street, Southampton, 1971–76,* Council British Archaeology Research Report 33, London.

Bourdillon, J. with Andrews, P. (1997) 'The animal bone', 242–5 in P. Andrews, *Excavations at Hamwic: Volume 2: Excavations at Six Dials,* Council for British Archaeology Research Report 109, York.

Bourne, W. R. P. (1981) 'The birds and animals consumed when Henry VIII entertained the King of France and the Count of Flanders at Calais in 1532', *Archives of Natural History* 10(2), 331–33.

Bowsher, D., Holder, N., Howell, I. and Dyson, T. (2008) *The London Guildhall: The Archaeology and History of the Guildhall Precinct from the Medieval Period to the 20th Century*, MoLAS Monograph Series 36, London.

Boyd, B. (2006) 'On sedentism in the Later Epipalaeolithic (Natufian) Levant', *World Archaeology* 38 (2), 164–78

Boyd Dawkins, W. B. (1910) 'The arrival of man in Britain in the Pleistocene Age', *Journal of the Royal Anthropological Institute of Great Britain and Ireland* 40, 233–63.

Boyeskorov, G. (1999) 'New data on moose (*Alces,* Artiodactyla) systematics', *Säugetierkundliche Mitteilungen* 44, 3–13.

Boyle, K. V. (2006) 'Neolithic wild game animals in Western Europe: the question of hunting', 10–23 in D. Serjeantson and D. Field (eds) *Animals in the Neolithic of Britain and Europe*, Oxbow, Oxford.

Bramwell, D. (1969) 'Identification of bird bones', 115 in P. A. Rahtz (ed.), *Excavations at King John's Hunting Lodge, Writtle, Essex, 1955–57*, Society for Medieval Archaeology Monograph No. 3, London.

Bramwell, D. (1975a) 'The bird bones', 340–42 in C. Platt and R. Coleman-Smith (eds.), *Excavations in Medieval Southampton, 1953–69, Volume 1*, Leicester University Press, London.

Bramwell, D. (1975b). 'Bird remains from medieval London', *London Naturalist* 54, 15–20.

Bramwell, D. (1983) 'The bird remains', 159–70 in J. W. Hedges, *Isbister: a chambered tomb in Orkney*, British Archaeological Report, British series 115, Oxford.

Bramwell, D. (1985) 'The bird bones', 94–95 in R. Shoesmith (ed.), *Hereford City Excavations, Volume 3: The finds,*

Council for British Archaeology Research Report 56, London.

Bramwell, D. (1986) 'The bird bones', 120–21 in J. Bateman and M. Redknap (eds), *Coventry: Excavations on The Town Wall 1976–78*, Coventry Museums Monograph Series No. 2, Coventry.

Bramwell, D. (1994) 'Bird bones' 121–122 in E. Greenfield, J. Poulsen and P. V. Irving, 'The Excavation of a Fourth-Century AD Villa and Bath-House at Great Staughton, Cambridgeshire, 1958 and 1959'. *Proceedings of the Cambridge Antiquarian Society* 83, 75–127.

Bramwell, D., Yalden, D. W. and Yalden, P. E. (1990) 'Ossum's Eyrie Cave: an archaeological contribution to the recent history of vertebrates in Britain', *Quaternary Journal of the Linnaean Society* 98, 1–25.

Branco, M., Monnerot, M., Ferrand, N. and Templeton, A. R. (2002) 'Postglacial dispersal of the European Rabbit (*Oryctolagus cuniculus*) on the Iberian Peninsula reconstructed from nested clade and mismatch analyses of mitochondrial DNA genetic variation', *Evolution* 56 (4), 792–803.

Breitenmoser, U. (1998) 'Large predators in the Alps: the fall and rise of Man's Competitors', *Biological Conservation* 83 (3), 279–289.

Britnell, R. (2004) *Britain and Ireland 1050–1530: Economy and Society*, Oxford University Press, Oxford.

Britnell, W. J. (1976) 'Antler cheekpieces of the British Late Bronze Age', *Antiquaries Journal* 56, 24–34.

Bronk Ramsey, C. (2001) 'Development of the Radiocarbon Program OxCal', *Radiocarbon* 43, 355–63.

Bronk Ramsey, C. (1995) 'Radiocarbon calibration and analysis of stratigraphy: The OxCal program', *Radiocarbon* 37, 425–30.

Bronk Ramsey, C., Pettit, P. B., Hedges, R. E. M., Hodgins, G. W. L. and Owen, D. C. (2000) 'Radiocarbon dates from the Oxford AMS system: Archaeometry datelist 30', *Archaeometry* 42 (2), 459–79.

Brothwell, D. R. (1981) 'The Pleistocene and Holocene archaeology of the House Mouse and related species', *Symposia of the Zoological Society, London* 47, 1–13.

Brothwell, D. and Jones, R. (1978) 'The relevance of small mammal studies to archaeology', 47–58 in D. R. Brothwell, K. D. Thomas and J. Clutton-Brock (eds) *Research Problems in Zooarchaeology,* (Occasional Publications 3), Insititute of Archaeology, London.

Brown, D. (2002) 'The foulmart: what's in a name?', *Mammal Review* 32 (2), 145–9.

Brown, D. and Anthony, D. (1998) 'Bit wear, horseback riding and the Botai site in Kazakstan', *Journal of Archaeological Science* 25, 331–47.

Bruce-Mitford and East, K. (1983) 'The drinking horns', 324–7 in R. Bruce-Mitford (ed.), *The Sutton Hoo Ship-*

Burial Vol. 3, British Museum Publications, London.

Bryant, J. P. and Kuropat, P. J. (1980) 'Selection of winter forage by subarctic browsing vertebrates', *Annual Review of Ecology and Systematics* 11, 261–285.

Buckland, P. C. (1979) *Thorne Moors: A Palaeoecological Study of a Bronze Age Site (A Contribution to the History of the British Insect Fauna)*, (Department of Geography Occasional Publications 8), University of Birmingham, Birmingham.

Buckland, P. C. (1981) 'The early dispersal of insect pests of stored products as indicated by archaeological records', *Journal of Stored Products Research* 17, 1–12.

Buckland, P. C. (1996) 'Insects', 165–70 in J. May (ed.), *Dragonby: Report on Excavations at an Iron Age and Romano-British Settlement in North Lincolnshire*, Oxbow Monograph 61, Oxford.

Buckland, P. C., Beal, C. J. and Heal, S. V. E. (1990) 'Recent work on the archaeological and environmental context of the Ferriby boats', 131–46 in S. Ellis and D. R. Crowther (eds), *Humber Perspectives: a region through the Ages*, Hull University Press, Hull.

Buckland, P. C., Holdsworth, P. and Monk, M. (1976) 'The interpretation of a group of Saxon pits in Southampton', *Journal of Archaeological Science* 3, 61–9.

Buckland, P. C. and Wagner, P. E. (2001) 'Is there an insect signal for the "Little Ice Age"?', *Climatic Change* 48, 137–49.

Budiansky, S. (2002) *The Character of Cats*, Weidenfeld and Nicolson, London.

Bullock, A. (1994) 'Evidence for fish exploitation from Tudor deposits excavated at Little Pickle, Surrey, England', 267–74 in D. Heinrich (ed.) *Archaeo-Ichthyological Studies. Papers Presented at the 6th Meeting of the ICAZ Fish Remains Working Group*, (OFFA 51), Wachholtz Verlag, Neumunster.

Burleigh, R., Currant, A., Jacobi, E. and Jacobi, R. (1991) 'A note on some British Late Pleistocene remains of horse (*Equus ferus*)', 233–37 in R. H. Meadows and H.-P. Uerpmann (eds.), *Equids in the Ancient World, Volume II*, Dr Ludwig Reichert Verlag, Wiesbaden.

Burnett, D. P. (1992) 'Animal bone from Great Linford Village', 231–9 in D. C. Mynard and R. J. Zeepvat (eds), *Great Linford: A Medieval Village at Milton Keynes*, Buckinghamshire Archaeological Society Monograph Series 3.

Butler, V. and Chatters, J. (1994) 'The role of fish density in structuring prehistoric salmon bone assemblages', *Journal of Archaeological Science* 21, 413–24.

Callou, C. (2003) *De la Garenne au Clapier: Etude Archéozoologique du Lapin en Europe Occidental*, (Mémoires du Muséum National d'Histoire Naturelle, Tome 189), Publications Scientifiques du Muséum, Paris.

Canby, J. I. (1977) *The Animal Bones from Hayton: An Illustration of the Possibilities of Bone Studies*, unpublished BA dissertation, University College, Cardiff.

Cantor, L. M. and Wilson, J. D. (1961) 'The mediaeval deer-parks of Dorset: I' *Dorset Natural History and Archaeology Society* 83, 109–16.

Carrott, J. and Kenward, H. K. (2001) 'Species associations among insect remains from urban archaeological deposits and their significance in reconstructing the past human environment', *Journal of Archaeological Science* 28(8), 887–905.

Carrott, J., Hall, A., Issitt, M., Jaques, D., Kenward, H., and Large, F. (1995) *Evaluation of biological remains from excavations at Tower Street, Hull (site code HCT95)*, Reports from the Environmental Archaeology Unit, York 95/37.

Carter, H. H. (1975) 'Fauna of an area of Mesolithic occupation in the Kennet valley, considered in relation to contemporary eating habits', *Berkshire Archaeological Journal* 68, 1–3.

Carter, J. (1874) 'On the skull of a *Bos primigenius* penetrated by a stone celt', *Geological Magazine*, Decade II, Volume I, 11, 1–4.

Cartmill, M. (1993) *A View to a Death in the Morning: Hunting and Nature Through History*, Harvard University Press, Cambridge.

Carus-Wilson, E. M. (1967) *Medieval Merchant Venturers: Collected Studies*, Meuthen, London.

Carver, M. (1998) *Sutton Hoo: Burial Ground of Kings?*, The British Museum Press, London.

Caseldine, C., Gearey, B., Hutton, J., Reilly, E., Stujs, I. and Casparie, W. (2001) 'From the wet to the dry: palaeoecological studies at Derryville, Co. Tipperary, Ireland', 99–115 in B. Raftery and J. Hickey (eds), *Recent Developments in Wetland Research*, (UCD/WARP Occasional Paper 14), University College Dublin, Dublin.

Cerón-Carrasco, R. (1994) 'Feathers from deposit F23 in the stone-lined pit (F22)', 414 in F. McCormick, 'Excavations at Pluscarden Priory, Moray', *Proceedings of the Society for Antiquaries Scotland* 124, 391–432.

Champion, T. (1999) 'The Later Bronze Age', 95–111 in J. R. Hunter and I. B. M. Ralston (eds.) *The Archaeology of Britain: An Introduction from the Upper Palaeolithic to the Industrial Revolution*, Routledge, London.

Chaplin, R. E. (1968–9) 'The animal bones from three late and post-medieval rubbish pits found at the Broad Street site, Worcester', in P. A. Barker, 'The origins of Worcester', *Transactions of Worcestershire Archaeological Society* 2, 89–91.

Chapman, N. and Chapman, D. (1975) *Fallow Deer: Their History, Distribution and Biology*, Terence Dalton, Lavenham.

Charles, B. and Ingrem, C. (2001) 'Animal bone', 76–82 in D. Poore and D. R. P. Wilkinson (eds), *Beaumont Palace and the White Friars: Excavations at the Sackler Library, Beaumont Street*, Oxford Archaeological Unit Occasional Paper 9, Oxford.

Charles, R. and Jacobi, R. M. (1994) 'The Lateglacial fauna from Robin Hood Cave, Cresswell: a re-assessment', *Oxford Journal of Archaeology* 13, 1–32.

Childe, V. G. (1935) *The Prehistory of Scotland*, Kegan, Paul, Trench and Trubner, London.

Childs, J. E. (1986) 'Size-dependent predation on rats (*Rattus norvegicus*) by house cats (*Felis catus*) in an urban setting', *Journal of Mammalogy* 67, 196–99.

Chowne, P., Girling, M. and Greig, J. (1986) 'Excavations at an Iron Age defended enclosure at Tattershall Thorpe, Lincolnshire', *Proceedings of the Prehistoric Society* 52, 159–88.

Clark, J. G. D. (1948) 'Fowling in prehistoric Europe', *Antiquity* 22, 116–30.

Clark, J. G. D. (1954) *Excavations at Star Carr*, Cambridge University Press, Cambridge.

Clark, J. M. (1976) 'Variation in coat colour gene frequencies and selection in the cats of Scotland', *Genetica* 46, 401–12.

Clark, W. B. (2006) *A Medieval Book of Beasts. The Second-Family Bestiary: Commentary, Art, Text and Translation*, Boydell, Woodbridge

Clavel, B. (2001) *L'Animal dans l'Alimentation Medievale et Moderne en France du Nord (XIIe – XVIIe siècles)*, Revue Archeolgique de Picardie No Spécial 19.

Clements, J. S. (1990) 'Bone report', 14 in D. Child (ed.), *The Excavations of a Stone-Lined Pit in the Garden of Richmond House, Cooks Green, Winchelsea, 1988–89*, HAARG Occasional Paper, Hastings.

Clevedon Brown, J. and Twigg, G. (1969) 'Studies on the pelvis in British Muridae and Cricetidae (Rodentia)', *Journal of Zoology, London* 158, 81–132.

Clutton-Brock, J. (1979) 'Report of the mammalian remains other than rodents from Quanterness', 112–134 in A. C. Renfrew (ed.), *Investigations in Orkney*, Society of Antiquaries, London.

Clutton-Brock, J. (1988) *The British Museum Book of Cats*, British Museum Publications, London.

Clutton-Brock, J. (1991) 'Extinct species', 571–5 in G. B. Corbet and S. Harris (eds), *Handbook of British Mammals* (3rd edition), Blackwell Scientific, Oxford.

Clutton-Brock, J. (1992) *Horse Power*, Natural History Museum, London.

Clutton-Brock, J. (1999) *The Natural History of Domestic Mammals* (2nd edition), Cambridge University Press and The Natural History Museum, London.

Clutton-Brock, J. and Burleigh, R. (1991a), 'The mandible of a Mesolithic horse from Seamer Carr, Yorkshire, England', 238–41 in R. H. Meadows and H.-P. Uerpmann (eds.), *Equids in the Ancient World, Volume II*, Dr Ludwig Reichert Verlag, Wiesbaden.

Clutton-Brock, J. and Burleigh, R. (1991b) 'The skull of a Neolithic horse from Grime's Graves, Norfolk, England' 242–49 in R. H. Meadows and H.-P. Uerpmann (eds.), *Equids in the Ancient World, Volume II*, Dr Ludwig Reichert Verlag, Wiesbaden.

Clutton-Brock, T. H., Coulson, T. and Milner, J. M. (2004) 'Red deer stocks in the Highlands of Scotland', *Nature* 429, 261–2.

Clutton-Brock, J. and Macgregor, A. (1988) 'An end to medieval reindeer in Scotland', *Proceedings of the Society of Antiquaries of Scotland* 118, 23–35.

Coakley, F. (2008) *A Manx notebook: Genealogy Pages on the Isle of Man – Diseases*. www.isle-of-man.com/manxnotebook/famhist/genealogy/diseases.htm

Coard, R. and Chamberlain, A. T. (1999) 'The nature and timing of faunal change in the British Isles across the Pleistocene Holocene transition', *Holocene* 9 (3), 372–376.

Cocker, M. and Mabey, R. (2005) *Birds Britannica*, Chatto and Windus, London.

Cohen, E. (1994) 'Animals in medieval perceptions: the image of the ubiquitous other', 59–80 in A. Manning and J. Serpell (eds) *Animals and Human Society: Changing Perspectives*, Routledge, London.

Coles, B. and Colville, B. (1980) 'A glacial relict mollusc', *Nature* (London) 286, 761.

Coles, B. J. (2000) 'Beaver territories: the resource potential for humans', 80–9 in G. Bailey, R. Charles and N. Winder (eds) *Human Ecodynamics*, Oxbow, Oxford.

Coles, B. J. (2006) *Beavers in Britain's Past*, Oxbow, Oxford.

Coles, J. M., Fleming, A. M. and Orme, B. J. (1980) 'The Baker Site: a Neolithic platform', *Somerset Levels Papers* 6, 6–23.

Coles, J. M. and Orme, B. J. (1982) 'Beaver in the Somerset Levels: some new evidence', *Somerset Levels Papers* 8, 67–73.

Connell, B., Davis, S. J. M. and Locker, A. (1997) *Animal Bones from Camber Castle East Sussex, 1963–1983*, (Ancient Monuments Laboratory Report 107/97), English Heritage, London.

Conroy, J. W. H., Kitchener, A. C. and Gibson, J. A. (1998) 'The history of the beaver in Scotland and its future reintroduction', 107–28 in R. A. Lambert (ed.), *Species History in Scotland*, Scottish Cultural Press, Edinburgh.

Coope, G. R. (1994) 'The response of insect faunas to

glacial-interglacial climatic fluctuations', *Philosophical Transactions of the Royal Society of London, Series B* 344, 19–26.

Coope, G. R. (1998) 'Insects', 213–33 in R. C. Preece and D. R. Bridgland (eds), *Late Quaternary Environmental Change in North-West Europe: Excavations at Hollywell Coombe, South-East England*, Chapman and Hall, London.

Copley, M. S., Berston, R., Dudd, N. S., Docherty, G., Mukerjee, A. J., Straker, V., Payne, S. and Evershed, R. P. (2003) 'Direct chemical evidence for widespread dairying in prehistoric Britain', *Proceedings of the National Academy of Sciences* 100 (4), 1524–9.

Corbet, G. B. (1961) 'Origin of the British insular races of small mammals and of the 'Lusitanian' fauna', *Nature* 191, 1037–40.

Corbet, G. B. and Harris, S. (1991) *The Handbook of British Mammals. 3rd Edition.* Blackwell, Oxford.

Corbet, G. C. and Southern, H. N. (1977) *Handbook of British Mammals* (2nd ed.), Blackwell, Oxford.

Cornwall, I. W. (1976) 'Report on the animal bone', in F. de M. Vatcher and H. L. Vatcher, 'The excavation of a round barrow near Poor's Heath, Risby, Suffolk', *Proceedings of the Prehistoric Society* 42, 289–92.

Cosh, R. S. and Neal, D. S. (2002) *Roman Mosaics of Britain Volume 1: Northern Britain, Incorporating the Midlands and East Anglia*, The Society of Antiquaries of London, London.

Cosh, R. S. and Neal, D. S. (2005) *Roman Mosaics of Britain Volume 2: South-west Britain*, The Society of Antiquaries of London, London.

Cotton, J., Elsden, N., Pipe, A. and Rayner, L. (2006) 'Taming the wild: a final Neolithic/Earlier Bronze Age aurochs deposit from West London', 149–67 in D. Serjeantson and D. Field (eds), *Animals in the Neolithic of Britain and Europe.* (Neolithic Studies Group Seminar Papers 7), Oxbow, Oxford.

Cowles, G. S. (1981) 'The first evidence of Demoiselle Crane (*Anthropoides virgo*) and pygmy cormorant (*Phalacrocorax pygmaeus*) in Britain', *Bulletin of the British Ornithological Club* 101(4), 383–5.

Cox, J. C. (1905) *The Royal Forests of England*, Methuen & Co, London.

Coy, J. (1977) *Bird Bones from Wirral Park Farm (The Mound), Glastonbury*, (Ancient Monuments Laboratory Report 2326), English Heritage, London.

Coy, J. (1980) 'The animal bones' 41–51 in J. Haslam 'A Middle Saxon Iron Smelting Site at Ramsbury, Wiltshire', *Medieval Archaeology* 24, 1–67.

Coy, J. (1983) 'Animal bone' 43–45 in S. M. Davies, 'Excavations at Christchurch, Dorset, 1981 to 1983', *Proceedings of the Dorset Natural History and Archaeological Society* 105, 21–56.

Coy, J. P. (1984) 'The small mammals and amphibia', 526–31 in B. Cunliffe (ed.), *Danebury: An Iron Age Hillfort in Hampshire. Vol. 2 The excavations 1968–1978: The Finds*, Council for British Archaeology Research Report 52, London.

Coy, J. (1985) *Animal Bones from Excavations at Wickham Glebe, Hampshire, 1976–80*, (Ancient Monuments Laboratory Report 4914), English Heritage, London.

Coy, J. (1986–90) 'Animal bones' 100–101 in P. J. Fasham and I. J. Stewart, 'Excavations at Reading Abbey, 1985–86', *The Berkshire Archaeological Journal* 73, 88–103.

Coy. J. (1995) 'Animal Bones', 132–9 and microfiche in P. J. Fasham and G. Keevil with D. Coe (eds), *Brighton Hill South: an Iron Age Farmstead and Deserted Medieval Village in Hampshire*, Wessex Archaeology Report 7, Salisbury.

Coy, J. (in press) 'Late Saxon and Medieval Animal Bone from the Western Suburbs', in D. Serjeantson and H. Rees (eds), *Food, Craft and Status in Medieval Winchester: the plant and animal remains from the suburbs and city defences*, Winchester Museums, Winchester.

Crabtree, P. (1985) 'The Faunal Remains' 85–9 in S. West (ed.), *West Stow: The Anglo-Saxon Village*, East Anglian Archaeology 24, Ipswich.

Crabtree, P. J. (1989) *West Stow: Early Anglo-Saxon Animal Husbandry*, East Anglian Archaeology 47, Bury St. Edmunds.

Crabtree, P. J. (1990) *West Stow: Early Anglo-Saxon Animal Husbandry*, East Anglian Archaeology 47, Bury St. Edmunds

Crabtree, P. J. (1996) 'Production and consumption in an early complex society: animal use in Middle Saxon East Anglia', *World Archaeology* 28(1), 58–75.

Crawford, R. D. (1984) 'Turkey', 325–34 in I. L. Mason (ed.), *Evolution of Domesticated Animals*, Longman, London.

Cronon, W. (1983) *Changes in the Land: Indians, Colonists and the Ecology of New England*, Hill and Wang, New York.

Crummy, P. (1993) 'The development of Roman Colchester', 34–45 in S. J. Greep (ed.), *Roman Towns: The Wheeler Inheritance*, Council for British Archaeology Research Report 93, London.

Cucchi, T. and Vigne, J.-D. (2006) 'Origin and diffusion of the house mouse in the Mediterraean', *Journal of Human Evolution* 21(2), 95–106.

Cucchi, T., Vigne, J.-D. and Auffray, J.-C. (2005) 'First occurrence of the house mouse (*Mus musculus domesticus* Schwarz & Schwarz, 1943) in the Western Mediterranean: a zooarchaeological revision of subfossil occurrences', *Biological Journal of the Linnean Society* 84, 429–45.

Cuisin, J. and Vigne, J. (1998) 'Présence de la Grande Outarde (*Otis tarda*) au boréal dans la région de Bonifacio (Corse-du-sud, France 8ème millenaire av. J. C.)', *Geobios* 31 (6), 831–7.

Cummins J. (1988) *The Hound and the Hawk: The Art of Medieval Hunting*, Phoenix, London.

Cunliffe, B. (1978) *Hengistbury Head*, Paul Elek, London.

Cunliffe, B. (1984) *Danebury: An Iron Age Hillfort in Hampshire. Volume 2 The Excavations, 1969–78: The Finds*, Council for British Archaeology Research Report 52, London.

Cunliffe, B. (1998) *Fishbourne Roman Palace*, Tempus, Stroud.

Cunliffe, B. (2004) 'Wessex cowboys', *Oxford Journal of Archaeology* 23, 61–81.

Cunliffe, B. (2005) *Iron Age Communities in Britain* (Fourth edition), Routledge, London.

Currant, A. P. and Jacobi, R. M. (2001) 'A formal mammalian biostratigraphy for the Late Pleistocene of Britain', *Quaternary Science Reviews* 20, 1707–16.

Currie, C. (1984) 'Tichfield Fishponds Project 1984: Interim report', *Hants Field Club Newsletter* NS4, 21–2.

Currie, C. (1989) 'The role of fishponds in the monastic economy', 147–72 in R. Gilchrist and H. Mytum (eds), *The Archaeology of Rural Monasteries*, British Archaeological Report, British series 203, Oxford.

Currie, C. (1991) 'The early history of the carp and its economic significance in England', *Agricultural History Review* 39, 97–107.

Curry-Lindahl K. (1951) 'Lons (Lynx lynx) historia och nuvarande förekomst i Sverige och övriga Europa', *Sveriges Natur* 11, 122–62.

Daly, P. (1969) 'Approaches to faunal analysis in archaeology', *American Antiquity* 34, 146–53.

D'Arcy, G. (1999) *Ireland's Lost Birds*, Four Courts Press, Dublin.

Dark, P. (2000) *The Environment of Britain in the First Millennium*, Duckworth, London.

Daniels, M. J., Beaumont, M. A., Johnson, P. J., Balharry, D., Macdonald, D. W. and Barratt, E. (2001) 'Ecology and genetics of wild-living cats in the north-east of Scotland and the implications for the conservation of the wildcat', *Journal of Applied Ecology* 38, 146–161.

Danielsson, B. (1977) *The Art of Hunting, 1327/William Twiti*, Almqvist & Wiksell International, Stockholm.

Davies, A. L. and Tipping, R. (2004) 'Sensing small-scale human activity in the palaeoecological record: fine spatial resolution pollen analyses from Glen Affric, northern Scotland', *The Holocene* 14(2), 233–245.

Davies, P. (2006) '*Cochlicopa nitens* (Gallenstein) from early postglacial tufa at Bossington, Hampshire, UK', *Journal of Conchology* 39 (2), 229.

Darvill, T. (1987) *Prehistoric Britain*, Batsford, London.

Davis, A. (2004) 'The plant remains', 54–7 in L. Dunwoodie (ed.), *Pre-Boudican and Later Activity on the Site of the Forum: Excavations at 168 Fenchurch Street, City of London*, MoLAS Archaeology Studies Series 13, London.

Davis, S., Wilkinson, D. and Clare, T. (2007) 'Putative ritual deposition of Neolithic stone axes in a wetland context in Cumbria: refining the narrative using beetle remains', *Journal of Wetland Archaeology* 7, 73–81.

Davis, S. J. M. (1987) *The Archaeology of Animals*, Batsford, London.

Davis, S. J. M. (1997) *Animal bones from the Roman site Redlands Farm, Stanwick, Northamptonshire, 1990 excavations*, (Ancient Monuments Laboratory Report 106/97), English Heritage, London

Davis, S. J. M. (2005) *Animal bones from Roman São Pedro, Fronteira, Alentejo*, (Trabalhos do CIPA 88), Instituto Português de Arqueologia, Lisbon.

Davison, A., Birks, J. D. S., Brookes, R. C., Messenger, J. E., and Griffiths, H. I. (2001) 'Mitochondrial phylogeography and population history of pine martens *Martes martes* compared with polecats *Mustela putorius*', *Molecular Ecology* 10, 2479–88.

Dawkins, W. B. and Jackson, J. W. (1917) 'The remains of the Mammalia found in the lake village of Glastonbury', 641–72 in A. Bullied and A. St G. Gray (eds), *The Glastonbury Lake Village*, Glastonbury Antiquarian Society, Taunton.

Degerbøl, M. (1940) 'Mammalia', *Zoology of the Faroes* 55, 11.

Degerbøl, M. and Fredskild, B. (1970) *The Urus (Bos primigenius* Bojanus*) and Neolithic Domestic Cattle (Bos taurus domesticus* Linné*) in Denmark*, Munksgaard, Copenhagen.

Dent, A. (1974) *Lost Beasts of Britain*, Harrap, London.

Dent, A. (1976) *Dieren in de Kunst*. De Haan, Bussum.

Dictionary of the Irish Language (1913–1976) L: 235. 33–56, Royal Irish Academy, Dublin

Dinnin, M. (1997), 'Holocene beetle assemblages from the Lower Trent floodplain at Bole Ings, Nottinghamshire, U. K.', *Quaternary Proceedings* 5, 83–104.

Dobney, K. M. (n.d.) *Northern Regional Review of Environmental Archaeology: Vertebrates,* unpublished report.

Dobney, K. and Harwood, J. (1998) 'Here to stay? Archaeological evidence for the introduction of commensal and economically important mammals to the North of England', 373–87 in N. Benecke (ed.), *The Holocene History of the European Vertebrate Fauna: Modern Aspects of Research Workshop 6th–9th April 1998*, Verlag Marie Leidorf GmbH, Rahden/Westf.

Dobney, K. M., Jacques, D., Barrett, J. and Johnstone, C. (2007) *Farmers, Monks and Aristocrats: The Environmental Archaeology of an Anglo-Saxon Estate Centre at Flixborough, North Lincolnshire, UK*, Oxbow, Oxford.

Dobney, K. M., Jaques, S. D. and Irving, B. G. (1996) *Of Butchers and Breeds: Report on Vertebrate Remains from Various Sites in the City of Lincoln*, Lincoln Archaeological Studies 5, Lincoln.

Donkin, R. A. (1991) *Meleagrides: An Historical and Ethnogeographical Study of the Guinea Fowl*, Ethnographica Ltd, London.

Drew, C. (2004) *Animal Bones from Uamh an Ard Achadh (High Pasture Cave), Skye: Intermediate Report.* http://www.high-pasture-cave.org/index.php/the_work/article/specialist_report_2004_animal_bone

Driscoll, C. A., Menotti-Raymond, M., Roca, A. L., Hupe, K., Johnson, W. E., Geffen, E., Harley, E., Delibes, M., Pontier, D., Kitchener, A. C., Yamaguchi, N., O'Brien, S. J. and Macdonald, D. (2007) 'The Near Eastern origin of cat domestication', *Science* 317 (5837), 519–23

Driver, J. C. (1990) 'Faunal remains', 228–257 in J.C. Driver, J. Rady and M. Sparks (eds), *Excavations in the Cathedral Precincts, 2 Linacre Garden, 'Meister Omers' and St Gabriel's Chapel*, Kent Archaeological Society, Maidstone.

Dudley, S. P., Gee, M., Kehoe, C., Melling, T. M. and the British Ornithologists' Union Records Committee. (2006) 'The British List: A Checklist of Birds in Britain (7th edition)', *Ibis* 148, 526–63.

Duffy, E. A. J. (1968) 'The status of *Cerambyx* L. (Col., Cerambycidae) in Britain', *Entomologist's Gazette* 19, 164–6.

Dumayne, L. and Barber, K. E. (1994) 'The impact of the Romans on the environment of northern England: pollen data from three sites close to Hadrian's Wall', *The Holocene* 4, 165–73.

Dumayne-Peaty, L. and Barber, K. E. (1997) 'Archaeological and environmental evidence for Roman impact on vegetation near Carlisle, Cumbria: a comment on McCarthy', *The Holocene* 7, 243–6.

Dunwoodie, L. (2004) *Pre-Boudican and Later Activity on the Site of the Forum: Excavations at 168 Fenchurch Street, City of London*, MoLAS Archaeology Studies Series 13, London.

Easterbee, N., Hepburn, L. V. and Jefferies, D. J. (1991) *Survey of the Status and Distribution of the Wildcat in Scotland 1983–1987*, Nature Conservancy Council for Scotland, Edinburgh.

Eastham, A. (1975) 'The bird bones', 409–415 in B. Cunliffe (ed.), *Excavations at Portchester Castle, Vol. I, Roman*,

Thames and Hudson, London.

Edwards, A and Horne, M. (1997) 'Animal bone', 117–29 in A. Whittle (ed.) *Sacred Mound, Holy Rings. Silbury Hill and the West Kennet Palisade Enclosures: a Later Neolithic Complex in North Wiltshire*, Oxbow Monograph 74, Oxford.

Edwards, A. J. H. (1933) 'Short cists in Roxburgh and Sutherland, and rock sculpturings in a cave at Wemyss, Fife', *Proceedings of the Society of Antiquaries of Scotland* 67, 164–76.

Edwards, C. J, Bollongo, R. and 38 others (2007) 'Mitochondrial DNA analysis shows a Near Eastern Neolithic origin for domestic cattle and no indication of domestication of European aurochs', *Proceedings of the Royal Society, Series B, Biological Sciences* 274 (1616), 1377–85.

Edwards, H. C. (1917) *Caesar's De Bello Gallico* VI, 28. Heinemann, London.

Edwards, K. (1996) 'A Mesolithic of the Western and Northern Isles of Scotland. Evidence from pollen and charcoal', 22–38, in T. Pollard and A. Morrison (eds.), *The Early Prehistory of Scotland*, Edinburgh University Press, Edinburgh.

Egan, G. (1998) *The Medieval Household: Daily Living c. 1150 – c. 1450*, The Stationary Office, London.

Ellis, C. J., Allen, M. J., Gardiner, J., Harding, P., Ingrem, C., Powell, A. and Scaife, R. G. (2003) 'An Early Mesolithic seasonal hunting site in the Kennet valley, southern England', *Proceedings of the Prehistoric Society* 69, 107–35.

Ellison, A. (1975) 'Animal skeletal material', 145–51 in P. Drewett, 'Excavations at Hadleigh Castle, Essex, 1971–2', *Journal British Archaeological Association* 38, 90–154.

Ekwall, E. (1960) *The Oxford Dictionary of English Place-names*, Oxford University Press, London.

Ervynk, A., Van Neer, W. and Lentacker, A. (1999) 'Introduction and extinction of wild animal species in historical times: the evidence from Belgium', 399–407 in N. Benecke (ed.), *The Holocene History of the European Vertebrate Fauna: Modern Aspects of Research Workshop, 6th to 9th April 1998, Berlin*, Verlag Marie Leidorf GmbH, Rahden.

Evans, J. G. (1971) 'Habitat changes on the calcareous soils of Britain: the impact of Neolithic man', 27–73 in D. D. A. Simpson (ed.), *Economy and Settlement in Neolithic and Early Bronze Age Britain and Europe*, Leicester University Press, Leicester.

Evans, J. G. (1975) *The Environment of Early Man in the British Isles*, Paul Elek, London.

Evans, J. G. (1990) 'Notes on some Late Neolithic and Bronze Age events in long barrow ditches in southern and eastern England', *Proceedings of the Prehistoric Society* 56, 111–16.

Evans, J. G. (1999) *Land and Archaeology: Histories of Human Environment in the British Isles*, Tempus, Stroud.

Evans, J. G., Rouse, A. J. and Sharples, N. M. (1988) 'The landscape setting of causewayed camps: recent work on the Maiden Castle enclosure', 73–84 in J. Barrett and I. Kinnes (eds), *The Archaeology of Context in the Neolithic and Bronze Age: Recent Trends*, Department of Archaeology and Prehistory, University of Sheffield, Sheffield.

Ewart, J. C. (1911) 'Animal remains' 362–77 in J. Curle (ed.), *A Roman Frontier Post and its People: The Fort of Newstead in the Parish of Melrose*, Maclehose and Sons, Glasgow.

Fairbarn, A. S. (2000) *Plants in Neolithic Britain and Beyond*, (Neolithic Studies Group Seminar Papers 5), Oxbow Books, Oxford.

Fairnell, E. (2003) *The Utilisation of Fur-bearing Animals in the British Isles: A Zooarchaeological Hunt for Data*, unpublished MSc dissertation, University of York.

Fairnell, E. H. and Barrett, J. H. (2007) 'Fur-bearing species and Scottish islands', *Journal of Archaeological Science* 34, 463–84.

Faure, E. and Kitchener, A. C. 2009 'An Archaeological and Historic Review of the Relationships between Felids and People', *Anthrozoos* 22(3), 221–238.

Fenton, A. (1978) *The Northern Isles*, John Donald, Edinburgh.

Finlay, J. (1984) *Faunal Evidence for prehistoric economy and settlement in the Outer Hebrides to 400AD,* unpublished PhD thesis, Edinburgh University.

Fisher, C. (1997) 'Past human exploitation of birds on the Isle of Man', *International Journal of Osteoarchaeology* 7 (4), 292–7.

Fisher, C. T. (1986) 'Bird bones from the excavation at Crown car parks Nantwich, Cheshire (with an Appendix on pathology by J. Baker)', *Circaea* 4 (1), 55–64.

Fisher, I. (2001) *Early Medieval Sculpture in the West Highlands and Islands*, Monograph Series 1 RCAHMS and SAS, Edinburgh.

Fisher, W. R. (1880) *The Forest of Essex: its History, Laws, Administration and Ancient Customs, and the Wild Deer which Lived in it*, Butterworths, London.

Fitzgerald, B. M. (1988) 'The diet of domestic cats and their impact on prey populations', 123–47 in D. C. Turner and P. Bateson (eds) *The Domestic Cat: The Biology of its Behaviour*, Cambridge University Press, Cambridge.

Fitzsimons, M. and Igoe, F. (2004) 'Freshwater fish conservation in the Irish Republic: a review of pressures and legislation impacting on conservation methods', *Biology and Environment. Proceedings of the Royal Irish Academy* 104B (3), 17–32.

Fletcher, J. (2000) 'The Re-introduction of Red Deer to South Uist in 1975' *Hebridean Naturalist, Curracag*, 23–6.

Fletcher, J. (2003) *Fletcher's Game*. Mercat Press, Edinburgh.

Forbes, C. L., Joysey K. A. and West, R. G. (1958) 'On post-glacial pelicans in Britain', *Geological Magazine* 95(2), 153–60.

Forester, E. S. and Heffner, E. H. (1955) *Columella, L. J. M.: On Agriculture*, (Loeb Classical Library 361), Heinemann, London.

Fox, C. (1923) *Archaeology of the Cambridge Region*, Cambridge University Press, Cambridge.

Franklin, A. (1996) 'On fox-hunting and angling: Norbert Elias and the "Sportisation" Process', *Journal of Historical Sociology* 9(4), 432–6.

Franzmann, A. W. (1981) '*Alces alces*', *Mammalian Species* 154, 1–7.

Frazer, F. C. and King, J. E. (1954) 'Faunal remains', 70–95 in J. G. D. Clark (ed.), *Excavations at Star Carr*, Cambridge University Press, Cambridge.

Frison, G. C. and Stanford, D. J. (1982) *The Agate Basin Site*, Academic Press, New York.

Frynta, D., Slábová, M., Váchová, H., Volfová, R. and Munclinger, P. (2005) 'Aggression and commensalism in House Mouse: a comparative study across Europe and the Near East', *Aggressive Behavior* 31, 283–93.

Fulford, M. (1991) 'Britain and the Roman Empire: the evidence for regional and long distance trade', 35–47 in R. F. J. Jones (ed.), *Roman Britain: Recent Trends*, University of Sheffield, Sheffield.

Fuller, E. (1999) *The Great Auk*, Erroll Fuller, Southborough.

Fuller, T. K., Mech, D. L. and Cochrane, J. F. (2003) 'Wolf population dynamics', 161–91 in D. L. Mech and L. Boitani (eds), *Wolves: Behavior, Ecology and Conservation*, University of Chicago Press, Chicago.

Fyfe, R. M., Brown, A. G. and Coles, B. J. (2003) 'Mesolithic to Bronze Age vegetation change and human activity in the Exe valley, Devon', *Proceedings of the Prehistoric Society* 69, 161–82.

Ganem G, and Searle J. B. (1996) 'Behavioral discrimination among chromosomal races of the house mouse (*Mus musculus domesticus*)', *Journal of Evolutionary Biology* 9, 817–30.

Garrard, A. N. (1984) 'The selection of South-West Asian animal domesticates' 117–32 in J. Clutton-Brock and C. Grigson (eds), *Animals and Archaeology 3: Early*

Herders and Their Flocks, British Archaeological Report, international series 202, Oxford.

Garrad, L. S. (1972) *The Naturalist in the Isle of Man*, David and Charles, Newton Abbot.

Gautier, A. (1984) 'Enkele dierresten uit de abdji Ter Duinen te Koksijde (ca. 1175–ca. 1250, ca. 1250–1318, 1593–1601 A.D)', *De Duinen* 13–14, 61–63.

Gautier, A. (2007) 'Deer parks in Sussex and the Godwinesons', *Anglo-Norman Studies* 29, 51–64.

Geist, V. (1998) *Deer of the World*, Stackpole Books, Mechanicsburg.

Gelling, M. (1984) *Place-names in the Landscape*, J. M. Dent & Sons, London.

Gentry, A, Clutton-Brock, J. and Groves, C. P. (2004) 'The naming of wild animal species and their domestic derivatives', *Journal of Archaeological Science* 31, 645–51.

Geraghty, S. (1996) *Viking Age Dublin: Botanical Evidence from Fishamble Street.* (Medieval Dublin Excavations 1962–81, Series C, vol. 2), National Museum of Ireland, Royal Irish Academy, Dublin.

Gidney, L. J. (1989) 'The animal bone' 69–70 in J. Nolan, R. Fraser, B. Harbottle and F. C. Burton, 'The Medieval town defences of Newcastle Upon Tyne: excavation and survey 1986–87', *Archaeologia Aeliana* 17, 29–78.

Gidney, L. J. (1992) *The Animal Bones from the Post-Medieval Deposits at St Peter's Lane*, (Ancient Monuments Laboratory Report 131/91), English Heritage, London.

Gidney, L. J. (1994) 'The animal bones' 177–84 in D. H. Heslop, L. Truman and J. E. Vaughan, 'Excavations at Westgate Road, Newcastle 1991', *Archaeologia Aeliana* 22, 153–84.

Gidney, L. J. (1995) *Two Groups of Animal Bones from Excavations at the Manor of Beaurepaire, County Durham*, Durham Environmental Archaeology Report (3/95), Durham.

Gilbert, J. M. (1979) *Hunting and Hunting Reserves in Medieval Scotland*, Donald, Edinburgh.

Gilbertson, D., Kent, M. and Grattan, J. (1996) *The Outer Hebrides; The Last 14,000 Years*, Sheffield Academic Press, Sheffield.

Gimbutas, M. (1982*) The Goddesses and Gods of Old Europe 6500–3500 BC: Myths and Cult Images*, Thames and Hudson, London.

Girling, M. A. (1976) 'Changes in the Meare Heath coleoptera fauna in response to flooding', *Proceedings of the Prehistoric Society* 42, 297–99.

Girling, M. A. (1979) 'The fossil insect assemblages from the Meare Lake Village', *Somerset Levels Papers* 5, 25–32.

Girling, M. A. (1982) 'The effect of the Meare Heath flooding episodes on the coleopteran succession', *Somerset Levels Papers* 8, 46–50.

Girling, M. A. (1985) 'Fly puparia', 31 and Fiche M1:A12 4 in S. M. Hirst (ed.), *An Anglo-Saxon Inhumation Cemetery at Sewerby, East Yorkshire*, York University Archaeological Publications, York.

Godwin, H. (1975) *The History of the British Flora* (2nd edition), Cambridge University Press, Cambridge.

Goodwin, H., Johnston, G. and Warburton, C. (2000) *Tourism and Carnivores: The Challenge Ahead*, WWF-UK, Godalming.

Götherström, A., Anderung, C., Hellborg, L., Elburg, L., Smith, C., Bradley, D. G. and Ellegren, H. (2005) 'Cattle domestication in the Near East was followed by hybridisation with aurochs bulls in Europe', *Proceedings of the Royal Society* Series B 272, 2345–50.

Goulding, M. (2001) 'Possible genetic sources of free-living Wild Boar (*Sus scrofa*) in southern England', *Mammal Review* 31 (3), 245–8.

Goulding, M. (2003) *Wild Boar in Britain*, Whittet Books, Stowmarket.

Goulding, M. and Roper, T. (2002) 'Press responses to the presence of free-living Wild Boar (*Sus scrofa*) in southern England', *Mammal Review* 32 (4), 272–82.

Gowlett, J. A. J., Hedges, R. E. M., Law, I. A. and Perry, C. (1987) 'Radiocarbon dates from the Oxford AMS system: archaeometry date-list 5', *Archeometry* 29, 125–55.

Grahame, I. (1984) 'Peafowl', 315–18 in I. L. Mason (ed.), *Evolution of Domesticated Animals*, Longman, London.

Graham-Stewart, A. (2007). 'Lost at sea, but why?', *Atlantic Salmon Trust Winter Journal* 2007/2008, 25–26.

Grant, A. (1975) 'The animal bones', 437–50 in B. W. Cunliffe (ed.), *Excavations at Portchester I: Roman*, Reports of the Research Committee of the Society of Antiquaries of London 32

Grant, A. (1978) 'Animal bones' 32–6 in R. Bradley (ed.), 'Rescue excavations in Dorchester-on-Thames 1972', *Oxoniensia* 43, 17–39

Grant, A. (1984) 'Animal husbandry', 496–547 in B. Cunliffe (ed.), *Danebury: An Iron Age Hillfort in Hampshire. Volume 2 The Excavations, 1969–78: The Finds*, Council for British Archaeology Research Report 52, London.

Grant, A. (1988) 'Animal resources', 149–87 in G. Astill and A. Grant (eds) *The Countryside of Medieval England*, Basil Blackwell, Oxford.

Grant, A. (1989) 'Animals in Roman Britain', 135–46 in M. Todd (ed.), *Research on Roman Britain 1960–1989*, Britannia Monograph Series 11, London.

Grant, A. and Sauer, E. (2006) 'The aurochs; nature worship and exploitation in Eastern Gaul', *Antiquity* 80 (309), 622–37.

Gray, A. P. (1974) *Mammalian Hybrids*, (Technical Communication 10), Commonwealth Agricultural Bureaux, Farnham Royal.

Gray, L. (2002) 'The botanical remains', 242–51 in J. Drummond-Murray and P. Thompson (eds), *Settlement in Roman Southwark: Archaeological Excavations (1991–8) for the London Underground Limited Jubilee Line Extension Project*, MoLAS Monograph Series 12, London.

Green, N. (2006) 'Ostrich eggs and peacock feathers: sacred objects as cultural exchange between Christianity and Islam', *Al-Masāq* 18 (1), 27–66.

Greene, J. P. (1989) *Norton Priory. The Archaeology of a Medieval Religious House*, Cambridge University Press, Cambridge.

Gregory, R., Murphy, E., Church, M., Edwards, K., Guttmann, E. and Simpson, D. (2005) 'Archaeological evidence for the first Mesolithic occupation of the Western Isles of Scotland', *The Holocene* 15 (7), 944–50.

Grieve, S. (1885) *The Great Auk or Garefowl – Its History, Archaeology and Remains*, Jack, London.

Grigson, C. (1976) 'Animal bones from pit 6', 11–18 in C. L. Matthews (ed.), *Occupation sites on a Chiltern Ridge Excavations at Puddlehill and Sites Near Dunstable, Bedfordshire*, British Archaeological Report, British series 29, Oxford.

Grigson, C. (1981) 'Mammals and man on Oronsay: some preliminary hypotheses concerning Mesolithic ecology in the Inner Hebrides', 163–80 in D. Brothwell and G. Dimbleby (eds), *Environmental Aspects of Coasts and Islands*, British Archaeological Reports, international Series 84, Oxford.

Grigson, C. (1989) 'Size and sex – evidence for the domestication of cattle in the Near East', 77–109 in A. Mills, D. Williams and N. Gardner (eds), *The Beginnings of Agriculture*, British Archaeological Report, international series 496, Oxford.

Grigson, C. (2000) 'The mammalian remains', 164–252 in A. Whittle, J. Pollard and C. Grigson (eds), *The Harmony of Symbols: The Windmill Hill Causewayed Enclosure*, Oxbow, Oxford.

Grigson, C. and Mellars, P. (1987) 'The mammalian remains from the middens', 243–89 in P. A. Mellars (ed.), *Excavations on Oronsay: Prehistoric Human Ecology on a Small Island*. Edinburgh University Press, Edinburgh.

Grimm, J. (in prep.) 'The animal bones', in V. Birbeck and K. Egging, Balkerne heights, Colchester: suburban development and cemetery use, *Transactions of the Essex Society for Archaeology and History*.

Gruffydd, R. G. (1990) 'Where was Rhaeadr Derwennydd (Canu Aneirin, Line 1114)?', 261–66 in A.T.E. Matonis and D. F. Melia (eds), *Celtic Language, Celtic Culture: A Festschrift for Eric P. Hamp*, Ford & Bailie, Van Nuys, California.

Grundy, G. B. (1932) 'The Saxon charters of Somerset Part IV', *Proceedings of the Somerset Archaeological and Natural History Society* 78, 186.

Grzimek, B. (1975) *Grzimek's Animal Life Encyclopedia: Mammals, I–IV*, Van Norstrand Reinhold, New York.

Guggisberg C. A. W. (1975) *Wild Cats of the World*. David & Charles, London.

Guilaine, J., Briois, F., Vigne, J.-D. and Carrère, I. (2000) 'Découverte d'un Néolithique précéramique ancien chypriote (fin 9e, début 8e millénaires cal. BC), apparenté au PPNB ancien/moyen du Levant nord', *Comptes Rendu de l'Académie de Science, Paris, Sciences de la Terre et des planètes* 330, 75–82.

Gurney, J. H. (1921/1972) 'Annals of Ornithology', Reprinted by Paul Minet, Chicheley.

Gwara, S. and Porter, D. W. (1997) *Anglo-Saxon Conversations: The Colloquies of Ælfric Bata*, Boydell, Woodbridge.

Hagen, A. (1995) *A Second Handbook of Anglo-Saxon Food and Drink: Production and Distribution*, Anglo Saxon Books, Frithgarth.

Hahn, D. (2003) *The Tower Menagerie*, Simon & Schuster, London.

Halard, X. (1983) 'Le loup en Normandie aux 14 et 15èmes siècles', *Annales de Normandie*, 33, 189–98.

Hall, A. R. and Kenward, H. K. (2004) 'Setting people in their environment: plant and animal remains from Anglo-Scandinavian York', 372–426 + references 507–521 in R. A. Hall, D. W. Rollason, M. Blackburn, D. N. Parsons, G. Fellows-Jensen, A. R. Hall, H. K. Kenward, T. P. O'Connor, D. Tweddle, A. J. Mainman and N. S. H. Rogers, *Aspects of Anglo-Scandinavian York*, (The Archaeology of York 8/4), Council for British Archaeology and York Archaeological Trust, York.

Hall, A., Kenward, H., Girvan, L. and McKenna, R. (2007) 'Investigations of plant and invertebrate macrofossil remains from excavations in 2004 at 62–8 Low Petergate, York (site code 2002.421)', *Reports from the Centre for Human Palaeoecology, University of York* 2007/06, 41.

Hall, A. R., Kenward, H. K. and Williams, D. (1980) *Environmental Evidence from Roman deposits in Skeldergate*, (The Archaeology of York 14/3), Council for British Archaeology, London.

Hall, R. A., Rollason, D. W, Blackburn, M., Parsons, D. N., Fellows-Jensen, G., Hall, A. R., Kenward, H. K., O'Connor, T. P., Tweddle, D., Mainman, A. J. and Rogers, N. S. H. (2004) *Aspects of Anglo-Scandinavian York*, Council for British Archaeology, York.

Hall, S. J. G. (2005) 'The horse in human society', 23–32 in D. Mills and S. McDonnell (eds), *The Domestic Horse: The Origins, Development and Management of its Behaviour*, Cambridge University Press, Cambridge.

Hall, S. J. G. (2008) 'A comparative analysis of the habitat of the extinct aurochs and other prehistoric mammals in Britain', *Ecography* 31 (2), 187–90.

Hallam, J. S., Edwards, B. J. N., Barnes, B. and Stuart, A. J. (1973) 'The remains of a Late Glacial elk with associated barbed points from High Furlong, near Blackpool, Lancashire', *Proceedings of the Prehistoric Society* 39, 100–28.

Hallowell, A. I. (1926) 'Bear ceremonialism in the northern hemisphere', *American Anthropologist* 28, 1–175.

Halpin, E. (1997) 'Animal, Bird and Fish Bone', 45–50 in J. Barber (ed.), *The Excavation of a Stalled Cairn at Point of Cott Westray, Orkney*, Scottish Trust for Archaeological Research, Edinburgh.

Halstead, P. (2003) 'The animal bones from Baleshare and Hornish Point', 142–8 in J. Barber (ed.), *Bronze Age Farms and Iron Farm Mounds of the Outer Hebrides*, Scottish Archaeology Internet Reports, www.sair.org.uk/sair, Edinburgh.

Hamilton, J. (2000) 'Animal husbandry', 131–45 in B. Cunliffe and C. Poole (eds.), *The Danebury Environs Programme: The Prehistory of a Wessex Landscape, Volume 2 – Part 6*, Oxford Committee for Archaeology, Oxford.

Hamilton, R. (1971) 'Animal remains', 165 in K. Branigan (ed.) *Latimer: Belgic, Roman, Dark Age and Early Modern Farm*, Chess Valley Archaeological Society, Bristol.

Hamilton-Dyer, S. (2005) 'Animal bones', 140–54 in V. Birbeck with R. J. C. Smith, P. Andrews and N. Stoodley, *The Origins of Mid-Saxon Southampton: Excavations at the Friends Provident St Mary's Stadium 198–2000*, Wessex Archaeology,.

Hamilton-Dyer, S. (2007) 'Exploitation of birds and fish in medieval and post medieval Ireland: A brief review of the evidence', 103–18 in E. M. Murphy and N. J. Whitehouse (eds), *Environmental Archaeology in Ireland*, Oxbow, Oxford.

Hamilton-Dyer (n.d.) *Animal Remains from Odiham Castle*, unpublished report.

Hamilton-Dyer, S., McCormick, F., Murray, H. K., and Murray, J. C. (1993) 'The bone assemblage and animal husbandry' 203–5 in H. K. Murray and J. C. Murray, 'Excavations at Rattray, Aberdeenshire: a Scottish deserted burgh', *Medieval Archaeology* 37, 109–218.

Hammon, A. (2005) *Late Romano-British – Early Medieval Socio-economic and Cultural Change: Analysis of the Mammal and Bird Bone Assemblages from the Roman City of Viroconium Cornoviorum, Shropshire*, unpublished PhD thesis, University of Sheffield.

Hammon, A. (2008) 'The animal bones', 150–61 in B. Cunliffe and C. Poole (eds): *The Danebury Environs Roman Programme: A Wessex landscape during the Roman era, volume 2 – part 3 Fullerton, Hants, 2000 and 2001*, English Heritage/Oxford University School of Archaeology (Monograph 71), Oxford, E-text 3.4, the animal bones: data (www.arch.ox.ac.uk/research_projects/danebury).

Hammond, P. M. (1974) 'Changes in the British coleopterous fauna', 323–69 in D. L. Hawksworth (ed.), *The changing flora and fauna of Britain*, (Systematics Association Special Volume 6), Academic Press, London.

Harcourt, R. (1979a) 'The animal bones' 150–60 in G. J. Wainwright (ed.) *Gussage All Saints: An Iron Age Settlement in Dorset*, (DoE Archaeological Reports 10), HMSO, London.

Harcourt, R. (1979b) 'The animal bones', 214–23 in G. J. Wainwright (ed.) *Mount Pleasant, Dorset: Excavations 1970–1971*, Thames and Hudson, London.

Harding, L. (2006) 'Bavarian hunters kill Bruno the bear', *The Guardian*. http://www.guardian.co.uk/animalrights/story/0,,1806320.html [accessed 10/7/06]

Harding, P. T. and Plant, R. A. (1978) 'A second record of *Cerambyx cerdo* L. (Coleoptera: Cerambycidae) from sub–fossil remains in Britain', *Entomologist's Gazette* 29, 150–52.

Hardy-Smith, T. and Edwards, P. C. (2004) 'The Garbage Crisis in prehistory: artifact patterns at the Early Natufian site of Wadi Hammeh 27 and the origins of household refuse disposal strategies', *Journal of Anthropological Archaeology* 23 (3), 253–89.

Harman, M. (1978) 'The animal bones', 177–88 in F. Pryor, *Excavations at Fengate, Peterborough, England: The Second Report*, Royal Ontario Museum Archaeology Monograph 5.

Harman, M. (1983) 'Animal remains from Ardnave, Islay', in G. Ritchie, and H. Welfare, (eds), 'Excavations at Ardnave, Islay', *Proceeding of the Society of Antiquaries of Scotland* 113, 302–36

Harman, M. (1985) 'The bird bones', 222–3 and microfiche in M. Atkin, A. Carter and D. H. Evans, *Excavations in Norwich 1971–1978, Part II*, East Anglian Archaeology Report 26, Norwich.

Harris, S., Morris, P., Wray, S. and Yalden, D. (1995) *A Review of British Mammals: Population Estimates and Conservation Status of British Mammals other than Cetaceans*. JNCC, Peterborough.

Harris, S. and Yalden, D. W. (2008) *Mammals of the British Isles: Handbook, 4th edition*. The Mammal Society, Southampton.

Harrison, C. J. O. and Cowles, G. S. (1977) 'The extinct large cranes of the North West palaeoartic', *Journal of Archaeological Science* 4, 15–17.

Harrison, C. J. O. (1988) 'The history of British birds', 9–25 in C. J. O. Harrison and D. Reid-Henry (eds), *The History of the Birds of Britain*, Collins, London.

Harrison, W. (1805) 'The description of England', 379 in R. Holinshed (ed.), *Holinshed's Chronicles of England, Scotland and Ireland,* Vol. 1

Hart, C. (1971) *The Verderers and Forest Laws of Dean*, David and Charles, Newton Abbot.

Harting, J. E. (1880a) *British Animals Extinct Within British Times, with some account of British Wild White Cattle*, Trübner & Co, London.

Harting, J. E. (1880b) *A Short History of the Wolf in Britain*, Pryor, Whitstable (republished 1994).

Hartley D. (1954) *Food in England*, Little, Brown, London [1999 ed.].

Haynes, S., Jaarola, M. and Searle, J. B. (2003) 'Phylogeography of the common vole (*Microtus arvalis*) with particular emphasis on the colonization of the Orkney archipelago', *Molecular Ecology* 12 (4), 951–6.

Hedges, R. E. M., Pettit, P. B., Bronk Ramsay, C. and Van Klinken, G. J. (1998). 'Radiocarbon dates from the Oxford AMS system, datelist 25', *Archaeometry* 40, 2, 437–55.

Helmer, D., Gourichon, L., Monchot, H., Peters, J. and Segui, M.S. (2005) 'Identifying early domestic cattle from Pre-Pottery Neolithic sites on the Middle Euphrates using sexual dimorphism', 86–95 in J.-D. Vigne, J. Peters and D. Helmer (eds), *The First Steps of Animal Domestication*, Oxbow, Oxford.

Hemmer, H. (1990) *Domestication: The Decline of Environmental Appreciation*, Cambridge University Press, Cambridge.

Henderson, A. (1997) 'From coney to rabbit: the story of a managed coloniser', *The Naturalist* 122, 101–21.

Henderson, I. (1998) '*Primus inter pares*: the St. Andrews Sarcophagus and Pictish Sculpture', 97–167 in S. M. Foster (ed.), *The St. Andrews Sarcophagus, A Pictish Masterpiece and its International Connections*, Four Courts Press, Dublin.

Heptner, V. G., Nasimovich, A. A. and Bannikov, A. G. (1989) *Mammals of the Soviet Union, vol. 1.* E.J. Brill, Leiden.

Hetherington, D. (2006) 'The lynx in Britain's past, present and future' *Ecos* 27, 68–74.

Hetherington, D. A. and Gorman, M.L. (2007) 'Using prey densities to estimate the potential size of reintroduced populations of Eurasian lynx', *Biological Conservation* 137, 37–44.

Hetherington, D. A, Lord, T. C., and Jacobi, R. M. (2006)

'New evidence for the occurrence of Eurasian lynx (*Lynx lynx*) in medieval Britain', *Journal of Quaternary Science* 21, 3–8.

Hetherington, D. A., Miller, D., Macleod, C. D., and Gorman, M. L. (2008) 'A potential habitat network for the Eurasian lynx in Scotland', *Mammal Review* 38, 285–303.

Hewitt, G. M. (1999) 'Post-glacial re-colonization of European biota', *Biological Journal of the Linnean Society* 68, 33–57.

Hickling, C. F. (1962) *Fish Culture,* Faber & Faber, London.

Hickling, C. F. (1971) 'Prior More's Fishponds', *Medieval Archaeology* 15–16, 118–23.

Higgs, E. S. (1961) 'Some faunas of the Mediterranean coastal areas', *Proceedings of the Prehistoric Society* 27, 144–52.

Hill, D. (2001) '150 years of the study of wics: 1841–1991', 3–6 in D. Hill and R. Cowie (eds), *The Early Medieval Trading Centres of Northern Europe*, Sheffield Academic Press, Sheffield.

Hill, J. and Rowsome, P. (2008) *Roman London and the Walbrook Stream Crossing: Excavations at 1 Poultry and Vicinity 1985–96,* MoLAS Monograph Series, London.

Hill, J. D. (1995) *Ritual and Rubbish in the Iron Age of Wessex*, British Archaeological Reports, British series 242, Oxford.

Hill, J. D. (2002) 'Just about the potter's wheel? Using, making and depositing Middle and Late Iron Age pots in East Anglia', 143–60 in A. Woodward and J. D. Hill (eds), *Prehistoric Britain: The Ceramic Basis*, Prehistoric Ceramics Research Group Occasional Publication 3, Oxford.

Hingley, R. (1992) 'Society in Scotland from 700 BC to AD 200', *Proceedings of the Society of Antiquaries of Scotland* 122, 7–53.

Hodges, R. (2000) *Towns and Trade in the Age of Charlemagne*, Duckworth, London.

Hoffman, R. R. (1986) 'Morphological evolutionary adaptations in the ruminant digestive system', 1–20 in A. Dobson and M. J. Dobson (eds), *Aspects of Digestive Physiology in Ruminants*, Ithaca University Press, Cornell.

Hoffmann, R. (1994) 'Remains and verbal evidence of carp (*Cyprinus carpio*) in Medieval Europe', 139–50 in W. van Neer (ed.) *Proceedings of the 7th Meeting of the ICAZ Fish Remains Working Group*, (Sciences Zoologiques 274), Annales de Musée Royal de l'Afrique Centrale, Tervuren.

Hoffmann, R. (1995) 'Environmental change and the culture of common carp in medieval Europe', *Guelph Ichthyology Reviews* 3, 57–85.

Hoffmann, R. (1996) 'Economic development and aquatic ecosystems in medieval Europe', *The American Historical Review* 101(3), 631–69.

Hooper, W. D. and Ash, H. B. (1979) *Marcus Terentius Varro On Agriculture* (Loeb Classical Library 283), Harvard University Press, London.

Hoppit, R. (2007) 'Hunting Suffolk's parks: towards a reliable chronology of imparkment', 146–64 in R. Liddiard (ed.), *The Medieval Park: New Perspectives*, Windgather Press, Macclesfield.

Horrox, R. (1994) *The Black Death*, Manchester University Press, Manchester.

Hough, C. (2001) 'Place-name evidence for an Anglo-Saxon animal name: OE *pohha/*pocca fallow deer', *Anglo-Saxon England* 30, 1–14.

Hughes, M., Montgomery, W. I., and Pródahl, P. (2007) *Population genetic structure of the Irish hare*, (Report Quo3–o4 to Heritage Service Northern Ireland), Quercus, Queen's University, Belfast.

Hull, R. (2007) *Scottish Mammals*. Birlinn Press, Edinburgh.

Humphrey, A. and Jones A. K. G. (2002) '*Fish Remains from Archaeological Excavations at the King's School, Ely, Cambridgeshire*', Department of Archaeological Sciences, University of Bradford, unpublished report for Cambridge Archaeological Unit.

Huntley, J. P. and Stallibrass, S. (1995) *Plant and Vertebrate Remains from Archaeological Sites in Northern England: Data Reviews and Future Directions*, Architectural and Archaeological Society of Durham and Northumberland, Durham.

Hurrell, H.G. (1979) 'The little-known rabbit', *Countryside* 23, 501–4.

Ingrem, C. (2003) 'Phase 4: the Post-Dissolution occupation', 406–427 in A. Hardy, A. Dodd and G. Keevill (eds), *Excavations at Eynsham Abbey, Oxfordshire, 1989–92*, (Thames Valley Landscape Volume 6), Oxford Archaeological Unit, Oxford.

Ingrem, C. (2004) *Assessment of the Animal bone from Roman deposits at Westward House, Chichester, Sussex*. Unpublished Centre for Applied Archaeological Analyses report to Sussex Archaeological Society.

Innes, C. (1837) *Liber Sancte Marie de Melros: munimenta vetustiora Monasterii Cisterciensis de Melros*, Bannatyne Club, Edinburgh.

Innes, J. B., Blackford, J., and Davey, P. J. (2003) 'Dating the introduction of cereal cultivation to the British Isles: early palaeoecological evidence from the British Isles', *Journal of Quaternary Science* 18(7), 603–13.

Iregren, E. and Ahlström, T. (1999) 'Geographical variation in the contemporaneous populations of brown bear (*Ursus arctos*) in Fennoscandia and the problem of immigration' 237–46 in N. Benecke (ed.), *The Holocene History of the European Vertebrate Fauna: Modern Aspects of Research Workshop, 6th to 9th April 1998, Berlin*, Verlag Marie Leidorf GmbH, Rahden.

Iregren, E., Bergström, M.-R. and Isberg, P.-E. (2001) 'The influence of age on metric values in the brown bear cranium (*Ursus arctos* L.)', 21–32 in H. Buitenhuis and W. Prummel (eds), *Animals and Man in the Past: Essays in Honour of Dr A. T. Clason Emeritus Professor of Archaeozoology Rijksuniversiteit Groningen*, Rijksuniversiteit (ARC-Publicatie 41), Groningen.

Irving, B. (1996) 'Fish', 53–6 in K. M. Dobney, S. D. Jacques and B. G. Irving, *Of Butchers and Breeds: Report on Vertebrate Remains from Various Sites in the City of Lincoln*, Lincoln Archaeological Studies 5, Lincoln.

Irving, B. (1998) 'Fish remains', 37–40 in G. Lucas (ed.), 'A medieval fishery on Whittlesea Mere, Cambridgeshire', *Medieval Archaeology* 42, 19–44.

IUCN (1998) *Guidelines for Re-introductions*. Prepared by the IUCN/SSC Re-introduction Specialist Group. IUCN, Gland, Switzerland and Cambridge.

Ijzereef, G. F. (1981) *Bronze Age Animal Bones from Bovenkarspel: The Excavation at Het Valkje*, (Nederlandse Oudheden 10), ROB, Amersfoort.

Jackson, C. E. (2006) *Peacock*, Reaktion Books, London.

Jacobi, R. (1978) 'Northern England in the eighth millenium: an essay', 295–32 in P. Mellars (ed.), *The Early Postglacial Settlement of Northern Europe*, Duckworth, London.

Jarman, A. O.H. (1988) '*Aneirin, Y Gododdin: Britain's oldest heroic poem*', (Welsh Classics 3), Gomer, Llandysul.

Jedrzejewski, W., Schmidt, K., Milkowski, L., Jedrzejewska, B. and Okarma H. (1993) 'Foraging by lynx and its role in ungulate mortality: the local (Bialowieza Forest) and the Palearctic viewpoints', *Acta Theriologica* 38, 385–403.

Jenkinson, R. D. S. (1983) 'The recent history of Northern Lynx (*Lynx lynx* Linné) in the British Isles', *Quaternary Newsletter* 41, 1–7.

Jewell, P. (1963) 'Cattle from British archaeological sites', 80–101 in A. E. Mourant and F. E. Zeuner (eds) *Man and Cattle*, (Occasional paper of the Royal Anthropological Institute 18), Royal Anthropological Institute, London.

Johnstone, C. J. (2004) *A Biometric Study of Equids in the Roman World*, unpublished PhD thesis, University of York.

Johnstone, C. J. (2006) 'Those elusive mules: investigating biometric methods for their identification', 183–91 in M. Mashkour (ed.) *Equids in Time and Space: Papers in Honour of Vera Eisenmann*, Oxbow, Oxford.

Johnstone, C. (2008) 'Commodities or logistics? The role of equids in Roman supply networks', 128–45, in S.

Stallibrass and R. Thomas (eds), *Feeding the Roman Army*, Oxbow, Oxford.

Jones, G. (1984) 'Animal Bones', 187–192 in A. Rogersen and C. Dallas (eds), *Excavations in Thetford 1948–59 and 1973–80*, East Anglian Archaeology Report 22, Norwich.

Jones, G. (1985) 'The zoological evidence' 171 in J. Hinchliffe and C. Sparey Green (eds), *Excavations At Brancaster 1974 and 1977*, East Anglian Archaeology Report 23, Gressenhall.

Jones, G. (1993) 'Animal and bird bones', 176–92 in C. Dallas (ed.) *Excavations in Thetford by B. K. Davidson between 1964 and 1970*, (East Anglian Archaeology 62), Norfolk Archaeological Unit, Dereham.

Jones, G. (2000) 'Evaluating the importance of cultivation and collecting in Neolithic Britain', 79–84 in A. S. Fairbairn (ed.), *Plants in Neolithic Britain and Beyond*, Oxbow, Oxford.

Jones, G. and Legge, A. J. (2008) 'Evaluating the role of cereal cultivation in the Neolithic: charred plant remains from Hambledon Hill', 469–76 in R. Mercer and F. Healey (eds), *Hambledon Hill, Dorset, England. Excavation and Survey of a Neolithic Monument Complex and its surrounding landscape. Volume 2*, English Heritage, Swindon.

Jones, R. L. and Keen, D. H. (1993) *Pleistocene Environments in the British Isles*, Chapman & Hall, London.

Jones, R. T., Reilly, K. and Pipe, A. R. (1997) 'The animal bones', 123–31 and microfiche in B. Morley and B. Gurney (eds), *Castle Rising Castle, Norfolk*, East Anglian Archaeology Report 81, Norwich.

Jones, R. T. and Ruben, I. (1987) 'Animal bones, with some notes on the effects of differential sampling' 197–206 in G. Beresford (ed.), *Goltho: The Development of an Early Medieval Manor c.850–1150*, English Heritage, London.

Jones, R. T., Sly, J., Simpson, D., Rackham, J. and Locker, A. (1985) *The Terrestrial Vertebrate Remains from The Castle, Barnard Castle*, (Ancient Monuments Laboratory Report 7/85), English Heritage, London.

Jones, W. H. S. (1963) *Pliny Natural History, Volume VIII, Books XXVIII–XXXII*, Harvard University Press, London.

Jope, M. and Grigson, C. (1965) 'Faunal remains', 141–67 in A. Keiller (ed.), *Windmill Hill and Avebury*, Clarendon Press, Oxford.

Kaagan, L. M. (2000) *The Horse in Late Pleistocene and Holocene Britain*, Unpublished PhD thesis, University College London.

Karns, P. D. (1998) 'Population, distribution, density and trends', 125–39 in A. W Franzmann and C. C. Schwartz (eds.), *Ecology and Management of the North American Moose*, Smithsonian Institution Press, Washington D.C.

Kasapidis, P., Suchentruck, F., Magoulas, A. and Kotoulas, G. (2005) 'The shaping of mitochondrial DNA phylogeographic patterns of the brown hare *Lepus europaeus* under the combined influence of Late Pleistocene climatic fluctuations and anthropogenic translocations', *Molecular Phylogenetics and Evolution* 34, 5–66.

Kelly, F. (2000) *Early Irish Farming. A study based mainly on the law-texts of the 7th and 8th centuries AD,* School of Celtic Studies, Dublin Institute for Advanced Studies, Dublin.

Kenward, H. K. (1997) 'Synanthropic decomposer insects and the size, remoteness and longevity of archaeological occupation sites: applying concepts from biogeography to past "islands" of human occupation', *Quaternary Proceedings* 5, 135–51.

Kenward, H. (2006) 'The visibility of past trees and woodland: testing the value of insect remains', *Journal of Archaeological Science* 33, 1368–80.

Kenward, H. K. (2009). *Invertebrates in archaeology in the north of England.* English Heritage Research Department Report Series 12/2009.

Kenward, H. K. and Allison, E. P. (1994) 'A preliminary view of the insect assemblages from the early Christian rath site at Deer Park Farms, Northern Ireland', 89–107 in D. J. Rackham (ed.) *Environment and Economy in Anglo-Saxon England*, Council for British Archaeology Research Report 89, London.

Kenward, H. and Carrott, J. (2003) 'Technical Report: the implications of invertebrates, mainly insects, from medieval and early post-medieval deposits at Morton Lane, Beverley, East Riding of Yorkshire', *Palaeoecology Research Services Report* 2003/58, 28.

Kenward, H. K. and Girling, M. (1986) *Arthropod Remains from Archaeological Sites in Southampton* (Ancient Monuments Laboratory Report 46/86), English Heritage, London.

Kenward, H. K. and Hall, A. R. (1995) *Biological Evidence from Anglo-Scandinavian Deposits at 16–22 Coppergate*, (The Archaeology of York 14/7), Council for British Archaeology, York.

Kenward, H. and Hall, A. (1997) 'Enhancing bio-archaeological interpretation using indicator groups: stable manure as a paradigm', *Journal of Archaeological Science* 24, 663–73.

Kenward, H., Hall, A. Allison, E. and Carrott, J. (in press). Environment, activity and living conditions at DPF: evidence from plant and invertebrate remains, Chapter 28 in Lynn, C. J. and McDowell, J. A., *The Excavation of a Raised Rath at Deer Park Farms, Glenarm, Co*

Antrim. Northern Ireland Archaeological Monograph.

Kenward, H. K., Hall, A. R. and Jones, A. K. G. (1986) *Environmental evidence from a Roman well and Anglian pits in the legionary fortress*, (The Archaeology of York 14/5), Council for British Archaeology, London.

Kenward, H., Hill, M., Jaques, D., Kroupa, A. and Large, F. (2000), 'Evidence from beetles and other insects', 76–78, 'Evidence for living conditions on the crannog', 99–101, 'Coleoptera analysis', 230–247, and bibliography, 300–320 in A. Crone (ed.) *The History of a Scottish Lowland Crannog: Excavations at Buiston, Ayrshire 1989–90*, (STAR Monograph 4), Scottish Trust for Archaeological Research, Edinburgh.

Kenward, H. K. and Williams, D. (1979) *Biological Evidence from the Roman Warehouses in Coney Street*, (The Archaeology of York 14/2), Council for British Archaeology, London.

Kerney, M. P. (1968) 'Britain's fauna of land mollusca and its relation to the post-glacial thermal optimum', *Symposia of the Zoological Society of London* 22, 273–91.

Kerney, M. P. (1976) 'Mollusca from an interglacial tufa in East Anglia, with the description of a new species of *Lyrodiscus* Pilsbry (Gastropoda: Zonitidae)', *Journal of Conchology* 29 (1), 47–50.

Kerney, M. P. (1977) 'A proposed zonation scheme for Late-glacial and Postglacial deposits using land Mollusca', *Journal of Archaeological Science* 4, 387–90.

Kerney, M. P. (1999) *Atlas of the Land and Freshwater Molluscs of Britain and Ireland*, Harley, Colchester.

Kerney, M. P., Preece, R. C. and Turner, C. (1980) 'Molluscan and plant biostratigraphy of some Late-Devensian and Flandrian deposits in Kent', *Philosophical Transactions of the Royal Society of London*, (B) 291, 1–43.

King, A. (1991) 'Food production and consumption – meat' 15–20 in R. Jones (ed.) *Britain in the Roman Period: Recent Trends*, J. R. Collis, Sheffield.

King, A. (2005) 'Animal remains from temples in Roman Britain', *Britannia* 36, 329–69.

King, J. (1987) 'The animal bones', 185–93 in G. B. Dannell and J. P. Wild (eds), *Longthorpe II: The Military Works-depot: An Episode in Landscape History*, Britannia Monograph Series 8, London.

King, J. (1996) 'The animal bones', 216–18 in D. F. Mackreth (ed.), *Orton Hall Farm: a Roman and Early Anglo-Saxon Farmstead*, East Anglian Archaeology report 76, Manchester.

King, J. E. (1962) 'Report on animal bones', 355–61 in J. Wymer, 'Excavations at the Maglemosian sites at Thatcham, Berkshire, England', *Proceedings of the Prehistoric Society* 28, 329–61.

Kirk, J. C. (1935) 'Wild and domestic cat compared', *The Scottish Naturalist* 216, 161–9

Kitchener, A. C. (1998) 'The Scottish wildcat: a cat with an identity crisis?', *British Wildlife* 9 (4), 232–42.

Kitchener, A. C. (2000) 'Are cats really solitary?', *Lutra* 43 (1), 1–10.

Kitchener, A. (2001) *Beavers*, Whittet Books, Stowmarket.

Kitchener, A. (2007) 'The fossil record of birds in Scotland', 21–36 in R. Forrester and I. Andrews (eds), *Birds of Scotland*, Scottish Ornithologists' Club, Aberlady.

Kitchener, A. C. and Bonsall, C. (1997) 'AMS radio-carbon dates for some extinct Scottish mammals', *Quaternary Newsletter* 83, 1–11.

Kitchener, A., Bonsall, C. and Bartosiewicz, L. (2004) 'Missing mammals from Mesolithic middens: a comparison of the fossil and archaeological records from Scotland', 73–82 in A. Saville (ed.), *Mesolithic Scotland and its Neighbours*, Society of Antiquaries of Scotland, Edinburgh.

Kitchener, A. C., Yamaguchi, N., Ward, J. M. and Macdonald, D. W. (2005) 'A diagnosis for the Scottish wildcat: a tool for conservation action for a critically-endangered felid', *Animal Conservation* 8, 223–37.

KORA (2007) http://www.kora.unibe.ch/en/proj/damage/damagemain.html).

Knight, A. (2007) http://www.glaucus.org.uk/sturgen.2htm

Kratochvil, J. (1968) 'Survey of the distribution of populations of the genus *Lynx* in Europe', *Acta Scientiarum Naturalium Academiae Scientiarum Bohemoslovocae Brno* 2 (4), 1–50.

Kratochvil, J. and Kratochvil, Z. (1976) 'The origin of the domesticated forms of the genus *Felis* (Mammalia)', *Zoologia Listy* 25, 193–208.

Kruuk, H. (2002) *Hunter and Hunted: Relationships Between Carnivores and People*, Cambridge University Press, Cambridge.

Kühn, R., Ludt, C. Manhart, H., Peters, J., Neumair, E. and Rottman, O. (2005) 'Close genetic relationship of early Neolithic cattle from Zeigelberg (Freising, Germany) with modern breeds', *Journal of Animal Breeding Genetics* 122 (Supplement 1), 36–44.

Kurtén, B. (1965) 'On the evolution of the European wild cat, *Felis silvestris* Schreber', *Acta Zoologica Fennica* 111, 1–29.

Kurtén, B. and Granqvist, E. (1987) 'Fossil pardel lynx (*Lynx pardina spelaea* Boule) from a cave in southern France', *Annales Zoologici Fennici* 24, 39–43.

Langbein, J. and Chapman, N. (2003) *Fallow Deer*, Mammal Society, London

Langley, P. J. W. and Yalden, D. W. (1977) 'The decline of the rarer carnivores in Great Britain during the nineteenth century', *Mammal Review* 7, 95–116.

Larson, G., Albarella, U. and Rowley-Conwy, P. A.

(2007) 'Current views on *Sus* phylogeography and pig domestication seen through modern mtDNA studies', 30–41 in U. Albarella, K. Dobney, A. Ervynck and P. Rowley-Conwy (eds), *Pigs and Humans: 10,000 Years of Interaction*. Oxford University Press, Oxford.

Larson, G., Albarella, U., Dobney, K., Rowley-Conwy, P., Schibler, J., Tresset, A., Vigne, J.-D., and 12 others (2007) 'Ancient DNA, pig domestication, and the spread of the Neolithic into Europe', *Proceedings of the National Academy of Sciences of the United States of America* 104 (39), 15276–81.

Lauwerier, R. C. G. M. and Zeiler, J. T. (2001) 'Wishful thinking and the introduction of the rabbit to the Low Countries', *Environmental Archaeology* 6, 87–90.

Lawrence, M. J. and Brown, R. W. (1973) *Mammals of Britain: Their Tracks, Trails and Signs,* Blandford Press, London.

Lawrence, P. (1982) 'Animal bones', 275–94 in J. G. Code and A. D. S. Streeten (eds), 'Excavations at Castle Acre, Norfolk 1972–77: county house and castle of the Norman earls of Surrey', *Archaeological Journal* 139, 138–301.

Lawrence, P. (1986) 'Zoological evidence: animal bone', 13 in T. Gregory and D. Gurney, *Excavations at Thornham, Wareham, Wighton and Caistor St. Edmund, Norfolk*, East Anglian Archaeology 30, Norwich.

Lawson, A. J. (2000) *Potterne 1982–5: Animal Husbandry in Later Prehistoric Wiltshire*, Trust for Wessex Archaeology, Salisbury.

Lawson, T. J. (1981) 'The 1926–7 excavations of the Creag nan Uamh bone caves, near Inchnadamph, Sutherland', *Proceedings of the Society of Antiquaries of Scotland* 111, 7–20.

Le Brun, A., Cliuzan, S., Davis, S. J. M., Hansen, J., and Renault-Miskovsky, J. (1987) 'Le neolithique preceramique de Chypre', *L'Anthropologie* 91, 283–316.

Legge, A. J. (1981) 'Aspects of cattle husbandry', 182–209 in R. Mercer (ed.), *Farming Practice in British Prehistory*, Edinburgh University Press, Edinburgh.

Legge, A. J. (1990) 'Animals, economy, and environment', 215–42 in R. Tringham and D. Krstić (eds), *Selevac: A Neolithic Village in Serbia*. (Monumenta Archaeologica 15), UCLA Institute of Archaeology, Los Angeles.

Legge, A. J. (1991a) 'The animal bones', 140–47 in I. M. Stead (ed.), *Iron Age cemeteries in East Yorkshire*, (English Heritage Archaeological Report 22), English Heritage, London.

Legge, A. J. (1991b) 'The animal remains from six sites at Down Farm, Woodcutts', 54–100 in J. Barrett, R. Bradby and M. Hall (eds), *Papers on the Prehistoric Archaeology of Cranborne Chase*, Oxbow Monograph 11, Oxford.

Legge, A. J. (1992) *Animals, Environment and the Bronze Age Economy. Fascicule 4 of Excavations at Grimes Graves, Norfolk 1972–1976*. The British Museum, London.

Legge, A. J. (1995) 'A horse burial and other grave offerings', 146–52 in K. Parfitt (ed.), *Iron Age Burials from Mill Hill, Deal*, British Museum Press, London.

Legge, A. J. (2006) 'Milk use in Prehistory: the osteological evidence', 8–13 in J. Mulville and A. K. Outram (eds), *The Zooarchaeology of Fats, Oils, Milk and Dairying,* Oxbow, Oxford.

Legge, A. (2008) 'Livestock and Neolithic society at Hambledon Hill', 536–85 in R. Mercer and F. Healey (eds), *Hambledon Hill, Dorset, England: Excavation and Survey of a Neolithic Monument Complex and its Surrounding Landscape. Volume 2,* English Heritage, Swindon.

Legge A. J. and Rowley-Conwy P. A. (1988) *Star Carr Revisited,* Birkbeck College, London.

Legge, A. J. and Rowley-Conwy, P. A. (2000) 'The exploitation of animals', 423–71 in A. M. T. Moore, G. C. Hillman and A. J. Legge (eds), *Village on the Euphrates: From Foraging to Farming at Abu Hureyra*, Oxford University Press, New York.

Legge, A. J., Williams, J. and Williams, P. (1989) 'Animal remains from Blackhorse Road, Letchworth' 90–95 in J. Moss-Eccardt, 'Archaeological investigations in the Letchworth area, 1958–1974'. *Proceedings of the Cambridge Antiquarian Society* 77, 35–103.

Lepetz, S. and Yvinec, J.-H. (2002) 'Présence d'espèces animals d'origine méditerranéenne en France du nord aux périodes romaine et médiévale: actions anthropiques et mouvements naturels', 33–42 in A. Gardeisen (ed.), *Mouvements ou déplacements de populations animals en Méditerranée au cours de l'Holocene*, British Archaeological Reports, international series 1017, Oxford.

Le Roy Ladurie, E. (1979) *Le Carnaval de Romans*, Gallimard, Paris.

Lever, C. (1977) *The Naturalised Animals of the British Isles.* Granada Publishing, St Albans.

Levine, M. A. (1983) 'Mortality models and the interpretation of horse populations structure', 23–46 in G. N. Bailey (ed.) *Hunter-gatherer Economy in Prehistory*, Cambridge University Press, Cambridge.

Levine, M. A. (2005) 'Origins and selection of horse behaviour', 5–22 in D. Mills and S. McDonnell (eds), *The Domestic Horse: The Origins, Development and Management of its Behaviour*, Cambridge University Press, Cambridge.

Levitan, B. (1984) 'The vertebrate remains', 108–148 in S. Rahtz and T. Rowley (eds), *Middleton Stoney: Excavation and Survey in a North Oxfordshire Parish 1970–1982*,

Oxford University Department for External Studies, Oxford.

Levitan, B. (1990) 'The vertebrate remains', 220–239 in M. Bell (ed.) *Brean Down Excavations 1983–1987*, (Historic Buildings and Monuments Commission Report 15), English Heritage, London.

Levitan, B. (1993) 'Vertebrate remains', 257–301 in A. Woodward and P. Leach (eds), *The Uley Shrines. Excavation of a Ritual Complex on West Hill, Uley, Gloucestershire: 1977–9*, British Museum Press, London.

Levitan, B. L., Audsley, A., Hawkes, C. J., Moody, A., Moody, P., Smart P. L. and Thomas, J. S. (1988) 'The Charterhouse Warren Farm Swallet, Mendip, Somerset: geomorphology, taphonomy, archaeology', *Proceedings of the Bristol Speleological Society* 18 (2), 171–239.

Liberg, O. and Sandell, M. (1988) 'Spatial organisation and reproductive tactics in the domestic cat and other felids', 159–77 in D. C. Turner and P. Bateson (eds), *The Domestic Cat: The Biology of its Behaviour*, Cambridge University Press, Cambridge.

Liddiard, R. (2003) 'The deer parks of Domesday Book', *Landscape* 4 (1), 4–23.

Liddiard, R. (2007) *The Medieval Park: New Perspectives*, Windgather Press, Oxford.

Liddle, J. (forthcoming) 'The animal bones' in A. Mackinder and J. Bowsher (eds), *Excavations at Riverside House and New Globe Walk, Bankside, Southwark*, Museum of London Archaeology Service, London.

Linnell, J. D. C., and 17 others (2002) 'The fear of wolves: a review of wolf attacks on humans', *NINA Oppdragsmelding* 731, 1–65.

Linseele, V., van Neer, W. and Hendricx, S. (2007) 'Evidence for early cat taming in Egypt', *Journal of Archaeological Science* 35 (9), 2672–3.

Linseele, V., van Neer, W. and Hendricx, S. (2008) 'Early cat taming in Egypt: a correction', *Journal of Archaeological Science* 35, 2672–2673.

Lister, A. M. (1984a) 'The fossil record of elk (*Alces alces* (L.).) in Britain', *Quaternary Newsletter* 44, 1–7.

Lister, A. M. (1984b) 'Evolutionary and ecological origins of British deer', *Proceedings of the Royal Society of Edinburgh*, Section B. 82 (4), 205–29.

Lister, A. M. (1995) 'Sea-levels and the evolution of island endemics: the dwarf red deer of Jersey', 151–72 in R. C. Preece (ed.), *Island Britain: A Quaternary Perspective*, Geological Society Special Publication No. 96, London.

Locker, A. (1990) 'The mammal, bird and fish bones', 205–12 in D. S. Neal, A. Wardle and J. Hunn (eds), *Excavation of the Iron Age, Roman and Medieval Settlement at Gorhambury, St Albans*, English Heritage Archaeological Report 14, London.

Locker, A. M. (1994) 'Animal bones', 107–110 in M. Papworth (ed.), 'Lodge Farm, Kingston Lacy estate, Dorset', *Journal of the British Archaeological Association* 147, 57–121.

Locker, A. (2000) 'Animal bone', 101–19 in A. J. Lawson (ed.), *Potterne 1982–5: Animal Husbandry in Later Prehistoric Wiltshire*, Wessex Archaeology Report 17, Salisbury.

Locker, A. (2005) 'Animal bone', 439–72 in M. Biddle (ed.), *Nonsuch Palace: The Material Culture of a Noble Restoration Household*, Oxbow, Oxford.

Locker, A. (2007) 'In piscibus diversis; the bone evidence for fish consumption in Roman Britain', *Britannia* 38, 141–80.

Locker, A. and Reilly, K. (1997) 'Animal bone' 52–55 in G. Malcolm (ed.), 'Excavations at Island Site, Finsbury Pavement, London EC2', *Transactions of the London and Middlesex Archaeological Society* 48, 33–58.

Long, J. R. (2003) *Introduced Mammals of the World: Their History, Distribution and Influence*, CABI Publishing, Wallingford.

Longfield, A. K. (1929) *Anglo-Irish Trade in the Sixteenth Century*, Routledge, London.

Lopez, B. H. (1978) *Of Wolves and Men*, Touchstone, New York.

Lopez-Martinez, N. (2007), 'The lagomorph fossil record and the origin of the European rabbit', 27–46 in P. C. Alves, N. Ferrand, and K. Hackländer (eds), *Lagomorph Biology Evolution, Ecology, and Conservation*, Springer, Berlin.

Lord, T. C., O'Connor, T. P., Siebrandt, D. and Jacobi, R. M. (2007) 'People and large carnivores as biostratinomic agents in Late Glacial cave assemblages', *Journal of Quaternary Science* 22(7), 681–694.

Loth, J. (1930) 'Notes étymologiques et lexicographiques', *Revue Celtique* 47, 160–75.

Lovegrove, R. (2007). *Silent Fields: The Long Decline of a Nation's Wildlife*, Oxford University Press, Oxford.

Lowe, E. J. (1853) *The Conchology of Nottingham*, Bartlett, London.

Lowe, J. J. and Walker, M. J. C. (1997) *Reconstructing Quaternary Environments (2nd ed.)*, Longman, Harlow.

Luff, R. M. (1993) *Animal Bones from Excavations in Colchester, 1971–85*, Colchester Archaeological Report 12, Colchester.

Luff, R. M. (1999) 'Animal and human bones', 204–23 in R. Turner (ed.), *Excavations of an Iron Age settlement and Roman religious complex at Ivy Chimneys, Witham, Essex 1978–83*, East Anglian Archaeology Report 88, Chelmsford.

Luff, R. M. and Moreno Garcia M. (1995) 'Killing cats in

the medieval period: an unusual episode in the history of Cambridge, England', *Archaeofauna* 4, 93–114.

Lumpkin, S. (1991) 'Cats and culture', 190–7 in J. Seidensticker and S. Lumpkin (eds), *Great Cats: Majestic Creatures of the Wild*, Merehurst, London.

Lyons, R. K., Forbes, T. D. A. and Machen, R. (n.d.) *What Range Herbivores Eat – and Why.* Texas A&M University, Texas Agricultural Extension Service. (on line at animalscience.tamu.edu/ansc/publications/sheeppubs/B6037-rangeherbivores.pdf)

MacDonald, D. and Barret, P. (1993) *Collins Field Guide to the Mammals of Britain and Europe*, Harper Collins, London.

Macdonald, D. W., Daniels, M. J., Driscoll, C., Kitchener, A. and Yamaguchi, N. (2004) *The Scottish Wildcat: Analyses for Conservation and an Action Plan*, Wildlife Conservation Research Unit, Oxford.

Macdonald, G. and Curle, A. O. (1929) 'The Roman fort at Mumrills', *Proceedinsg of the Society of Antiquaries of Scotland* 63, 396–575.

Macdonald, J. D. (1958) 'The bird bones', 143 in M. A. Cotton and P. W. Gathercole (eds), *Excavations at Clausentum, Southampton, 1951–4*, Her Majesty's Stationary Office, London.

Macholán, M. (2006) 'A geometric morphometric analysis of the shape of the first upper molar in mice of the genus *Mus* (Muridae, Rodentia)', *Journal of Zoology* 270, 672–81.

Mackinnon, M. (2004) *Production and Consumption of Aimals in Roman Italy: Integrating the Zooarchaeological and Textual Evidence*, (Journal of Roman Archaeology, supplementary series no. 54), Journal of Roman Archaeology, Portsmouth.

Macphail, S. R. (1881) *History of the Religious House of Pluscardyn: Convent of the Vale of Saint Andrew, in Morayshire*, Oliphant, Anderson & Ferrier, Edinburgh.

Madox, T. (1969) *The History and Antiquities of the Exchequer of the Kings of England*, Augustus M. Kelley, New York.

Mainland, I., Ewens, V. and Davis, G. (2004) *A preliminary report on the hand collected mammal bone assemblages from 2000 and 2002 excavations at the Iron Age site of Mine Howe, Tankerness, Orkney,* Department of Archaeological Sciences, University of Bradford.

Mainland, I., and Ewens, V. (2005) *A preliminary report on the hand collected mammal bone assemblages from 2003 excavations at the Iron Age site of Mine Howe, Tankerness, Orkney*, Department of Archaeological Sciences, University of Bradford.

Mainland, I. (1995) 'A Preliminary discussion of the animal bone assemblage from the 1979–1993 excavations at the Earl's Bu, Orphir, Orkney', Sheffield Environmental Facility Report.

Mainland, I. (2005) *The mammalian, avian and amphibian remains from Moaness.* Department of Archaeological Sciences, University of Bradford, Unpublished Report.

Maitland. P. S. and Campbell, R. N. (1992) *Freshwater Fishes of the British Isles,* Harper Collins, London.

Malek, J. (1993) *The Cat in Ancient Egypt*, British Museum Press, London.

Maltby M. (1979) *The Animal Bones from Exeter 1971–1975,* Department of Prehistory and Archaeology, Sheffield.

Maltby, M. (1982) 'Animal and bird bones', 114–34 in R. A. Higham, J. P. Allan, and S. R. Blaylock, 'Excavations at Okehampton Castle, Devon. Part 2 – the Bailey', *Devon Archaeological Society* 40, 19–151.

Maltby, M. (1984) 'The animal bones', 199–212 in M. G. Fulford (ed.), *Silchester: Excavations on the Defences 1974–80*, Britannia Monograph Series 5, London.

Maltby, M. (1994) 'The meat supply in Roman Dorchester and Winchester', 85–102 in A. R. Hall and H. K. Kenward (eds), *Urban-rural Connexions: Perspectives from Environmental Archaeology*, Oxbow, Oxford.

Maltby, M. (1996) 'The exploitation of animals in the Iron Age: the archaeozoological evidence', 17–27 in T. C. Champion and J. R. Collis (eds), *The Iron Age in Britain and Ireland: Recent Trends*, J. R. Collis Publications, Sheffield.

Maltby, M. (1997) 'Domestic fowl on Romano-British sites: inter-site comparisons of abundance', *International Journal of Osteoarchaeology* 7, 402–444.

Manceau, V., Després, L., Bouvet, J. and Taberlet, P. (1999) 'Systematics of the genus *Capra* inferred from mitochondrial DNA sequence data', *Molecular phylogenetics and Evolution* 13, 504–510.

Mannino, M. and Thomas K. D. (2002) 'Depletion of a resource? The impact of prehistoric human foraging on intertidal mollusc communities and its significance for human settlement, mobility and dispersal', *World Archaeology* 33(3), 452–74.

Maroo, S. and Yalden, D. W. (2000) 'The Mesolithic mammal fauna of Great Britain', *Mammal Review* 30, 243–248.

Marshall, J. T. Jr. and Sage, R. D. (1981) 'Taxonomy of the house mouse', *Symposia of the Zoological Society of London* 47, 15–25.

Martinková, N., McDonald, R. A., and Searle, J. B. (2007) 'Stoats (*Mustela erminea*) provide evidence of natural overland colonization of Ireland', *Proceedings of the Royal Society London B* 274, 1387–93.

Mascheretti, S., Rogatcheva, M. B., Gunduz, I., Fredga, K., and Searle, J. B. (2003) 'How did pygmy shrews colonise Ireland? Clues from a phylogenetic analysis of mitochondrial cytochrome b sequences', *Proceedings of the Royal Society, London, B* 270, 1593–9.

Masseti, M. (1996) The postglacial diffusion of the genus *Dama* Frisch, 1775, in the Mediterranean region. *Supplemento alle Ricerche di Biologia della Selvaggina* 25, 7–29.

Masseti, M., Cavallaro, A., Pecchioli, E. and Vernesi, C. (2006) 'Artificial occurrence of the Fallow Deer. *Dama dama dama* (L., 1758), on the Island of Rhodes (Greece): Insight from mtDNA Analysis', *Human Evolution*, 21, 2, 167–176.

Mather, A. S. (1990) *Global Forest Resources*, Timber Press, Portland, Oregon.

Matheus, P., Burns, J., Weinstock, J. and Hofreiter, M. (2004) 'Pleistocene brown bears in the mid-continent of North America', *Science* 306, 1150.

Matthews, J. (2002) *Celtic Totem Animals,* Gothic Image, Glastonbury.

May, E. (1985) 'Wideristhöhe und langknochenmaße bei pferd – ein immer noch aktuelles problem', *Zeitschrift für Säugertierkunde* 50, 368–82.

McCarthney, E. (1984) 'Analysis of Faunal Remains', 133–47 in H. Fairhurst (ed.), *Excavations at Crosskirk Broch, Caithness,* Society of Antiquaries of Scotland (Monograph Series 3), Edinburgh.

McCarthy, M. R. (1995) 'Archaeological and environmental evidence for the Roman impact on vegetation near Carlisle, Cumbria', *The Holocene* 5, 491–5

McCormick, F. (1981) 'The animal bones from Ditch 1', 313–318 in J. Barber (ed.), 'Excavations in Iona', *Proceedings of the Society of Antiquaries of Scotland* 111, 282–380.

McCormick, F. (1984) 'Large Mammal Bone', 75–125, Fiche 2: D10 in N. Sharples (ed.), 'Excavations at Pierowall Quarry, Westray, Orkney', *Proceedings of the Society of Antiquaries of Scotland,* 114, 108–110.

McCormick, F. (1987) 'The animal bones', 99–100 in R. M. Cleary, M. F. Hurley and E. A. Twohig (eds), *Archaeological Excavations in the Cork-Dubling gas pipeline 1981–1982,* University College, Cork.

McCormick, F. (1988) 'The domesticated cat in early Christian and Medieval Ireland', 218–28 in G. Mac Niocaill and P. F. Wallace (eds), *Keimelia. Studies in Medieval Archaeology and History in Memory of Tom Delaney,* Galway University Press, Galway.

McCormick, F. (1997) 'The animal bones', 819–53 in M. F. Hurley, O. M. B. Scully with S. W. J. McCutcheon (eds), *Late Viking Age and Medieval Waterford: Excavations 1986–1992,* Waterford Corporation, Waterford.

McCormick, F. (1999) 'Early evidence for wild animals in Ireland', 355–71 in N. Benecke (ed.), *The Holocene History of the European Vertebrate Fauna: Modern Aspects*

of Research Workshop, 6th to 9th April 1998, Berlin, Verlag Marie Leidorf GmbH, Rahden.

McCormick, M. (2003) 'Rats, communications, and plague: toward an ecological history', *Journal of Interdisciplinary History* 34 (1), 1–25.

McCormick, F. (2006) 'Animal Bones', 61–180 in I. Armit (ed.), *Anatomy of an Iron Age Roundhouse: The Cnip Wheelhouse Excavations, Lewis,* Society of Antiquaries of Scotland, Edinburgh.

McCormick, F. and Buckland, P.C. (1997) 'The vertebrate fauna', 83–103 in K. J. Edwards and I. B. M. Ralston (eds), *Scotland After the Ice Age: Environment, Archaeology and History, 8,000 B.C.–A.D. 1000,* Edinburgh University Press, Edinburgh.

McDonnell, J. (1981) *Inland Fisheries in Medieval Yorkshire 1066–1300,* (Borthwick Papers, no. 60), University of York, York.

McIllroy, A. (2006) 'Gallivanting grizzly', *The Guardian.* http://www.guardian.co.uk/elsewhere/journalist/story/0,,1817056,00.html [accessed 10/7/06]

McLaren, D., Wigen, R. J., Mackie, Q. and Fedje, D. W. (2005) 'Bear hunting at the Pleistocene/Holocene transition on the nothern northwest coast of America', *Canadian Zooarchaeology* 22, 3–29.

McOrist, S. and Kitchener, A. C. (1994) 'Current threats to the European wildcat, *Felis silvestris,* in Scotland', *Ambio* 23, 243–5.

Mead, W. E. (1967) *The English Medieval Feast,* Allen and Unwin, London.

Meaney, A. (1981) *Anglo-Saxon Amulets and Curing Stones,* British Archaeological Report, British series 96, Oxford.

Meddens, B. (2000) 'The animal bone', 315–55 in P. Ellis (ed.), *The Roman Baths at MACELLUM at Wroxeter: Excavations by Graham Webster 1955–85,* English Heritage Archaeological Report 9, London.

Meddens, B. (2002) 'Animal bones from Catterick Bridge (Site 240)', 425–31 in P. R. Wilson (ed.) *Cataractonium: Roman Catterick and its Hinterland. Excavations and Research 1958–1997. Part II,* Council for British Archaeology Report 129, London.

Mellars, P. and Dark, P. (1998) *Star Carr in Context,* McDonald Institute for Archaeological Research, Cambridge.

Mellor, D. J. and Stafford, K. J. (2004) 'Animal welfare implications of neonatal mortality and morbidity in farm animals', *The Veterinary Journal* 168, 118–133.

Met Office http://www.metoffice.gov.uk/climate/uk/averages/19712000/mapped.html

Monaghan, N. T. (1989) 'The elk in Irish Quaternary deposits', *Irish Naturalists' Journal* 23, 97–101.

Middleton, P. (1979) 'Army surplus in Gaul: a hypothesis

for Roman Britain', 81–97, in B. C. Burnham and H. B. Johnson (eds), *Invasion and Response: The Case for Roman Britain*, British Archaeological Report, British series 73, Oxford.

Miles, D. (1984) *Archaeology at Barton Court Farm, Abingdon, Oxon*, Council for British Archaeology Research Report 50, Oxford.

Millais, J. G. (1906) *Mammals of Great Britain and Ireland*, Longman, London.

Milne, G, (1985) *The Port of Roman London*, Batsford, London

Mitchell, F. J. G. (2005) 'How open were European primeval forests? Hypothesis testing using palaeoecological data', *Journal of Ecology* 93, 168–177.

Mithen, S. and Finlayson, B. (1991) 'Red deer hunters on Colonsay: Staosnaig and its implications for the interpretation of the Oronsay middens', *Proceedings of the Prehistoric Society* 57, 1–8.

Montgomery, D. R. (2003) *King of Fish. The Thousand-year Run of Salmon*, Westview Press, Boulder Colorado.

Moore, A. M. T., Hillman, G. C. and Legge, A. J. (2000) *Village on the Euphrates: From Foraging to Farming at Abu Hureyra*, Oxford University Press, Oxford.

Moore, P. D. (1993) 'The origin of blanket mire, revisited', 218–44 in F. M. Chambers (ed.), *Climate Change and Human Impact on the Landscape*, Chapman and Hall, London.

Morales Muñiz, A., Pecharroman, M. A. C., Carrasquilla, F. H. and von Lettow-Vorbeck, L. (1995) 'Of mice and sparrows: commensal faunas from the Iberian Iron Age in the Duero Valley (Central Spain)', *International Journal of Osteoarchaeology* 5, 127–38.

Mulkeen, S. and O'Connor, T. P. (1997) 'Raptors in towns: towards an ecological model', *International Journal of Osteoarchaeology* 7 (4), 440–9.

Müller, H.-H. (1971) 'De braunbär *Ursus arctos* L. im Mittlealter', *Hercynia* 8 (1), 52–7.

Mulville, J. (1999) 'The faunal remains', 234–274 in M. Parker Pearson and N. Sharples. (eds), *Between Land and Sea: Excavations at Dun Vulan, South Uist*, Sheffield Academic Press, Sheffield.

Mulville, J. (2000) 'The faunal remains', 250–265, 285–290, 299–305 in K. Branigan and P. Foster (eds), *From Barra to Berneray: SEARCH Volume 5*, Sheffield Academic Press, Sheffield.

Mulville, J. (2005) 'Mammalian bone; resource exploitation; site activities and discussion' 165–169, 190–1, in N. Sharples (ed.), *A Norse Farmstead in the Outer Hebrides: Excavations at Mound 3, Bornais, South Uist*, Oxbow Books, Oxford.

Mulville, J. (forthcoming) 'Social zooarchaeology of a Norse-period farmstead' in M. Parker-Pearson, P.

Marshall, J. Mulville and H. Smith '*A Norse-period farmstead at Cille Pheadair, South Uist, c. 950–1300*', Oxbow, Oxford.

Mulville, J. and Ingrem, C. (forthcoming) 'Animal Resources at Cille Donnain Wheelhouse', Cardiff Archaeological Specialist Reports, Cardiff.

Mulville, J. and Grigson, C. (2007) 'The animal bones', 237–54 in D. Benson and A. Whittle (eds), *Building Memories: The Neolithic Cotswold Long Barrow at Ascott-under-Wychwood, Oxfordshire*, Oxbow Books, Oxford.

Mulville, J. and Levitan, B. (2004) 'The animal bone' 463–78 in G. Lambrick and T. Allen (eds), *Gravelly Guy, Stanton Harcourt: The Development of a Prehistoric and Romano-British Community*, Oxford University School of Archaeology, Oxford.

Mulville, J. and Powell, A. (forthcoming) 'Mammalian bone; resource exploitation; site activities and discussion' in N. Sharples (ed.), *A Norse Farmstead in the Outer Hebrides. Excavations at Mound 1, Bornais, South Uist*, Oxbow Books, Oxford.

Mulville, J., Parker Pearson, M., Sharples, N, Smith, H. and Chamberlain, A. (2003) 'Quarters, arcs and squares: human and animal remains in the Hebridean Late Iron Age', 21–34 in J. Downes and A. Ritchie (eds), *Sea Change: Orkney and Northern Europe in the Later Iron Age AD 300–800*, The Pinkfoot Press, Balgavies, Angus.

Mynors, R. A. B., Thomson, R. M. and Winterbottom, M. (1998) Gesta Regum Anglorum: *Vol. 1: History of the English Kings/William of Malmesbury*, Clarendon Press, Oxford.

Nachtsheim, H. (1949) *Vom Wildtier zum Haustier*, Paul Parey, Hamburg and Berlin

National Archive – Public Records Office. E101/390/11 folio 91.

Nicastro, N. (2004) 'Perceptual and acoustic evidence for species-level differences in meow vocalisations by domestic cats (*Felis catus*) and African wild cats (*Felis silvestris lybica*)', *Journal of Comparative Psychology* 118 (3), 287–96.

Nicholson, R. and Davies, G. (2007) 'The mammal bone', 169–227 in S. J. Dockrill, J. M. Bond, R. Nicholson and A. Smith *Investigations in Sanday, Orkney: Island Landscape Through Three 3000 years of Prehistory – Tofts Ness, Sanday (Volume 2)*, Oxbow, Oxford.

Nielsen, K. H. (2002) 'Ulv, hest og drage. Ikonografisk analyse af dyrene i stil II–III', *Hikuin* 29, 187–218.

Noddle, B. (1976) 'Report on the animal bones from Walton, Aylesbury', 269–287 in M. Farley, 'Saxon and Medieval Walton, Aylesbury: excavations 1973–4', *Records of Buckinghamshire* 20 (2), 153–290.

Noddle, B. (1976–77) 'The animal bones from Buckquoy,

Orkney', 201–209 in A. Ritchie (ed.), 'Excavations of Pictish and Viking-age farmsteads at Buckquoy, Orkney', *Proceedings of the Society of Antiquaries of Scotland* 108, 174–227.

Noddle, B. (1978–80) 'Animal bones from Dun Cul Bhuirg, Iona' 225–7 in J. N. Ritchie and A. M. Lane (eds), 'Dun Cul Bhuirg, Iona, Argyll', *Proceedings of the Society of Antiquaries of Scotland* 110, 209–29.

Noddle, B. (1981) 'A comparison of mammalian bones found in the midden deposit with others from the Iron Age site of Dun Bhuirg', 38–50 in R. Reece (ed.), *Excavations in Iona 1964 to 1974*, Institute of Archaeology Occasional publication 5, London.

Noddle, B. (1982) 'The size of red deer in Britain – past and present, with some reference to fallow deer' 315–33 in M. Bell and S. Limbray (eds), *Archaeological Aspects of Woodland Ecology*, British Archaeological Report, international series 146, Oxford.

Noddle, B. (1983) 'Animal bones from Knap of Howar', 92–100 in A. Ritchie (ed.), 'Excavation of a Neolithic farmstead at Knap of Howar, Papa Westray, Orkney', *Proceedings of the Society of Antiquaries of Scotland* 113, 40–121.

Noddle, B. (1985a) 'Animal bones', 84–94 in R. Shoesmith (ed.), *Hereford City Excavations, Vol. 3. The Finds*, Council for British Archaeology Research Report 56, London.

Noddle, B. (1985b) 'The animal bones: Bewell House', fiche M8.F1. in R. Shoesmith (ed.) *Hereford City Excavations. Vol. 3: The Finds*, Council for British Archaeology Research Report 56, London.

Noddle, B. (1986) 'Animal Bones', 132 in A. Whittle (ed.), *Scord of Brouster an Early Agricultural Settlement on Shetland, Excavations 1977–79*, (Committee for Archaeology Monograph no 9), Oxford University, Oxford.

Noddle, B. A. (1993) 'The animal bones', 97–103 in P. J. Casey and J. L. Davies (eds), *Excavations at Segontium (Caernarfon) Roman Fort, 1975–197*, Council for British Archaeology Research Report 90, London.

Noddle, B. (1997) 'Animal Bones', 234–36 in S. Buteux (ed.), *Settlements at Skaill, Deerness, Orkney: Excavation by Peter Gellings of the Prehistoric, Pictish, Viking and later Periods, 1963–198*, British Archaeological Report, British series 260, Oxford.

Noddle, B. (forthcoming) *The Animal Bones from Skara Brae*.

Noddle, B. and Bramwell, D. (1975) 'The animal bones', 332–39 in C. Platt and R. Coleman-Smith (eds) *Excavations in Medieval Southampton 1953–1969 Vol. I: The Excavation Reports*, Leicester University Press, Leicester.

Noddle, B. and Hamilton-Dyer, S. (2002) 'The bird bones', 115–116, in A. Thomas and A. Boucher (eds), *Hereford City Excavations Vol. 4, 1976–1990. Further Sites and Evolving Interpretations*, Hereford City and County Archaeological Trust, Logaston.

Noe-Nygaard, N. (1975) 'Two shoulder blades with healed lesions from Star Carr', *Proceedings of the Prehistoric Society* 41, 10–16.

Noe-Nygaard, N., Price, T. D. and Hede, S.U. (2005) 'The diet of aurochs and domestic cattle in Southern Scandinavia; evidence from 15^N and 13^C stable isotopes', *Journal of Archaeological Science* 32, 855–71.

Nowak, R. M. (1999a) *Walker's Mammals of the World Volume 1*, John Hopkins University Press, London.

Nowak, R. M. (1999b) *Walker's Mammals of the World. Volume II*, The John Hopkins University Press, Baltimore and London.

O'Connor, T. (1982) *Animal bones from Flaxengate, Lincoln, c 870–1500*, (The Archaeology of Lincoln 18 –1), Lincolnshire Archaeological Trust, Lincoln.

O'Connor, T. P. (1984a) *Bones from Aldwark, York*, (Ancient Monuments Laboratory Report 4391), English Heritage, London.

O'Connor, T. P. (1984b) *Selected Groups of Bones from Skeldergate and Walmgate*, (The Archaeology of York 15/1), Council for British Archaeology, London.

O'Connor, T. P. (1986a) 'The garden dormouse *Eliomys quercinus* from Roman York', *Journal of Zoology, London* 210, 620–2.

O'Connor, T. P. (1986b) 'The animal bones', 223–46 in D. Zienkiewicz (ed.), *The Legionary Fortress Baths at Caerleon. Volume II: The Finds*, National Museum of Wales, Cardiff

O'Connor, T. P. (1988) *Bones from the General Accident Site*, (The Archaeology of York 15/2: The Animal Bones), Council for British Archaeology, London.

O'Connor, T. P. (1989) *Bones from the Anglo-Scandinavian levels at 16–22 Coppergate*, (The Archaeology of York 15/3: The Animal Bones), Council for British Archaeology, London.

O'Connor, T. P. (1991a) 'On the lack of bones of the ship rat *Rattus rattus* from Dark Age York', *Journal of Zoology, London* 224, 318–320.

O'Connor, T. (1991b) *Bones from 46–54 Fishergate*, (The Archaeology of York: The animal Bones 15/4), Council for British Archaeology, London.

O'Connor, T. P. (1991c) 'The animal bone', 88–91. In D. Stocker, *St Mary's Guildhall, Lincoln The survey and excavation of a medieval building complex*. City of Lincoln Archaeology Unit (The Archaeology of Lincoln XII–1), Lincoln.

O'Connor, T. P. (1992) 'Pets and pests in Roman and medieval Britain', *Mammal Review* 22 (2), 107–13.

O'Connor, T. P. (2000) 'Human refuse as a major ecological

factor in medieval urban vertebrate communities', 15–20 in G. Bailey, R. Charles and N. Winder (eds), *Human Ecodynamics*, Oxbow, Oxford.

O'Connor, T. P. (2001) 'Collecting, sieving, and animal bone quantification', 7–16 in H. Buitenhuis and W. Prummel (eds) *Animals and Man in the Past.* Rijksuniversiteit Groningen, Groningen.

O'Connor, T. P. (2002) 'Bird bones and small mammal bones', 262 in G. Webster (ed by J. Chadderton), *The Legionary Fortress at Wroxeter: Excavations by Graham Webster 1955–85*, (English Heritage Archaeological Reports 19), English Heritage, London.

O'Connor, T. P. (2003) *The Analysis of Urban Animal Bone Assemblages*, (Archaeology of York 19/2), Council for British Archaeology, York.

O'Connor, T. P. (2007a) 'Wild or domestic? Biometric variation in the cat *Felis silvestris* Schreber', *International Journal of Osteoarchaeology* 17, 581–595

O'Connor, T. P. (2007b) 'Thinking about beastly bodies', 1–10 in A. Pluskowski (ed.) *Breaking and Shaping Beastly Bodies: Animals as Material Culture in the Middle Ages*, Oxbow, Oxford.

O'Connor, T. P. and Barrett, J. H. (2006) 'Animal bones', 260–95 in J. Balme and A. Patterson (eds) *A Student Guide to Archaeological Analysis*, Blackwell, Oxford.

Oddy, W. and Grigson, C. (1983) 'Scientific report on the dimensions of the drinking-horns from the Sutton Hoo ship burial', 406–8 in R. Bruce-Mitford (ed.), *The Sutton Hoo Ship-Burial Vol. 3*, British Museum Publications, London.

Onions, C. T. (1966) *The Oxford Dictionary of English Etymology*, Oxford University Press, Oxford.

Olsen, S. L. (2006) 'Early horse domestication on the Eurasian Steppe', 245–69 in M. A. Zeder, D. G. Bradley, E. Emshwiller and B. D. Smith (eds), *Documenting Domestication: New Genetic and Archaeological Paradigms*, University of California Press, Berkeley.

O'Meara, J. J. (1982) *Gerald of Wales: The History and Topography of Ireland*, Penguin, Harmondsworth.

O'Neil, H. E. (1945) 'The Roman villa at Park Street near St Albans, Herts. Report on the excavations of 1943–45', *Archaeological Journal* 102, 21–110.

O'Regan, H. J. and Kitchener, A. C. (2005) 'The effects of captivity on the morphology of captive, domesticated and feral mammals', *Mammal Review* 35 (3/4), 215–30.

Osborne, P. J. (1965) 'The effect of forest clearance on the distribution of the British Insect fauna', 556–7 in, *Proceedings XII International Congress of Entomology, London, 8–16th July 1964*.

Osborne, P. J. (1969) 'An insect fauna of Late Bronze Age date from Wilsford, Wiltshire', *Journal of Animal Ecology* 38, 555–66.

Osborne, P. J. (1974) '*Airaphilus elongatus* (Gyll.) (Col., Cucujidae) present in Britain in Roman times', *Entomologist's Monthly Magazine* 109, 239.

Osborne, P. J. (1979) 'Insect remains'85–7 and 189–93 in C. Smith (ed.), *Fisherwick: The Reconstruction of an Iron Age Landscape*, British Archaeological Reports, British series 61, Oxford.

Osborne, P. J. (1988) 'A Late Bronze Age insect fauna from the River Avon, Warwickshire, England: its implications for the terrestrial and fluvial environment and for climate', *Journal of Archaeological Science* 15, 715–27.

Osborne, P. J. (1989) 'Insects', 96–9 in P. Ashbee, M. Bell and E. Proudfoot (eds), *Wilsford Shaft: Excavations 1960–2*, HBMC, London.

Osborne, P. J. (1994) 'The insects', 266 in P. Bidwell and S. Speak (eds), *Excavations at South Shields Roman Fort I,* Society of Antiquaries of Newcastle upon Tyne with Tyne and Wear Museums Monograph Series 4, Newcastle upon Tyne.

Osborne, P. J. (1996) 'An insect fauna of Roman date from Stourport, Worcestershire, U. K., and its environmental implications', *Circaea, the Journal of the Association for Environmental Archaeology* 12, 183–9.

Osgood, R. (1998) *Warfare in the Late Bronze Age of North Europe*, British Archaeological Reports, international series 694, Oxford.

O'Sullivan, T. (1998) 'Mammals', 91–130 in N. Sharples (ed.), *Scalloway,* Oxbow, Oxford.

Outen, A. (1979) 'The animal bones', 113–120 in A. Down (ed.), *Chichester Excavations IV: The Roman Villas At Chilgrove And Upmarden*, Chichester, Phillimore.

Owen, A. (1841). *Ancient Laws and Institutes of Wales*, The Commissioners on the Public Records of the Kingdom, London.

Owen, C. (1969) 'The domestication of the ferret', 489–93 in P. J. Ucko and G. W. Dimbleby (eds) *The Domestication and Exploitation of Plants and Animals*, Duckworth, London.

Palk, N. A. (1984) *Iron Age Bridle-bits from Britain*, (Department of Archaeology Occasional Paper No. 10), University of Edinburgh, Edinburgh.

Panagiotakopulu, E. (2000) *Archaeology and Entomology in the Eastern Mediterranean: Research into the History of Insect Synanthropy in Greece and Egypt*, British Archaeological Reports, international series 836, Oxford.

Parker, A. J. (1988) 'The birds of Roman Britain', *Oxford Journal of Archaeology* 7(2), 197–226.

Parkes, R. and Barrett, J. (n.d.) *The Zooarchaeology of Sand – interim report*. University of York.

Partridge, E. (1966) *Origins: A Short Etymological Dictionary of Modern English*. Routledge & Kegan Paul, London.

Peacock, D. P. S. (1978) 'The Rhine and the problem of Gaulish wine in Roman Britain', 49–57 in J. du Plat Taylor and H. Cleere (eds), *Roman Shipping and Trade: Britain and the Rhine provinces*, Council for British Archaeology Research Report 24, London.

Peek, J. M. (1998) 'Habitat relationships' 351–75 in A. W. Franzmann and C. C. Schwartz (eds.), *Ecology and Management of the North American Moose*, Smithsonian Institution Press, Washington D.C.

Pemberton, J. M. and Smith, R. H. (1985) 'Lack of biochemical polymorphism in British fallow deer', *Heredity* 55, 199–207.

Philpott, R. (1991) *Burial Practices in Roman Britain: A Survey of Grave Treatment and Furnishing A.D. 43–410*, British Archaeological Reports, British series 219, Oxford.

Pierpaoli, M., Birò, Z. S., Herrmann, M., Hupe, K., Fernandes, M., Ragni, B., Szemethy, L. and Randi, E. (2003) 'Genetic distinction of wildcat (*Felis silvestris*) populations in Europe, and hybridization with domestic cats in Hungary', *Molecular Ecology* 12, 2585–98.

Pipe, A. (2003) 'The animal bone', 175–82 in C. Cowan (ed.), *Urban Development in North-west Roman Southwark: Excavations 1974–90*, MoLAS Monograph Series 16, London.

Pipe, A. (2007) 'The animal bones', 246–50 in P. Miller and D. Saxby (eds), *The Augustinian Priory of St Mary Merton, Surrey: Excavations 1976–90*, MoLAS Monograph Series 34, London.

Pipe, A. (in prep) 'The animal bones', in J. Hill and P. Rowsome, *Roman London and the Walbrook stream crossing: excavations at 1 Poultry and vicinity 1985–96*. MoLAS Monograph Series, London.

Pitts, M. (2006) 'Flight of the eagles', *British Archaeology* 86, 6.

Platt, M. I. (1934) 'Report on the animal bones', 515–516 in G. J. Callander, and W. G. Grant (eds), 'A long stalled chambered cairn or mausoleum (Rousay type) near Midhowe, Rousay, Orkney', *Proceeding of the Society of Antiquaries of Scotland* 10, 348–516.

Platt, M. I. (1935) 'Report on the animal bones', 341–3 in G. J. Callander and G. G. Walter (eds), 'A long, stalled cairn, The Knowe of Yarso, in Rousay, Orkney', *Proceeding of the Society of Antiquaries of Scotland* 69, 235–41.

Platt, M. I. (1936) 'Report on the animal bones found in the chambered cairn, Knowe of Ramsay, Rousay, Orkney', 415–9 in G. J. Callander and G. G.Walter (eds), 'the Knowe of Ramsay, at Hullion, Rousay, Orkney', *Proceedings of the Society of Antiquaries of Scotland* 70, 407–419.

Platt, M. I. (1937a) 'Report on the animal bone' 152–4 in C. Calder (ed.), 'A Neolithic double-chambered cairn of the stalled type and later structures on the Calf of Eday, Orkney', *Proceedings of the Society of Antiquaries of Scotland* 71,115–54.

Platt, M. I. (1937b) 'Report on the animal bones', 306–8 in G. J. Callander and G. G. Walter (eds), 'A long stalled Cairn at Blackhammer, Rousay, Orkney', *Proceedings of the Society of Antiquaries of Scotland* 71, 297–308.

Platt, M. I. (1956) 'Report on the animal bones', 212–5 in J. C. R. Hamilton (ed.) *Excavations at Jarlshof*, HMSO, Edinburgh.

Pluskowski. A. G. (2004) 'Lupine apocalypse: the wolf in pagan and Christian cosmology in medieval Britain and Scandinavia', *Cosmos* 17, 113–131.

Pluskowski, A. G. (2006a) 'Where are the wolves? Investigating the scarcity of European grey wolf (*Canis lupus lupus*) remains in medieval archaeological contexts and its implications', *International Journal of Osteoarchaeology* 16(4), 279–95.

Pluskowski, A. G. (2006b) *Wolves and the Wilderness in the Middle Ages*, Boydell, Woodbridge.

Pocock, R. I. (1951) *Catalogue of the Genus Felis*, British Museum, London.

Pollard, A. J. (2004) *Imagining Robin Hood*, Routledge, New York.

Poole, K. (n.d.) *Status, Economy and Diet at Twelfth-century Ludgershall Castle: A Zooarchaeological Study*, unpublished BA dissertation, University of Southampton.

Pope, S. (1925) *Hunting with the Bow and Arrow*. G. P. Puttnam's Sons, New York.

Poplin, F. (1984) 'Contribution osteo-archéologique à la connaissance des astragales de l'Antre corycien', *Bulletin de Correspondences Helléniques Supplément* 9, 381–93.

Potter, T. W. and Johns, C. (1992) *Roman Britain*, British Museums Publications, London.

Powell, A. and Clark, K. M. (1996) *Exploitation of Domestic Animals in the Iron Age at Rooksdown*, unpublished Centre for Human Ecology report, University of Southampton.

Powell, A. and Serjeantson, D. (n.d.) *Pevensey Castle: The Animal Bones*, Faunal Remains Unit, unpublished report, university of Southampton.

Preece, R. C. (1980) 'The biostratigraphy and dating of the tufa deposit at the Mesolithic site at Blashenwell, Dorset, England', *Journal of Archaeological Science* 7, 345–62.

Preece, R. C. (1992) 'Cochlicopa nitens (Gallenstein) in the British Isles Late-Glacial', *Journal of Conchology* 34, 215–24.

Preece, R. C. (1995) *Island Britain: A Quaternary Perspective*, The Geological Society, London.

Preece, R. C. and Bridgland, D. R. (1998) *Late-Quaternary Environmental Change in North-west Europe: Excavations at Holywell Coombe, South-east England*, Chapman and Hall, London.

Preece, R. C. and Bridgland, D. R. (1999) 'Holywell Coombe, Folkestone: a 13,000 year history of an English chalkland valley', *Quaternary Science Reviews* 18, 1075–125.

Preece, R. C., Coxon, P., and Robinson, J. E. (1986) 'New biostratigraphic evidence of the Post-glacial colonization of Ireland and for Mesolithic forest disturbance', *Journal of Biogeography* 13, 487–509.

Price, C. (2003) *Late Pleistocene and Early Holocene Small Mammals in South West Britain*, British Archaeological Report, British series 347, Oxford.

Rackham, D. J. (1979) '*Rattus rattus*: the introduction of the black rat into Britain', *Antiquity* 53, 112–120.

Rackham, D. J. (1982) 'The smaller mammals in the urban environment: their recovery and interpretation from archaeological deposits', 86–93 in A. R. Hall and H. K. Kenward (eds), *Environmental Archaeology in the Urban Context*, Council for British Archaeology Research Report 43, London.

Rackham, D. J. (1985) *An Analysis and Interpretation of the Sample of Animal Bones from Thorpe Thewles, Cleveland*, (Ancient Monuments Laboratory Report 4567). English Heritage, London.

Rackham, J., Locker, A. and West, B. (1989) 'Animal remains', 148–70 in R. L. Whytehead and R. Cowie, with L. Blackmore, 'Excavations at the Peabody site, Chandos Place, and the National Gallery', *Transactions of the London and Middlesex Archaeological Society* 40, 35–177.

Rackham, J. (1983) 'The animal remains', 240–56 in M. Ellison and B. Harbottle, The excavation of a 17th-Century Bastion in the Castle of Newcastle Upon Tyne, 1976–81. *Archaeologia Aeliana* 11, 136–263.

Rackham, J. (1986) 'An analysis of the animal remains', Fiche A1–4, G7 in C. D Morris and N. Emery (eds), 'The chapel and enclosure on the Brough of Deerness, Orkney: survey and excavation, 1975–1977', *Proceedings of the Society of Antiquaries of Scotland* 116, 301–374.

Rackham, J, (1989) 'The biological assemblage' 77–80, 87–91, 99–107, 232–247 in C. D. Morris (ed.), *The Birsay Bay Project Volume 1. Coastal Sites Beside the Brough Road, Birsay, Orkney Excavations 1976–82*. University of Durham, (Department of Archaeology Monograph series 1), Durham.

Rackham, J. (1994) 'Economy and Environment in Saxon London', 126–36 in J. Rackham (ed.), *Environment and Economy in Anglo-Saxon England*, Council for British Archaeology Research Report 89, London.

Rackham, J. (2005) 'The animal bone', 374–380 in C. Woodfield (ed.), *The Church of Lady of Mount Carmel and Some Conventual Buildings at the Whitefriars,*

Coventry, British Archaeological Report British Series 389, Oxford.

Rackham, O. (1989) *The Last Forest: The Story of Hatfield Forest*. Dent, London.

Rackham, O. (1993) *Trees and Woodland in the British Landscape*, J. M. Dent, London.

Rackham, O. (1997) *The History of the Countryside: The Classic History of Britain's Landscape, Flora and Fauna*, Phoenix, London.

Randall, J. (2005) *Traditions of Seabird Fowling in the North Atlantic Region*, The Islands Book Trust, Stornaway.

Reeves, H. M. and McCabe, R. E. (1998) 'Of moose and man', 1–75 in A. W. Franzmann and C. C. Schwartz (eds.), *Ecology and Management of the North American Moose*, Smithsonian Institution Press, Washington D.C.

Reimer, P. J. and 28 others (2004) 'IntCal04 terrestrial radiocarbon age calibration, 0–26 cal kyr BP', *Radiocarbon* 46, 1029–58.

Renecker, L. A. and Schwartz, C. C. (1998) 'Food habits and feeding behaviour', 403–39 in A. W. Franzmann and C. C. Schwartz (eds.), *Ecology and Management of the North American Moose*, Smithsonian Institution Press, Washington D.C.

Reumer, J. W. F. and Sanders, E. A. C. (1984) 'Changes in the vertebrate fauna of Menorca in prehistoric and classical times', *Zeitschrift für Säugetierkunde* 49, 321–5.

Reynolds, S. H. (1934) *A Monograph of the British Pleistocene Mammalia, Vol. III, Part VIIa. Alces* (supplement*)*, Palaeontographical Society, London.

Rielly, K. (1997) 'Animal bone', 270–3 in J. C. Smith, F. Healy, M. J. Allen, E.L. Morris, I. Barnes and P. J. Woodward (eds), *Excavations Along the Route of the Dorchester By-pass, Dorset, 1986–88,* Wessex Archaeology Report 11, Salisbury.

Rielly, K. (2004) 'The animal bones', 57–9 in L. Dunwoodie (ed.), *Pre-Boudican and later activity on the site of the forum: excavations at 168 Fenchurch Street, City of London*, MoLAS Archaeology Study Series 13, London.

Rielly, K. (2006) 'Animal bone', 202–10 in C. Thomas, R. Cowie and J. Sidell (eds), *The Royal Palace, Abbey and Town of Westminster on Thorney Island*, MoLAS Monograph Series 22, London.

Rielly, K. (2007) 'Vertebrate remains', 477–9 and CD in D. Bowsher, T. Dyson, N. Holder and I. Howell (eds), *The London Guildhall. An Archaeological History of a Neighbourhood from Early Medieval to Modern Times, Part II*, MoLAS Monograph Series 36, London.

Rielly, K. (forthcoming) 'The animal bones' in J. Bowsher and P. Miller (eds) *The Rose and the Globe – playhouses of Tudor Bankside, Southwark: Excavations 1988–91*, MoLAS Monograph Series, London.

Rielly, K. (in prep a) 'The distribution of the black rat in Roman, saxon and early medieval Britain', for submission to Internet Archaeology.

Rielly, K, (in prep b) 'The animal bones', in L. Casson, J. Drummond-Murray and A. Francis (eds), *Roman and Medieval Development South of Cripplegate: Excavations at 10 Gresham Street, City of London*, MoLAS Monograph Series, London

Rielly, K. and Davis, D. (in prep) *The animal bones and seeds from a 1st century well at Fish Street Hill, London EC3*.

Ritchie, J. (1920) *The Influence of Man on Animal Life in Scotland: A Study of Faunal Evolution*, Cambridge University Press, Cambridge.

Roberts, A. F. (1986) 'Faunal remains from Bewsey Old Hall, Warrington', *Circaea* 4 (1), 26–27.

Robinson, M. A. (1979) 'The biological evidence', 77–133 in G. Lambrick and M. A. Robinson (eds), *Iron Age and Roman Riverside Settlements at Farmoor, Oxfordshire*, Council for British Archaeology Research Report 32, London.

Robinson, M. A. (1981) 'The Iron Age to Early Saxon environment of the Upper Thames terraces', 251–86 in M. Jones and G. Dimbleby (eds), *The Environment of Man: The Iron Age to the Anglo-Saxon Period*, British Archaeological Report, British series 87, Oxford.

Robinson, M. A. (2000), 'Middle Mesolithic to Late Bronze Age insect assemblages and an Early Neolithic assemblage of waterlogged macroscopic plant remains', 146–67 in S. P. Needham (ed.), *The Passage of the Thames. Holocene Environment and Settlement at Runnymede*, (Runnymede Bridge Research Excavations, Volume 1), British Museum Press, London.

Robinson, M. A. (2003) 'Environmental investigations at the British Telcom tunnel', 378–83 in A. Dodd (ed.), *Oxford Before the University: The Late Saxon and Norman Archaeology of the Defences and the Town*, (Thames Valley Landscapes Monograph 17), Oxford Archaeology, Oxford.

Robinson, M. and Lambrick, G. H. (1984) 'Holocene alluviation and hydrology in the Upper Thames basin', *Nature* 308, 809–14.

Rogers, P. M., Arthur, C. P. and Soriguer, R. C. (1994) 'The rabbit in continental Europe', 64–107 in H. V. Thompson and C. M. King (eds), *The European Rabbit: The History and Biology of a Successful Colonizer*, Oxford University Press, Oxford.

Rooney, A. (1993) *Hunting in Middle English Literature*, D. S. Brewer, Cambridge.

Ross, A. (1967) *Pagan Celtic Britain*, Routledge and Kegan Paul, London.

Rossel, S., Marshall, F., Peters, J., Pilgram, T., Adams, M.

D. and O'Connor, D. (2008) 'Domestication of the donkey: timing, processes and indicators', *Proceedings of the National Academy of Sciences* 105 (10), 3715–20.

Rotherham, I. D. (2007) 'The historical ecology of medieval parks and the implications for conservation', in R. Liddiard (ed.), *The Medieval Park: New Perspectives*, Windgather Press, Macclesfield.

Rowley, T. (1997) *Norman England: An Archaeological Perspective on the Norman Conquest*, Batsford/English Heritage, London.

Rowley-Conwy, P. (2003) 'Early domestic animals in Europe: imported or locally domesticated?', 99–117 in A. Ammerman and P. Biagi (eds), *The Widening Harvest. The Neolithic Transition in Europe: Looking Forward, Looking Back*, (Colloquia and Conference Papers 6), Archaeological Institute of America, Boston.

Rowley-Conwy, P. (2004) 'How the West was lost: a re-appraisal of agricultural origins in Britain, Ireland and southern Scandinavia', *Current Anthropology* 45(4), 83–111.

Ryder, M. L. (1975) 'Some Phoenician animal remains from Sicily', 213–18 in A. T. Clason (ed.), *Archaeozoological Studies: Papers of the Archaeozoological Conference 1974, held at the Biologisch-Archaeologisch Institut of the State University of Groningen*, North Holland Publishing, Amsterdam.

Ryder, P. (1996) 'The development of the cat flap – an example of the *portfelix* in the Roman Wall', *Archaeology in Northumberland* 1995–6, 36

Sadler, J. P. (1991) *Archaeological and Palaeoecological Implications of Palaeoentomological Studies in Orkney and Iceland*, unpublished PhD thesis, University of Sheffield.

Sadler, P. (1990) 'The faunal remains', 462–508 in J. R. Fairbrother (ed.) *Faccombe Netherton: Excavtions of a Saxon and Medieval Manorial Complex II*, British Museum Occasional Paper 74, London.

Salisbury, J. E. (1994) *The Beast Within: Animals in the Middle Ages*, Routledge, New York.

Samuels, J. and Buckland, P. C. (1978), 'A Romano-British settlement at Sandtoft, South Humberside', *Yorkshire Archaeological Journal* 50, 65–75.

Savage, R. J. G. (1966) 'Irish Pleistocene mammals' *Irish Naturalists' Journal* 15, 117–30.

Scharff, R. F. (1906) 'On the former occurrence of the African wild cat (*Felis ocreata*, Gmel.) in Ireland', *Proceedings of the Royal Irish Academy* 26B, 1–12.

Schauenberg, P. (1981) 'Élements d'écologie du chat forestier d'Europe *Felis silvestris* Schreber, 1777', *Terre et la Vie* 35, 3–36.

Schönfelder, M. (1994) 'Bear-claws in Germanic graves', *Oxford Journal of Archaeology* 13, 217–27.

Schreve, D. and Currant, A. (in prep). *Pleistocene Vertebrates of Great Britain*, Geological Conservation Review Series, Joint Nature Conservation Committee, Peterborough.

Schwarz, E. and Schwarz, H. K. (1943) 'The wild and commensal stocks of the house mouse *Mus musculus* Linnaeus', *Journal of Mammalogy* 24, 59–72.

Scott, S. (1992) 'The animal bones', 236–51 in D. H. Evans and D. G. Tomlinson (eds), *Excavations at 33–35 Eastgate, Beverly 1983–86*, Sheffield Excavation Reports 3, Sheffield

Sellar, T. J. (1989) 'Bone report', Fiche C1–G2 in B. Bell and C. Dickson (eds), 'Excavations at Warebeth (Stromness cemetery) Broch, Orkney', *Proceedings of the Society of Antiquaries of Scotland* 119, 101–131.

Serjeantson, D. (1985) 'Evidence of *c.* 16th–17th century diet from Shaftesbury, Dorset: the animal remains from No. 8 Gold Hill' 53–54 in M. Cox, 'Excavations within No. 8 Gold Hill, Shaftesbury, Dorset'. *Proceedings of the Dorset Natural History and Archaeological Society* 107, 47–54.

Serjeantson, D. (1988) 'Archaeological and ethnographic evidence for seabird exploitation in Scotland', *Archaeozoologia* II/1 (2), 209–24.

Serjeantson, D. (1990) 'The introduction of mammals to the Outer Hebrides and the role of boats in stock management', *Anthropozoologica* 13, 7–18.

Serjeantson, D. (1996) 'The animal bones', 194–223 in S. Needham and T. Spence (eds), *Refuse and Disposal at Area 16 East Runnymede. Runnymede Bridge Research Excavations, Volume 2*, British Museum Press, London.

Serjeantson, D. (2000a) 'The bird bones', 484–500 in M. Fulford and J. Timby, *Late Iron Age and Roman Silchester. Excavations on the site of the Forum-Basilica 1977, 1980–86*, Britannia Monograph Series 15, London.

Serjeantson, D. (2000b) 'Bird bones', 182–185 in C. J. Young (ed.), *Excavations at Carisbrooke Castle, Isle of Wight. 1921–1990*, Trust for Wessex Archaeology Limited, Salisbury.

Serjeantson, D. (2001) 'The Great Auk and the Gannet: a prehistoric perspective on the extinction of the great auk', *International Journal of Osteoarchaeology* 11, 43–55.

Serjeantson, D. (2005) 'Archaeological records of a gadfly petrel *Pterodroma* sp. from Scotland in the first millennium AD', *Documenta Archaeobiologiae* 3, 235–46.

Serjeantson, D. (2006a) 'Birds as food and markers of status', 131–47 in C. M. Woolgar, D. Serjeantson and T. Waldron (eds), *Food in Medieval England: Diet and Nutrition,* Oxford University Press, Oxford.

Serjeantson, D. (2006b) 'Animal bones', 213–46 in C. Evans (ed.), *Marshland Communities and Cultural Landscapes from the Bronze Age to the Present Day: The Haddenham Project Volume* 2, McDonald Institute, Cambridge.

Serjeantson, D. (n.d) *Mammal, bird and fish remains from the Udal (north), North Uist:* Interim report, Unpublished report.

Serjeantson, D., Smithson, V. and Waldron, T. (2005) 'Animal husbandry and the environmental context', 151–67 in A. Ritchie (ed.), *Kilellan Farm, Ardnave, Islay: Excavations of a Prehistoric to Early Medieval Site by Colin Burgess and Others 1954–76*, Society of Antiquaries of Scotland, Edinburgh.

Serjeantson, D and Woolgar, C. M. (2006) 'Fish consumption in medieval England', 102–130 in C. M. Woolgar, D. Serjeantson and T. Waldron (eds), *Food in Medieval England: Diet and Nutrition*, Oxford University Press, Oxford.

Shaler, N. S. (1876) *The Age of the Bison in the Ohio Valley*, Kentucky Geological Survey, Kentucky.

Sharples, N. (2000) 'Antlers and Orcadian Rituals: an ambiguous role for red deer in the Neolithic', 107–116 in A. Ritchie (ed.), *Neolithic Orkney in its European Context,* MacDonald Institute Monographs, Cambridge.

Sharples, N. and Smith, R. (2009) 'Norse Settlement in the Western Isles', 103–30 in A. Wolf (ed.), '*Scandinavian Scotland – Twenty years after*', St Andrews Dark Age Studies Committee, St John House papers No. 12, St Andrews.

Sheail, J. (1971) *Rabbits and their History*. Davis and Charles, Newton Abbot.

Sheail, J. (1984) 'The Rabbit', *Biologist* 31 (3), 135–140.

Shennan, I., Lambeck, K., Flather, R., Horton, B., McArthur, J., Innes, J., Lloyd, J., Rutherford, M. and Wingfield, R. (2000) 'Modelling western North Sea palaeogeographies and tidal changes during the Holocene', 299–319 in I. Shennan and J. Andrews (eds), *Holocene Land-ocean Interaction and Environmental Change around the North Sea*, Geological Society Special Publications 166, London.

Shirley, E. P. (1867) *Some Accounts of English Deer Parks with Notes on the Management of Deer*, John Murray, London.

Simon, A. L. (1944) *Birds and Their Eggs: A Concise Encyclopedia of Gastronomy, Section VI*, Wine and Food Society, London.

Simoons, F. J. (1994) *Eat Not This Flesh: Food Avoidances from Prehistory to the Present*, University of Wisconsin Press, Wisconsin.

Smith, C. (2000) 'A grumphie in the sty: an archaeological

view of pigs in Scotland, from the earliest domestication to the agricultural revolution', *Proceedings of the Society of Antiquaries of Scotland* 130, 705–24.

Smith, C. with the late Hodgson, G. W. I., Armitage, P., Clutton-Brock, J., Dickson, C., Holden, T. and Smith, B. B. (1994) 'Animal bone report', 139–53 in B. B. Smith (ed.), *Howe: Four Millennia of Orkney Prehistory*, Society of Antiquaries of Scotland Monograph Series 9, Edinburgh.

Smith D. N. (2001) 'The insect remains from Invereskgate', *University of Birmingham Environmental Archaeology Services Report* 30.

Smith, D. N. and Howard, A. (2004) 'Identifying changing fluvial conditions in low gradient alluvial archaeological landscapes: can coleoptera provide insights into changing discharge rates and floodplain evolution?', *Journal of Archaeological Science* 31, 109–20.

Smith, D. N., Osborne, P. J. and Barrett, J. (2000) 'Beetles as indicators of past environments and human activity at Goldcliff', 245–61 in M. Bell, A. Caseldine and H. Neumann (eds), *Prehistoric Intertidal Archaeology in the Welsh Severn Estuary*, Council for British Archaeology Research Report 120, York.

Smith, J. A. (1872) 'Notice of the discovery of the remains of the elk (*Cervus alces* Linn., *Alces machilis* Gray) in Berwickshire; with notes on its occurrence in the British islands, more particularly in Scotland', *Proceedings of the Society of Antiquaries of Scotland* 9, 384–410.

Smith, J. C., Healy, F., Allen, M. J., Morris, E. L., Barnes, I. and Woodward, P. J. (1997) *Excavations Along the Route of the Dorchester By-pass, Dorset, 1986–88,* (Wessex Archaeology Report 11), Trust for Wessex Archaeology, Salisbury.

Snow, D. W. and Perrins, C. M. (1998) *The Birds of the Western Palearctic*, Oxford University Press, Oxford.

Sommer, R. S. and Benecke, N. (2006) 'Late Pleistocene and Holocene development of the felid fauna (Felidae) of Europe: a review', *Journal of Zoology* 269, 7–19.

Spiegel Online (2007) 'Diplomatic row rages over Bruno', *Spiegel Online*. http://www.spiegel.de/international/zeitgeist/0,1518,474419,00.html [accessed 3/4/07]

Stace, C. (1997) *New Flora of the British Isles*, Cambridge University Press, Cambridge.

Staines, B.W. (1991) 'Red deer', 492–504 in G. B. Corbet and S. Harris (eds), *The Handbook of British Mammals*, Blackwell Publications, Oxford.

Stallibrass, S. (1992) *Animal bone from excavations at Annetwell Street, Carlisle, 1982–4. Period 3: the earlier timber fort,* (Ancient Monuments Laboratory Report 132/91), English Heritage, London.

Stallibrass, S. (1993) *Animal Bones from Excavations in the Southern Area of The Lanes, Carlisle, Cumbria, 1981–2,* (Ancient Monuments Laboratory Report 96/93), English Heritage, London.

Stallibrass, S. (2002) 'An overview of animal bones: What would we like to know, what we do know so far, and where do we go from here?', 392–415 in P. R. Wilson (ed.) *Cataractonium: Roman Catterick and its Hinterland. Excavations and Research 1958–1997. Part II*, Council for British Archaeology Report 129, London.

Starr, R. J. (1992) 'Silvia's deer (Vergil, Aeneid 7.479–502): game parks and Roman law', *The American Journal of Philology* 113 (3), 435–9.

Steane, J. (1988) 'The Royal fishponds of medieval England', 39–68 in M. Aston (ed.), *Medieval Fish, Fisheries and Fishponds in England*, British Archaeological Reports, British series 182 (i), Oxford.

Steane, J. (1985) *The Archaeology of Medieval England and Wales*, Croom Helm, London.

Stelfox, A. W. (1965) 'Notes on the Irish "wild cat"', *The Irish Naturalists' Journal* 15 (3), 57–60.

Stephenson, R. O., Gerlach, S. C., Guthrie, R. D., Harrington, C. R., Mills, R. O. and Hare, G. (2001) 'Woodland bison in late Holocene Alaska and adjacent Canada; palaeontological, archaeological and historical records' 124–58 in S. Craig Gerlach and M. S. Murray (eds), *People and Wildlife in North America*, British Archaeological Report, international series 944, Oxford.

Stewart, M. (2003) 'Using the woods, 1650–1850 (1): the community resource', 82–104 in T. C. Smout (ed.) *People and Woods in Scotland*, Edinburgh University Press, Edinburgh.

Stocker, D. and Stocker, M. (1996) 'Sacred profanity: the theology of rabbit breeding and the symbolic landscape of the warren', *World Archaeology* 28 (2), 265–72.

Stone, D. J. (2006) 'The consumption and supply of birds in late medieval England', 148–61 in C. M. Woolgar, D. Serjeantson and T. Waldron (eds), *Food in Medieval England: Diet and Nutrition,* Oxford University Press, Oxford.

Stoves, J. L. (1983) 'Examination of hairs from the Sutton Hoo musical instrument', 723–25 in R. Bruce-Mitford (ed.), *The Sutton Hoo Ship Burial Vol. 3*, British Museum Press, London.

Stuart, A. J. (1976) 'The nature of the lesions on the elk skeleton from High Furlong near Blackpool, Lancashire', *Proceedings of the Prehistoric Society* 42, 323–4.

Stuart, A. J. (1982) *Pleistocene Vertebrates in the British Isles*, Longman, London.

Stuart, J. and Burnett, G. (1878) *The Exchequer Rolls of Scotland*, vol 1, General Register House, Edinburgh.

Suchentruck, F., Jaschke, C., and Haiden, A. (2001) 'Little allozyme and mtDNA variability in brown hares (*Lepus europaeus*) from New Zealand and Britain – a legacy of bottlenecks?', *Mammalian Biology* 66, 48–59.

Sutcliffe, A. J. (1960) 'Joint Mitnor Cave, Buckfastleigh', *Transactions and Proceedings of the Torquay Natural History Society* 13, 1–26.

Sutcliffe, A. J. (1964) 'The mammalian fauna', 85–111 in C. D. Ovey (ed.), *The Swanscombe Skull: A Survey of Research on a Pleistocene Site*, Royal Anthropological Institute of Great Britain and Ireland, London.

Sutcliffe, A. J. and Zeuner, F. E. (1962) 'Excavations in the Torbryan Caves, Devonshire. 1. Tornewton Cave', *Proceedings of the Devon Archaeological and Exploration Society* 5, 127–45.

Sutermeister, H. (1976) 'Burpham: A settlement site within the Saxon defences', *Sussex Archaeological Collections* 114, 194 207.

Sutterby, R. and Greenhalgh M. (2005) *Atlantic Salmon: An Illustrated Natural History*, Merlin Unwin Books, Ludlow.

Suzuki, H., Shimada, T., Terashima, M., Tsuchiya, K. and Aplin, K. (2004) 'Temporal, spatial, and ecological modes of evolution of Eurasian *Mus* based on mitochondrial and nuclear gene sequences', *Molecular Phylogenetics and Evolution* 33, 626–46.

Sykes, N. J. (2001) *The Norman Conquest: A Zooarchaeological Perspective*, unpublished PhD thesis, University of Southampton.

Sykes, N. J. (2004a) 'The introduction of fallow deer (*Dama dama*) to Britain: a zooarchaeological perspective' *Environmental Archaeology* 9, 75–83.

Sykes, N. (2004b) 'Neolithic and Saxon animal bone', 87–91 in C. J. Ellis (ed.), *A Prehistoric Ritual Complex at Eynesbury, Cambridgeshire: Excavations of a Multi-period Site in the Great Ouse Valley, 2000–2001*, East Anglian Archaeology 17, Salisbury.

Sykes, N. (2005) 'The dynamics of status symbols: wildfowl exploitation in England AD 410–1450', *The Archaeological Journal* 161, 82–105.

Sykes, N. J. (2006) 'The impact of the Normans on hunting practices in England', 162–75 in C. Woolgar, D. Serjeantson and T. Waldron (eds), *Food in Medieval England: Diet and Nutrition*, Oxford University Press, Oxford.

Sykes, N. J. (2007) *The Norman Conquest: A Zooarchaeological Perspective*, British Archaeological Report, international series 1656, Oxford.

Sykes, N. J. (forthcoming) 'Woods and the wild' in D. Hinton and H. Hamerow (eds), *A Handbook of Anglo-Saxon Archaeology*, Oxford University Press, Oxford

Sykes, N. J. (n.d.) *The Animal Remains from Clay Hill,*

Sussex, unpublished report for the Sussex Archaeological Society.

Sykes, N. J. (in prep) 'Husbandry, Hares and Feasting: The Animal Remains from Whitehall Roman Villa, Northamptonshire' Bioarchaeology Research Laboratory Report to CLASP.

Sykes, N. J., Ingrem, C. and Ayres K. (2005) 'The bones and shell', 116–32 in R. Poulton (ed.) *A Medieval Royal Complex at Guildford: Excavations at the Castle and Palace*, Surrey Archaeological Society, Guildford.

Sykes, N. J., White, J., Hayes, T. and Palmer, M. (2006) 'Tracking animals using strontium isotopes in teeth: the role of fallow deer (*Dama dama*) in Roman Britain', *Antiquity* 80, 948–59.

Tabor, R. (1991) *Cats: The Rise of the Cat*, BBC Books, London.

Tapper, S. (1992) *Game Heritage*, The Game Conservancy, Fordingbridge.

Tchernov E. (1984) 'Commensal animals and human sedentism in the Middle East' 91–115 in J. Clutton-Brock and C. Grigson (eds) *Animals and Archaeology 3: Early Herders and Their Flocks*, British Archaeological Report, international series 202, Oxford.

Tchernov E. (1991) 'Biological evidence for human sedentism in Southwest Asia during the Natufian', 315–40 in O. Bar-Yosef and F. R. Valla (eds) *The Natufian Culture in the Levant*, , International Monographs in Prehistory 1, Ann Arbor.

Tchernov E. (1993) 'The effect of sedentism on the exploitation of the environment in Southern Levant', 137–59 in J. Desse and F. Audoin-Rouzeau (eds), *Exploitation des Animaux Sauvages à Travers le Temps*, Editions APDCA, Juan-les-Pins.

Tchernov E. (1994) *An Early Neolithic Village in the JordanValley Part II: The Fauna of Netiv Hagdud*, Peabody Museum of Archaeology and Ethnology, Harvard University, Cambridge MA.

Tertullianus, Q. Septimus Florens (1977) *Apology: De Spectaculis*. Trans. T. R. Glover, (Loeb Classical Library), William Heinemann Ltd, London.

Tetlow, E. A. (2003) 'A "wildwood" insect fauna from Goldcliff East, Gwent', *Archaeology in the Severn Estuary* 14, 41–7.

Thaw, S., Jaarola, M., Searle, J. B., and Dobney, K. (2004) 'The origin of the Orkney Vole *Microtus arvalis orcadensis*: a proxy for reconstructing human movements', 114–20 in R. A. Housley and G. Coles (eds), *Atlantic Connections and Adaptations Vol. 21*, Oxbow Books, Oxford.

Thomas, J. (2004) 'Thoughts on the 'repacked' Neolithic Revolution', *Antiquity* 78, 67–74.

Thomas, R. (1999) 'Feasting at Worcester Cathedral in the

seventeenth century: a zooarchaeological and historical approach, *Archaeological Journal* 156, 342–358.

Thomas, R. (2001) 'The Medieval management of fallow deer: A pathological line of enquiry', 287–93 in M. La Verghetta and L. Capasso (eds), *Proceedings of the XIIIth European Meeting of the Palaeopathology Association Cheiti, Italy: 18th–23rd September 2000*, S.P.A. Teramo, Italy.

Thomas, R. M. (2005) *Animals, Economy and Status: The Integration of Historical and Zooarchaeological Evidence in the Study of a Medieval Castle*, British Archaeological Report, British series 392, Oxford.

Thompson, A. P. D. (1951) 'A history of the ferret', *Journal of History of Medicine and Allied Sciences* 6 (4), 471–80.

Thompson, H. V. (1994) 'The rabbit in Britain', 64–107 in H. V. Thompson and C. M. King (eds), *The European Rabbit: The History and Biology of a Successful Colonizer*, Oxford University Press, Oxford.

Thoms, J. E. (2003) *Aspects of Economy and Environment of North West Lewis in the First Millennium AD: the Non-marine Faunal Evidence form Bostadh and Beirgh Considered within the Framework of north Atlantic Scotland*, unpublished PhD thesis, University of Edinburgh.

Thorpe, I. J. (2006) 'Fighting and feuding in Neolithic and Bronze Age Britain and Ireland', 141–66 in T. Otto, H. Thrane and H. Vandkilde (eds), *Warfare and Society: Archaeological and Social Anthropological Perspectives*, Aarhus University Press, Aarhus.

Thorpe, L. (1978) *Gerald of Wales: The Journey Through Wales and The Description of Wales*, Penguin Books, London.

Thulin, C.-G. (2003) 'The distribution of mountain hares *Lepus timidus* in Europe: a challenge from brown hares *L. europaeus*?', *Mammal Review* 33, 29–42.

Tipping, R. (1994) 'The form and fate of Scotland's woodlands', *Proceedings of the Society of Antiquaries of Scotland* 124, 1–54.

Tittensor, A. M. and Tittensor, R. M. (1985) 'The rabbit warren at West Dean near Chichester', *Sussex Archaeological Collections* 123, 151–85.

Todd, N. B. (1977) 'Cats and commerce', *Scientific American* 237, 100–107.

Todd, N. B. (1978) 'An ecological, behavioural genetic model for the domestication of the cat', *Carnivore* 1, 52–60.

Toynbee, J. M. C. (1973) *Animals in Roman Life and Art*, Thames and Hudson, London.

Trechmann, C. T. (1939) 'A skeleton of elk (*Cervus alces*) from Neasham, near Darlington', *Proceedings of the Yorkshire Geological Society* 24, 100–102.

Troy, C. S., MacHugh, D. E., Bailey, J. F., Magee, D. A., Loftus, R. T., Cunningham, P., Chamberlain, A. T., Sykes, B. C. and Bradley, D. G. (2001) 'Genetic evidence for Near-Eastern origins of European domestic cattle', *Nature* 410, 1088–91.

Turk, F. A. (1964) 'Blue and brown hares associated together in a Bronze Age fissure cave burial', *Proceedings of the Zoological Society of London* 142, 185–8.

Uerpman, H.-P. (1987) *The Ancient Distribution of Ungulate Mammals in the Middle East*, (Beihefte zum Tübunger Atlas des Vorderen Orients, Reihe A Naturwissenschaften 27), Dr. Ludwig Reichert Verlag, Wiesbaden.

Vallentine, J. F. (1990) *Range Management*, Academic Press, San Diego.

Van Bree, P. J. H. and Clason, A. T. (1971) 'On the skull of a lynx *Lynx lynx* (Linnaeus, 1758), found in the Roman castellum at Valkenburg, Province of Zuid-Holland, the Netherlands', *Bijdragen Tot de Dierkunde* 41, 130–5.

Van Bree, P. H., Van Soest, R. W. M. and Vetter, J. C. M. (1970). 'Biometric analysis of the effect of castration on the skull of the male domestic cat (*Felis catus* L., 1758)', *Publicaties van het Natuurhistorisch Genootschap in Limburg* 20 (3/4), 11–14.

Van Dam, P. J. E. M. (2001) 'Status loss due to ecological success: landscape change and the spread of the rabbit', *Innovation* 14 (2), 157–70.

Van Damme, D. and Ervynck, A. (1988) 'Medieval ferrets and rabbits in the castle of Laarne (East Flanders Belgium): a contribution to the history of a predator and its prey', *Helinium* 28 (2), 278–84

Van Vuure, C. (2005) *Retracing the Aurochs: History, Morphology and Ecology of an Extinct Wild Ox*, Pensoft, Sofia and Moscow.

Van Wijngaarden-Bakker, L. H. (1974) 'The animal remains from the Beaker settlement at Newgrange, Co. Meath – first report', *Proceedings of the Royal Irish Academy* 74 (Section C), 313–85.

Van Wijngaarden-Bakker, L. (1986) 'The faunal remains', 70–76 in P.C.Woodman (ed.), *Excavations at Mount Sandel, Ireland 1975–1977*, H.M.S.O., Belfast.

Van Wijngaarden-Bakker, L. H. (1989) 'Faunal remains and the Irish Mesolithic', 125–33 in C. Bonsall (ed.), *The Mesolithic in Europe*, John Donald, Edinburgh.

Veale, E. M. (1957) 'The rabbit in England', *English History Review* 5, 85–90.

Vera, F. W. M. (2002) *Grazing Ecology and Forest History*, CABI Publishing, Wallingford.

Vickers, K. (1988) *A Review of Irish Salmon and Salmon Fisheries*, Atlantic Salmon Trust, Pitlochry.

Vigne, J.-D. (1992) 'Zooarchaeological and biogeographical history of the mammals of Corsica and Sardinia', *Mammal Review* 22, 87–96.

Vigne, J.-D., Guilane, J., Debue, K., Haye, L. and Gérard, P. (2004) 'Early taming of the cat in Cyprus', *Science* 304, 259.

Vila, C., Leonard, J. A., Gothertson, A., Markland, S., Sandberg, K., Liden, K., Wayne, R. K., and Ellegren, H. (2001) 'Widespread origins of domestic horse lineages, *Science* 291, 474–7.

Von Arx, M., Breitenmoser-Würsten, C., Zimmermann, F. and Breitenmoser, U. (2004) *Status and Conservation of the Eurasian lynx* (Lynx lynx*) in Europe in 2001*, KORA Bericht No. 19.

Von den Driesch, A. (1999) 'The crane, *Grus grus*, in prehistoric Europe and its relation to the Pleistocene crane, *Grus primigenia*', 201–7 in N. Benecke (ed.), *Archäologie in Eurasien*. Marie Leidorf, Rahden.

Waites, B. (1997) *Monasteries and Landscape in North East England: The Medieval Colonisation of the North York Moors*, Multum in Parvo Press, Rutland.

Wallace, G. (2005) 'The faunal assemblage from the grooved ware pit F538' 147–151 in C. French and F. Pryor (eds), *Archaeology and Environment of the Etton Landscape,* East Anglian Archaeology 109, Peterborough.

Walton, I. (1653) *The Compleat Angler*, (ed. B. Loughrey 1985), Penguin Country Library, Harmondsworth, Middlesex.

Warren, C. (2002) *Managing Scotland's Environment,* Edinburgh University Press, Edinburgh.

Warren, C. (2004). *The Microfaunal Remains from Chapel Cave, North Yorkshire as a Reflection of Local Environmental Conditions*, unpublished MSc thesis, University of Bradford.

Warry, J. (1988) 'The ancient history of rabbits', *The Local Historian* 18, 13–15.

Waters, B. (1987) *Severn Tide,* Alan Sutton, Gloucester.

Webster, J. A. (2001) 'A review of the historical evidence of the habitat of the pine marten in Cumbria', *Mammal Review* 31, 17–31.

Wells, C. E., Hodgkinson, D. and Huckerby, E. (2000) 'Evidence for the possible role of beaver (*Castor fiber*) in the prehistoric ontogenesis of a mire in northwest England, UK', *The Holocene* 10 (4), 503–8.

West, B. (1983) *The Roman Buildings West of the Walbrook Project: Human, Animal and Bird Bones, Level III,* unpublished manuscript, Department of Urban Archaeology, Museum of London.

West, B. (1995) 'The case of the missing victuals', *Historical Archaeology* 29(2), 20–42.

West, B. and Zhou, B. (1988) 'Did chickens go north? New evidence for domestication,' *Journal of Archaeological Science* 15, 515–533.

Weinstock, J. (2002) *The Medieval and Post-Medieval Bone Remains from Heigham Street, Norwich,* (Centre for Archaeology Report 33/2002), English Heritage, Portsmouth.

Wheeler, A. (1977) 'The origin and distribution of the freshwater fishes of the British Isles', *Journal of Biogeography* 4, 1–24.

Wheeler, A. (1979) *The Tidal Thames,* Routledge and Kegan Paul, London.

Wheeler, R. E. M. and Wheeler, T. V. (1932) *Report on the Excavation of the Prehistoric, Roman and Post-Roman site in Lydney Oak, Gloucester*, Report of the Research Committee of the Society of Antiquaries of London 9, London.

White, D. A. (1964) 'Excavations at War Ditches, Cherry Hinton', *Proceedings of the Cambridge Antiquity Society* 56, 9–29.

White, J. (n.d.) *The 14th-Century Faunal Remains from Wells Museum Garden: Reflections of Status, Religion and Feasting in the Late Medieval Period*, unpublished BA dissertation, University of Southampton.

White, K. D. (1970) *Roman Farming*, Thames and Hudson, London.

Whitehead, G. K. (1950) *Deer and Their Management in the Deer Parks of Great Britain and Ireland*, Country Life, London.

Whitehead, G. K. (1953) *Ancient White Cattle of Britain and their Descendants*. Faber and Faber, London.

Whitehead, G. K. (1972) *Deer of the World*, Constable, London.

Whitehead, G. K. (1993) *The Whitehead Encyclopaedia of Deer*, Swan Hill, Shrewsbury.

Whitehouse, N. J. (1997) 'Insect faunas associated with *Pinus sylvestris* L. from the mid-Holocene of the Humberhead Levels, Yorkshire, UK', *Quaternary Proceedings* 5, 293–303.

Whitehouse, N. J. (2000) 'Forest fires and insects: palaeoentomological research from a sub-fossil burnt forest', *Palaeogeography, Palaeoclimatology, Palaeoecology* 164, 231–46.

Whitehouse N. J. (2004) 'Mire ontogeny, environmental and climate change inferred from fossil beetle successions from Hatfield Moors, eastern England', *The Holocene* 14, 79–93.

Whitehouse, N. J. (2006) 'The Holocene British and Irish ancient forest fossil beetle fauna: implications for forest history, biodiversity and faunal colonisation', *Quaternary Science Reviews* 25, 1755–89.

Whitehouse, N. J. (2007) 'Fossil insect remains in environmental investigations', 136–63 in E. Murphy and N. J. Whitehouse (eds), *Environmental Archaeology in Ireland*, Oxbow, Oxford.

Whitehouse, N. J. and Smith, D. N. (2010) How fragmented was the British wildwood? Perspectives on the 'Vera' grazing debate using fossil beetles. *Quaternary Science Reviews.* doi: 10.1016/j.quascirev.2009.10.010

Whitehouse, N. J. and Rodgers, K. (2008) 'Greyabbey Bay, Strangford Lough: palaeoentomology', 147–54 in N. J. Whitehouse, H. Roe, S. McCarron and J. Knight (eds), *North of Ireland: Field Guide*, Quaternary Research Association, London.

Whittle, A. (1986) *Scord of Brouster an Early Agricultural Settlement on Shetland, Excavations 1977–79,* (Committee for Archaeology Monograph no. 9), Oxford University, Oxford.

Widdowson, E. (1980) 'Growth in animals', 1–9 in T. L/ J. Lawrence (ed.), *Growth in Animals*, Elsevier, London.

Willcox, G., Buxo, R. and Herveux, L. (2009) 'Late Pleistocene and early Holocene climate and the beginnings of cultivation in northern Syria', *The Holocene* 19, 151–8.

Wilcox, H. A. (1933) *The Woodlands and Marshlands of England*, Hodder & Stoughton, London.

Williams, J. J. (1998) *Hunting in Early Modern England: An Examination with Special Reference to the Reign of Henry VIII,* unpublished PhD thesis, University of Birmingham.

Williamson, M. (1996) *Biological Invasions*, (Population and community biology series 15), Chapman and Hall, London.

Williamson, R. (1991) *Salmon Fisheries in Scotland,* Atlantic Salmon Trust, Pitlochry.

Williamson, T. (2006) *The Archaeology of Rabbit Warrens*, Shire Publications, Princes Risborough.

Wilson, C. A. (1973) *Food and Drink in Britain,* Constable, London.

Wilson, D. (2004) 'Multi-use management of the medieval Anglo-Norman forest', *Journal of the Oxford University History Society* 1, 1–16.

Wilson, R. (1984) 'Medieval and Post-Medieval animal bones and marine shells' 265–268 and microfiche in T. G. Hassall, C. E. Halpin and M. Mellor (eds), 'Excavations in St Ebbe's, Oxford, 1967–1976. Part II: Post-Medieval domestic tenements and the post-dissolution site of the Greyfriars', *Oxoniensia* 49, 153–275.

Wilson, R. (1990) *Sicily under the Roman Empire*: *The Archaeology of a Roman Province, 36 BC–AD 535*, Aris and Phillips, Warminster.

Witts, P. (2005) *Mosaics in Roman Britain*, Tempus, Stroud.

Wolff, P., Herzig-Straschil, B. and Bauer, K. (1980) '*Rattus rattus* (Linné 1758) und *Rattus norvegicus* (Berkenhout 1769) in Österreich und deren Unterscheidung am Schädel und postcranialem Skelett', *Mammalia Austriaca 4. Mitt. Abt. Zool. Landesmus. Joanneum* 9 (3), 141–188.

Wood, N. J. and Phua, S. H. (1996) 'Variation in the control region sequence of the sheep mitochondrial genome', *Animal Genetics* 27, 25–33

Wood, J. G. (1864) *A Natural History. (New Edition)*. Routledge, Warne & Routledge, London.

Woodman, P. (1978) 'The chronology and the economy of the Irish Mesolithic', 333–70 in P. Mellars (ed.), *The Early Postglacial Settlement of Northern Europe,* Duckworth, London.

Woodman, P., McCarthy, M. and Monaghan, N. (1997) 'The Irish Quaternary fauna project', *Quaternary Science Reviews* 16, 129–59.

Woolgar, C. (1999) *The Great Household in Late Medieval England*, Yale University Press, New Haven and London.

Worley, F. and Evans, E.-J. (2006) 'Animal bone', 311–21 in D. Poore, D. Score and A. Dodd (eds), 'Excavations at No. 4A Merton St., Merton College, Oxford: the evolution of a medieval stone house and tenement and an early college property', *Oxoniensia* 71, 211–342.

Worsop, C. (2000) 'Plants by proxy: plant resources on a Neolithic crannog as indicated by insect remains', 37–47 in A. Fairbairn (ed.) *Plants in Neolithic Britain and Beyond*, (Neolithic studies group seminar papers 5), Oxbow, Oxford.

Wright, T. (1884) *Anglo-Saxon and Old English Vocabularies*, Trübner & Co., London.

Wymer, J. (1962) 'Excavations at the Maglemosian sites at Thatcham, Berkshire, England', *Proceedings of the Prehistoric Society* 28, 255–361.

Yalden, D. W. (1977) 'Small mammals and the archaeologist', *Bulletin of the Peakland Archaeological Society* 30, 18–25.

Yalden, D. W. (1981) 'The occurrence of the pigmy shrew *Sorex minutus* on moorland, and the implications for its presence in Ireland', *Journal of Zoology* 195, 147–156.

Yalden, D. (1982) 'When did the mammal fauna of the British Isles arrive?' *Mammal Review* 12, 1–57.

Yalden, D. W. (1995) 'Small mammals from Viking-Age Repton', *Journal of Zoology* 237, 655–7.

Yalden, D. W. (1999) *The History of British Mammals*, T. & A. D. Poyser, London

Yalden, D. W. (2002) 'Place-name and archaeological evidence on the recent history of birds in Britain', *Acta Zoologica Cracoviensia* 45, 415–29.

Yalden, D. W. and Albarella, U. (2009) *The History of British Birds*, Oxford, Oxford University Press.

Yalden, D. W. and Kitchener, A. (2008). 'History of the fauna', 17–31 in S. Harris and D. W. Yalden (eds), *Mammals of the British Isles, 4th edition,* The Mammal Society, Southampton.

Yalden, D. W. and McCarthy, R. I. (2004) 'The archaeological record of birds in Britain and Ireland compared:

extinctions or failures to arrive?', *Environmental Archaeology* 9, 123–6.

Yamaguchi, N., Driscoll, C., Kitchener, A. C., Ward, J. M. and Macdonald, D. W. (2004) 'Craniological differentiation between European wildcats (*Felis silvestris silvestris*), African wildcats (*F. s. lybica*) and Asian wildcats (*F. s. ornata*): implications for their evolution and conservation', *Biological Journal of the Linnaean Society* 83, 47–63.

Yannouli, E and Trantalidou, K. (1999) 'The fallow deer (*Dama dama* Linnaeus, 1758): archaeological presence and representation in Greece', 247–82 in N. Benecke (ed.), *The Holocene History of the European Vertebrate Fauna: Modern Aspects of Research Workshop 6th–9th April 1998*, Verlag Marie Leidorf GmbH, Rahden/Westf.

Yapp, B. (1981) *Birds in Medieval Manuscripts*, British Library, London.

Yates, D. (2001) 'Bronze Age agricultural intensification in the Thames Valley and Estuary', 65–82 in J. Brück (ed.), *Bronze Age Landscapes: Tradition and Transformation*, Oxbow Books, Oxford.

Zavatsky, B. P. (1976) 'The use of the skull in age determination of the brown bear', 275–79 in M. R. Pelton, J. W. Lentfer and G. E. (eds), *Folk Bears – Their Biology and Management*, International Union for the Conservation of Nature and Natural Resources (New Series 40), Morges.

Zeuner, F. E. (1963) *A History of Domesticated Animals*, Hutchinson, London.

Index

Note: animal species that are mentioned other than passim are indexed under both 'Latin' and vernacular names regardless of which form is used on the indexed page